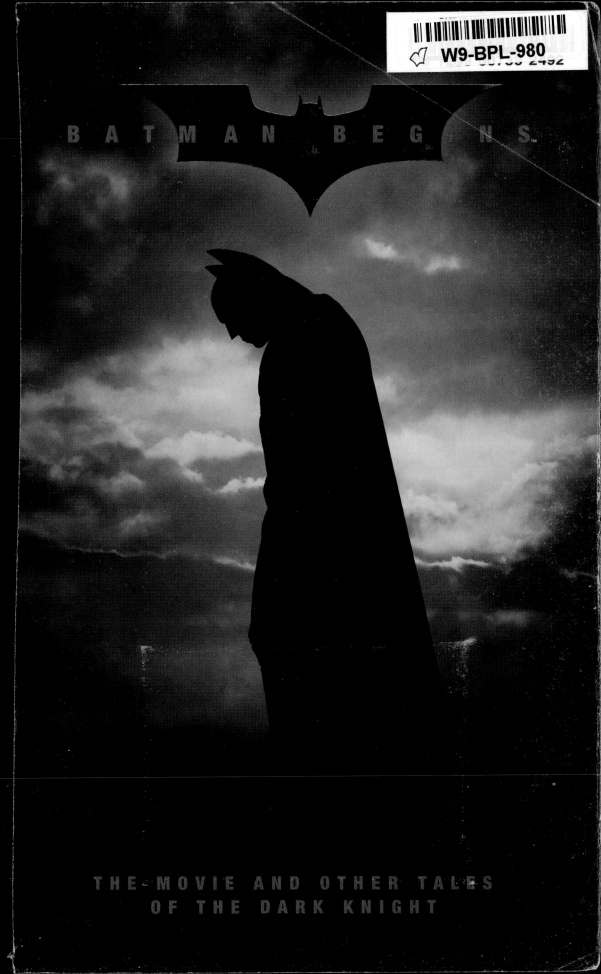

BATMAN BEGINS™

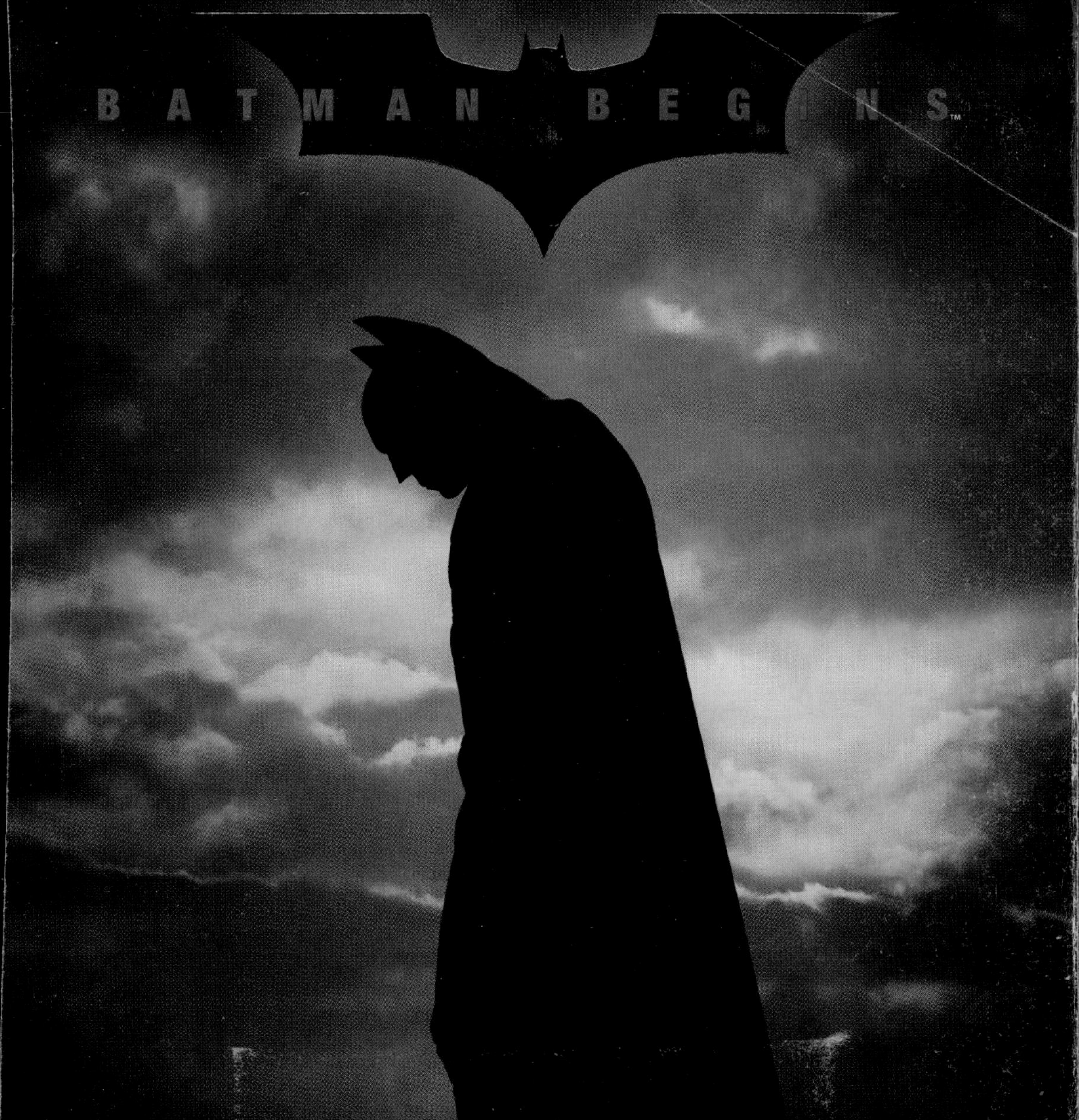

THE MOVIE AND OTHER TALES OF THE DARK KNIGHT

BATMAN BEGINS: THE MOVIE & OTHER TALES OF THE DARK KNIGHT

Published by DC Comics. Cover and compilation copyright © 2005 DC Comics. All Rights Reserved.

Originally published in single magazine form in BATMAN BEGINS: THE MOVIE, SECRET ORIGINS OF THE WORLD'S GREATEST SUPER-HEROES, DETECTIVE COMICS #757, BATMAN #604, BATMAN: LEGENDS OF THE DARK KNIGHT #168. Copyright © 1989, 2001, 2002, 2003, 2005 DC Comics. All Rights Reserved. All characters, their distinctive likenesses and related elements featured in this publication are trademarks of DC Comics. The stories, characters and incidents featured in this publication are entirely fictional. DC Comics does not read or accept unsolicited submissions of ideas, stories or artwork.

DC Comics, 1700 Broadway, New York, NY 10019 A Warner Bros. Entertainment Company Printed in Canada. First Printing. ISBN: 1-4012-0440-6 Publication design by Peter Hamboussi.

BATMAN CREATED BY **BOB KANE**

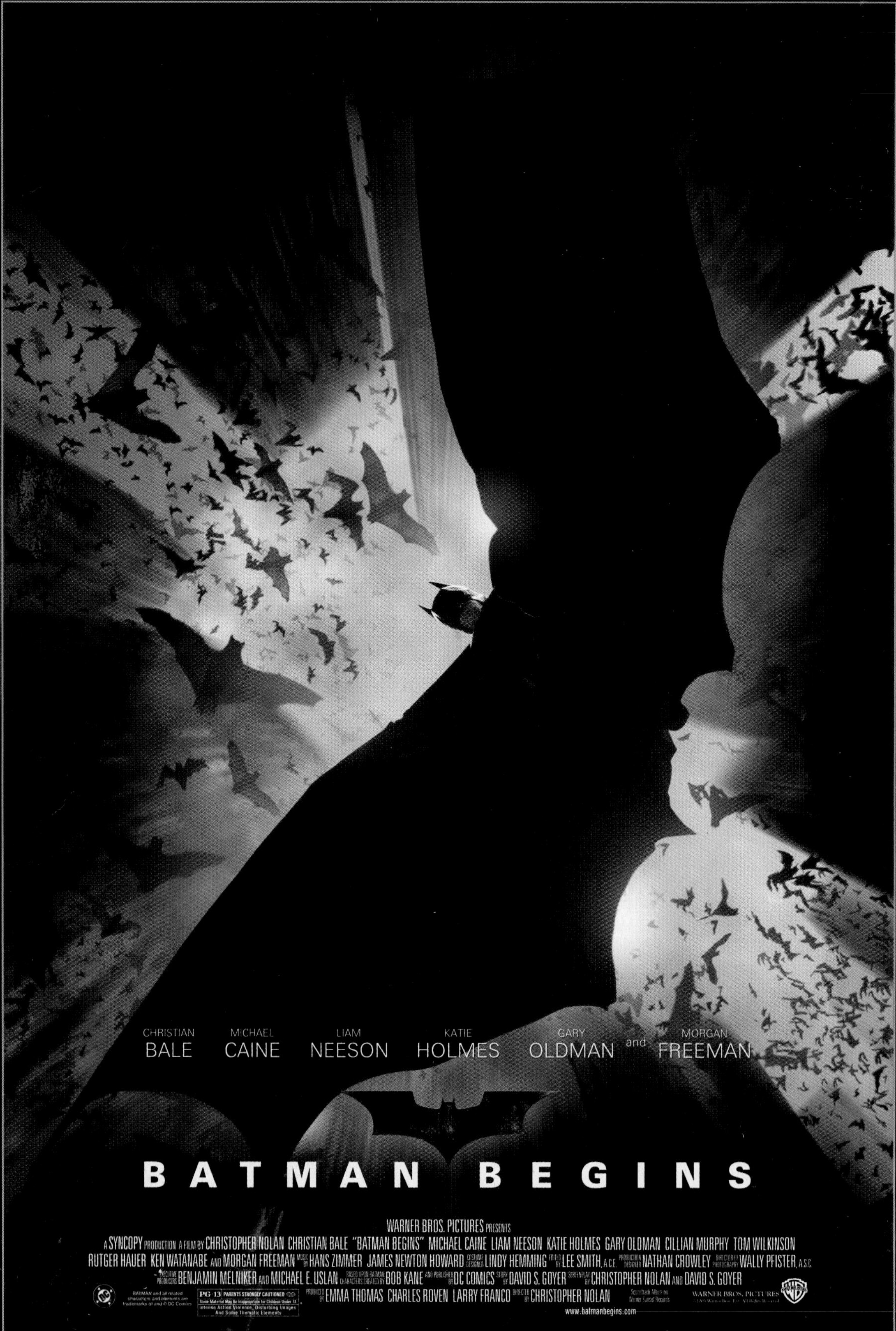

CHRISTIAN BALE
MICHAEL CAINE
LIAM NEESON
KATIE HOLMES
GARY OLDMAN
and
MORGAN FREEMAN
BATMAN BEGINS
WARNER BROS. PICTURES PRESENTS
A SYNCOPY PRODUCTION A FILM BY CHRISTOPHER NOLAN CHRISTIAN BALE "BATMAN BEGINS" MICHAEL CAINE LIAM NEESON KATIE HOLMES GARY OLDMAN CILLIAN MURPHY TOM WILKINSON
RUTGER HAUER KEN WATANABE AND MORGAN FREEMAN MUSIC BY HANS ZIMMER JAMES NEWTON HOWARD COSTUME DESIGNER LINDY HEMMING EDITED BY LEE SMITH, A.C.E. PRODUCTION DESIGNER NATHAN CROWLEY DIRECTOR OF PHOTOGRAPHY WALLY PFISTER, A.S.C.
EXECUTIVE PRODUCERS BENJAMIN MELNIKER AND MICHAEL E. USLAN BASED UPON BATMAN CHARACTERS CREATED BY BOB KANE AND PUBLISHED BY DC COMICS STORY BY DAVID S. GOYER SCREENPLAY BY CHRISTOPHER NOLAN AND DAVID S. GOYER
BATMAN and all related characters and elements are trademarks of and © DC Comics
PG-13 PARENTS STRONGLY CAUTIONED
Some Material May Be Inappropriate for Children Under 13.
Intense Action Violence, Disturbing Images And Some Thematic Elements
PRODUCED BY EMMA THOMAS CHARLES ROVEN LARRY FRANCO DIRECTED BY CHRISTOPHER NOLAN
WARNER BROS. PICTURES
www.batmanbegins.com

BATMAN BEGINS: The Movie

SCOTT BEATTY writer **KILIAN PLUNKETT** penciller **SERGE LaPOINTE** inker
JOSE VILLARRUBIA colorist **JARED K. FLETCHER** letterer

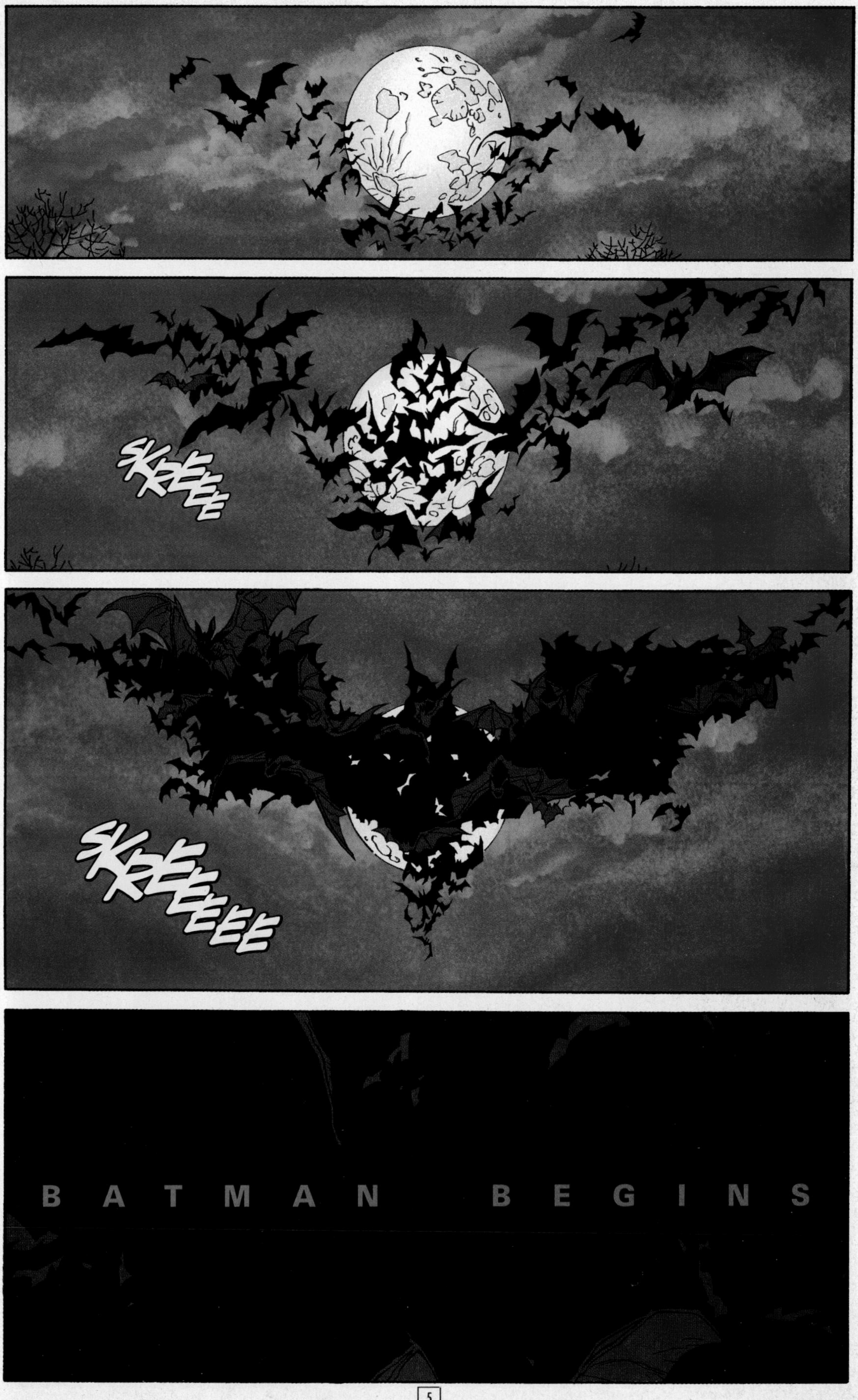
SKREEEE
SKREEEEEEE
BATMAN BEGINS

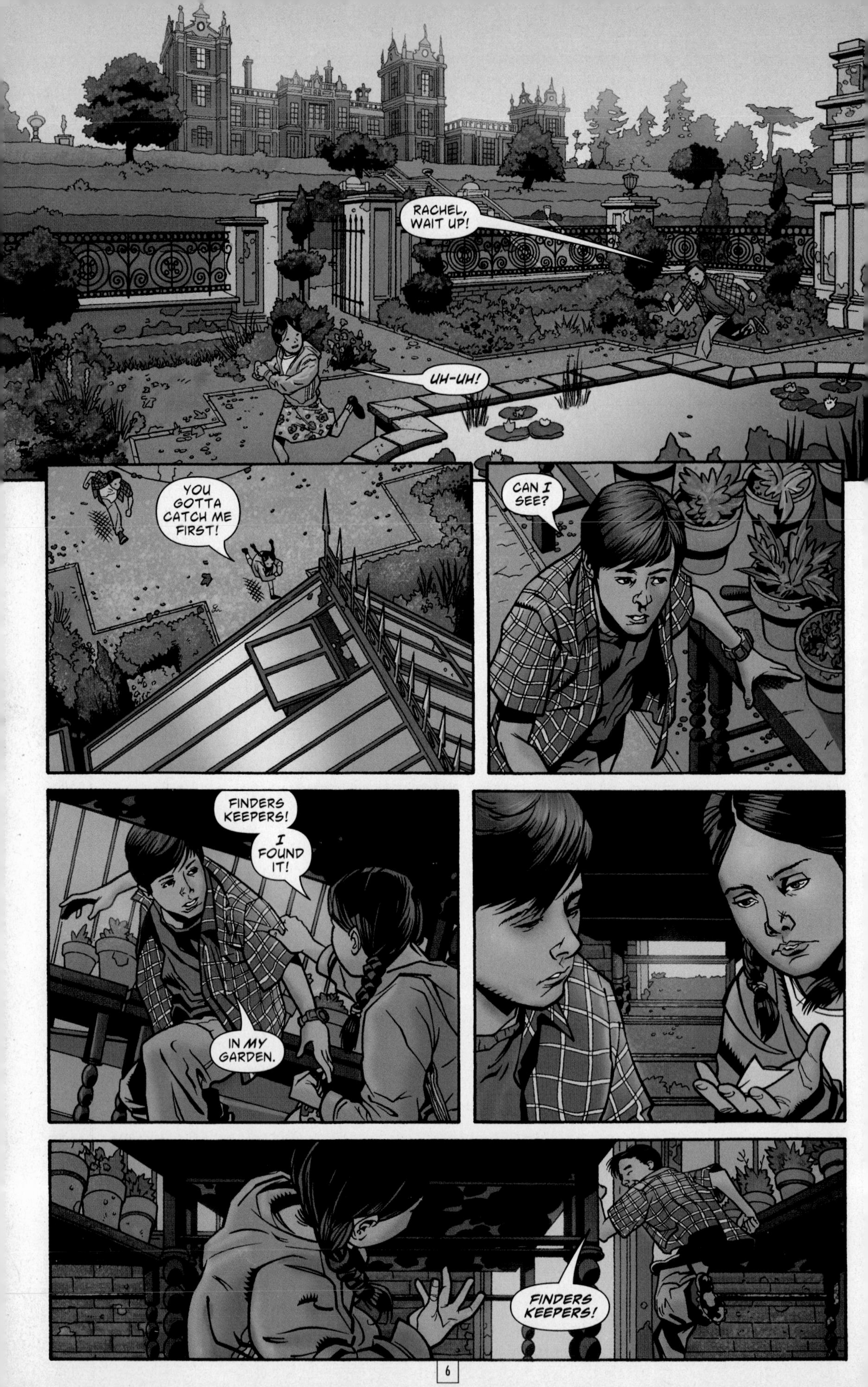
RACHEL, WAIT UP!
UH-UH!
YOU GOTTA CATCH ME FIRST!
CAN I SEE?
FINDERS KEEPERS!
I FOUND IT!
IN MY GARDEN.
FINDERS KEEPERS!

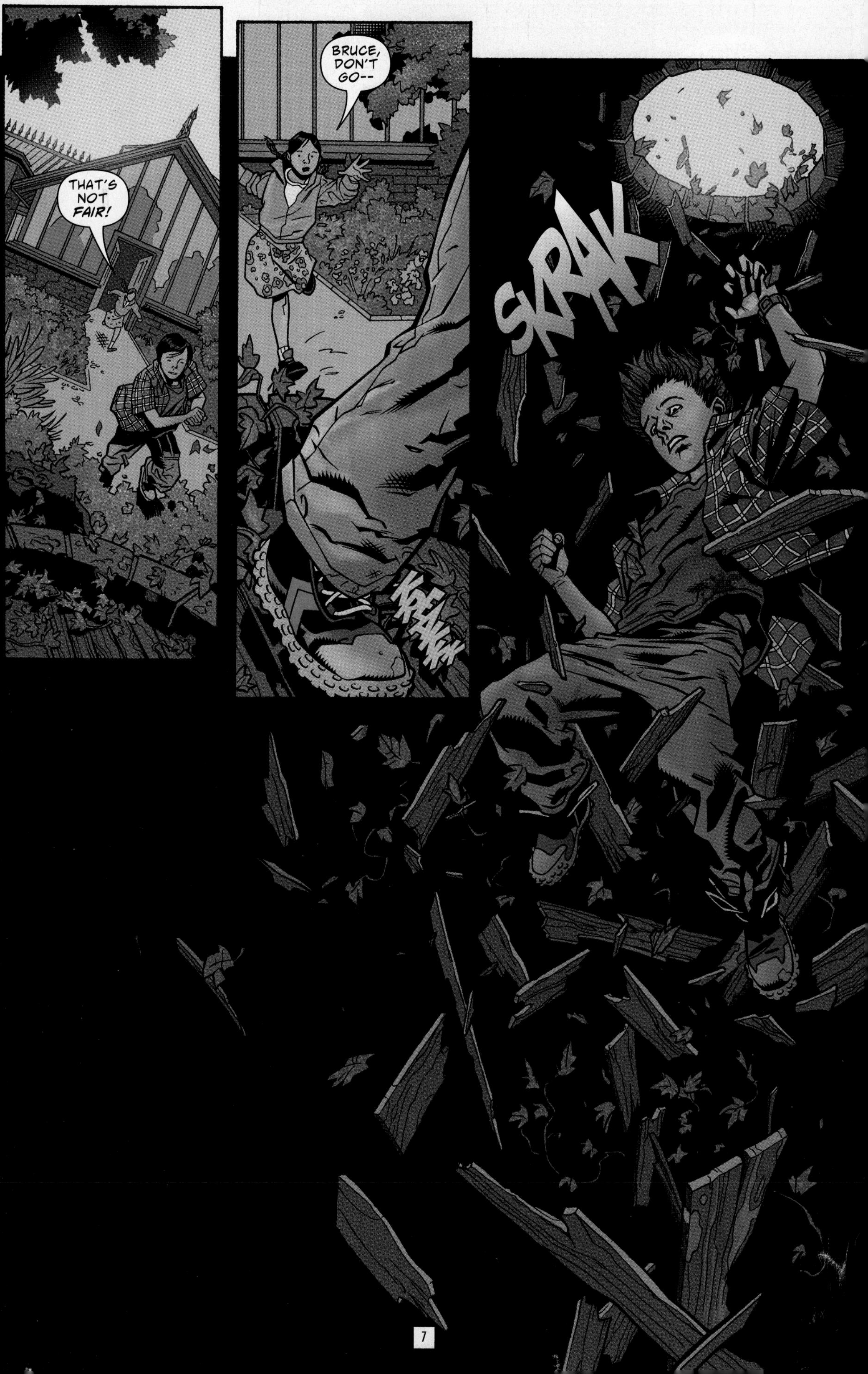
THAT'S NOT FAIR!
BRUCE, DON'T GO--
KRANK
SKRAK

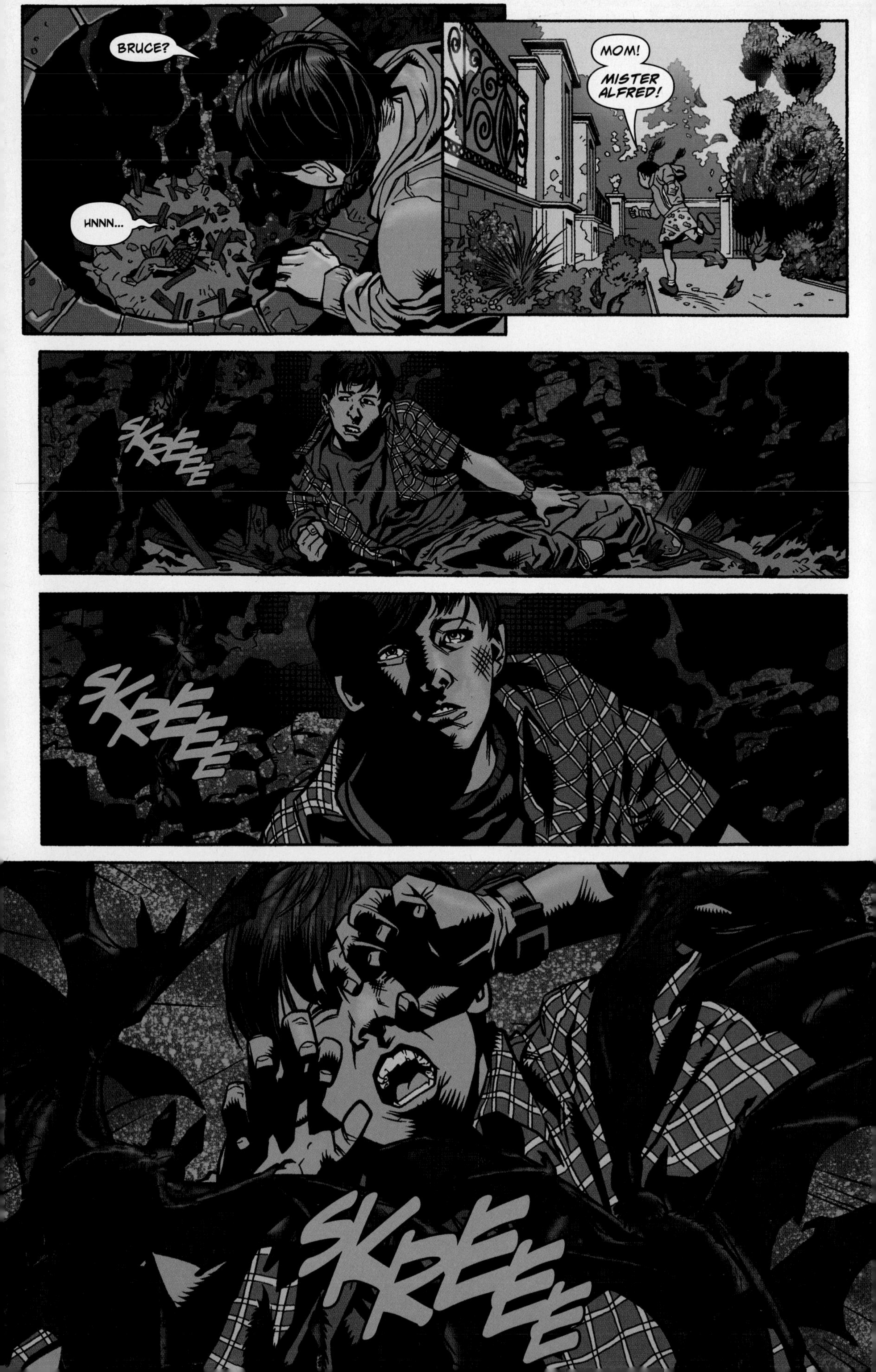
BRUCE?
HNNN...
MOM!
MISTER ALFRED!
SKREEE
SKREEE
SKREEE

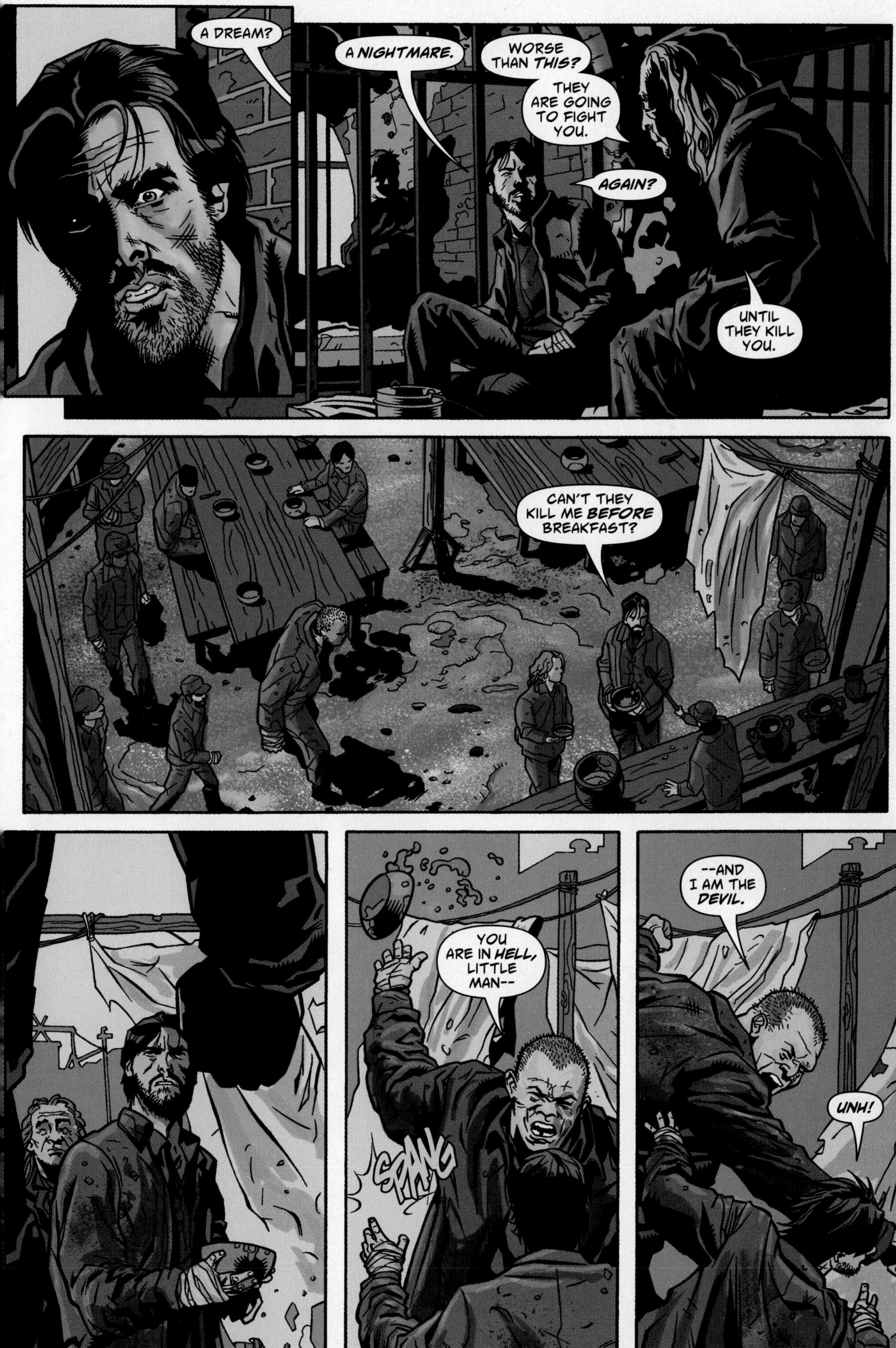
A DREAM?
A NIGHTMARE.
WORSE THAN THIS?
THEY ARE GOING TO FIGHT YOU.
AGAIN?
UNTIL THEY KILL YOU.
CAN'T THEY KILL ME BEFORE BREAKFAST?
YOU ARE IN HELL, LITTLE MAN--
SPANG
--AND I AM THE DEVIL.
UNH!

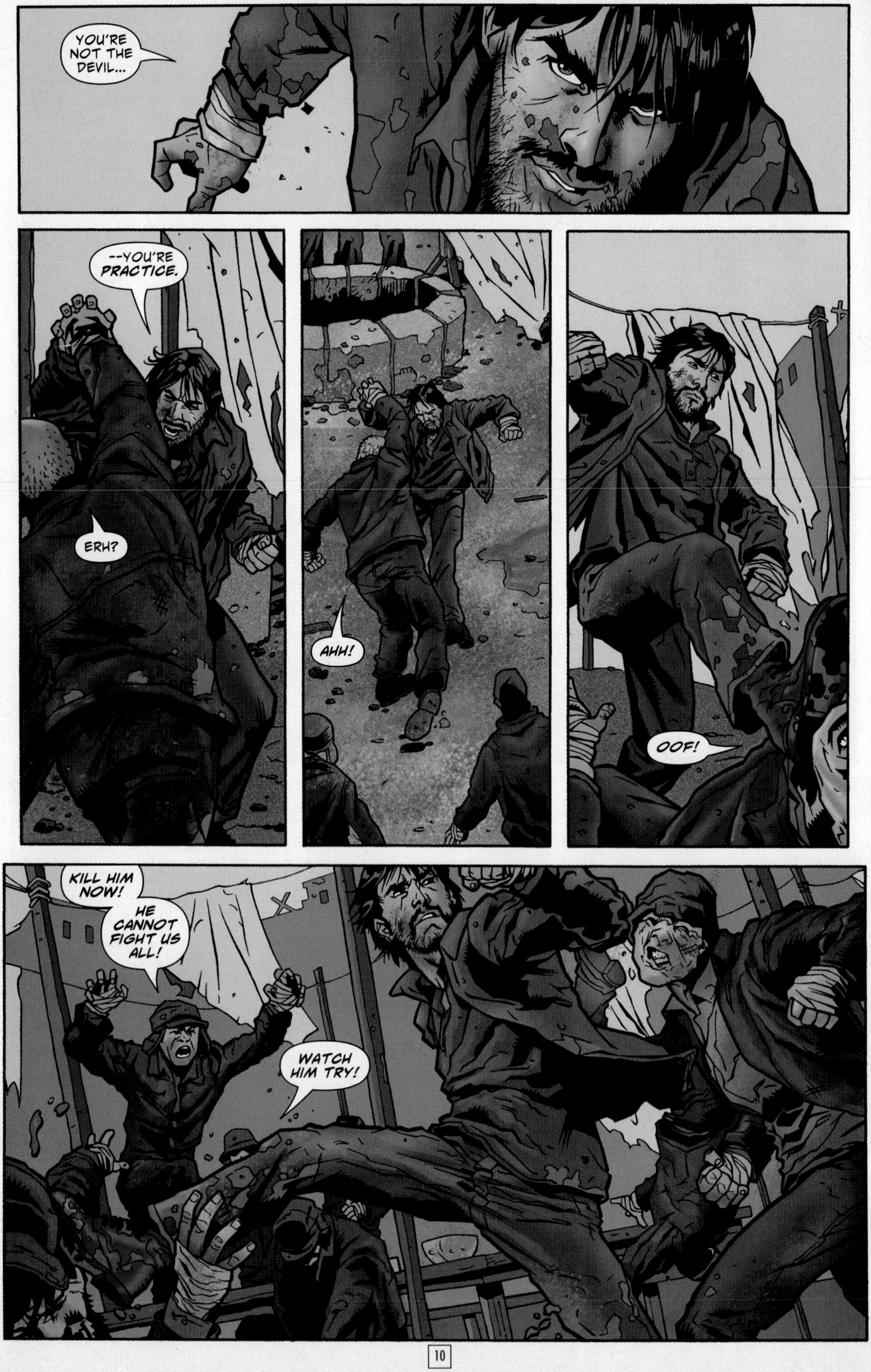
YOU'RE NOT THE DEVIL...
--YOU'RE PRACTICE.
ERH?
AHH!
OOF!
KILL HIM NOW!
HE CANNOT FIGHT US ALL!
WATCH HIM TRY!

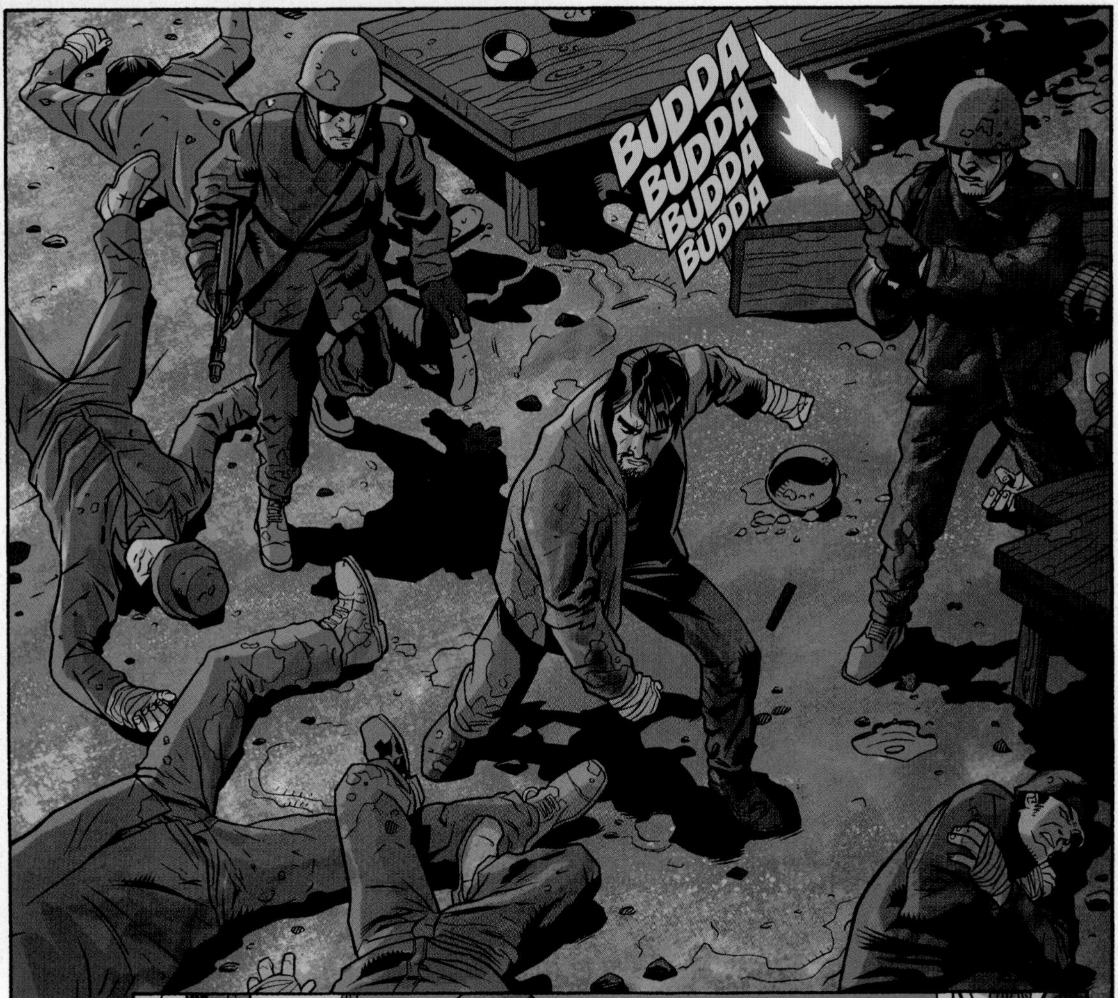
BUDDA BUDDA BUDDA BUDDA

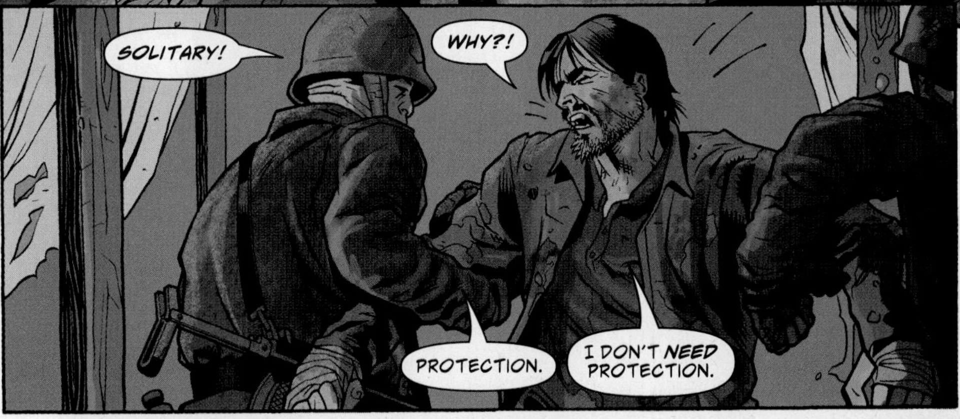
SOLITARY!
WHY?!
PROTECTION.
I DON'T NEED PROTECTION.

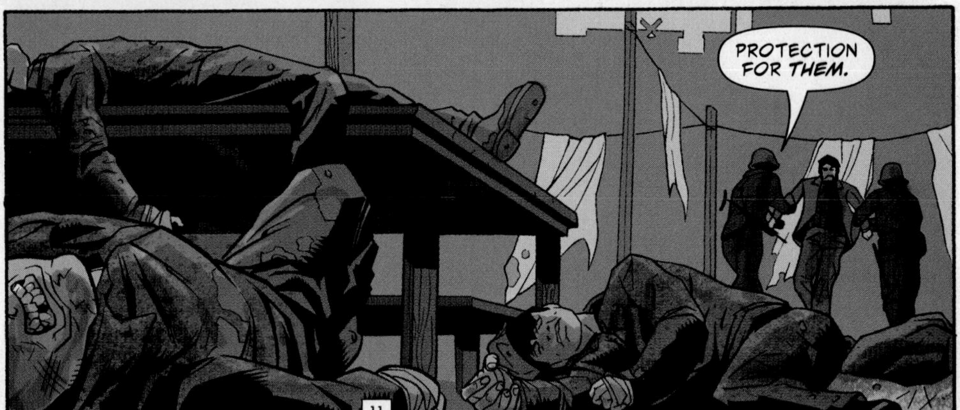
PROTECTION FOR THEM.

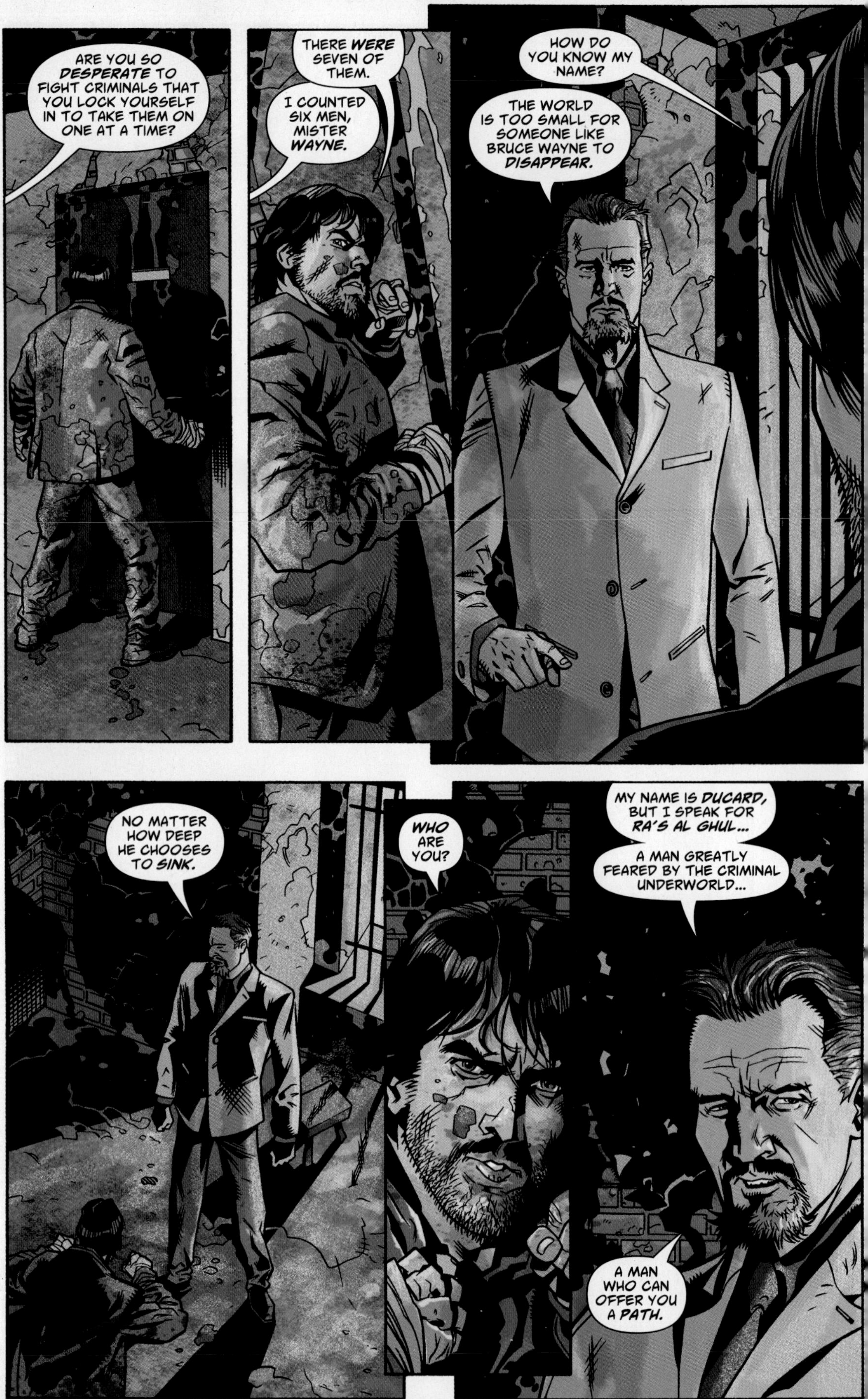
ARE YOU SO DESPERATE TO FIGHT CRIMINALS THAT YOU LOCK YOURSELF IN TO TAKE THEM ON ONE AT A TIME?
I COUNTED SIX MEN, MISTER WAYNE.
THERE WERE SEVEN OF THEM.
HOW DO YOU KNOW MY NAME?
THE WORLD IS TOO SMALL FOR SOMEONE LIKE BRUCE WAYNE TO DISAPPEAR.
NO MATTER HOW DEEP HE CHOOSES TO SINK.
WHO ARE YOU?
MY NAME IS DUCARD, BUT I SPEAK FOR RA'S AL GHUL...
A MAN GREATLY FEARED BY THE CRIMINAL UNDERWORLD...
A MAN WHO CAN OFFER YOU A PATH.

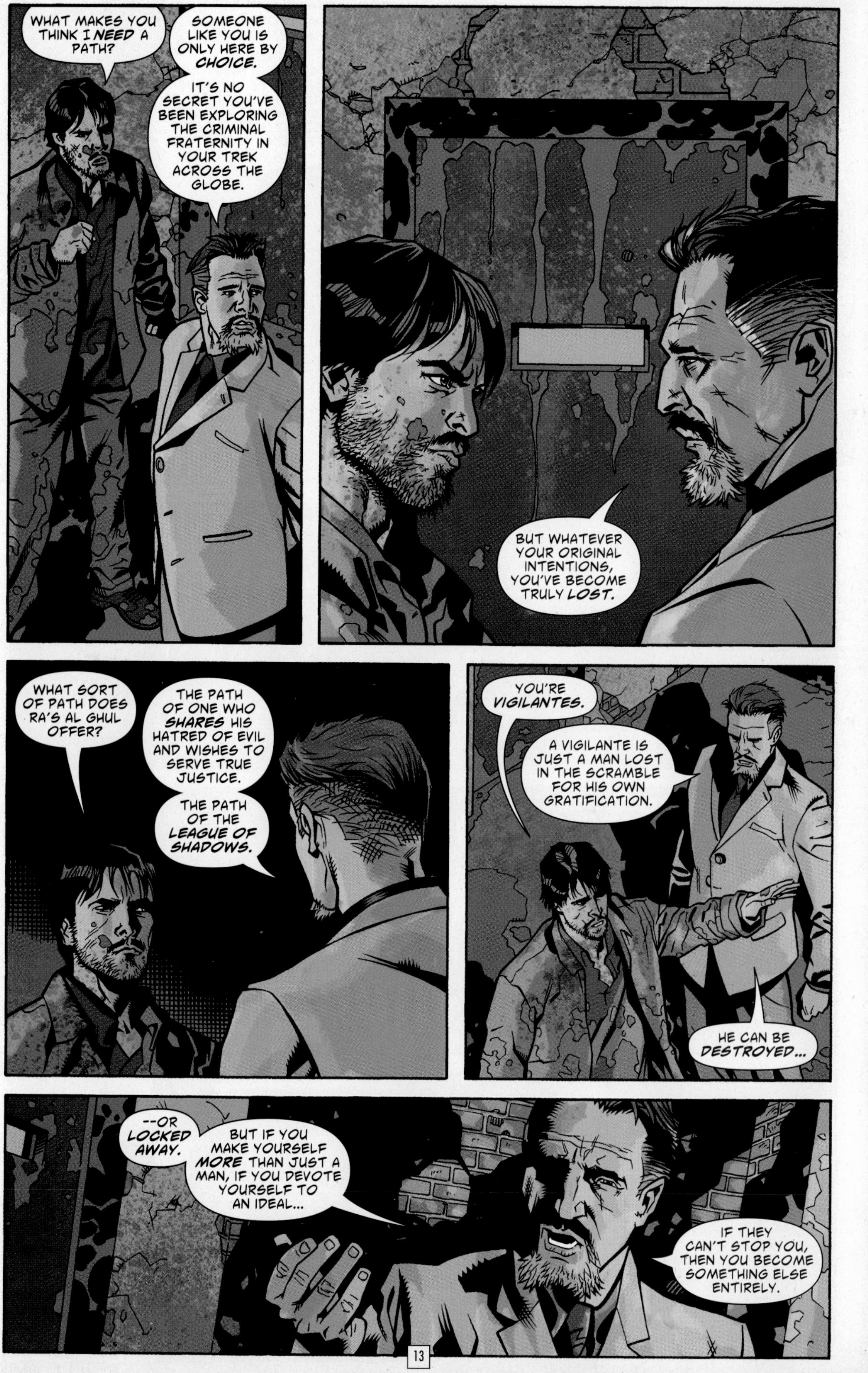
WHAT MAKES YOU THINK I NEED A PATH?
SOMEONE LIKE YOU IS ONLY HERE BY CHOICE.
IT'S NO SECRET YOU'VE BEEN EXPLORING THE CRIMINAL FRATERNITY IN YOUR TREK ACROSS THE GLOBE.
BUT WHATEVER YOUR ORIGINAL INTENTIONS, YOU'VE BECOME TRULY LOST.
WHAT SORT OF PATH DOES RA'S AL GHUL OFFER?
THE PATH OF ONE WHO SHARES HIS HATRED OF EVIL AND WISHES TO SERVE TRUE JUSTICE.
THE PATH OF THE LEAGUE OF SHADOWS.
YOU'RE VIGILANTES.
A VIGILANTE IS JUST A MAN LOST IN THE SCRAMBLE FOR HIS OWN GRATIFICATION.
HE CAN BE DESTROYED...
--OR LOCKED AWAY.
BUT IF YOU MAKE YOURSELF MORE THAN JUST A MAN, IF YOU DEVOTE YOURSELF TO AN IDEAL...
IF THEY CAN'T STOP YOU, THEN YOU BECOME SOMETHING ELSE ENTIRELY.

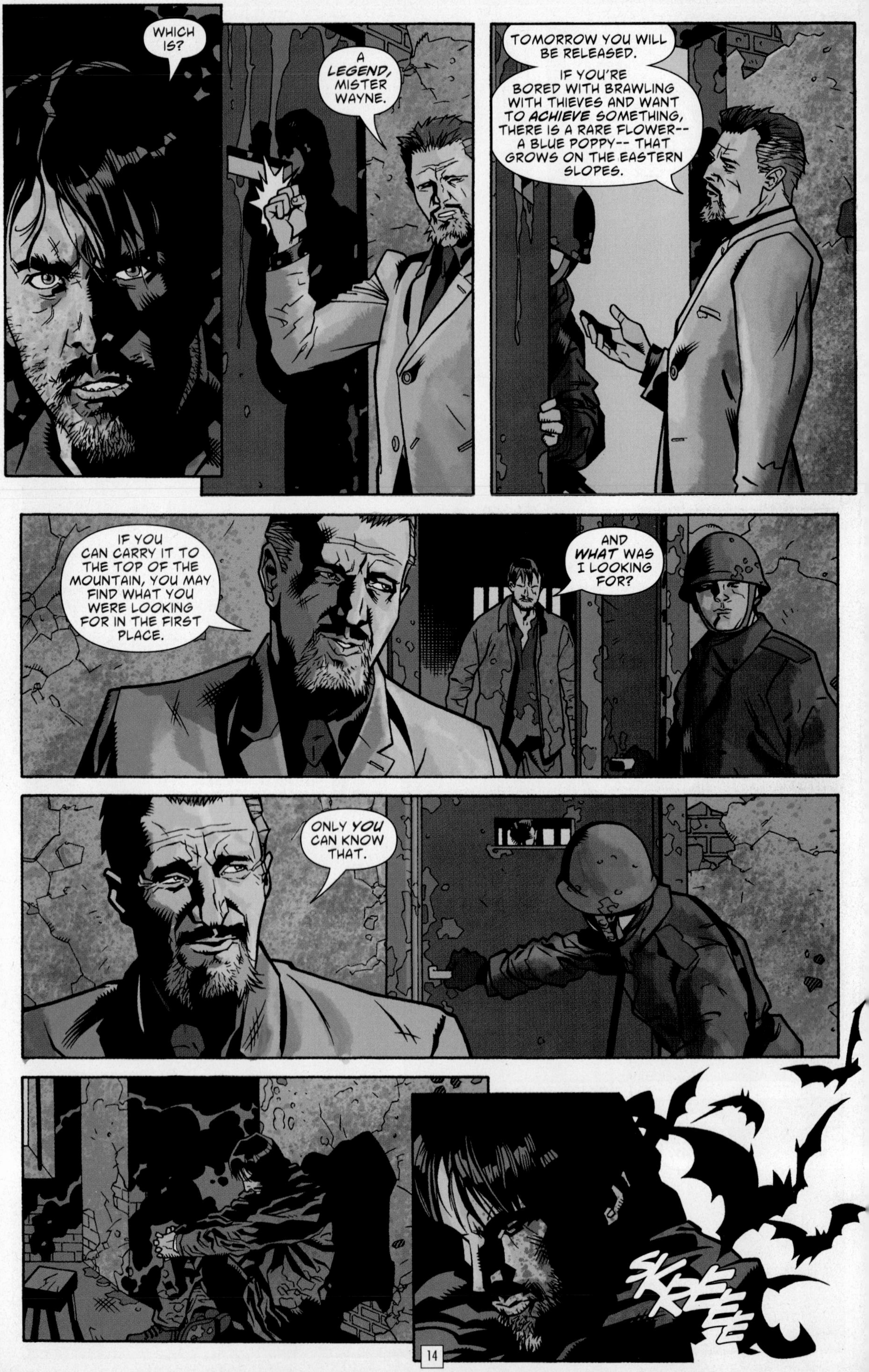
WHICH IS?
A LEGEND, MISTER WAYNE.
TOMORROW YOU WILL BE RELEASED.
IF YOU'RE BORED WITH BRAWLING WITH THIEVES AND WANT TO ACHIEVE SOMETHING, THERE IS A RARE FLOWER-- A BLUE POPPY-- THAT GROWS ON THE EASTERN SLOPES.
IF YOU CAN CARRY IT TO THE TOP OF THE MOUNTAIN, YOU MAY FIND WHAT YOU WERE LOOKING FOR IN THE FIRST PLACE.
AND WHAT WAS I LOOKING FOR?
ONLY YOU CAN KNOW THAT.
SKREEEE

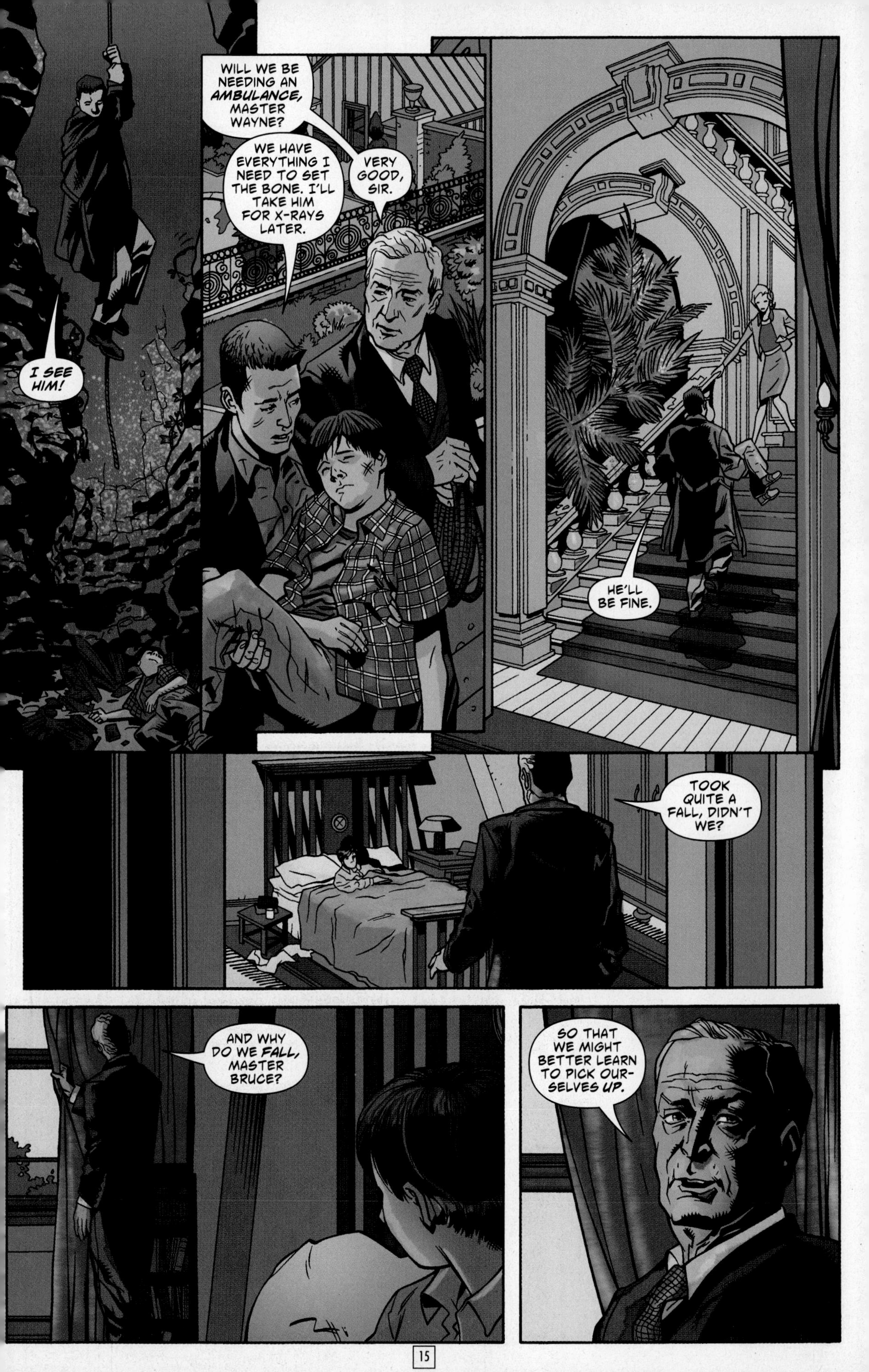
I SEE HIM!
WILL WE BE NEEDING AN AMBULANCE, MASTER WAYNE?
WE HAVE EVERYTHING I NEED TO SET THE BONE. I'LL TAKE HIM FOR X-RAYS LATER.
VERY GOOD, SIR.
HE'LL BE FINE.
TOOK QUITE A FALL, DIDN'T WE?
AND WHY DO WE FALL, MASTER BRUCE?
SO THAT WE MIGHT BETTER LEARN TO PICK OURSELVES UP.

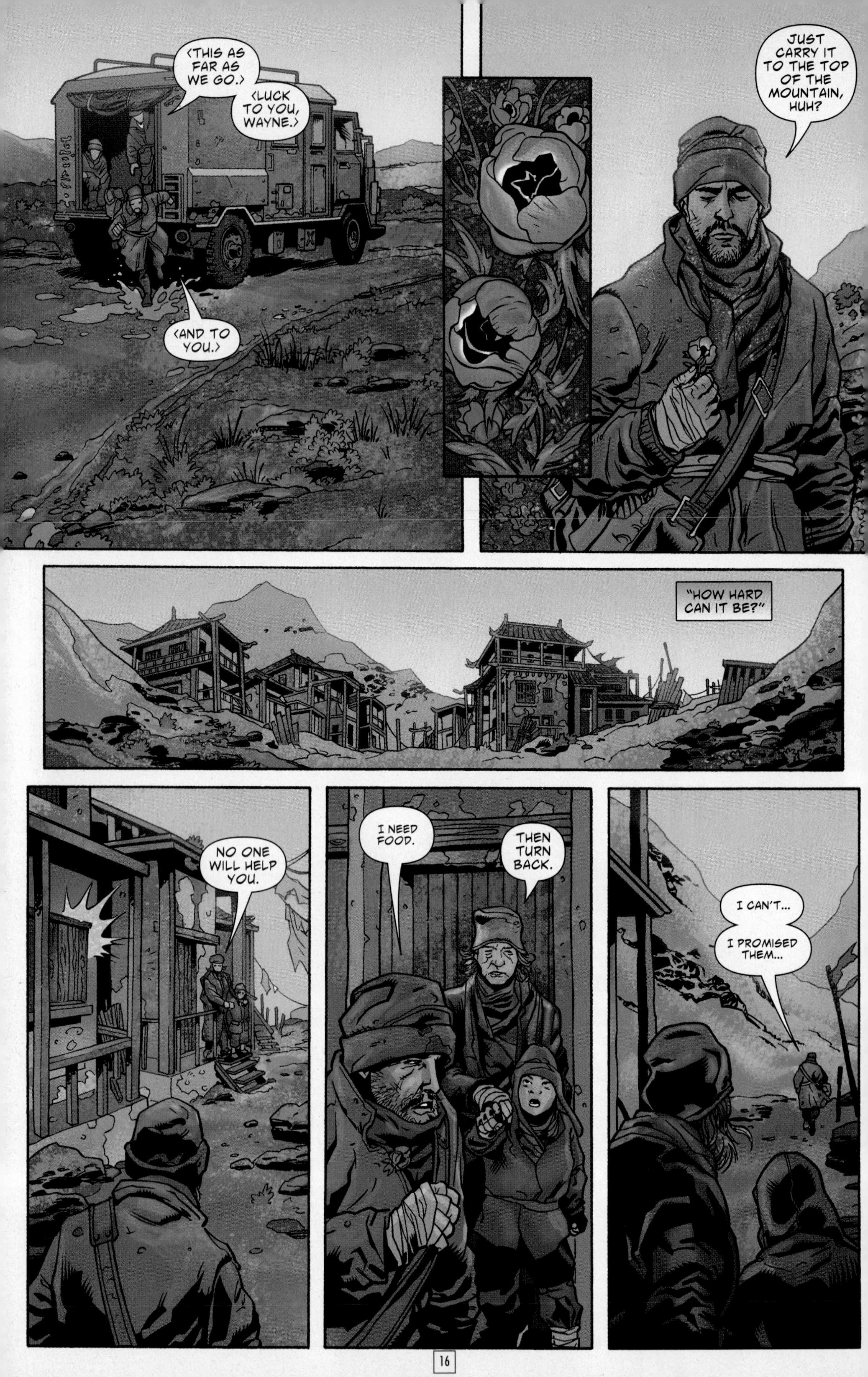
<THIS AS FAR AS WE GO.>
<LUCK TO YOU, WAYNE.>
<AND TO YOU.>
JUST CARRY IT TO THE TOP OF THE MOUNTAIN, HUH?
"HOW HARD CAN IT BE?"
NO ONE WILL HELP YOU.
I NEED FOOD.
THEN TURN BACK.
I CAN'T...
I PROMISED THEM...

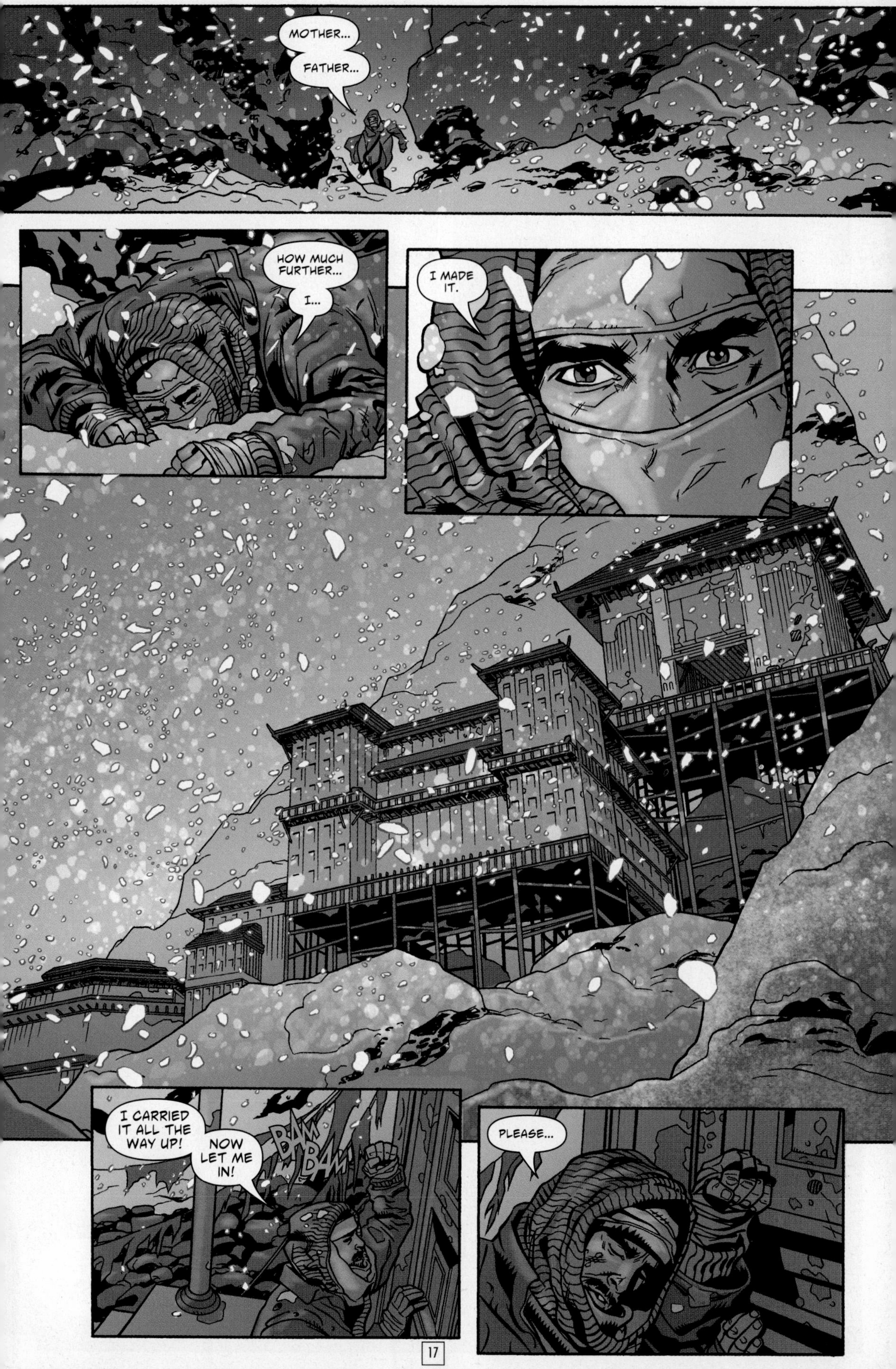
MOTHER...
FATHER...
HOW MUCH FURTHER...
I...
I MADE IT.
I CARRIED IT ALL THE WAY UP!
NOW LET ME IN!
BAM BAM
PLEASE...

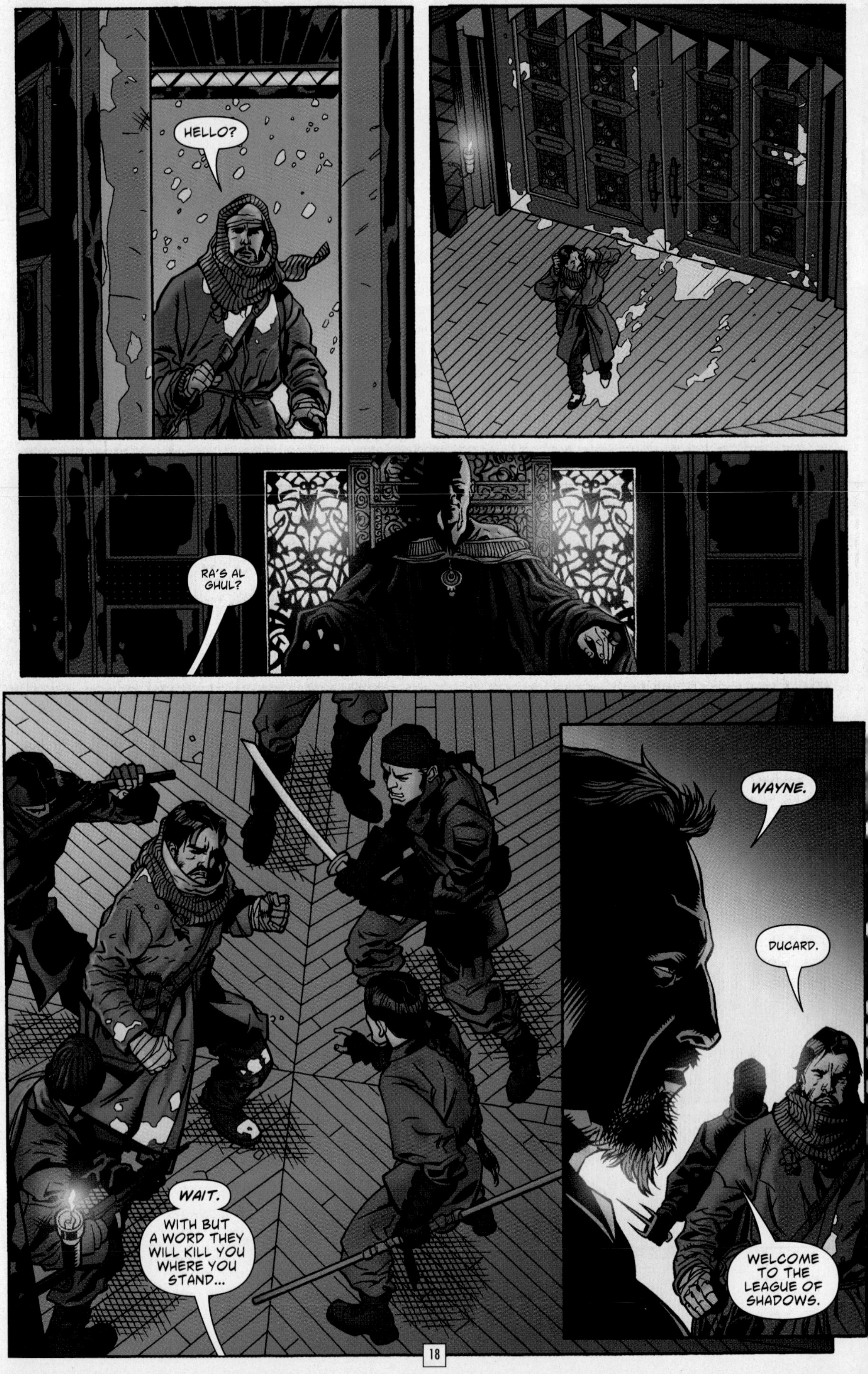
HELLO?
RA'S AL GHUL?
WAIT.
WITH BUT A WORD THEY WILL KILL YOU WHERE YOU STAND...
WAYNE.
DUCARD.
WELCOME TO THE LEAGUE OF SHADOWS.

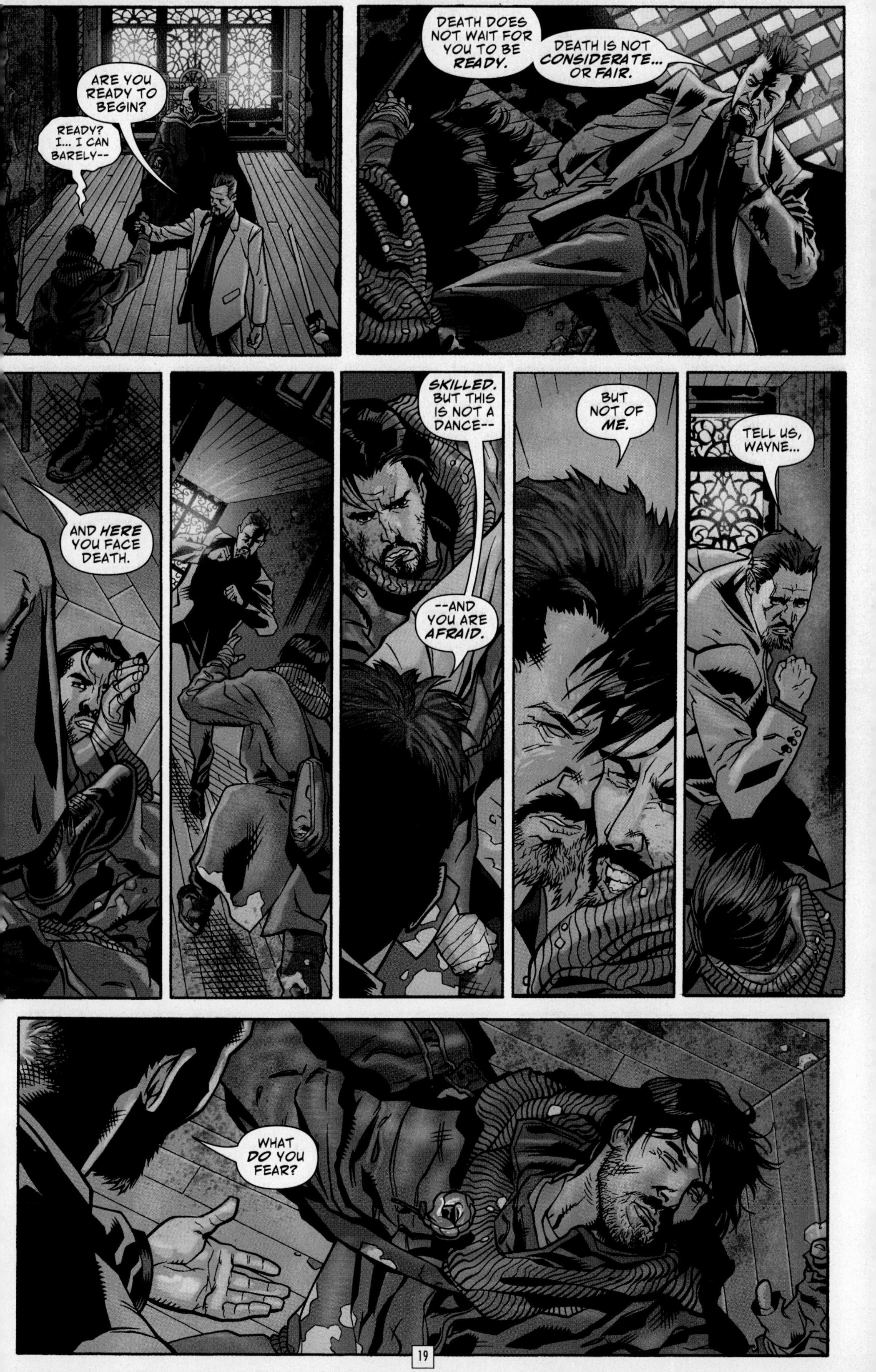
ARE YOU READY TO BEGIN?
READY? I... I CAN BARELY--
DEATH DOES NOT WAIT FOR YOU TO BE READY.
DEATH IS NOT CONSIDERATE... OR FAIR.
AND HERE YOU FACE DEATH.
SKILLED. BUT THIS IS NOT A DANCE--
--AND YOU ARE AFRAID.
BUT NOT OF ME.
TELL US, WAYNE...
WHAT DO YOU FEAR?

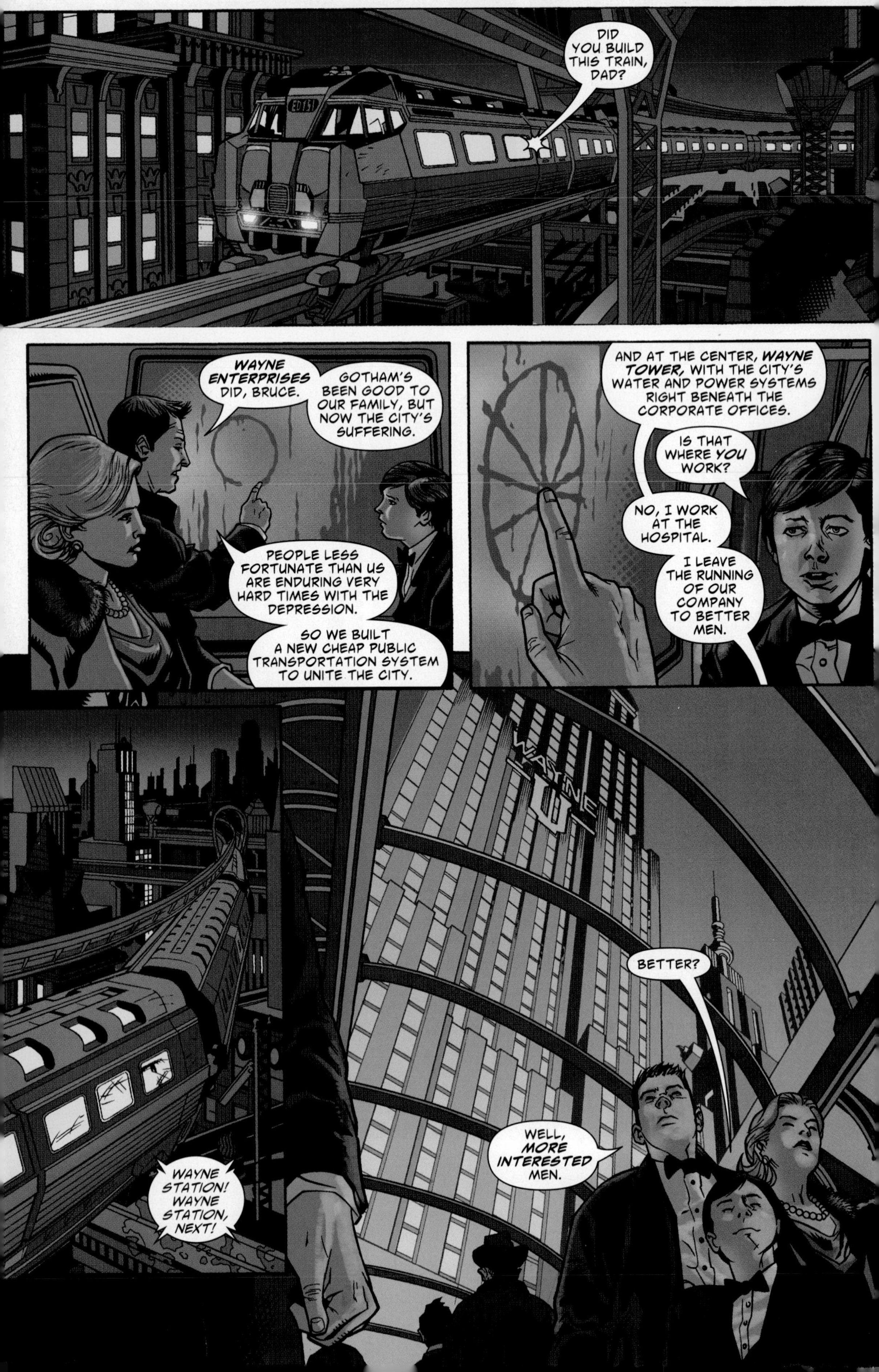
DID YOU BUILD THIS TRAIN, DAD?
WAYNE ENTERPRISES DID, BRUCE.
GOTHAM'S BEEN GOOD TO OUR FAMILY, BUT NOW THE CITY'S SUFFERING.
PEOPLE LESS FORTUNATE THAN US ARE ENDURING VERY HARD TIMES WITH THE DEPRESSION.
SO WE BUILT A NEW CHEAP PUBLIC TRANSPORTATION SYSTEM TO UNITE THE CITY.
AND AT THE CENTER, WAYNE TOWER, WITH THE CITY'S WATER AND POWER SYSTEMS RIGHT BENEATH THE CORPORATE OFFICES.
IS THAT WHERE YOU WORK?
NO, I WORK AT THE HOSPITAL.
I LEAVE THE RUNNING OF OUR COMPANY TO BETTER MEN.
WAYNE
BETTER?
WELL, MORE INTERESTED MEN.
WAYNE STATION! WAYNE STATION, NEXT!

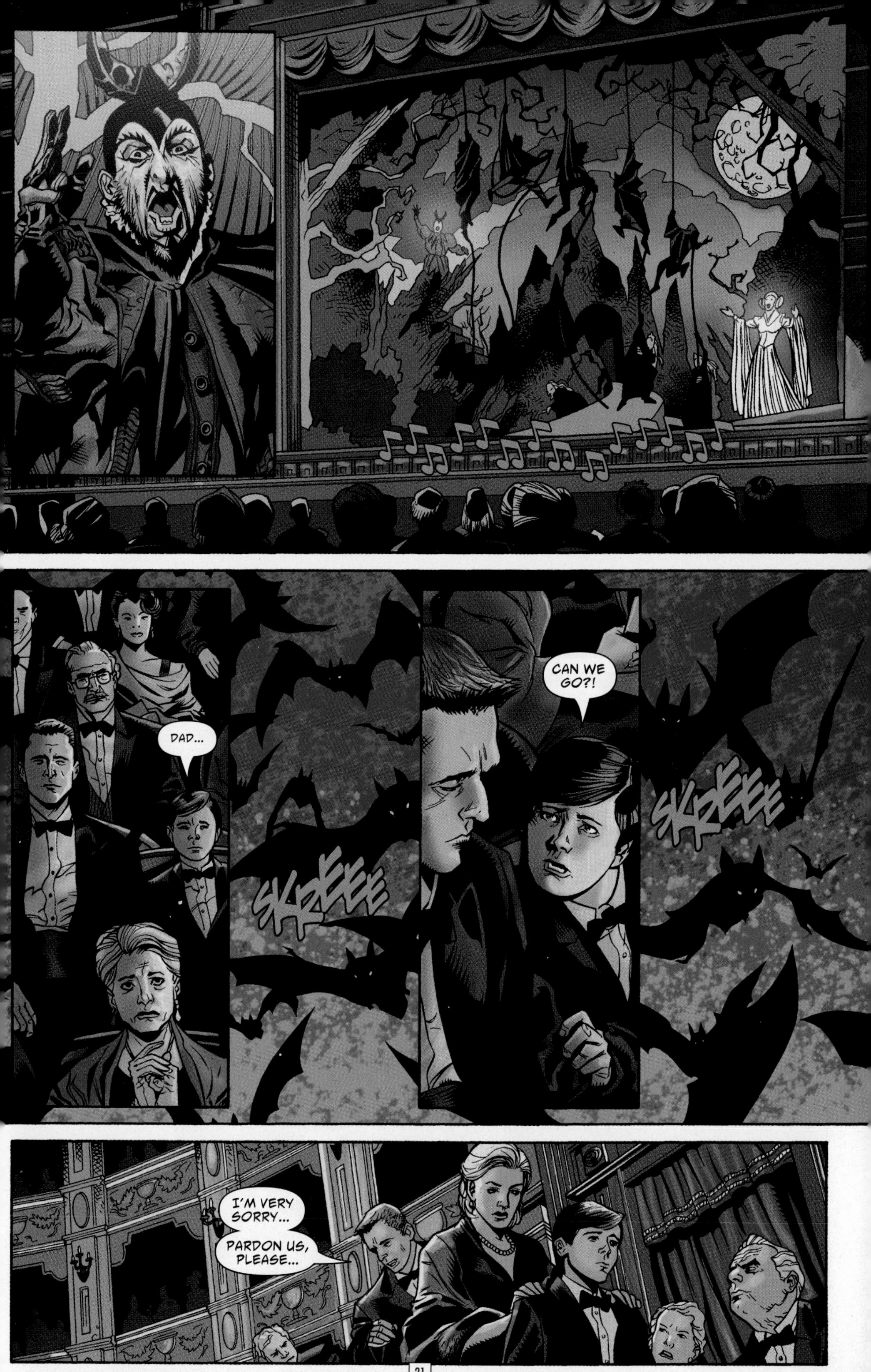
DAD...
CAN WE GO?!
SKREEE
SKREEE
I'M VERY SORRY...
PARDON US, PLEASE...

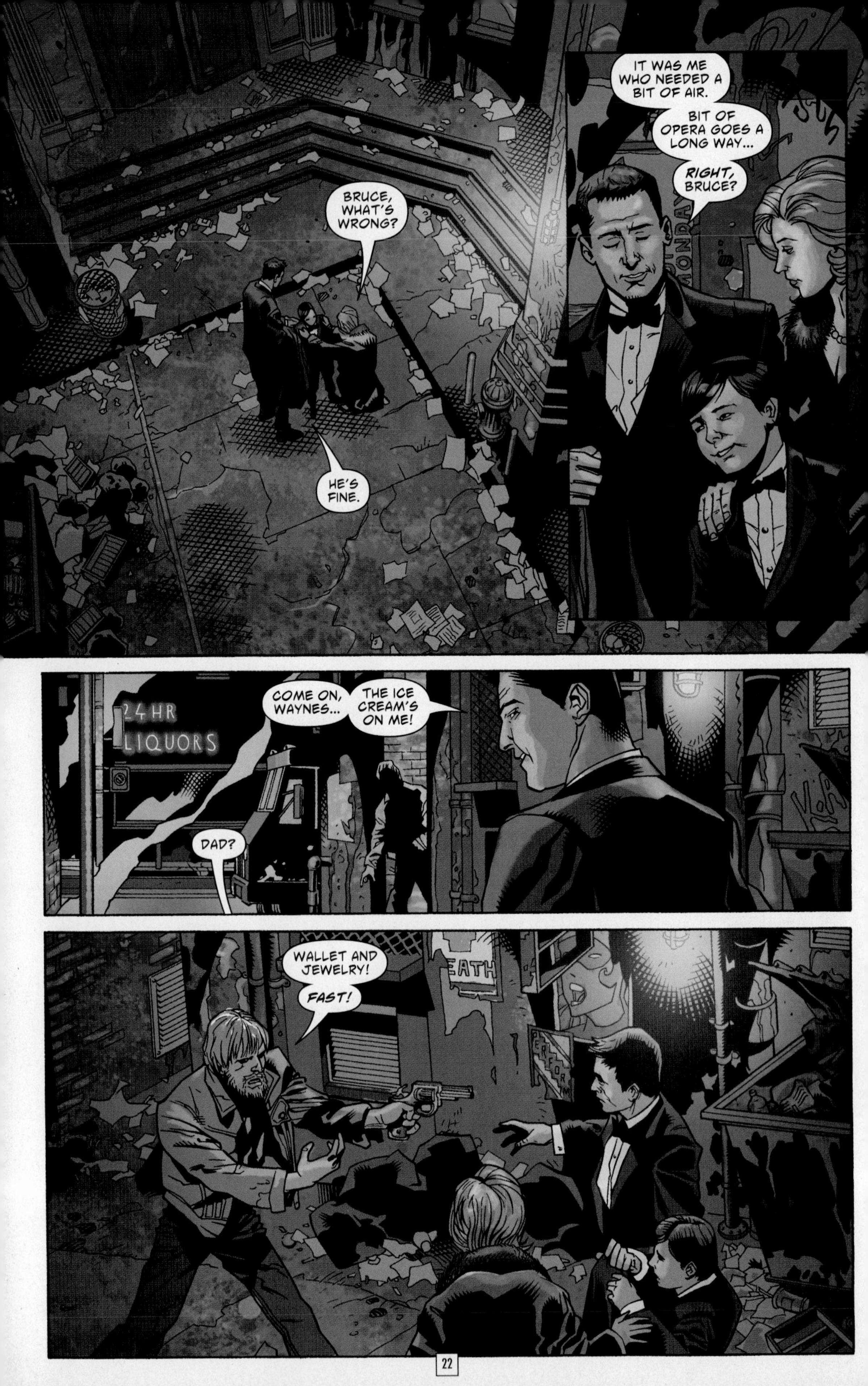

BRUCE, WHAT'S WRONG?
HE'S FINE.
IT WAS ME WHO NEEDED A BIT OF AIR.
BIT OF OPERA GOES A LONG WAY...
RIGHT, BRUCE?
24HR LIQUORS
COME ON, WAYNES...
THE ICE CREAM'S ON ME!
DAD?
WALLET AND JEWELRY!
FAST!

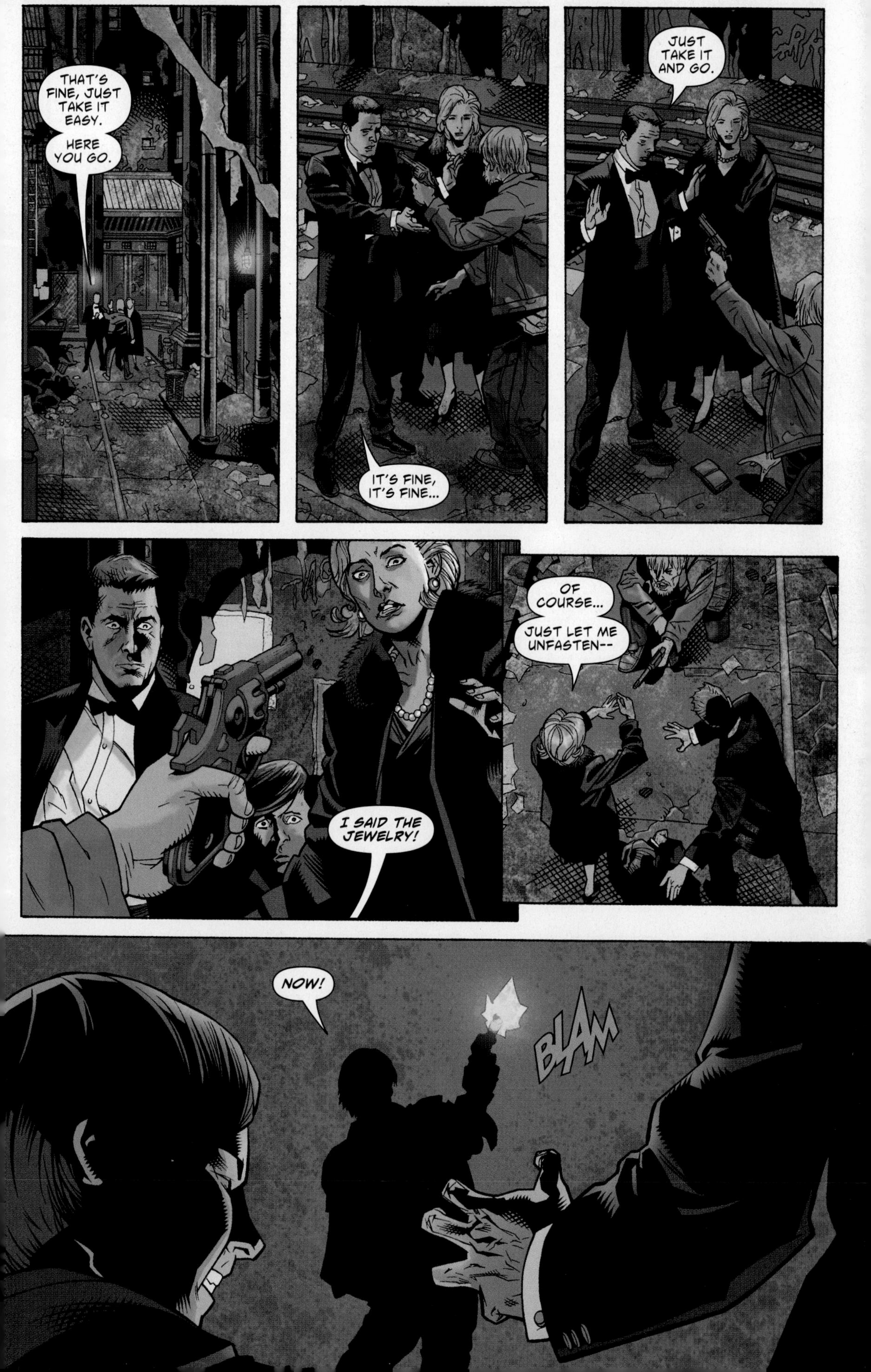
THAT'S FINE, JUST TAKE IT EASY.
HERE YOU GO.
IT'S FINE, IT'S FINE...
JUST TAKE IT AND GO.
I SAID THE JEWELRY!
OF COURSE...
JUST LET ME UNFASTEN--
NOW!
BLAM

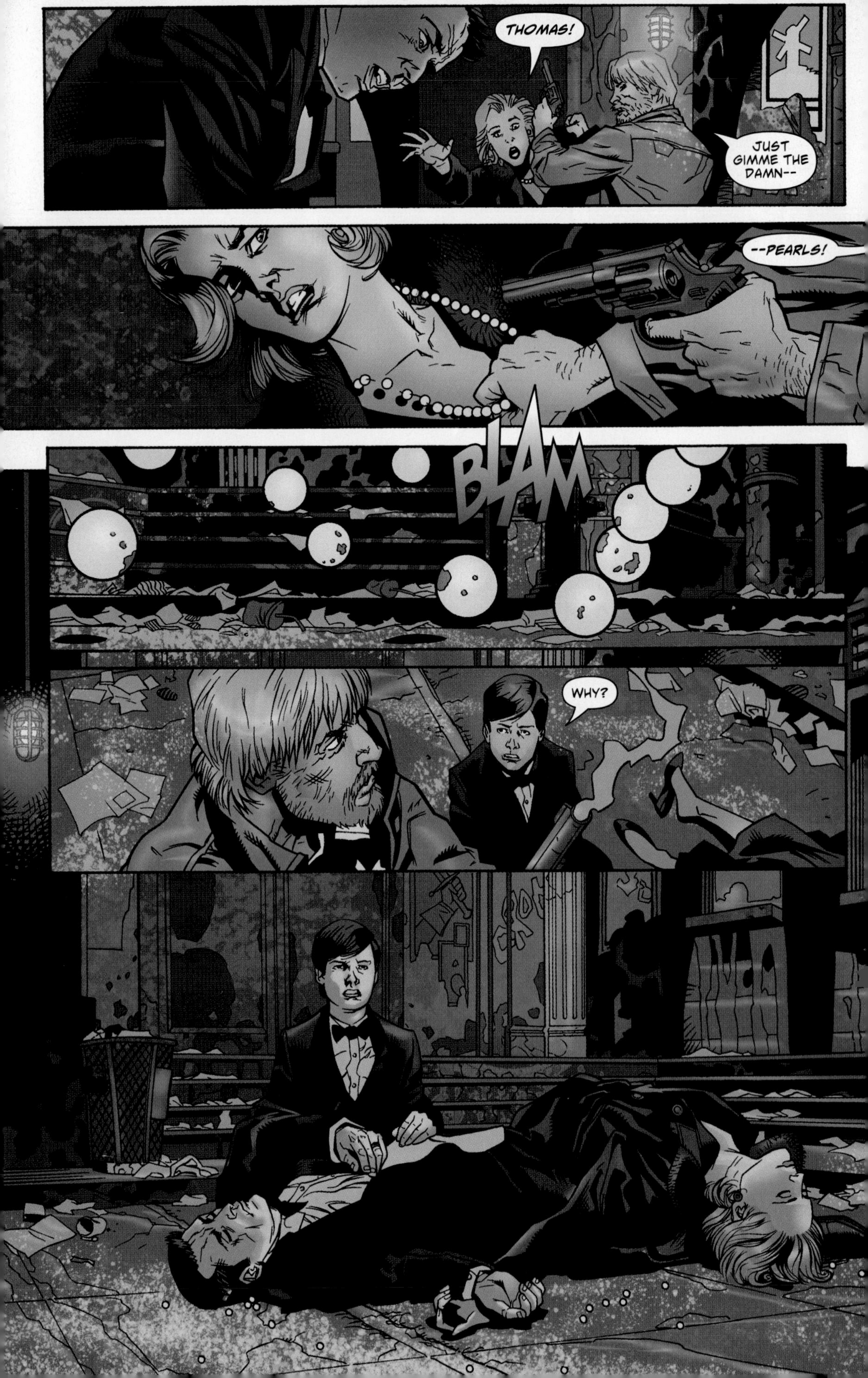
THOMAS!
JUST GIMME THE DAMN--
--PEARLS!
BLAM
WHY?

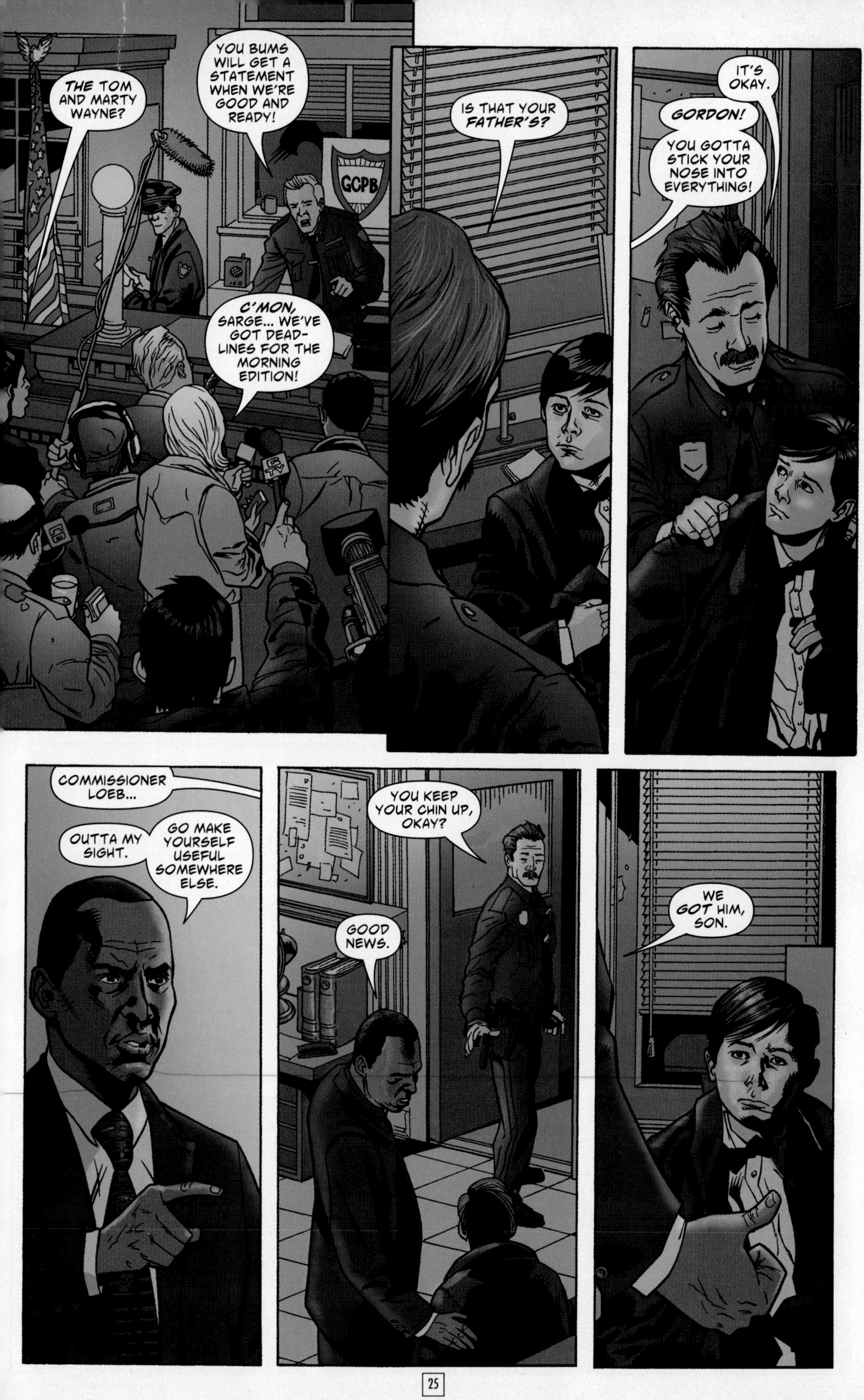
THE TOM AND MARTY WAYNE?
YOU BUMS WILL GET A STATEMENT WHEN WE'RE GOOD AND READY!
C'MON, SARGE... WE'VE GOT DEAD-LINES FOR THE MORNING EDITION!
IS THAT YOUR FATHER'S?
IT'S OKAY.
GORDON!
YOU GOTTA STICK YOUR NOSE INTO EVERYTHING!
COMMISSIONER LOEB...
OUTTA MY SIGHT.
GO MAKE YOURSELF USEFUL SOMEWHERE ELSE.
YOU KEEP YOUR CHIN UP, OKAY?
GOOD NEWS.
WE GOT HIM, SON.

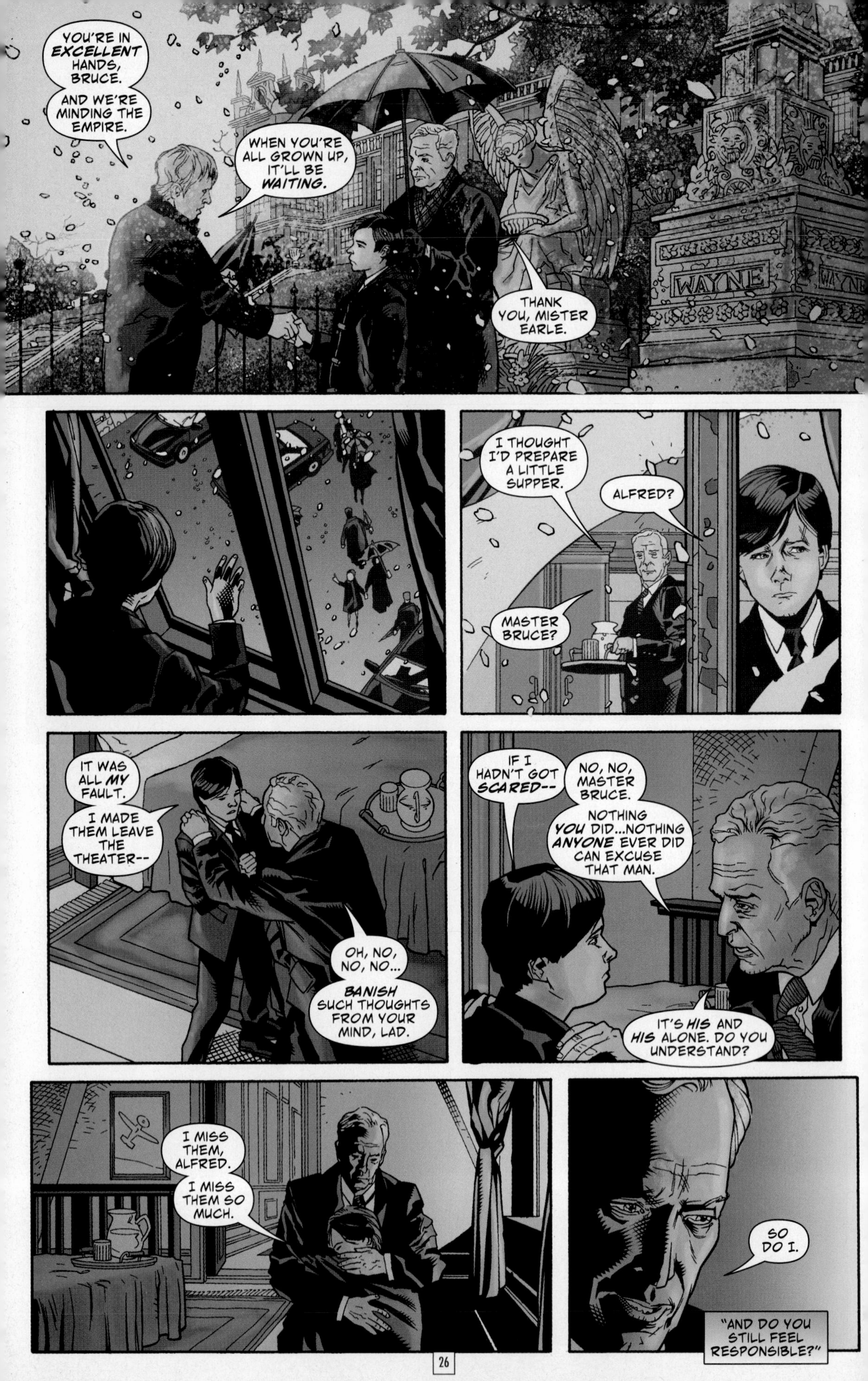

YOU'RE IN EXCELLENT HANDS, BRUCE.
AND WE'RE MINDING THE EMPIRE.
WHEN YOU'RE ALL GROWN UP, IT'LL BE WAITING.
THANK YOU, MISTER EARLE.
WAYNE
WAYNE
I THOUGHT I'D PREPARE A LITTLE SUPPER.
ALFRED?
MASTER BRUCE?
IT WAS ALL MY FAULT.
I MADE THEM LEAVE THE THEATER--
OH, NO, NO, NO...
BANISH SUCH THOUGHTS FROM YOUR MIND, LAD.
IF I HADN'T GOT SCARED--
NO, NO, MASTER BRUCE.
NOTHING YOU DID...NOTHING ANYONE EVER DID CAN EXCUSE THAT MAN.
IT'S HIS AND HIS ALONE. DO YOU UNDERSTAND?
I MISS THEM, ALFRED.
I MISS THEM SO MUCH.
SO DO I.
"AND DO YOU STILL FEEL RESPONSIBLE?"

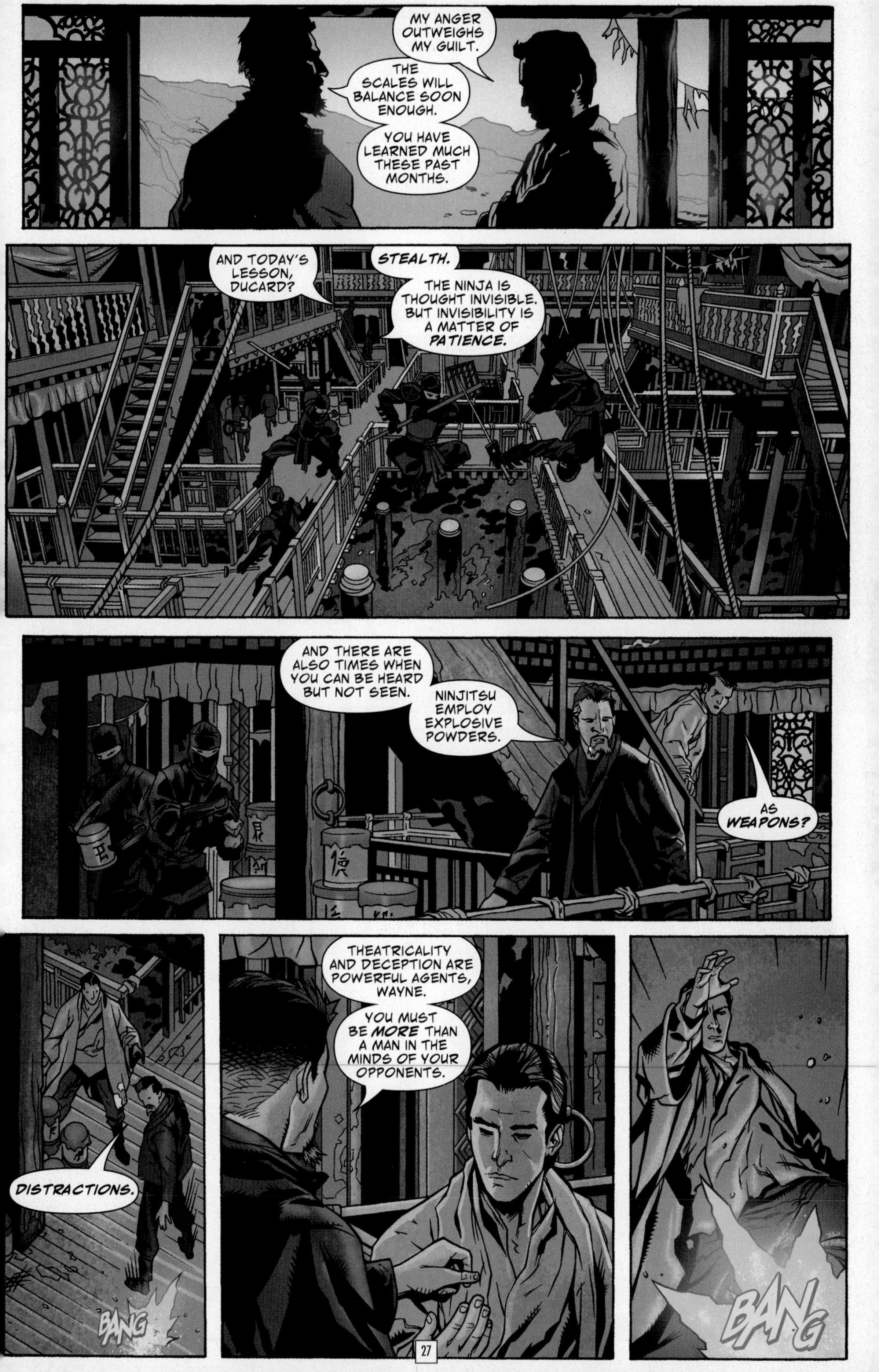
MY ANGER OUTWEIGHS MY GUILT.
THE SCALES WILL BALANCE SOON ENOUGH.
YOU HAVE LEARNED MUCH THESE PAST MONTHS.
AND TODAY'S LESSON, DUCARD?
STEALTH.
THE NINJA IS THOUGHT INVISIBLE. BUT INVISIBILITY IS A MATTER OF PATIENCE.
AND THERE ARE ALSO TIMES WHEN YOU CAN BE HEARD BUT NOT SEEN.
NINJITSU EMPLOY EXPLOSIVE POWDERS.
AS WEAPONS?
DISTRACTIONS.
BANG
THEATRICALITY AND DECEPTION ARE POWERFUL AGENTS, WAYNE.
YOU MUST BE MORE THAN A MAN IN THE MINDS OF YOUR OPPONENTS.
BANG

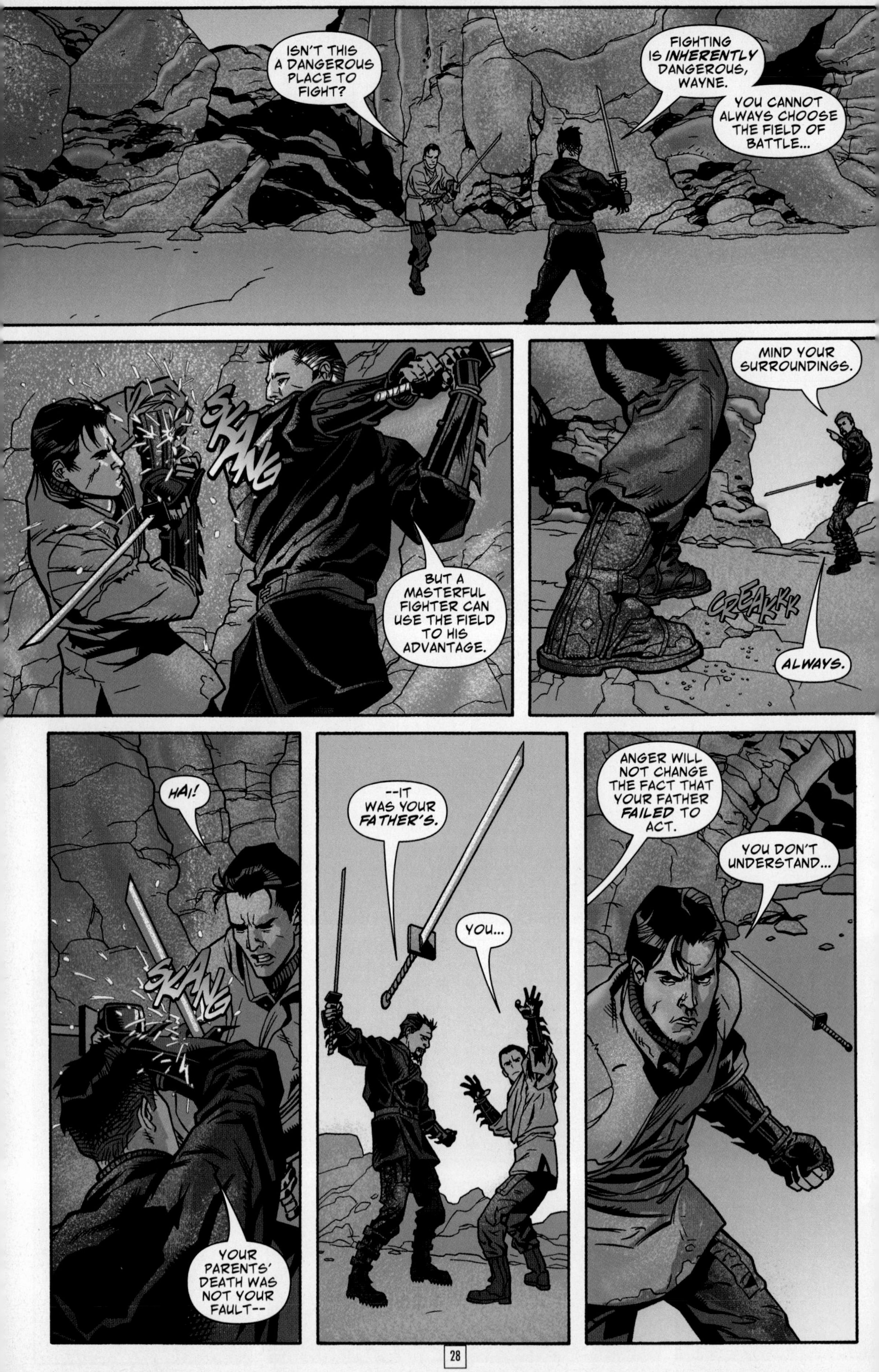
ISN'T THIS A DANGEROUS PLACE TO FIGHT?
FIGHTING IS *INHERENTLY* DANGEROUS, WAYNE.
YOU CANNOT ALWAYS CHOOSE THE FIELD OF BATTLE...
SKRANG
BUT A MASTERFUL FIGHTER CAN USE THE FIELD TO HIS ADVANTAGE.
MIND YOUR SURROUNDINGS.
CREAKKK
ALWAYS.
HAI!
SKRANG
YOUR PARENTS' DEATH WAS NOT YOUR FAULT--
--IT WAS YOUR *FATHER'S.*
YOU...
ANGER WILL NOT CHANGE THE FACT THAT YOUR FATHER *FAILED* TO ACT.
YOU DON'T UNDERSTAND...

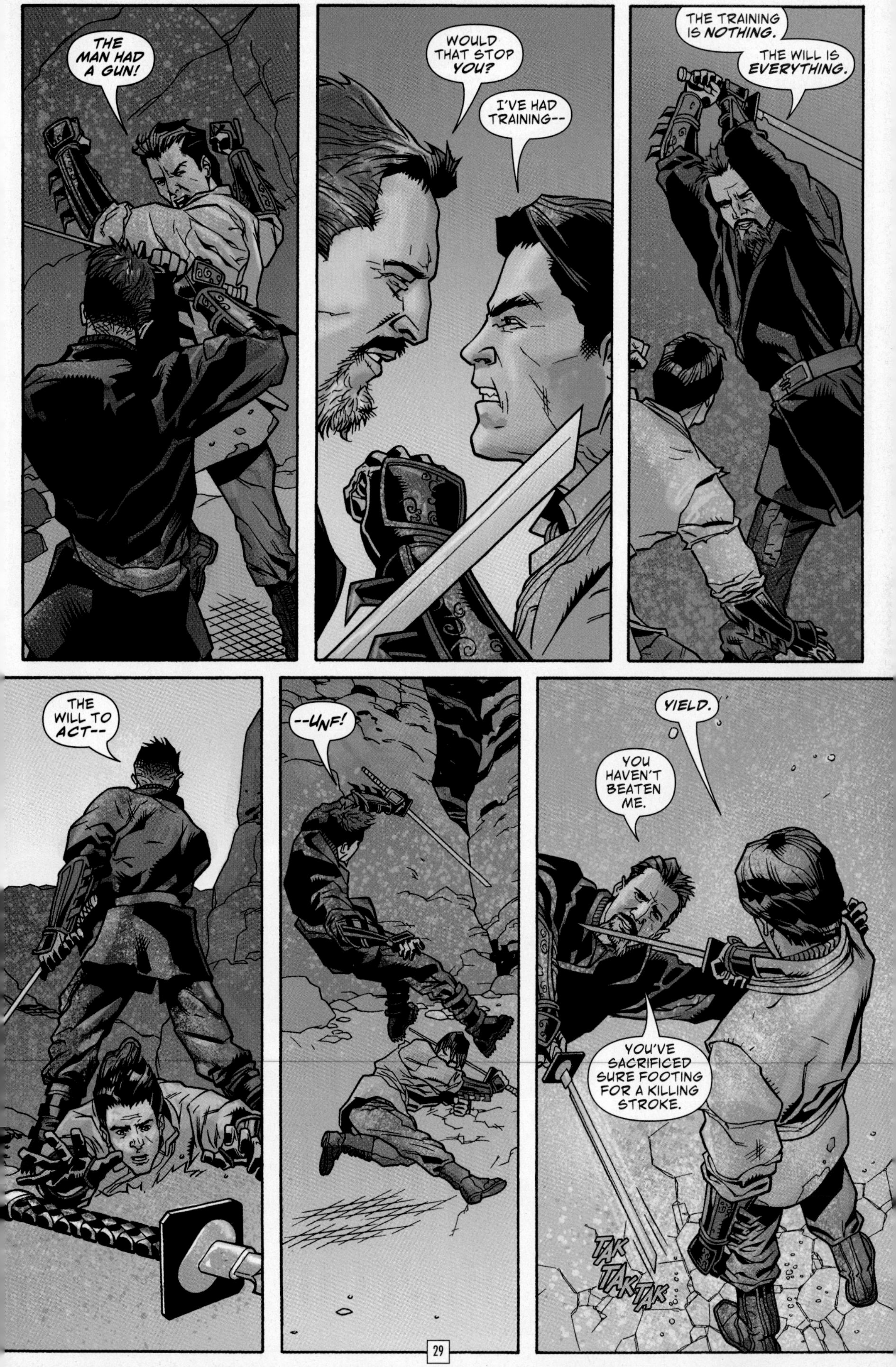
THE MAN HAD A GUN!
WOULD THAT STOP YOU?
I'VE HAD TRAINING--
THE TRAINING IS NOTHING.
THE WILL IS EVERYTHING.
THE WILL TO ACT--
--UNF!
YIELD.
YOU HAVEN'T BEATEN ME.
YOU'VE SACRIFICED SURE FOOTING FOR A KILLING STROKE.
TAK TAK TAK

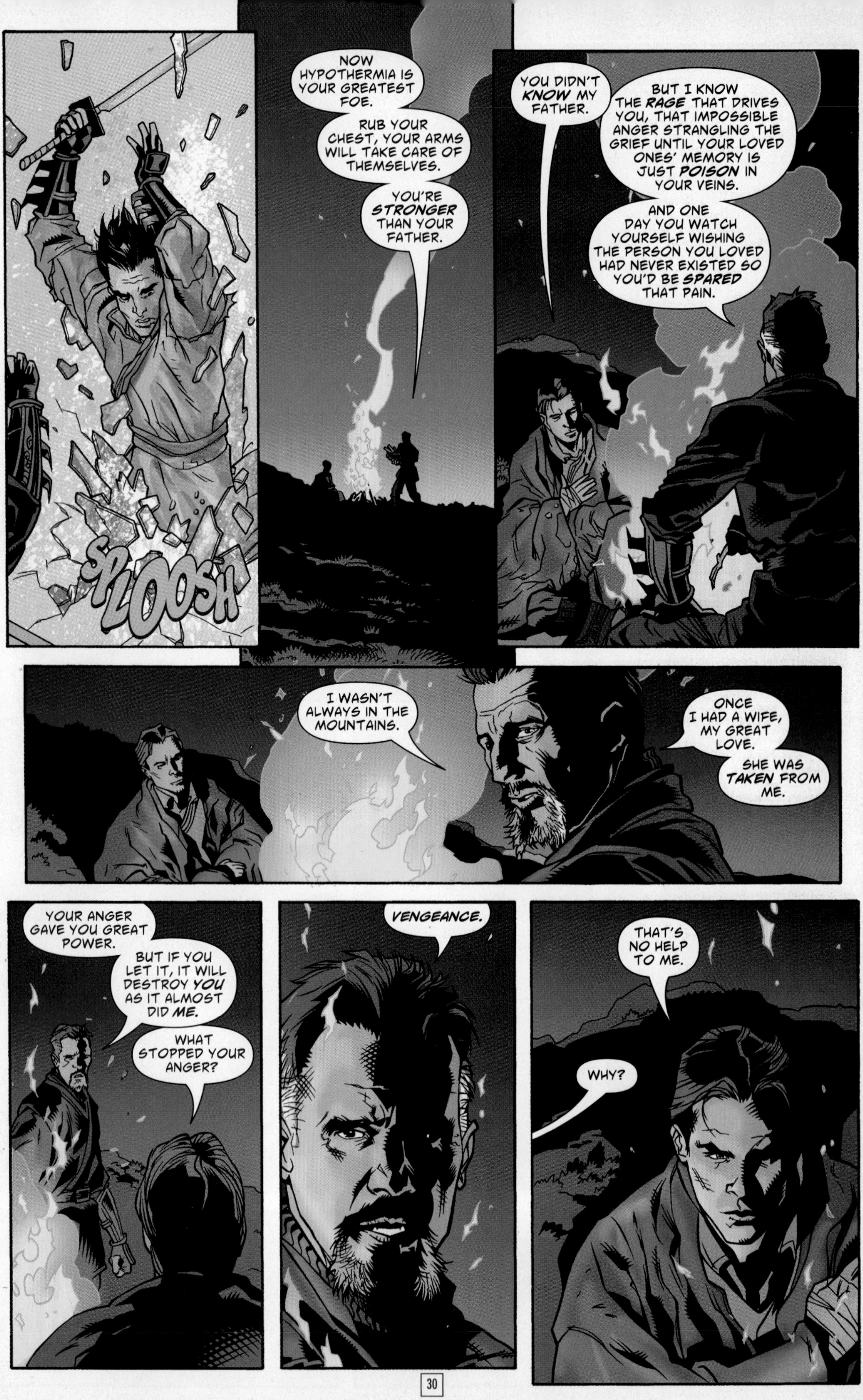
SPLOOSH
NOW HYPOTHERMIA IS YOUR GREATEST FOE.
RUB YOUR CHEST, YOUR ARMS WILL TAKE CARE OF THEMSELVES.
YOU'RE STRONGER THAN YOUR FATHER.
YOU DIDN'T KNOW MY FATHER.
BUT I KNOW THE RAGE THAT DRIVES YOU, THAT IMPOSSIBLE ANGER STRANGLING THE GRIEF UNTIL YOUR LOVED ONES' MEMORY IS JUST POISON IN YOUR VEINS.
AND ONE DAY YOU WATCH YOURSELF WISHING THE PERSON YOU LOVED HAD NEVER EXISTED SO YOU'D BE SPARED THAT PAIN.
I WASN'T ALWAYS IN THE MOUNTAINS.
ONCE I HAD A WIFE, MY GREAT LOVE.
SHE WAS TAKEN FROM ME.
YOUR ANGER GAVE YOU GREAT POWER.
BUT IF YOU LET IT, IT WILL DESTROY YOU AS IT ALMOST DID ME.
WHAT STOPPED YOUR ANGER?
VENGEANCE.
THAT'S NO HELP TO ME.
WHY?

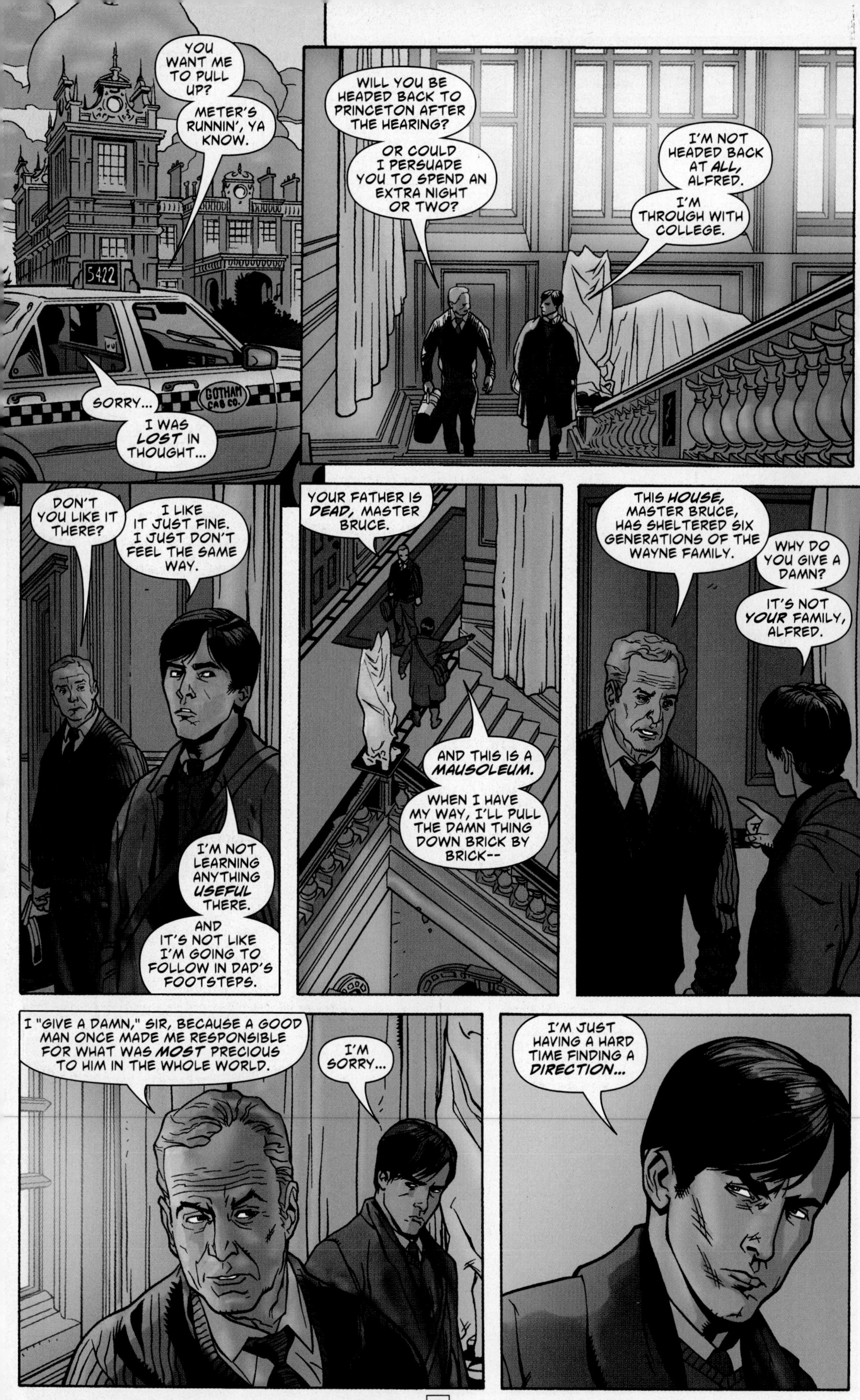
YOU WANT ME TO PULL UP?
METER'S RUNNIN', YA KNOW.
5422
SORRY...
I WAS LOST IN THOUGHT...
GOTHAM CAB CO.
WILL YOU BE HEADED BACK TO PRINCETON AFTER THE HEARING?
OR COULD I PERSUADE YOU TO SPEND AN EXTRA NIGHT OR TWO?
I'M NOT HEADED BACK AT ALL, ALFRED.
I'M THROUGH WITH COLLEGE.
DON'T YOU LIKE IT THERE?
I LIKE IT JUST FINE. I JUST DON'T FEEL THE SAME WAY.
I'M NOT LEARNING ANYTHING USEFUL THERE.
AND IT'S NOT LIKE I'M GOING TO FOLLOW IN DAD'S FOOTSTEPS.
YOUR FATHER IS DEAD, MASTER BRUCE.
AND THIS IS A MAUSOLEUM.
WHEN I HAVE MY WAY, I'LL PULL THE DAMN THING DOWN BRICK BY BRICK--
THIS HOUSE, MASTER BRUCE, HAS SHELTERED SIX GENERATIONS OF THE WAYNE FAMILY.
WHY DO YOU GIVE A DAMN?
IT'S NOT YOUR FAMILY, ALFRED.
I "GIVE A DAMN," SIR, BECAUSE A GOOD MAN ONCE MADE ME RESPONSIBLE FOR WHAT WAS MOST PRECIOUS TO HIM IN THE WHOLE WORLD.
I'M SORRY...
I'M JUST HAVING A HARD TIME FINDING A DIRECTION...

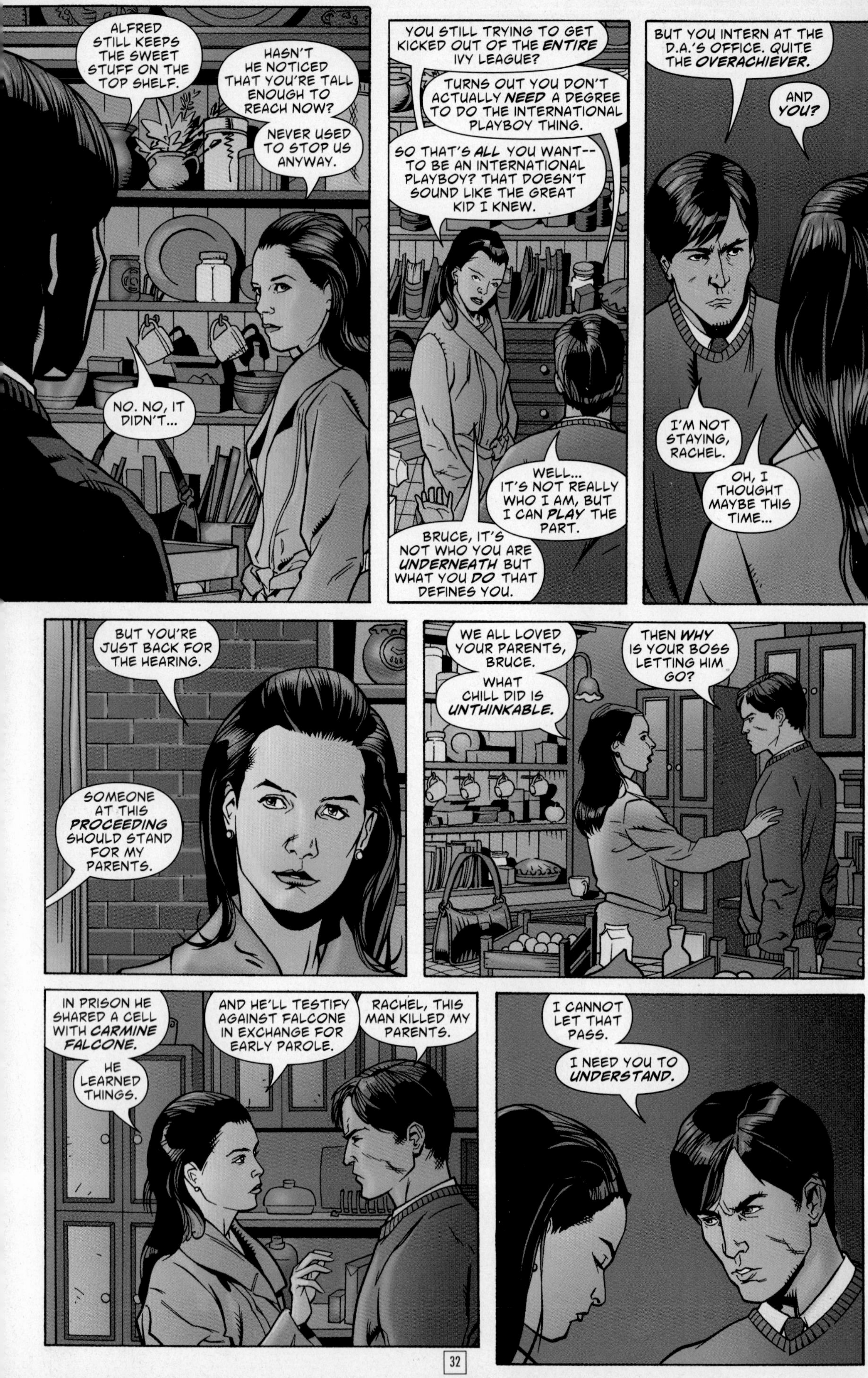
ALFRED STILL KEEPS THE SWEET STUFF ON THE TOP SHELF.
HASN'T HE NOTICED THAT YOU'RE TALL ENOUGH TO REACH NOW?
NEVER USED TO STOP US ANYWAY.
NO. NO, IT DIDN'T...
YOU STILL TRYING TO GET KICKED OUT OF THE ENTIRE IVY LEAGUE?
TURNS OUT YOU DON'T ACTUALLY NEED A DEGREE TO DO THE INTERNATIONAL PLAYBOY THING.
SO THAT'S ALL YOU WANT-- TO BE AN INTERNATIONAL PLAYBOY? THAT DOESN'T SOUND LIKE THE GREAT KID I KNEW.
WELL... IT'S NOT REALLY WHO I AM, BUT I CAN PLAY THE PART.
BRUCE, IT'S NOT WHO YOU ARE UNDERNEATH BUT WHAT YOU DO THAT DEFINES YOU.
BUT YOU INTERN AT THE D.A.'S OFFICE. QUITE THE OVERACHIEVER.
AND YOU?
I'M NOT STAYING, RACHEL.
OH, I THOUGHT MAYBE THIS TIME...
BUT YOU'RE JUST BACK FOR THE HEARING.
SOMEONE AT THIS PROCEEDING SHOULD STAND FOR MY PARENTS.
WE ALL LOVED YOUR PARENTS, BRUCE.
WHAT CHILL DID IS UNTHINKABLE.
THEN WHY IS YOUR BOSS LETTING HIM GO?
IN PRISON HE SHARED A CELL WITH CARMINE FALCONE.
HE LEARNED THINGS.
AND HE'LL TESTIFY AGAINST FALCONE IN EXCHANGE FOR EARLY PAROLE.
RACHEL, THIS MAN KILLED MY PARENTS.
I CANNOT LET THAT PASS.
I NEED YOU TO UNDERSTAND.

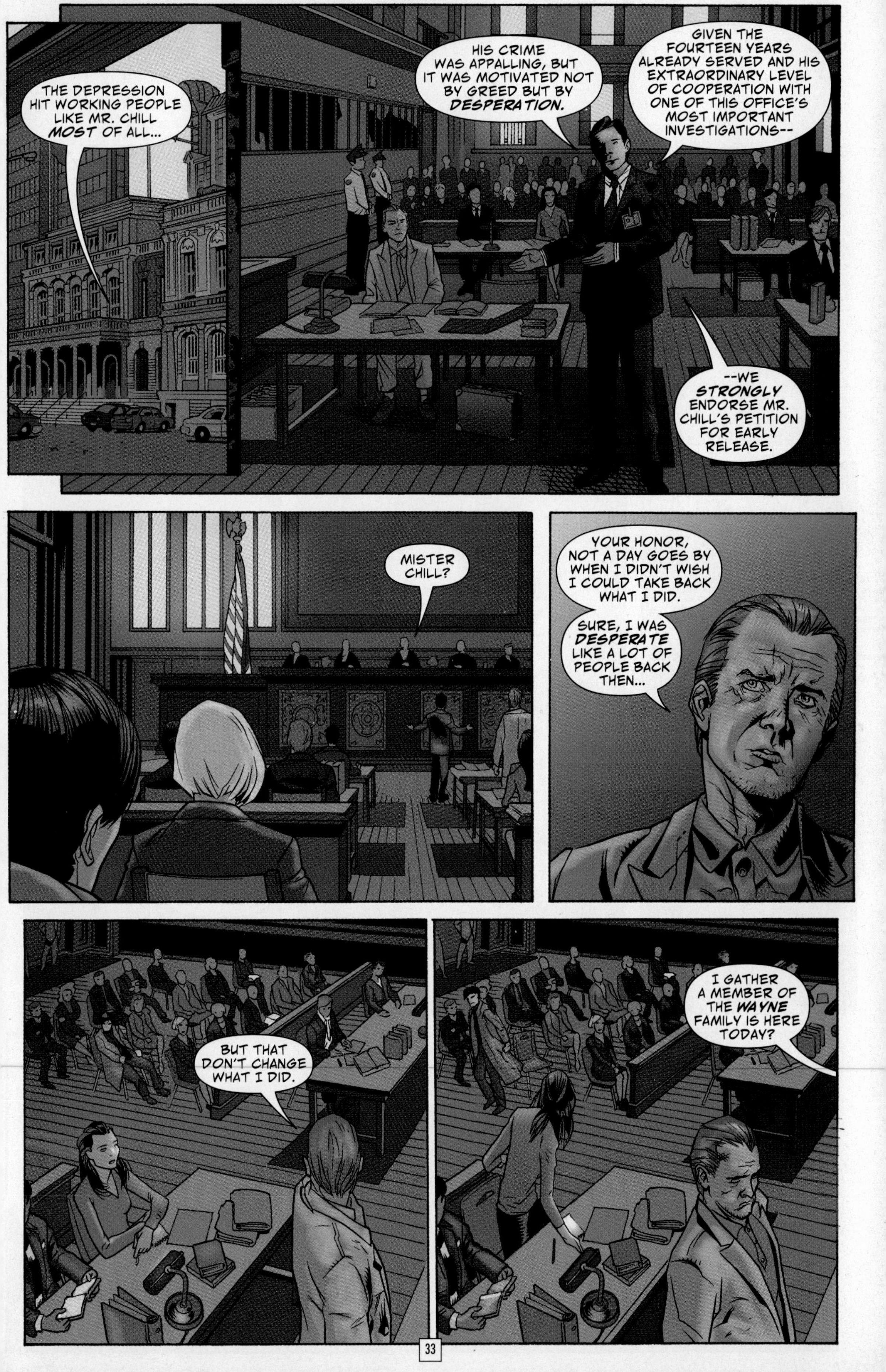
THE DEPRESSION HIT WORKING PEOPLE LIKE MR. CHILL MOST OF ALL...
HIS CRIME WAS APPALLING, BUT IT WAS MOTIVATED NOT BY GREED BUT BY DESPERATION.
GIVEN THE FOURTEEN YEARS ALREADY SERVED AND HIS EXTRAORDINARY LEVEL OF COOPERATION WITH ONE OF THIS OFFICE'S MOST IMPORTANT INVESTIGATIONS--
--WE STRONGLY ENDORSE MR. CHILL'S PETITION FOR EARLY RELEASE.
MISTER CHILL?
YOUR HONOR, NOT A DAY GOES BY WHEN I DIDN'T WISH I COULD TAKE BACK WHAT I DID.
SURE, I WAS DESPERATE LIKE A LOT OF PEOPLE BACK THEN...
BUT THAT DON'T CHANGE WHAT I DID.
I GATHER A MEMBER OF THE WAYNE FAMILY IS HERE TODAY?

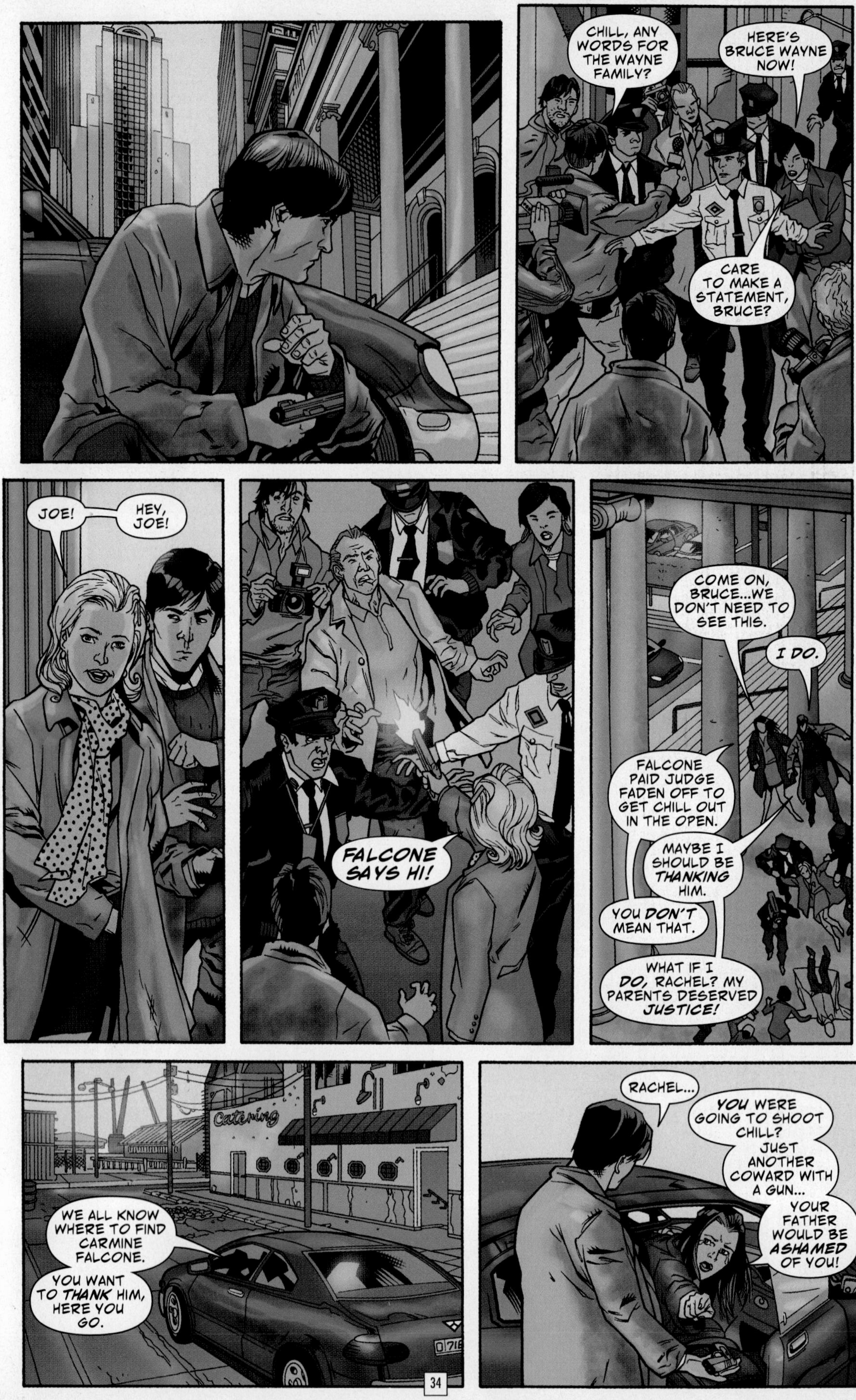
CHILL, ANY WORDS FOR THE WAYNE FAMILY?
HERE'S BRUCE WAYNE NOW!
CARE TO MAKE A STATEMENT, BRUCE?
JOE!
HEY, JOE!
FALCONE SAYS HI!
COME ON, BRUCE...WE DON'T NEED TO SEE THIS.
I DO.
FALCONE PAID JUDGE FADEN OFF TO GET CHILL OUT IN THE OPEN.
MAYBE I SHOULD BE THANKING HIM.
YOU DON'T MEAN THAT.
WHAT IF I DO, RACHEL? MY PARENTS DESERVED JUSTICE!
Catering
WE ALL KNOW WHERE TO FIND CARMINE FALCONE.
YOU WANT TO THANK HIM, HERE YOU GO.
RACHEL...
YOU WERE GOING TO SHOOT CHILL?
JUST ANOTHER COWARD WITH A GUN...
YOUR FATHER WOULD BE ASHAMED OF YOU!

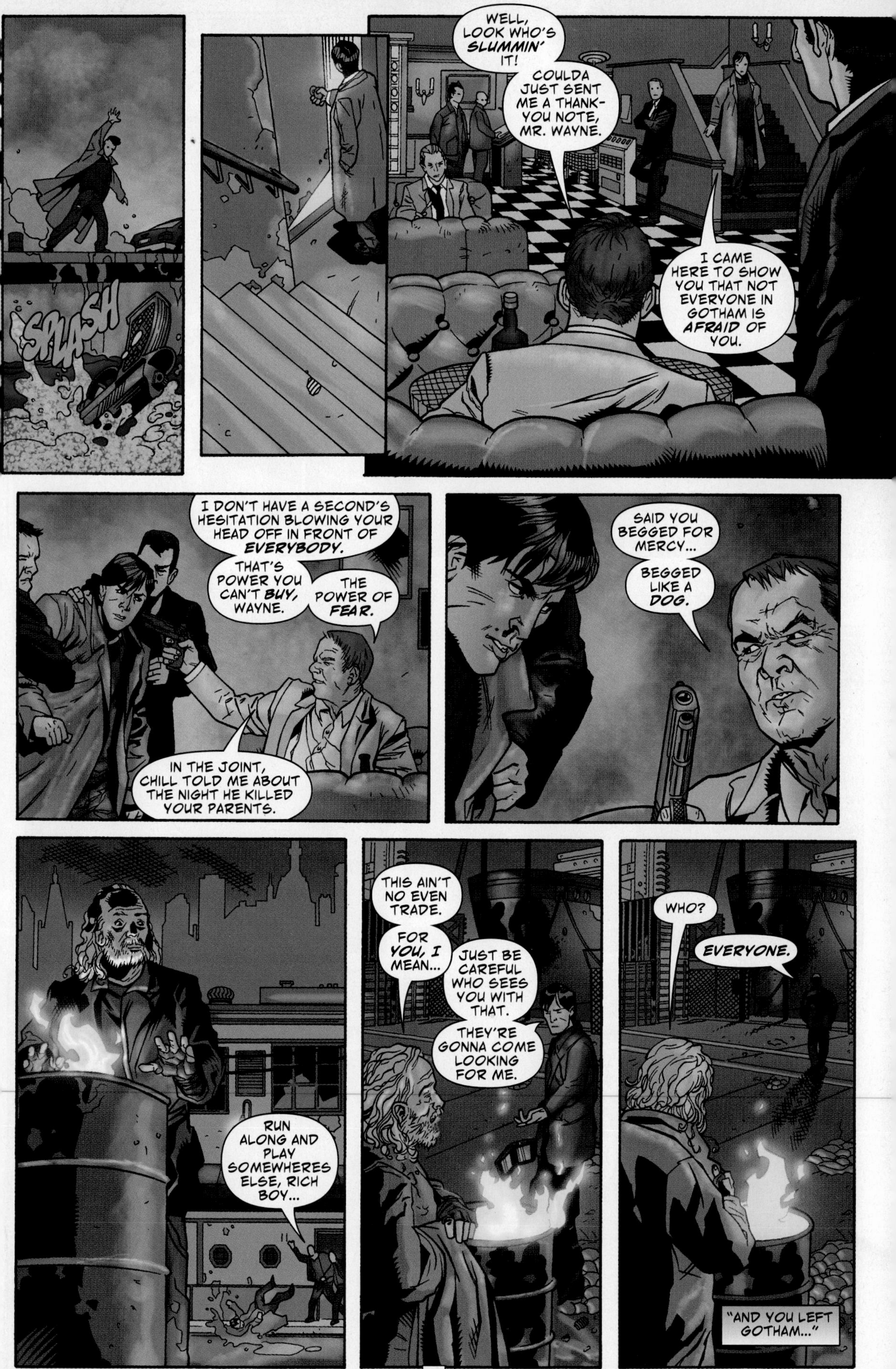
SPLASH
WELL, LOOK WHO'S SLUMMIN' IT!
COULDA JUST SENT ME A THANK-YOU NOTE, MR. WAYNE.
I CAME HERE TO SHOW YOU THAT NOT EVERYONE IN GOTHAM IS AFRAID OF YOU.
I DON'T HAVE A SECOND'S HESITATION BLOWING YOUR HEAD OFF IN FRONT OF EVERYBODY.
THAT'S POWER YOU CAN'T BUY, WAYNE.
THE POWER OF FEAR.
IN THE JOINT, CHILL TOLD ME ABOUT THE NIGHT HE KILLED YOUR PARENTS.
SAID YOU BEGGED FOR MERCY...
BEGGED LIKE A DOG.
RUN ALONG AND PLAY SOMEWHERES ELSE, RICH BOY...
THIS AIN'T NO EVEN TRADE.
FOR YOU, I MEAN...
JUST BE CAREFUL WHO SEES YOU WITH THAT.
THEY'RE GONNA COME LOOKING FOR ME.
WHO?
EVERYONE.
"AND YOU LEFT GOTHAM..."

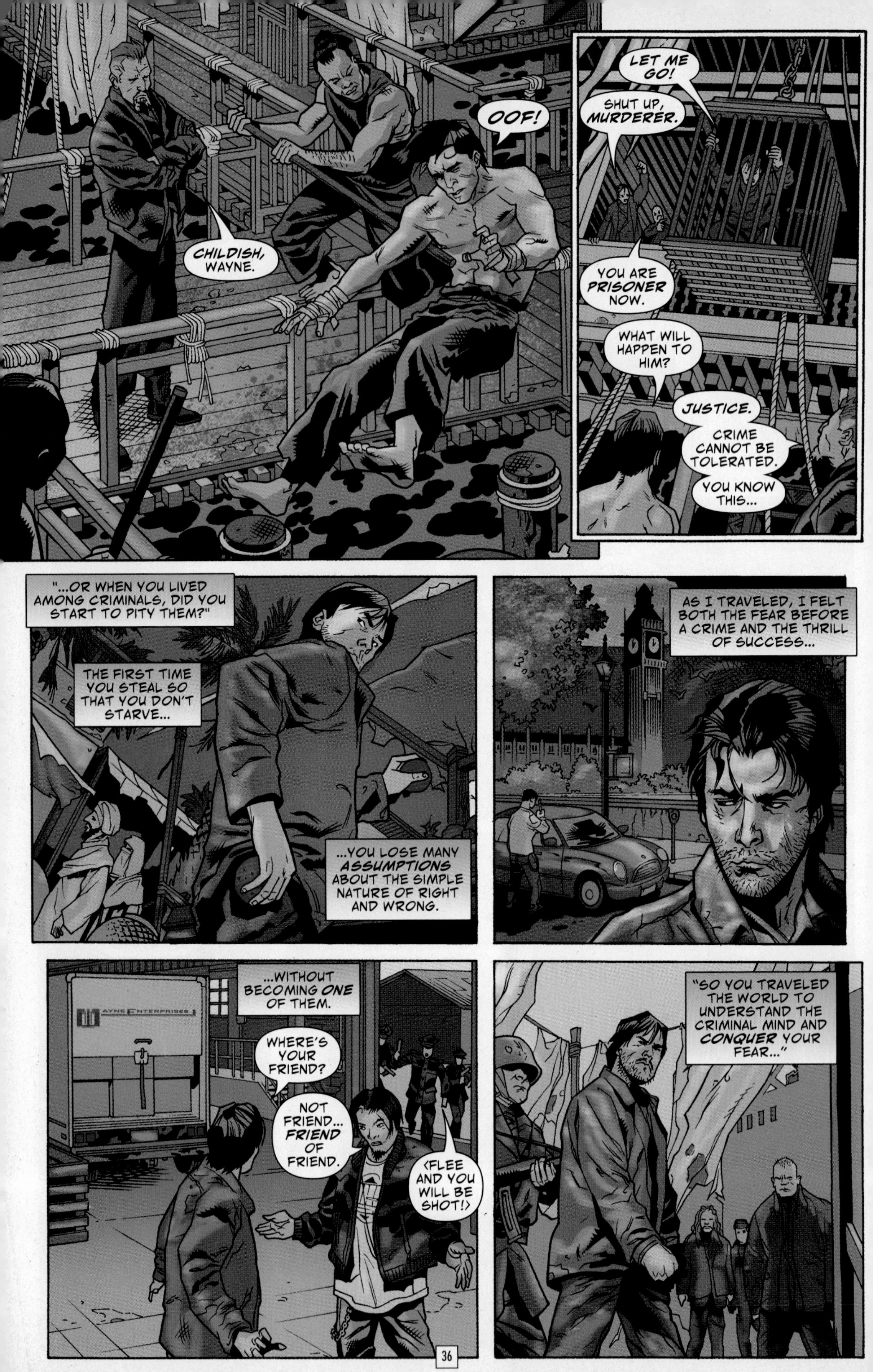
OOF!
CHILDISH, WAYNE.
LET ME GO!
SHUT UP, MURDERER.
YOU ARE PRISONER NOW.
WHAT WILL HAPPEN TO HIM?
JUSTICE.
CRIME CANNOT BE TOLERATED.
YOU KNOW THIS...
"...OR WHEN YOU LIVED AMONG CRIMINALS, DID YOU START TO PITY THEM?"
THE FIRST TIME YOU STEAL SO THAT YOU DON'T STARVE...
...YOU LOSE MANY ASSUMPTIONS ABOUT THE SIMPLE NATURE OF RIGHT AND WRONG.
AS I TRAVELED, I FELT BOTH THE FEAR BEFORE A CRIME AND THE THRILL OF SUCCESS...
...WITHOUT BECOMING ONE OF THEM.
AYNE ENTERPRISES
WHERE'S YOUR FRIEND?
NOT FRIEND... FRIEND OF FRIEND.
<FLEE AND YOU WILL BE SHOT!>
"SO YOU TRAVELED THE WORLD TO UNDERSTAND THE CRIMINAL MIND AND CONQUER YOUR FEAR..."

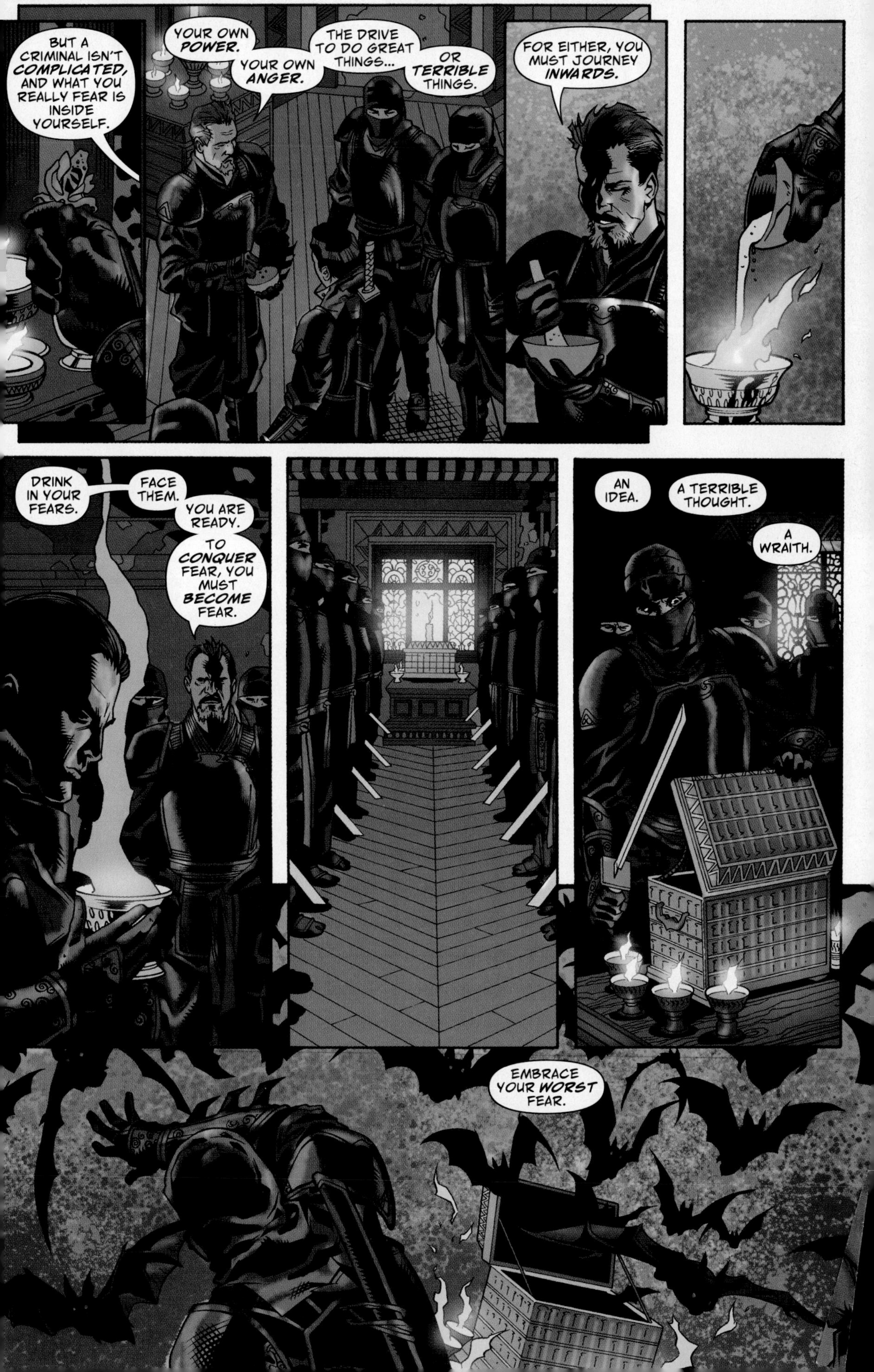

BUT A CRIMINAL ISN'T COMPLICATED, AND WHAT YOU REALLY FEAR IS INSIDE YOURSELF.
YOUR OWN POWER.
YOUR OWN ANGER.
THE DRIVE TO DO GREAT THINGS...
OR TERRIBLE THINGS.
FOR EITHER, YOU MUST JOURNEY INWARDS.
DRINK IN YOUR FEARS.
FACE THEM.
YOU ARE READY.
TO CONQUER FEAR, YOU MUST BECOME FEAR.
AN IDEA.
A TERRIBLE THOUGHT.
A WRAITH.
EMBRACE YOUR WORST FEAR.

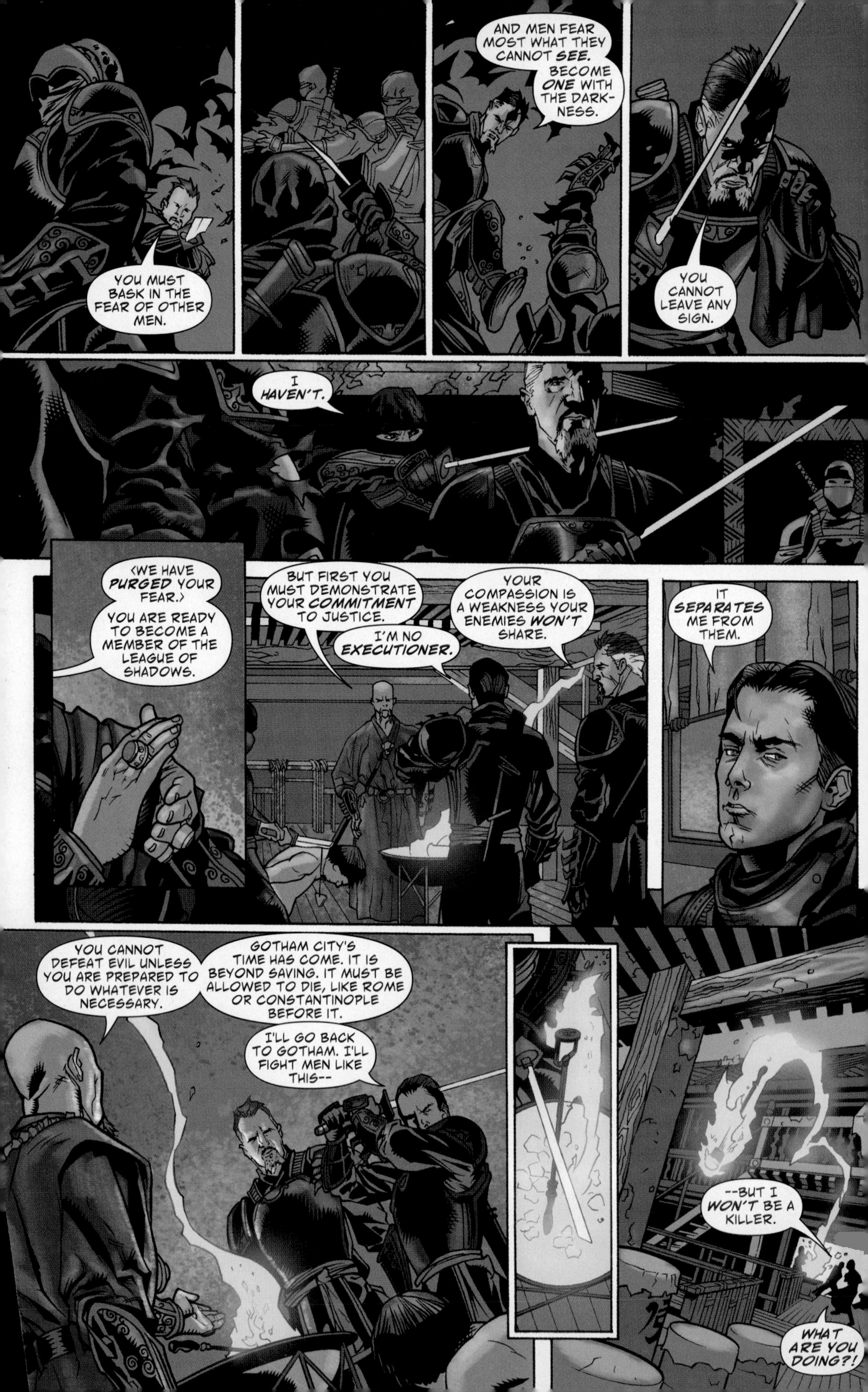
YOU MUST BASK IN THE FEAR OF OTHER MEN.
AND MEN FEAR MOST WHAT THEY CANNOT SEE.
BECOME ONE WITH THE DARK-NESS.
YOU CANNOT LEAVE ANY SIGN.
I HAVEN'T.
<WE HAVE PURGED YOUR FEAR.>
YOU ARE READY TO BECOME A MEMBER OF THE LEAGUE OF SHADOWS.
BUT FIRST YOU MUST DEMONSTRATE YOUR COMMITMENT TO JUSTICE.
I'M NO EXECUTIONER.
YOUR COMPASSION IS A WEAKNESS YOUR ENEMIES WON'T SHARE.
IT SEPARATES ME FROM THEM.
YOU CANNOT DEFEAT EVIL UNLESS YOU ARE PREPARED TO DO WHATEVER IS NECESSARY.
GOTHAM CITY'S TIME HAS COME. IT IS BEYOND SAVING. IT MUST BE ALLOWED TO DIE, LIKE ROME OR CONSTANTINOPLE BEFORE IT.
I'LL GO BACK TO GOTHAM. I'LL FIGHT MEN LIKE THIS--
--BUT I WON'T BE A KILLER.
WHAT ARE YOU DOING?!

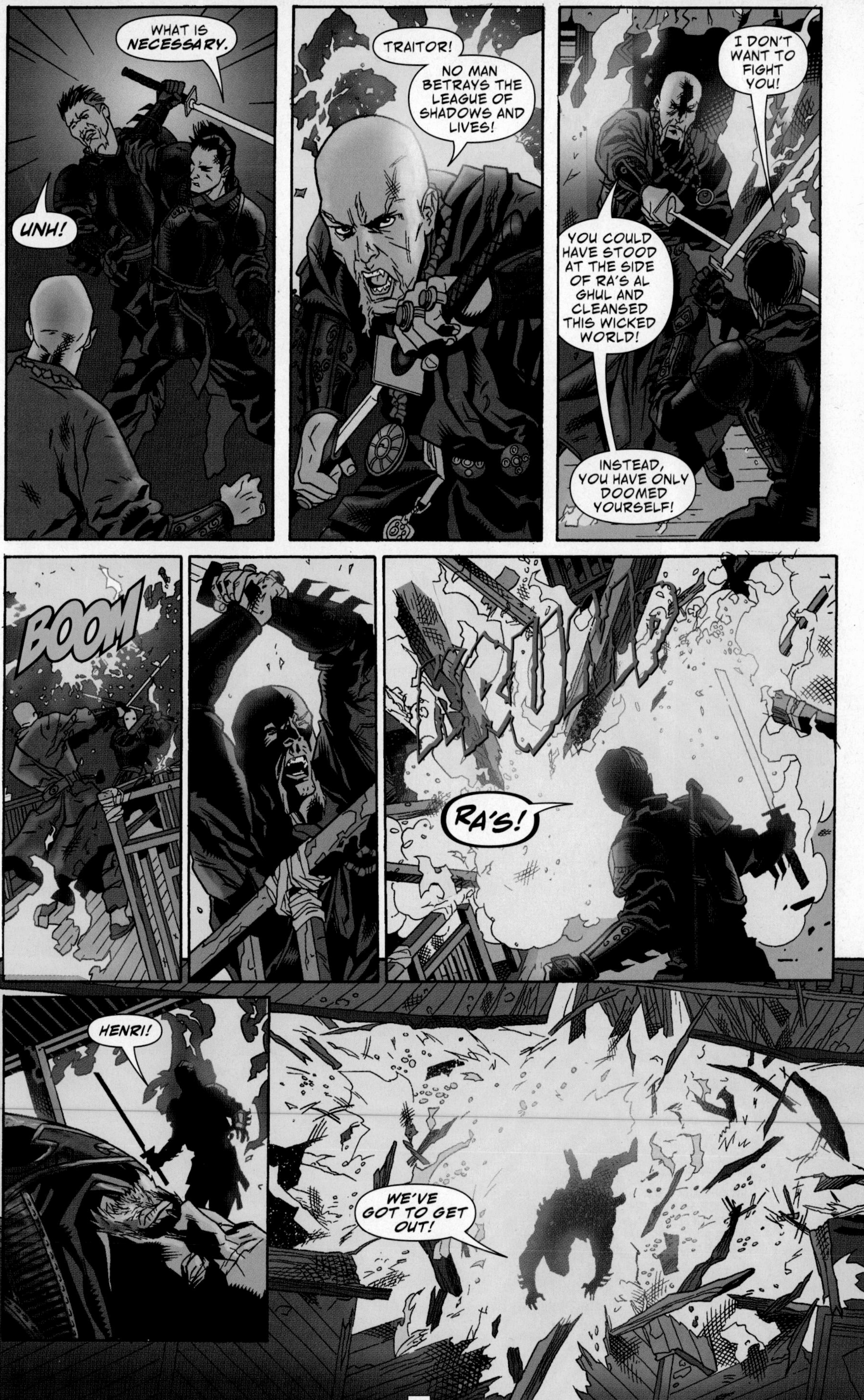

WHAT IS NECESSARY.
UNH!
TRAITOR!
NO MAN BETRAYS THE LEAGUE OF SHADOWS AND LIVES!
I DON'T WANT TO FIGHT YOU!
YOU COULD HAVE STOOD AT THE SIDE OF RA'S AL GHUL AND CLEANSED THIS WICKED WORLD!
INSTEAD, YOU HAVE ONLY DOOMED YOURSELF!
BOOM
RA'S!
HENRI!
WE'VE GOT TO GET OUT!

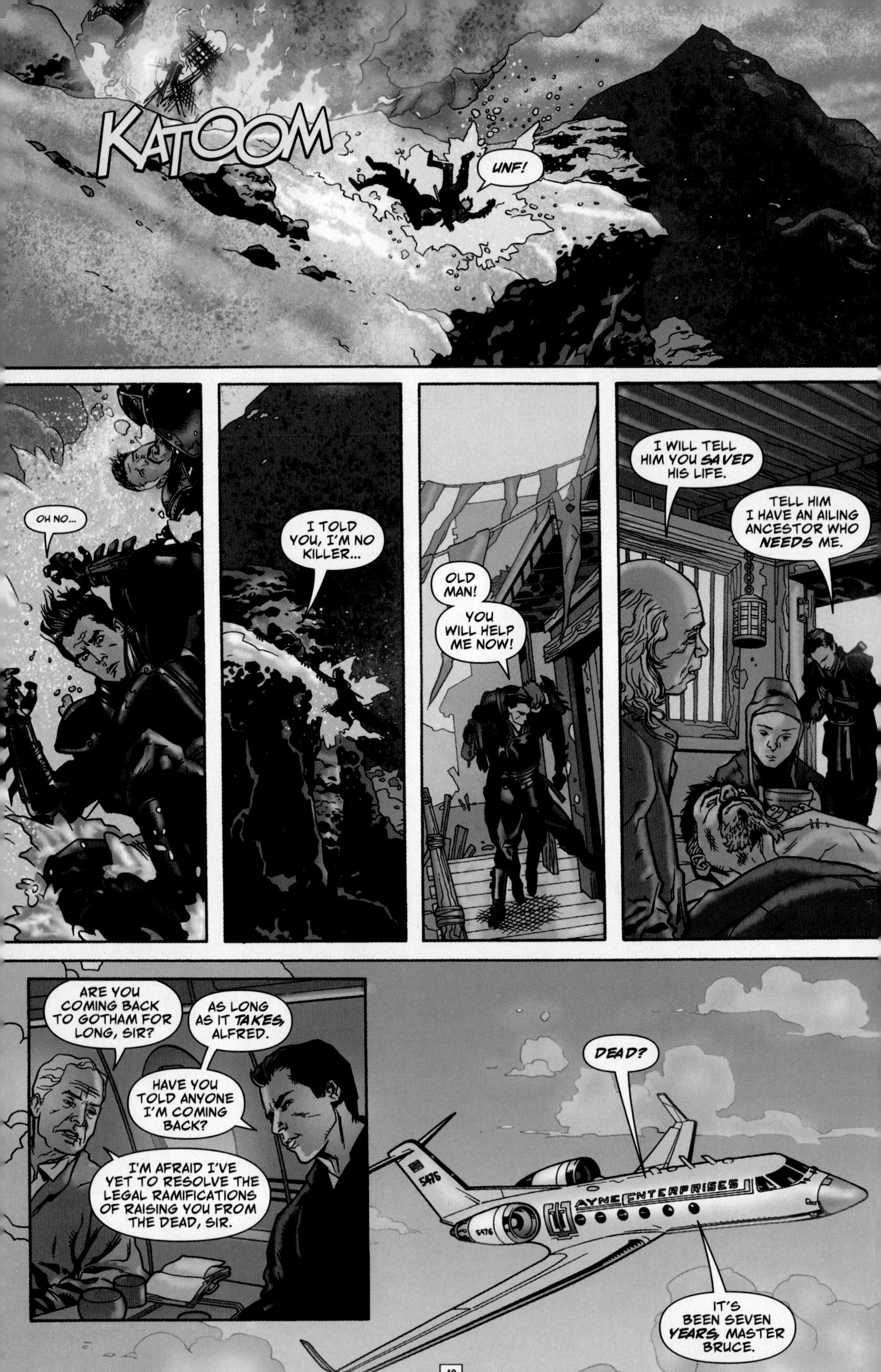
KATOOM
UNF!
OH NO...
I TOLD YOU, I'M NO KILLER...
OLD MAN!
YOU WILL HELP ME NOW!
I WILL TELL HIM YOU *SAVED* HIS LIFE.
TELL HIM I HAVE AN AILING ANCESTOR WHO *NEEDS* ME.
ARE YOU COMING BACK TO GOTHAM FOR LONG, SIR?
AS LONG AS IT *TAKES,* ALFRED.
HAVE YOU TOLD ANYONE I'M COMING BACK?
I'M AFRAID I'VE YET TO RESOLVE THE LEGAL RAMIFICATIONS OF RAISING YOU FROM THE DEAD, SIR.
DEAD?
IT'S BEEN SEVEN *YEARS,* MASTER BRUCE.
5476
AYNE ENTERPRISES

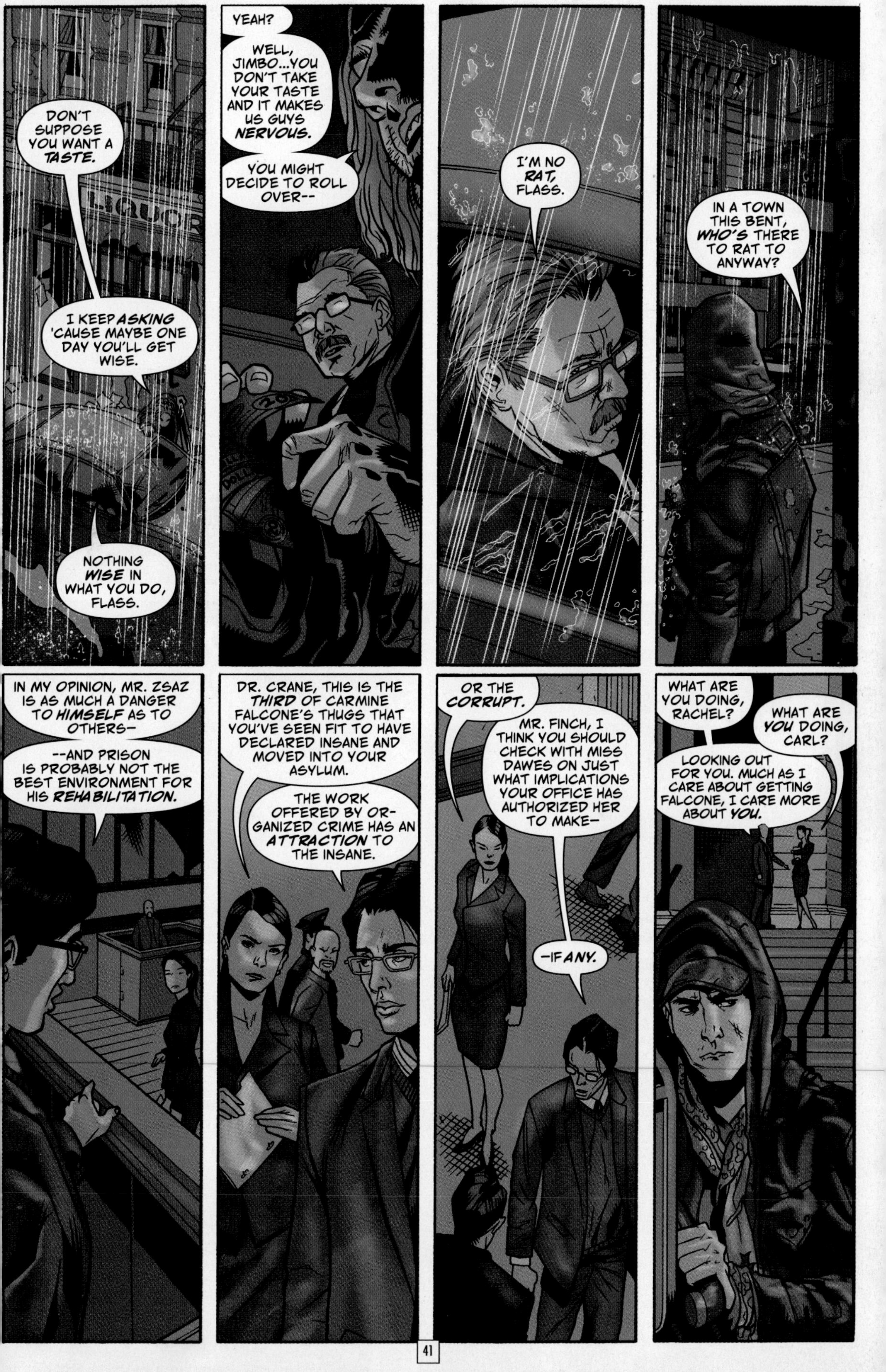
DON'T SUPPOSE YOU WANT A TASTE.
I KEEP ASKING 'CAUSE MAYBE ONE DAY YOU'LL GET WISE.
NOTHING WISE IN WHAT YOU DO, FLASS.
YEAH?
WELL, JIMBO...YOU DON'T TAKE YOUR TASTE AND IT MAKES US GUYS NERVOUS.
YOU MIGHT DECIDE TO ROLL OVER--
I'M NO RAT, FLASS.
IN A TOWN THIS BENT, WHO'S THERE TO RAT TO ANYWAY?
IN MY OPINION, MR. ZSAZ IS AS MUCH A DANGER TO HIMSELF AS TO OTHERS—
--AND PRISON IS PROBABLY NOT THE BEST ENVIRONMENT FOR HIS REHABILITATION.
DR. CRANE, THIS IS THE THIRD OF CARMINE FALCONE'S THUGS THAT YOU'VE SEEN FIT TO HAVE DECLARED INSANE AND MOVED INTO YOUR ASYLUM.
THE WORK OFFERED BY ORGANIZED CRIME HAS AN ATTRACTION TO THE INSANE.
OR THE CORRUPT.
MR. FINCH, I THINK YOU SHOULD CHECK WITH MISS DAWES ON JUST WHAT IMPLICATIONS YOUR OFFICE HAS AUTHORIZED HER TO MAKE—
—IF ANY.
WHAT ARE YOU DOING, RACHEL?
WHAT ARE YOU DOING, CARL?
LOOKING OUT FOR YOU. MUCH AS I CARE ABOUT GETTING FALCONE, I CARE MORE ABOUT YOU.

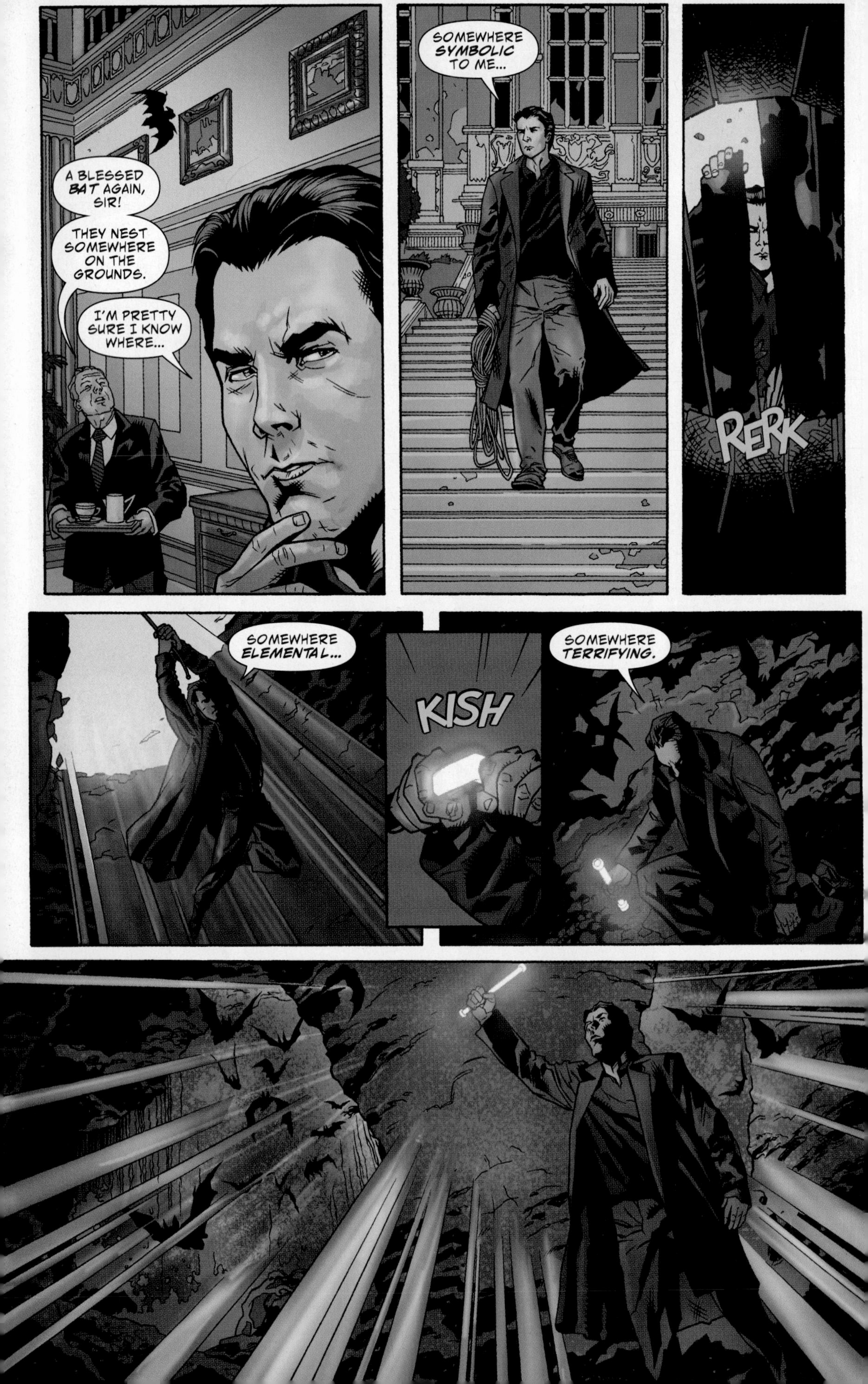
A BLESSED BAT AGAIN, SIR!
THEY NEST SOMEWHERE ON THE GROUNDS.
I'M PRETTY SURE I KNOW WHERE...
SOMEWHERE SYMBOLIC TO ME...
RERK
SOMEWHERE ELEMENTAL...
KISH
SOMEWHERE TERRIFYING.

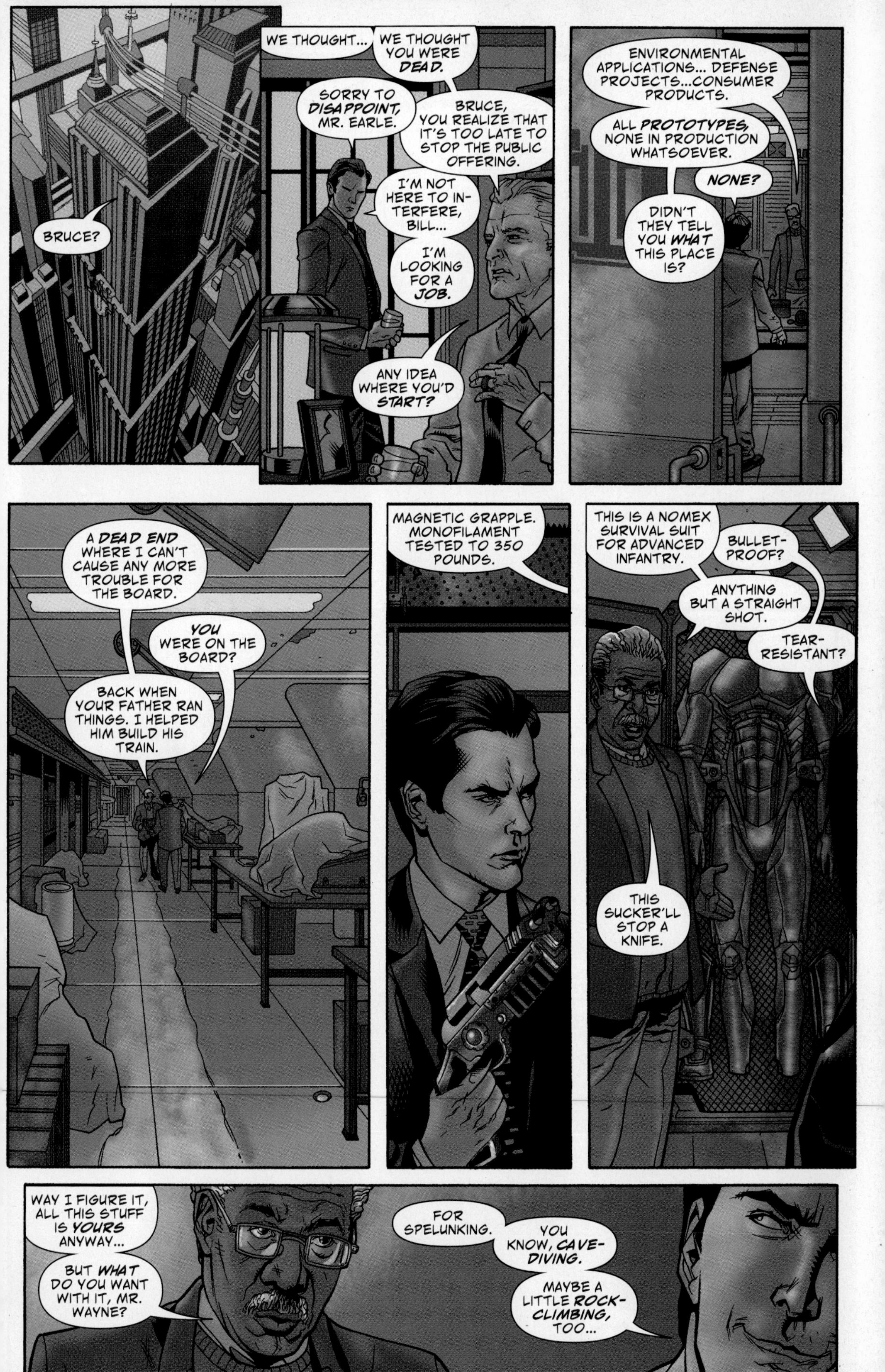
BRUCE?
WE THOUGHT...
WE THOUGHT YOU WERE DEAD.
SORRY TO DISAPPOINT, MR. EARLE.
BRUCE, YOU REALIZE THAT IT'S TOO LATE TO STOP THE PUBLIC OFFERING.
I'M NOT HERE TO IN-TERFERE, BILL...
I'M LOOKING FOR A JOB.
ANY IDEA WHERE YOU'D START?
ENVIRONMENTAL APPLICATIONS... DEFENSE PROJECTS...CONSUMER PRODUCTS.
ALL PROTOTYPES, NONE IN PRODUCTION WHATSOEVER.
NONE?
DIDN'T THEY TELL YOU WHAT THIS PLACE IS?
A DEAD END WHERE I CAN'T CAUSE ANY MORE TROUBLE FOR THE BOARD.
YOU WERE ON THE BOARD?
BACK WHEN YOUR FATHER RAN THINGS. I HELPED HIM BUILD HIS TRAIN.
MAGNETIC GRAPPLE. MONOFILAMENT TESTED TO 350 POUNDS.
THIS IS A NOMEX SURVIVAL SUIT FOR ADVANCED INFANTRY.
BULLET-PROOF?
ANYTHING BUT A STRAIGHT SHOT.
TEAR-RESISTANT?
THIS SUCKER'LL STOP A KNIFE.
WAY I FIGURE IT, ALL THIS STUFF IS YOURS ANYWAY...
BUT WHAT DO YOU WANT WITH IT, MR. WAYNE?
FOR SPELUNKING.
YOU KNOW, CAVE-DIVING.
MAYBE A LITTLE ROCK-CLIMBING, TOO...

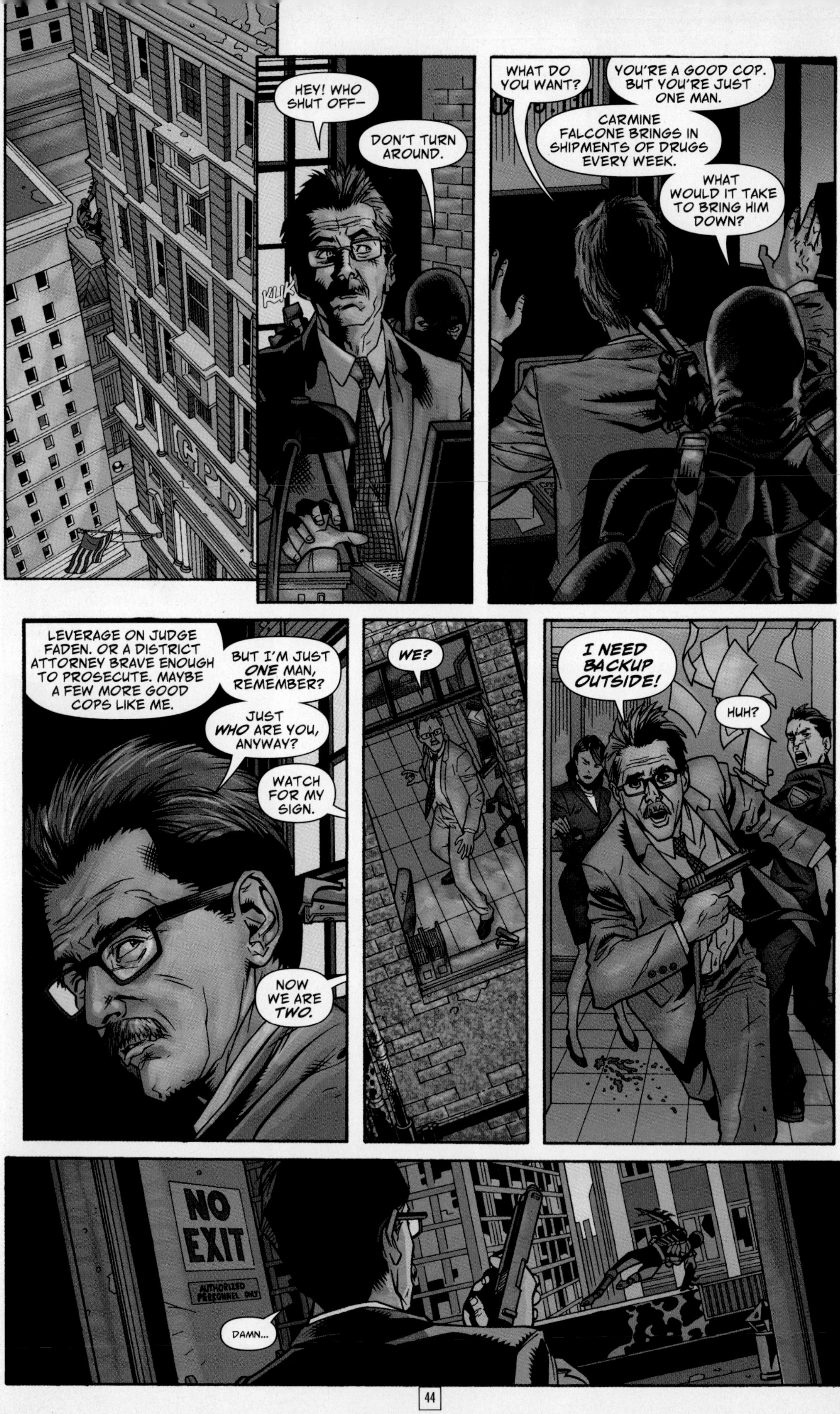
HEY! WHO SHUT OFF–
DON'T TURN AROUND.
KLIK
WHAT DO YOU WANT?
YOU'RE A GOOD COP. BUT YOU'RE JUST ONE MAN.
CARMINE FALCONE BRINGS IN SHIPMENTS OF DRUGS EVERY WEEK.
WHAT WOULD IT TAKE TO BRING HIM DOWN?
LEVERAGE ON JUDGE FADEN. OR A DISTRICT ATTORNEY BRAVE ENOUGH TO PROSECUTE. MAYBE A FEW MORE GOOD COPS LIKE ME.
BUT I'M JUST *ONE* MAN, REMEMBER?
JUST *WHO* ARE YOU, ANYWAY?
WATCH FOR MY SIGN.
NOW WE ARE *TWO.*
WE?
I NEED BACKUP OUTSIDE!
HUH?
NO EXIT
AUTHORIZED PERSONNEL ONLY
DAMN...

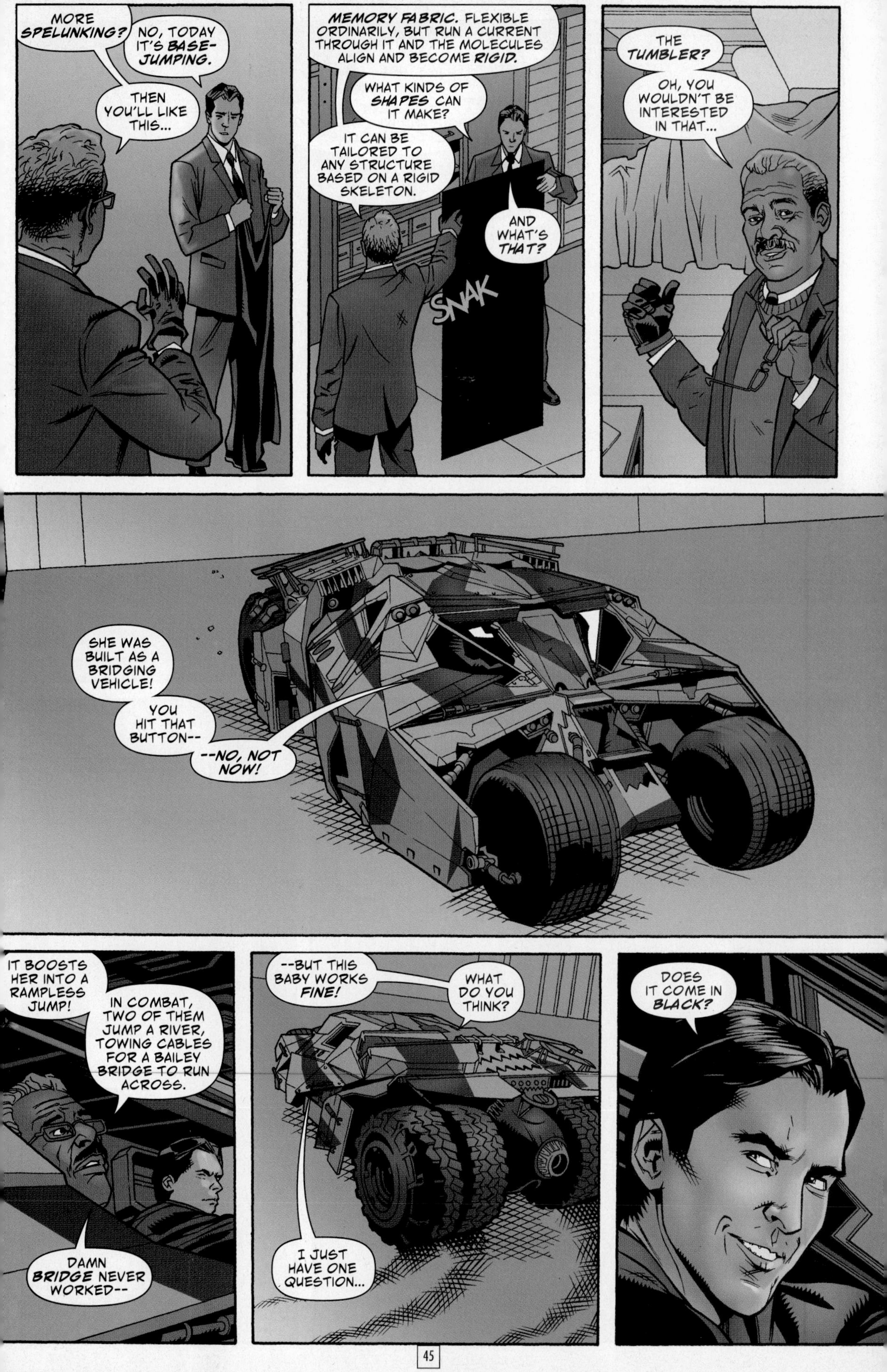
MORE SPELUNKING?
NO, TODAY IT'S BASE-JUMPING.
THEN YOU'LL LIKE THIS...
MEMORY FABRIC. FLEXIBLE ORDINARILY, BUT RUN A CURRENT THROUGH IT AND THE MOLECULES ALIGN AND BECOME RIGID.
WHAT KINDS OF SHAPES CAN IT MAKE?
IT CAN BE TAILORED TO ANY STRUCTURE BASED ON A RIGID SKELETON.
SNAK
AND WHAT'S THAT?
THE TUMBLER?
OH, YOU WOULDN'T BE INTERESTED IN THAT...
SHE WAS BUILT AS A BRIDGING VEHICLE!
YOU HIT THAT BUTTON--
--NO, NOT NOW!
IT BOOSTS HER INTO A RAMPLESS JUMP!
IN COMBAT, TWO OF THEM JUMP A RIVER, TOWING CABLES FOR A BAILEY BRIDGE TO RUN ACROSS.
DAMN BRIDGE NEVER WORKED--
--BUT THIS BABY WORKS FINE!
WHAT DO YOU THINK?
I JUST HAVE ONE QUESTION...
DOES IT COME IN BLACK?

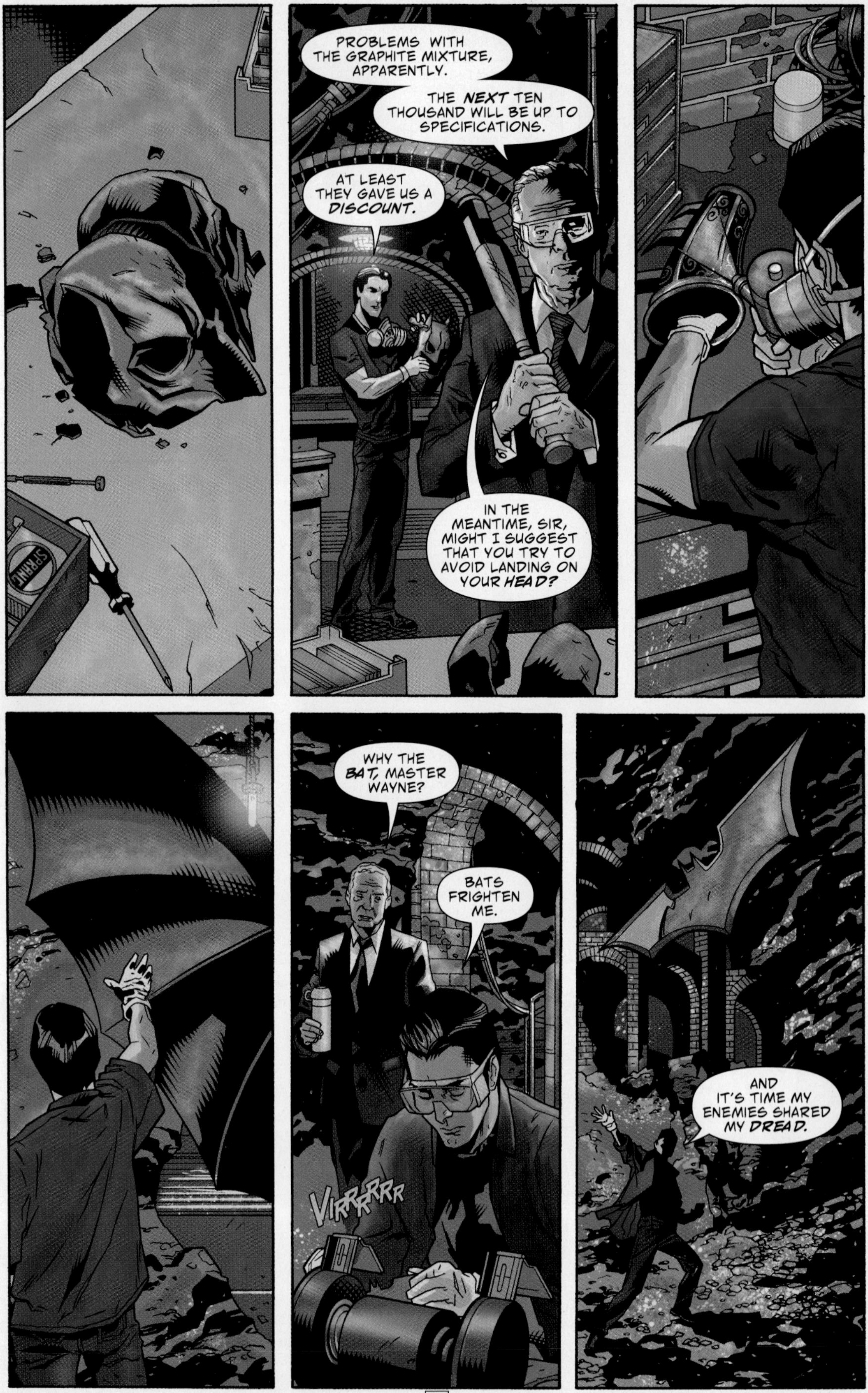
SPRING
PROBLEMS WITH THE GRAPHITE MIXTURE, APPARENTLY.
THE NEXT TEN THOUSAND WILL BE UP TO SPECIFICATIONS.
AT LEAST THEY GAVE US A DISCOUNT.
IN THE MEANTIME, SIR, MIGHT I SUGGEST THAT YOU TRY TO AVOID LANDING ON YOUR HEAD?
WHY THE BAT, MASTER WAYNE?
BATS FRIGHTEN ME.
VIRRRRRR
AND IT'S TIME MY ENEMIES SHARED MY DREAD.

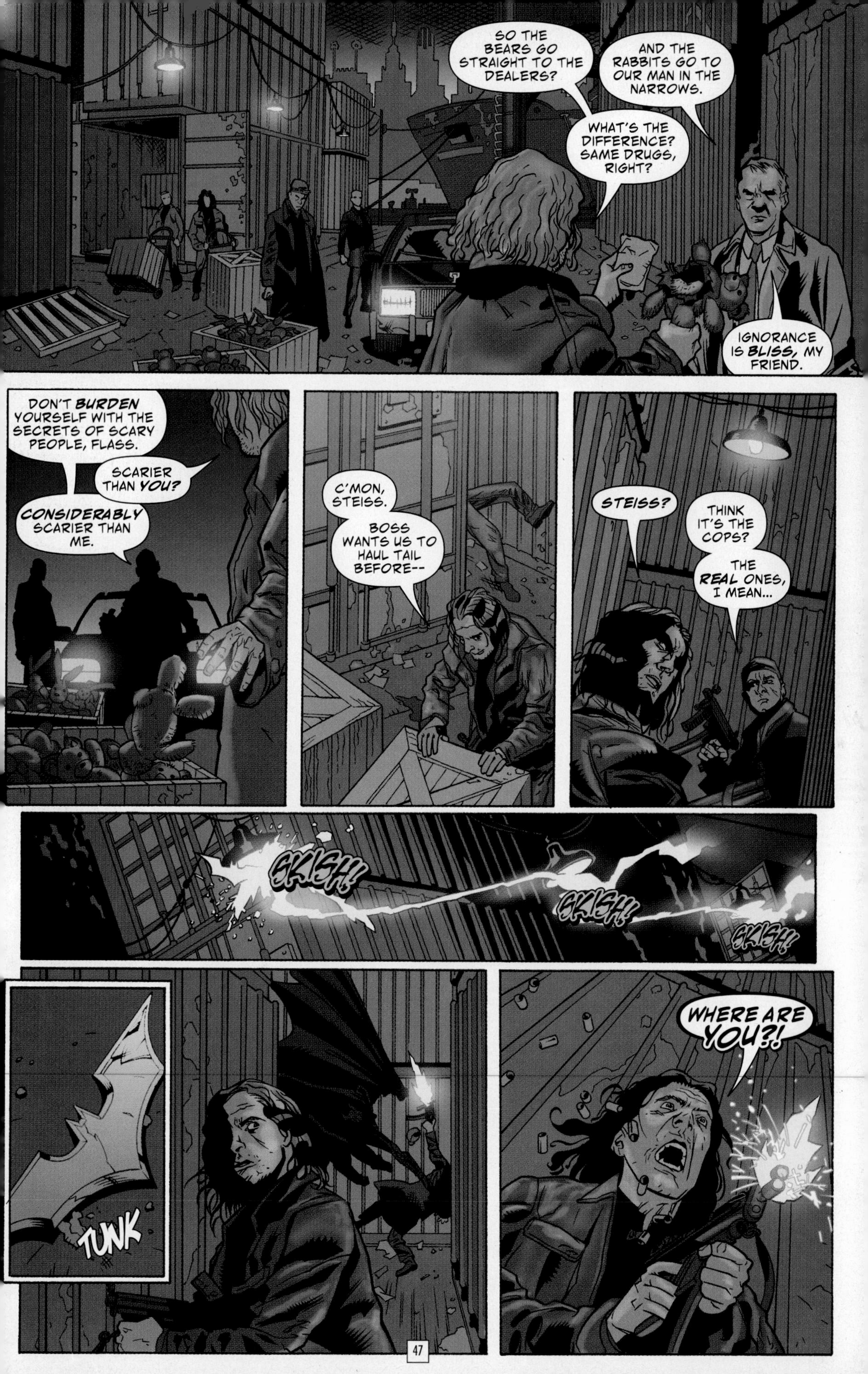
SO THE BEARS GO STRAIGHT TO THE DEALERS?
AND THE RABBITS GO TO OUR MAN IN THE NARROWS.
WHAT'S THE DIFFERENCE? SAME DRUGS, RIGHT?
IGNORANCE IS BLISS, MY FRIEND.
DON'T BURDEN YOURSELF WITH THE SECRETS OF SCARY PEOPLE, FLASS.
SCARIER THAN YOU?
CONSIDERABLY SCARIER THAN ME.
C'MON, STEISS.
BOSS WANTS US TO HAUL TAIL BEFORE--
STEISS?
THINK IT'S THE COPS?
THE REAL ONES, I MEAN...
SKISH!
SKISH!
SKISH!
TUNK
WHERE ARE YOU?!

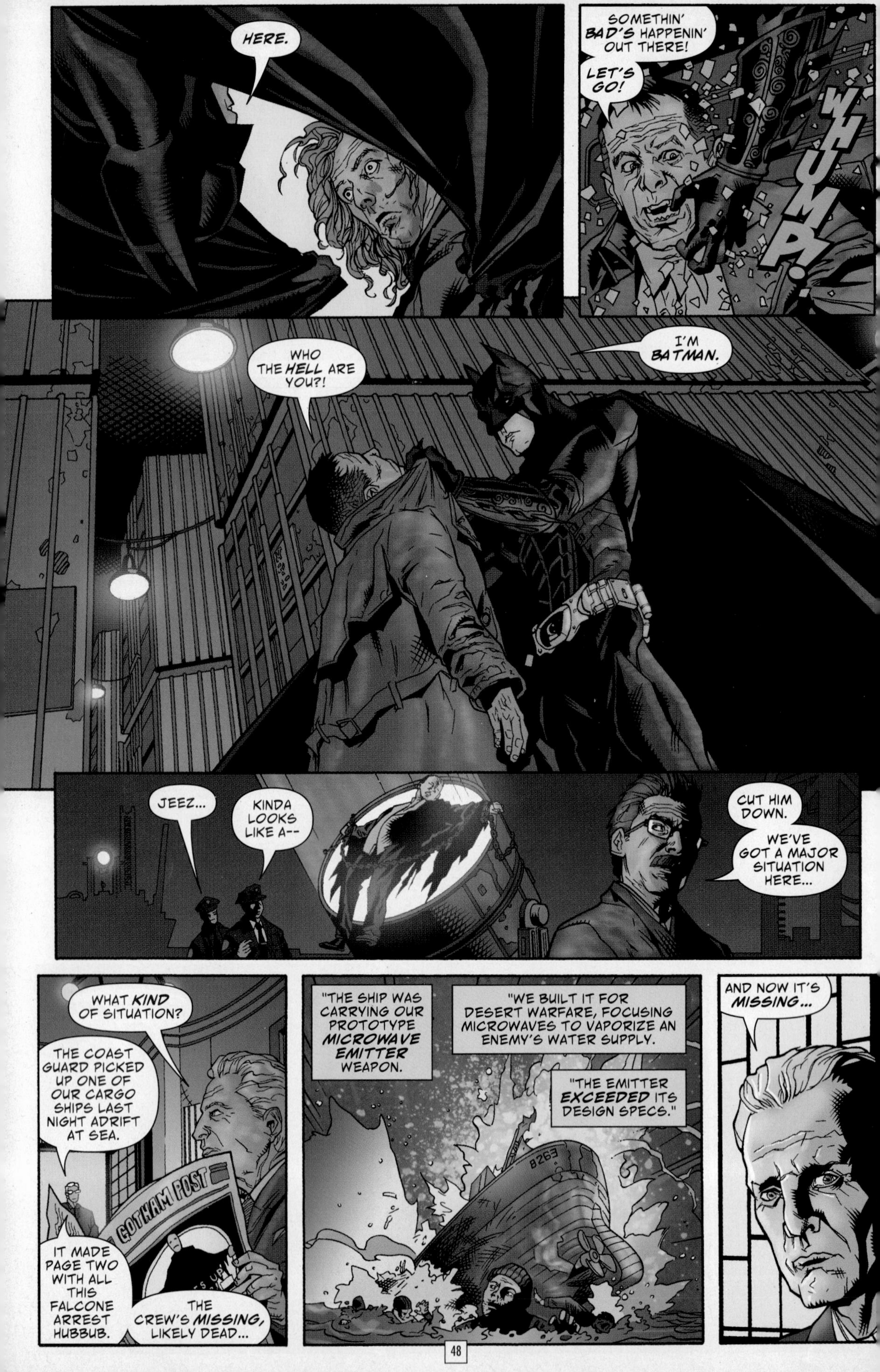
HERE.
SOMETHIN' BAD'S HAPPENIN' OUT THERE!
LET'S GO!
WHUMP!
WHO THE HELL ARE YOU?!
I'M BATMAN.
JEEZ...
KINDA LOOKS LIKE A--
CUT HIM DOWN.
WE'VE GOT A MAJOR SITUATION HERE...
WHAT KIND OF SITUATION?
THE COAST GUARD PICKED UP ONE OF OUR CARGO SHIPS LAST NIGHT ADRIFT AT SEA.
GOTHAM POST
IT MADE PAGE TWO WITH ALL THIS FALCONE ARREST HUBBUB.
THE CREW'S MISSING, LIKELY DEAD...
"THE SHIP WAS CARRYING OUR PROTOTYPE MICROWAVE EMITTER WEAPON.
"WE BUILT IT FOR DESERT WARFARE, FOCUSING MICROWAVES TO VAPORIZE AN ENEMY'S WATER SUPPLY.
"THE EMITTER EXCEEDED ITS DESIGN SPECS."
8263
AND NOW IT'S MISSING...

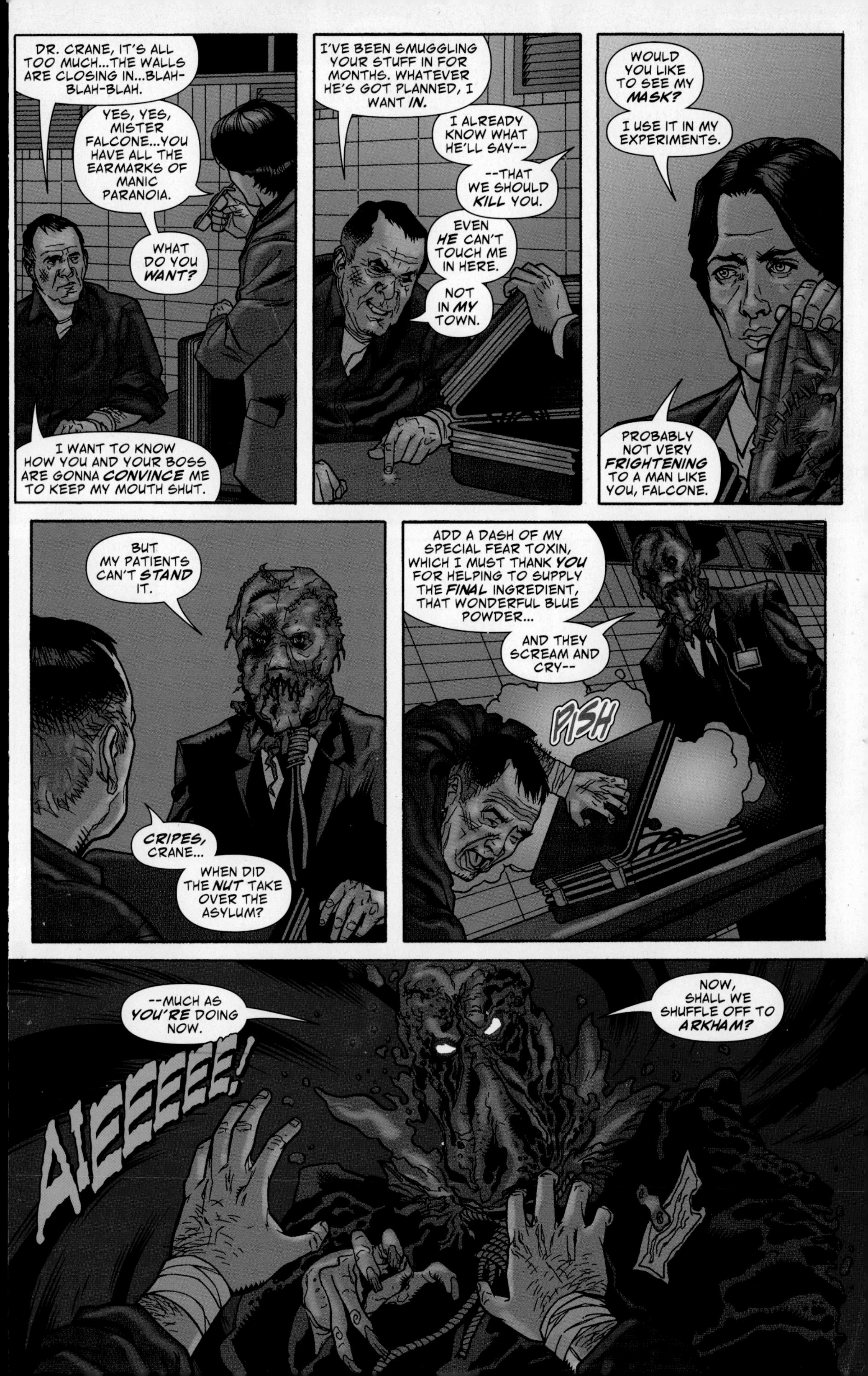
DR. CRANE, IT'S ALL TOO MUCH...THE WALLS ARE CLOSING IN...BLAH-BLAH-BLAH.
YES, YES, MISTER FALCONE...YOU HAVE ALL THE EARMARKS OF MANIC PARANOIA.
WHAT DO YOU WANT?
I WANT TO KNOW HOW YOU AND YOUR BOSS ARE GONNA CONVINCE ME TO KEEP MY MOUTH SHUT.
I'VE BEEN SMUGGLING YOUR STUFF IN FOR MONTHS. WHATEVER HE'S GOT PLANNED, I WANT IN.
I ALREADY KNOW WHAT HE'LL SAY--
--THAT WE SHOULD KILL YOU.
EVEN HE CAN'T TOUCH ME IN HERE.
NOT IN MY TOWN.
WOULD YOU LIKE TO SEE MY MASK?
I USE IT IN MY EXPERIMENTS.
PROBABLY NOT VERY FRIGHTENING TO A MAN LIKE YOU, FALCONE.
BUT MY PATIENTS CAN'T STAND IT.
CRIPES, CRANE...
WHEN DID THE NUT TAKE OVER THE ASYLUM?
ADD A DASH OF MY SPECIAL FEAR TOXIN, WHICH I MUST THANK YOU FOR HELPING TO SUPPLY THE FINAL INGREDIENT, THAT WONDERFUL BLUE POWDER...
AND THEY SCREAM AND CRY--
PISH
--MUCH AS YOU'RE DOING NOW.
NOW, SHALL WE SHUFFLE OFF TO ARKHAM?
AIEEEEE!

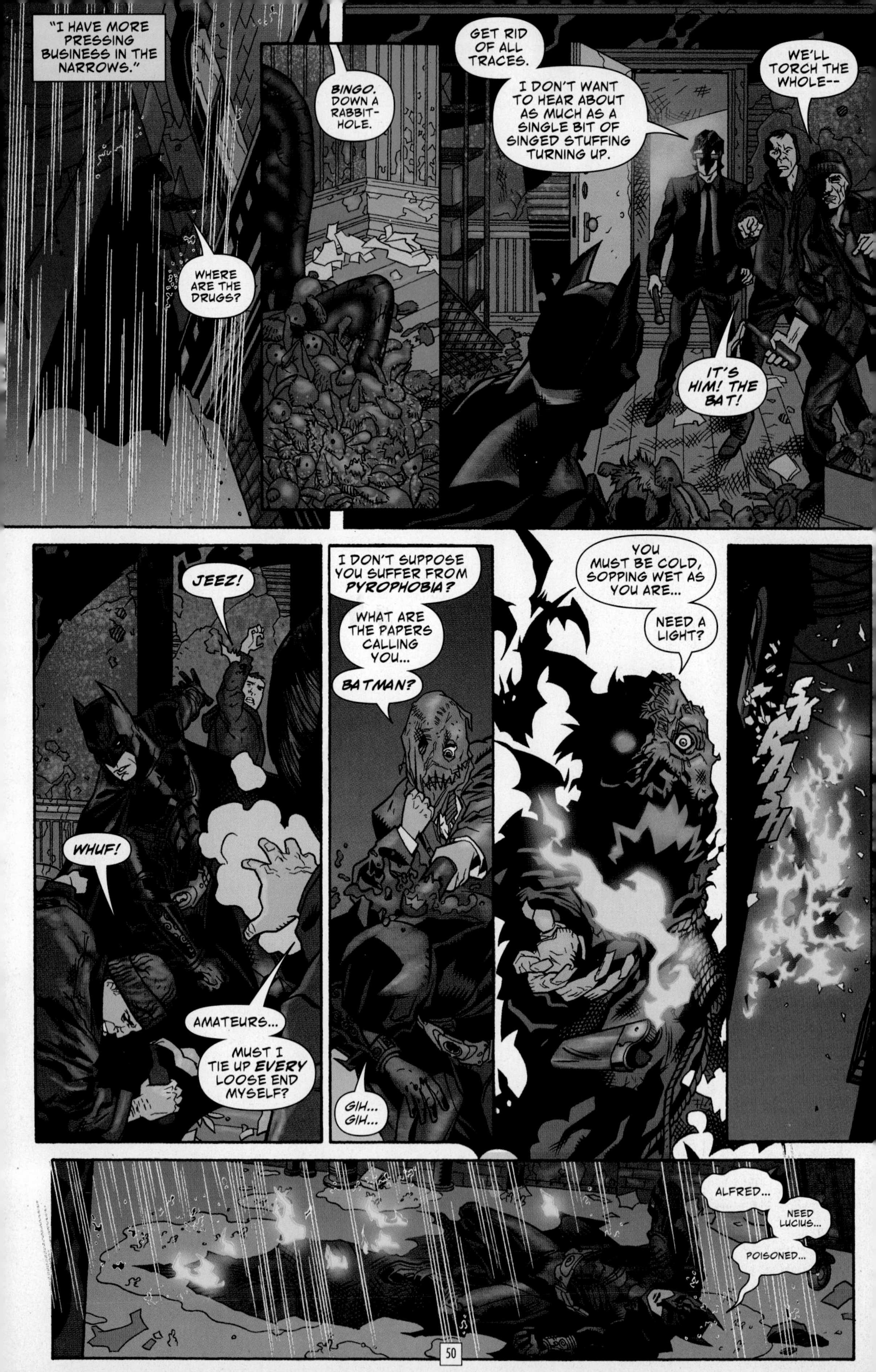
"I HAVE MORE PRESSING BUSINESS IN THE NARROWS."
WHERE ARE THE DRUGS?
BINGO. DOWN A RABBIT-HOLE.
GET RID OF ALL TRACES.
I DON'T WANT TO HEAR ABOUT AS MUCH AS A SINGLE BIT OF SINGED STUFFING TURNING UP.
WE'LL TORCH THE WHOLE--
IT'S HIM! THE BAT!
JEEZ!
WHUF!
AMATEURS...
MUST I TIE UP EVERY LOOSE END MYSELF?
I DON'T SUPPOSE YOU SUFFER FROM PYROPHOBIA?
WHAT ARE THE PAPERS CALLING YOU...
BATMAN?
GIH... GIH...
YOU MUST BE COLD, SOPPING WET AS YOU ARE...
NEED A LIGHT?
ALFRED...
NEED LUCIUS...
POISONED...

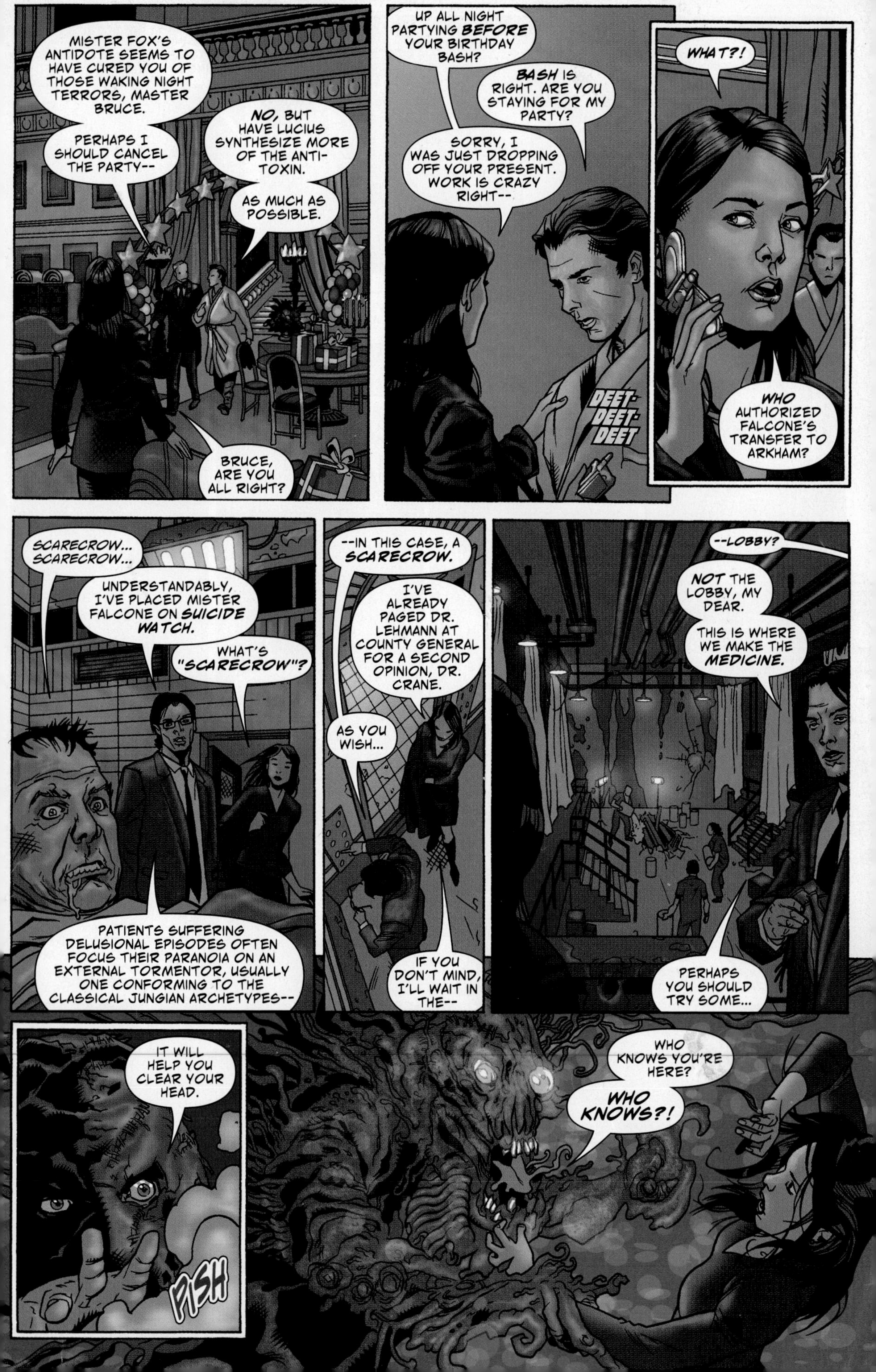
MISTER FOX'S ANTIDOTE SEEMS TO HAVE CURED YOU OF THOSE WAKING NIGHT TERRORS, MASTER BRUCE.
PERHAPS I SHOULD CANCEL THE PARTY--
NO, BUT HAVE LUCIUS SYNTHESIZE MORE OF THE ANTI-TOXIN.
AS MUCH AS POSSIBLE.
BRUCE, ARE YOU ALL RIGHT?
UP ALL NIGHT PARTYING BEFORE YOUR BIRTHDAY BASH?
BASH IS RIGHT. ARE YOU STAYING FOR MY PARTY?
SORRY, I WAS JUST DROPPING OFF YOUR PRESENT. WORK IS CRAZY RIGHT--
DEET-DEET-DEET
WHAT?!
WHO AUTHORIZED FALCONE'S TRANSFER TO ARKHAM?
SCARECROW... SCARECROW...
UNDERSTANDABLY, I'VE PLACED MISTER FALCONE ON SUICIDE WATCH.
WHAT'S "SCARECROW"?
PATIENTS SUFFERING DELUSIONAL EPISODES OFTEN FOCUS THEIR PARANOIA ON AN EXTERNAL TORMENTOR, USUALLY ONE CONFORMING TO THE CLASSICAL JUNGIAN ARCHETYPES--
--IN THIS CASE, A SCARECROW.
I'VE ALREADY PAGED DR. LEHMANN AT COUNTY GENERAL FOR A SECOND OPINION, DR. CRANE.
AS YOU WISH...
IF YOU DON'T MIND, I'LL WAIT IN THE--
--LOBBY?
NOT THE LOBBY, MY DEAR.
THIS IS WHERE WE MAKE THE MEDICINE.
PERHAPS YOU SHOULD TRY SOME...
IT WILL HELP YOU CLEAR YOUR HEAD.
PISH
WHO KNOWS YOU'RE HERE?
WHO KNOWS?!

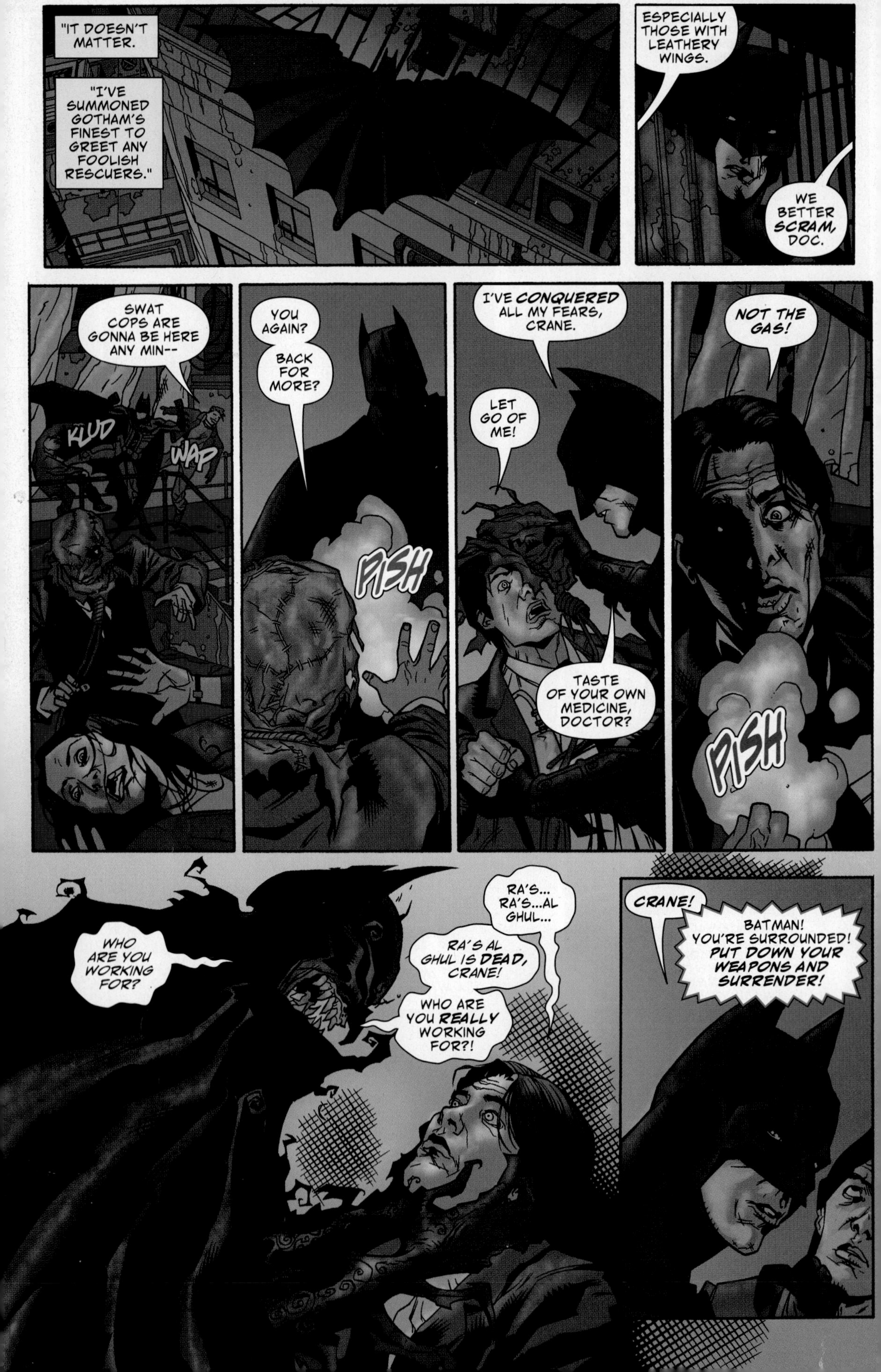
"IT DOESN'T MATTER.
"I'VE SUMMONED GOTHAM'S FINEST TO GREET ANY FOOLISH RESCUERS."
ESPECIALLY THOSE WITH LEATHERY WINGS.
WE BETTER SCRAM, DOC.
SWAT COPS ARE GONNA BE HERE ANY MIN--
KLUD
WAP
YOU AGAIN?
BACK FOR MORE?
PISH
I'VE CONQUERED ALL MY FEARS, CRANE.
LET GO OF ME!
TASTE OF YOUR OWN MEDICINE, DOCTOR?
NOT THE GAS!
PISH
WHO ARE YOU WORKING FOR?
RA'S... RA'S...AL GHUL...
RA'S AL GHUL IS DEAD, CRANE!
WHO ARE YOU REALLY WORKING FOR?!
CRANE!
BATMAN! YOU'RE SURROUNDED! PUT DOWN YOUR WEAPONS AND SURRENDER!

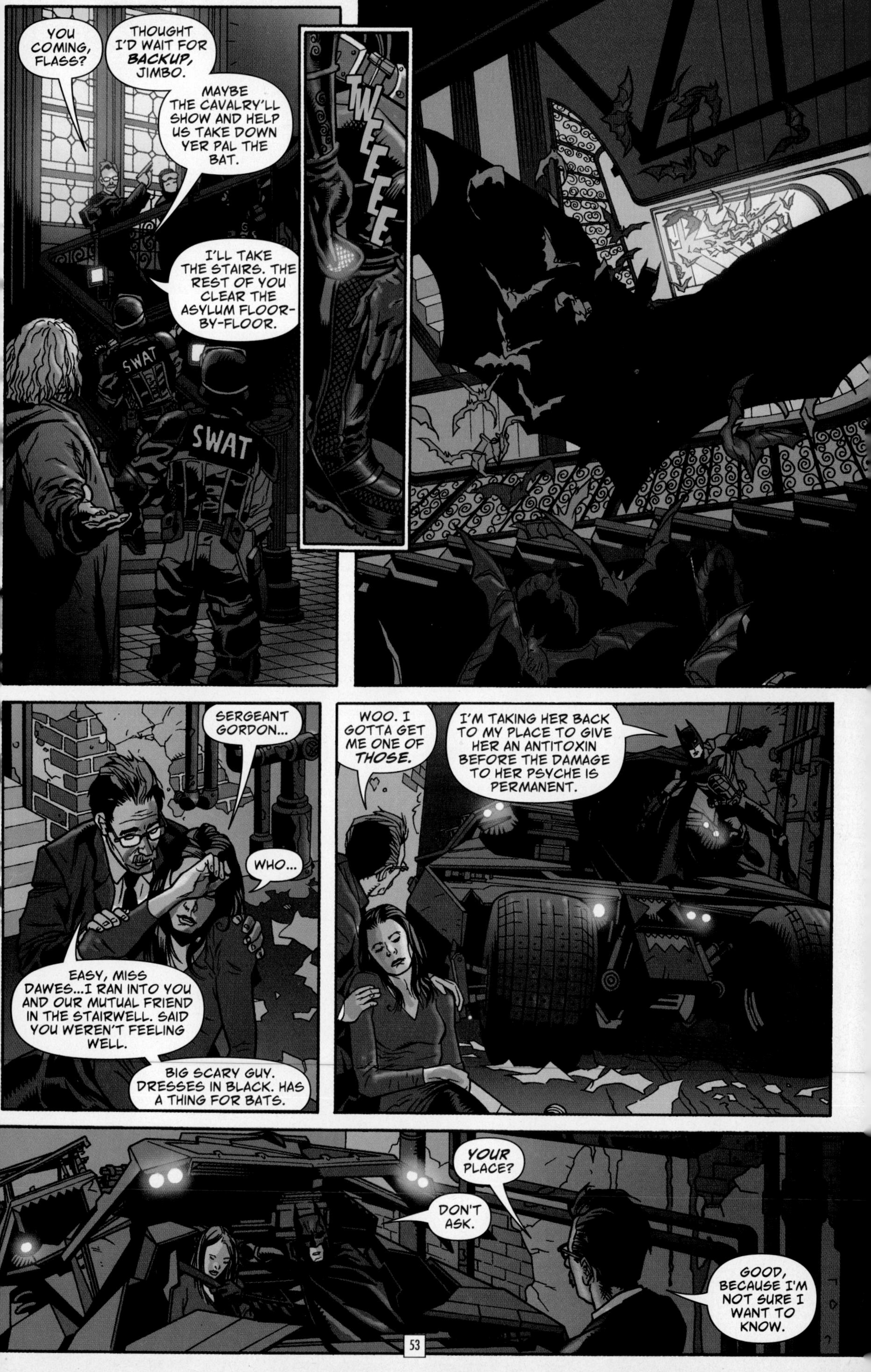
YOU COMING, FLASS?
THOUGHT I'D WAIT FOR *BACKUP,* JIMBO.
MAYBE THE CAVALRY'LL SHOW AND HELP US TAKE DOWN YER PAL THE BAT.
I'LL TAKE THE STAIRS. THE REST OF YOU CLEAR THE ASYLUM FLOOR-BY-FLOOR.
SWAT
SWAT
TWEEEE
SERGEANT GORDON...
WHO...
EASY, MISS DAWES...I RAN INTO YOU AND OUR MUTUAL FRIEND IN THE STAIRWELL. SAID YOU WEREN'T FEELING WELL.
BIG SCARY GUY. DRESSES IN BLACK. HAS A THING FOR BATS.
WOO. I GOTTA GET ME ONE OF *THOSE.*
I'M TAKING HER BACK TO MY PLACE TO GIVE HER AN ANTITOXIN BEFORE THE DAMAGE TO HER PSYCHE IS PERMANENT.
YOUR PLACE?
DON'T ASK.
GOOD, BECAUSE I'M NOT SURE I WANT TO KNOW.

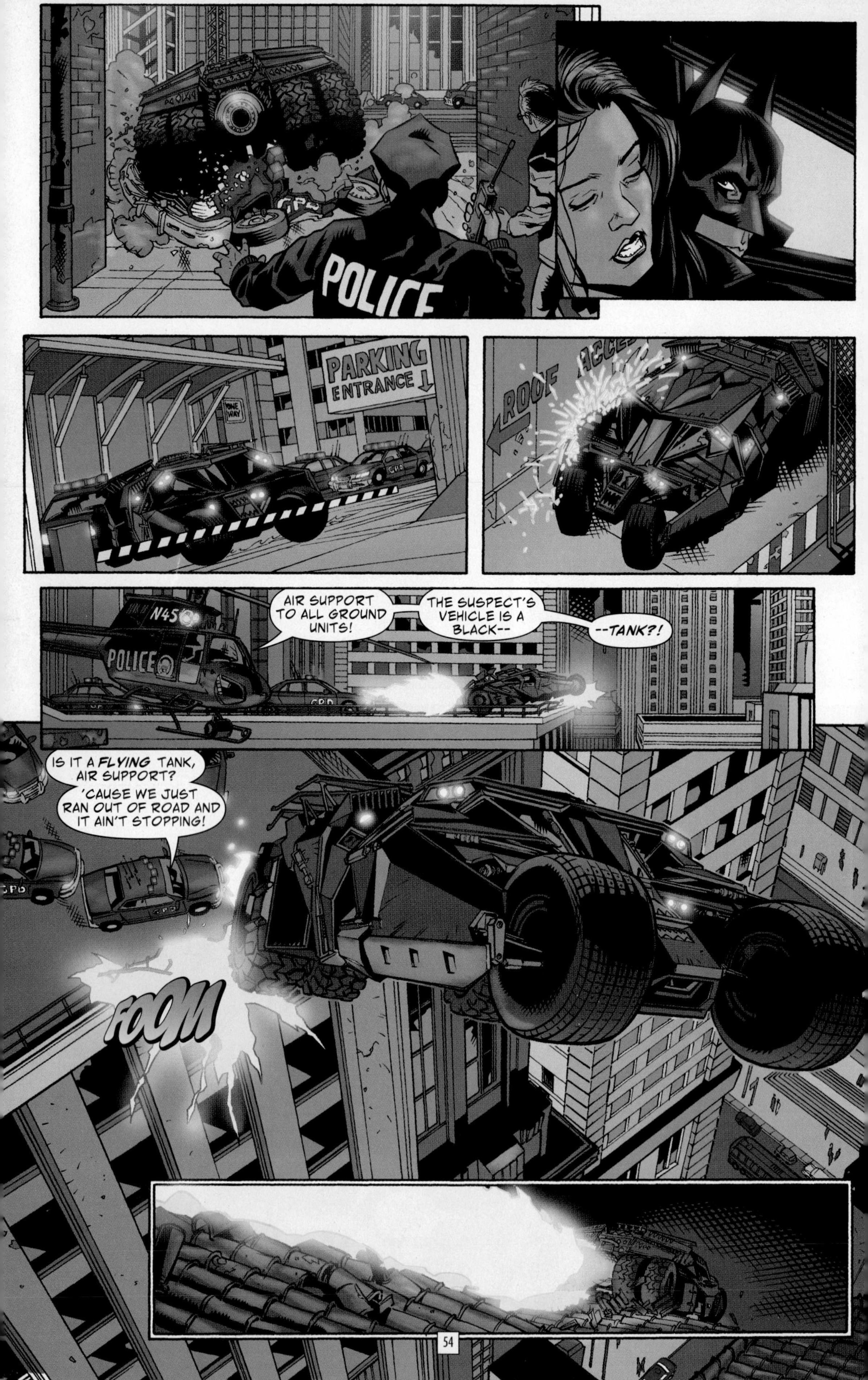
POLICE
PARKING ENTRANCE
ONE WAY
ROOF ACCE
N45
POLICE
AIR SUPPORT TO ALL GROUND UNITS!
THE SUSPECT'S VEHICLE IS A BLACK--
--TANK?!
IS IT A *FLYING* TANK, AIR SUPPORT?
'CAUSE WE JUST RAN OUT OF ROAD AND IT AIN'T STOPPING!
FOOM

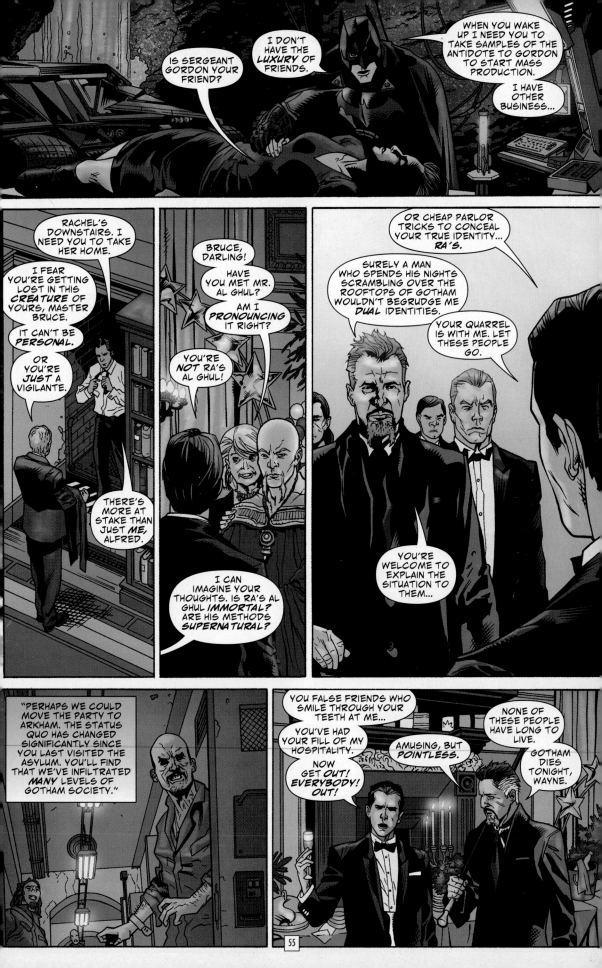

IS SERGEANT GORDON YOUR FRIEND?

I DON'T HAVE THE LUXURY OF FRIENDS.

WHEN YOU WAKE UP I NEED YOU TO TAKE SAMPLES OF THE ANTIDOTE TO GORDON TO START MASS PRODUCTION.

I HAVE OTHER BUSINESS...

RACHEL'S DOWNSTAIRS. I NEED YOU TO TAKE HER HOME.

I FEAR YOU'RE GETTING LOST IN THIS *CREATURE* OF YOURS, MASTER BRUCE.

IT CAN'T BE *PERSONAL.*

OR YOU'RE JUST A VIGILANTE.

THERE'S MORE AT STAKE THAN JUST *ME*, ALFRED.

BRUCE, DARLING! HAVE YOU MET MR. AL GHUL?

AM I *PRONOUNCING* IT RIGHT?

YOU'RE *NOT* RA'S AL GHUL!

I CAN IMAGINE YOUR THOUGHTS. IS RA'S AL GHUL *IMMORTAL?* ARE HIS METHODS *SUPERNATURAL?*

OR CHEAP PARLOR TRICKS TO CONCEAL YOUR TRUE IDENTITY... *RA'S.*

SURELY A MAN WHO SPENDS HIS NIGHTS SCRAMBLING OVER THE ROOFTOPS OF GOTHAM WOULDN'T BEGRUDGE ME *DUAL* IDENTITIES.

YOUR QUARREL IS WITH ME. LET THESE PEOPLE GO.

YOU'RE WELCOME TO EXPLAIN THE SITUATION TO THEM...

"PERHAPS WE COULD MOVE THE PARTY TO ARKHAM. THE STATUS QUO HAS CHANGED SIGNIFICANTLY SINCE YOU LAST VISITED THE ASYLUM. YOU'LL FIND THAT WE'VE INFILTRATED *MANY* LEVELS OF GOTHAM SOCIETY."

YOU FALSE FRIENDS WHO SMILE THROUGH YOUR TEETH AT ME...

YOU'VE HAD YOUR FILL OF MY HOSPITALITY.

NOW GET *OUT!* EVERYBODY! OUT!

AMUSING, BUT *POINTLESS.*

NONE OF THESE PEOPLE HAVE LONG TO LIVE.

GOTHAM DIES TONIGHT, WAYNE.

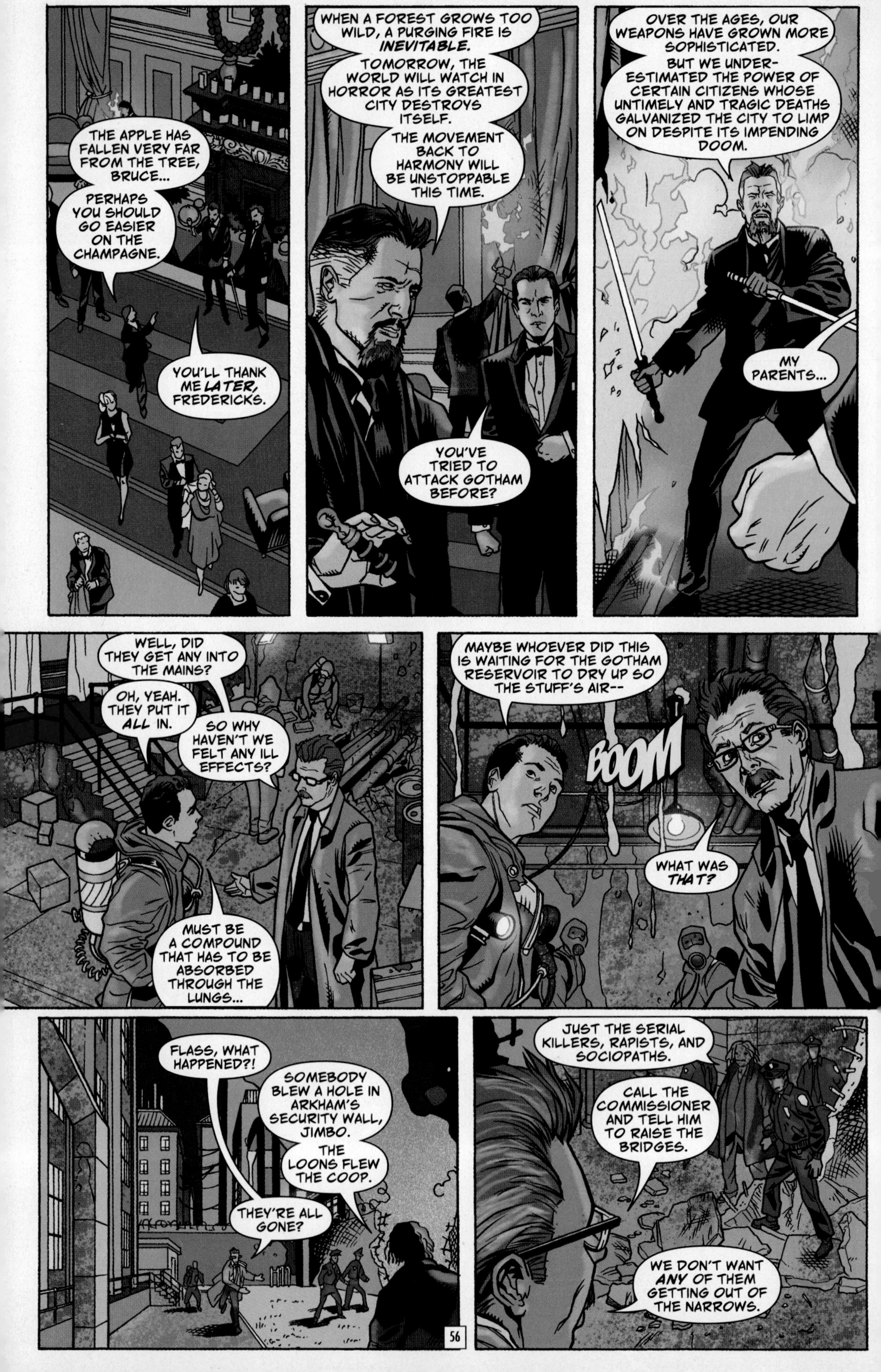
THE APPLE HAS FALLEN VERY FAR FROM THE TREE, BRUCE...
PERHAPS YOU SHOULD GO EASIER ON THE CHAMPAGNE.
YOU'LL THANK ME LATER, FREDERICKS.
WHEN A FOREST GROWS TOO WILD, A PURGING FIRE IS INEVITABLE.
TOMORROW, THE WORLD WILL WATCH IN HORROR AS ITS GREATEST CITY DESTROYS ITSELF.
THE MOVEMENT BACK TO HARMONY WILL BE UNSTOPPABLE THIS TIME.
YOU'VE TRIED TO ATTACK GOTHAM BEFORE?
OVER THE AGES, OUR WEAPONS HAVE GROWN MORE SOPHISTICATED.
BUT WE UNDER-ESTIMATED THE POWER OF CERTAIN CITIZENS WHOSE UNTIMELY AND TRAGIC DEATHS GALVANIZED THE CITY TO LIMP ON DESPITE ITS IMPENDING DOOM.
MY PARENTS...
WELL, DID THEY GET ANY INTO THE MAINS?
OH, YEAH. THEY PUT IT ALL IN.
SO WHY HAVEN'T WE FELT ANY ILL EFFECTS?
MUST BE A COMPOUND THAT HAS TO BE ABSORBED THROUGH THE LUNGS...
MAYBE WHOEVER DID THIS IS WAITING FOR THE GOTHAM RESERVOIR TO DRY UP SO THE STUFF'S AIR--
BOOM
WHAT WAS THAT?
FLASS, WHAT HAPPENED?!
SOMEBODY BLEW A HOLE IN ARKHAM'S SECURITY WALL, JIMBO.
THE LOONS FLEW THE COOP.
THEY'RE ALL GONE?
JUST THE SERIAL KILLERS, RAPISTS, AND SOCIOPATHS.
CALL THE COMMISSIONER AND TELL HIM TO RAISE THE BRIDGES.
WE DON'T WANT ANY OF THEM GETTING OUT OF THE NARROWS.

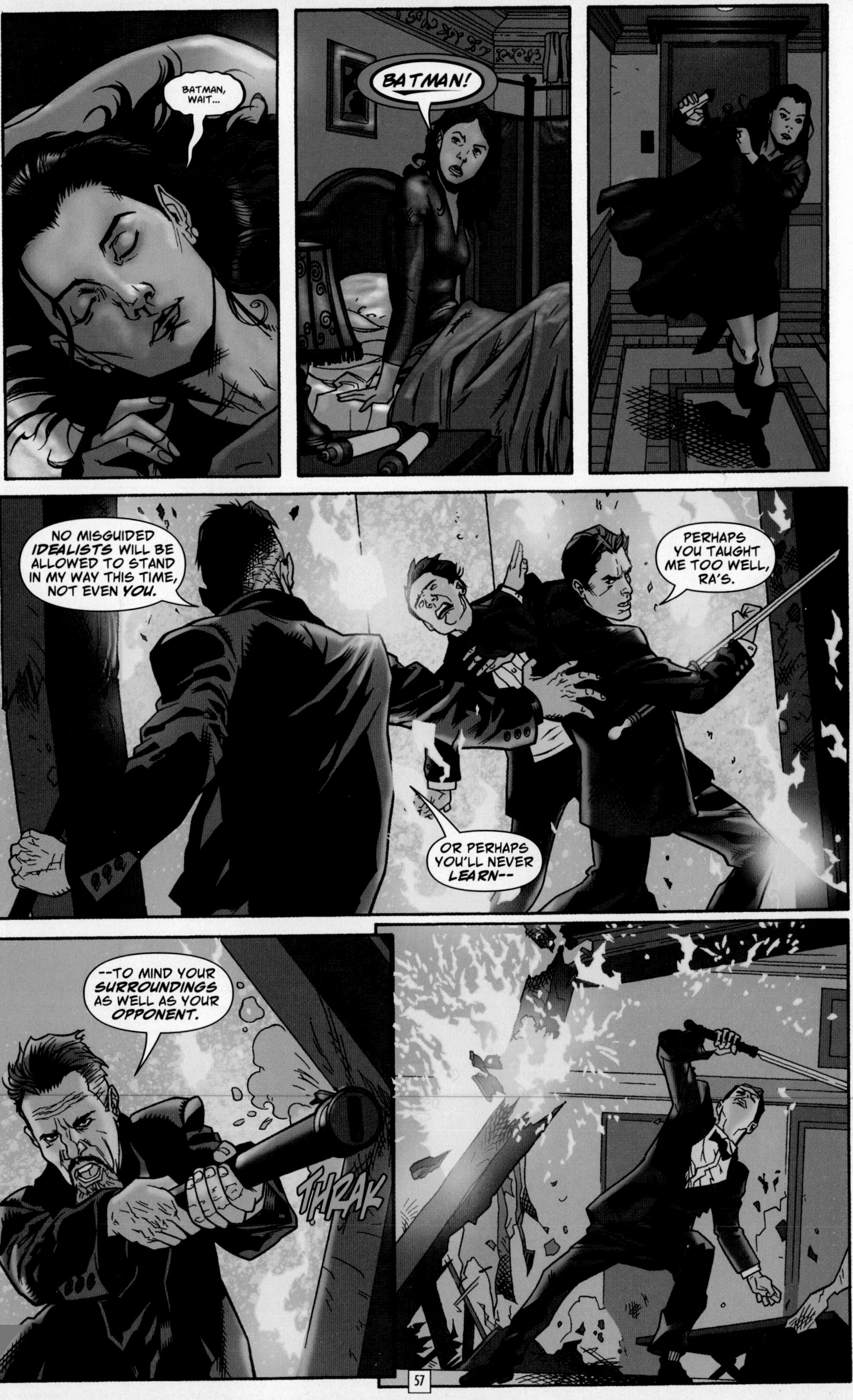
BATMAN, WAIT...
BATMAN!
NO MISGUIDED IDEALISTS WILL BE ALLOWED TO STAND IN MY WAY THIS TIME, NOT EVEN YOU.
PERHAPS YOU TAUGHT ME TOO WELL, RA'S.
OR PERHAPS YOU'LL NEVER LEARN--
--TO MIND YOUR SURROUNDINGS AS WELL AS YOUR OPPONENT.
THRAK

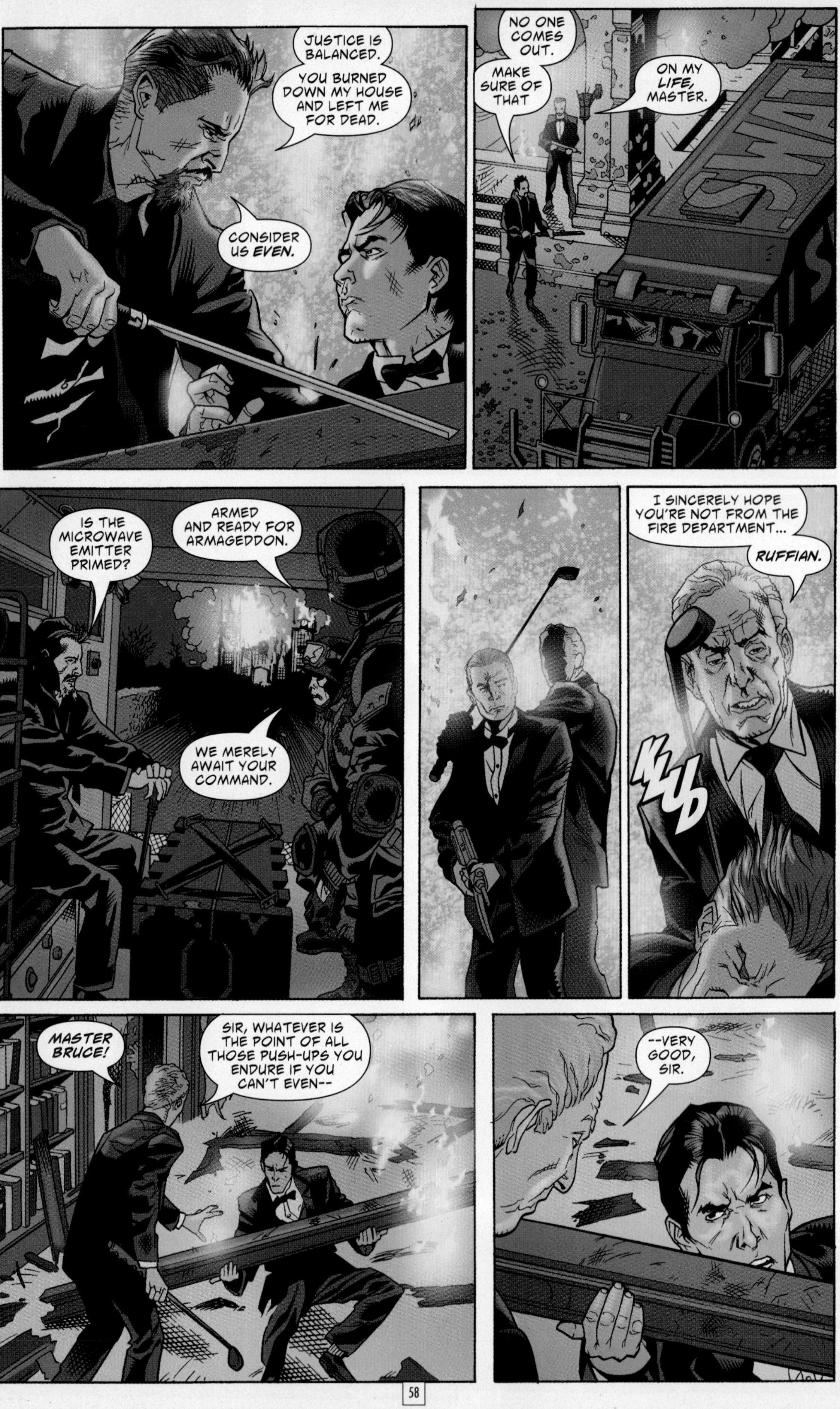
JUSTICE IS BALANCED.
YOU BURNED DOWN MY HOUSE AND LEFT ME FOR DEAD.
CONSIDER US EVEN.
NO ONE COMES OUT.
MAKE SURE OF THAT
ON MY LIFE, MASTER.
IS THE MICROWAVE EMITTER PRIMED?
ARMED AND READY FOR ARMAGEDDON.
WE MERELY AWAIT YOUR COMMAND.
I SINCERELY HOPE YOU'RE NOT FROM THE FIRE DEPARTMENT...
RUFFIAN.
KLUD
MASTER BRUCE!
SIR, WHATEVER IS THE POINT OF ALL THOSE PUSH-UPS YOU ENDURE IF YOU CAN'T EVEN--
--VERY GOOD, SIR.

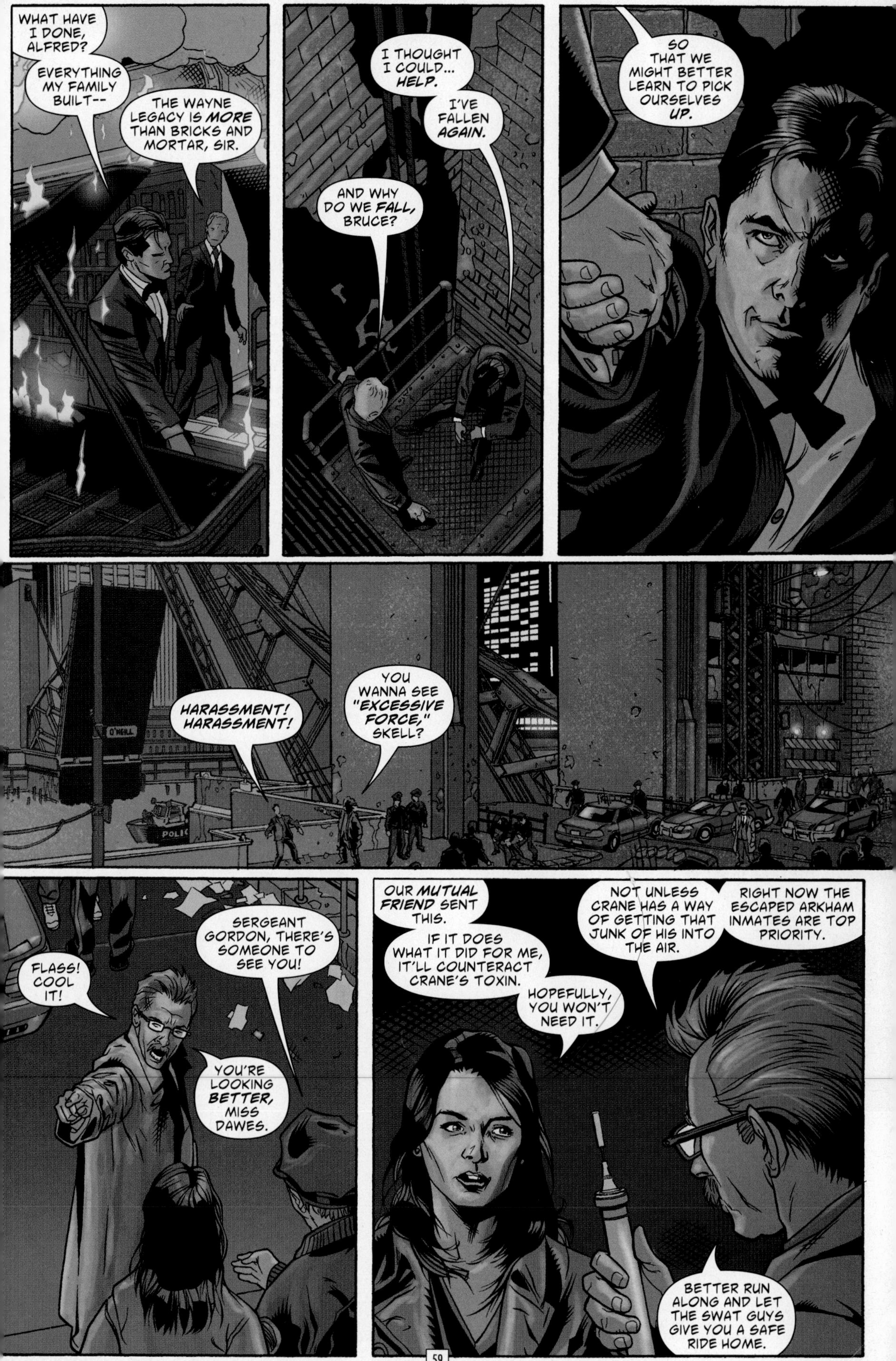
WHAT HAVE I DONE, ALFRED?
EVERYTHING MY FAMILY BUILT--
THE WAYNE LEGACY IS MORE THAN BRICKS AND MORTAR, SIR.
I THOUGHT I COULD... HELP.
I'VE FALLEN AGAIN.
AND WHY DO WE FALL, BRUCE?
SO THAT WE MIGHT BETTER LEARN TO PICK OURSELVES UP.
O'NEILL
HARASSMENT! HARASSMENT!
YOU WANNA SEE "EXCESSIVE FORCE," SKELL?
POLIC
FLASS! COOL IT!
SERGEANT GORDON, THERE'S SOMEONE TO SEE YOU!
YOU'RE LOOKING BETTER, MISS DAWES.
OUR MUTUAL FRIEND SENT THIS.
IF IT DOES WHAT IT DID FOR ME, IT'LL COUNTERACT CRANE'S TOXIN.
HOPEFULLY, YOU WON'T NEED IT.
NOT UNLESS CRANE HAS A WAY OF GETTING THAT JUNK OF HIS INTO THE AIR.
RIGHT NOW THE ESCAPED ARKHAM INMATES ARE TOP PRIORITY.
BETTER RUN ALONG AND LET THE SWAT GUYS GIVE YOU A SAFE RIDE HOME.

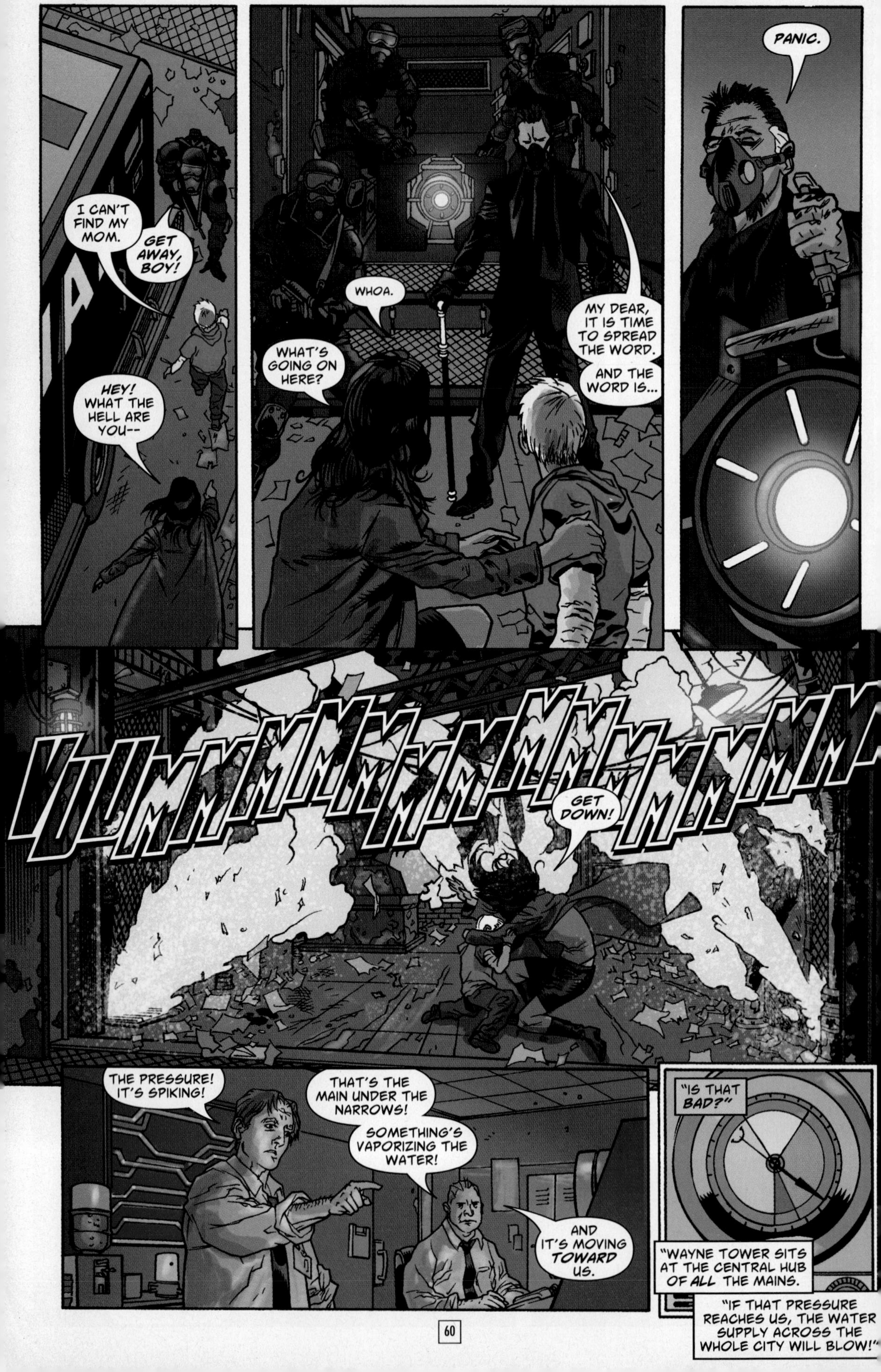
I CAN'T FIND MY MOM.
GET AWAY, BOY!
HEY! WHAT THE HELL ARE YOU--
WHOA.
WHAT'S GOING ON HERE?
MY DEAR, IT IS TIME TO SPREAD THE WORD.
AND THE WORD IS...
PANIC.
VUUMMMMMMMMMMMMMMMMM
GET DOWN!
THE PRESSURE! IT'S SPIKING!
THAT'S THE MAIN UNDER THE NARROWS!
SOMETHING'S VAPORIZING THE WATER!
AND IT'S MOVING TOWARD US.
"IS THAT BAD?"
"WAYNE TOWER SITS AT THE CENTRAL HUB OF ALL THE MAINS.
"IF THAT PRESSURE REACHES US, THE WATER SUPPLY ACROSS THE WHOLE CITY WILL BLOW!"

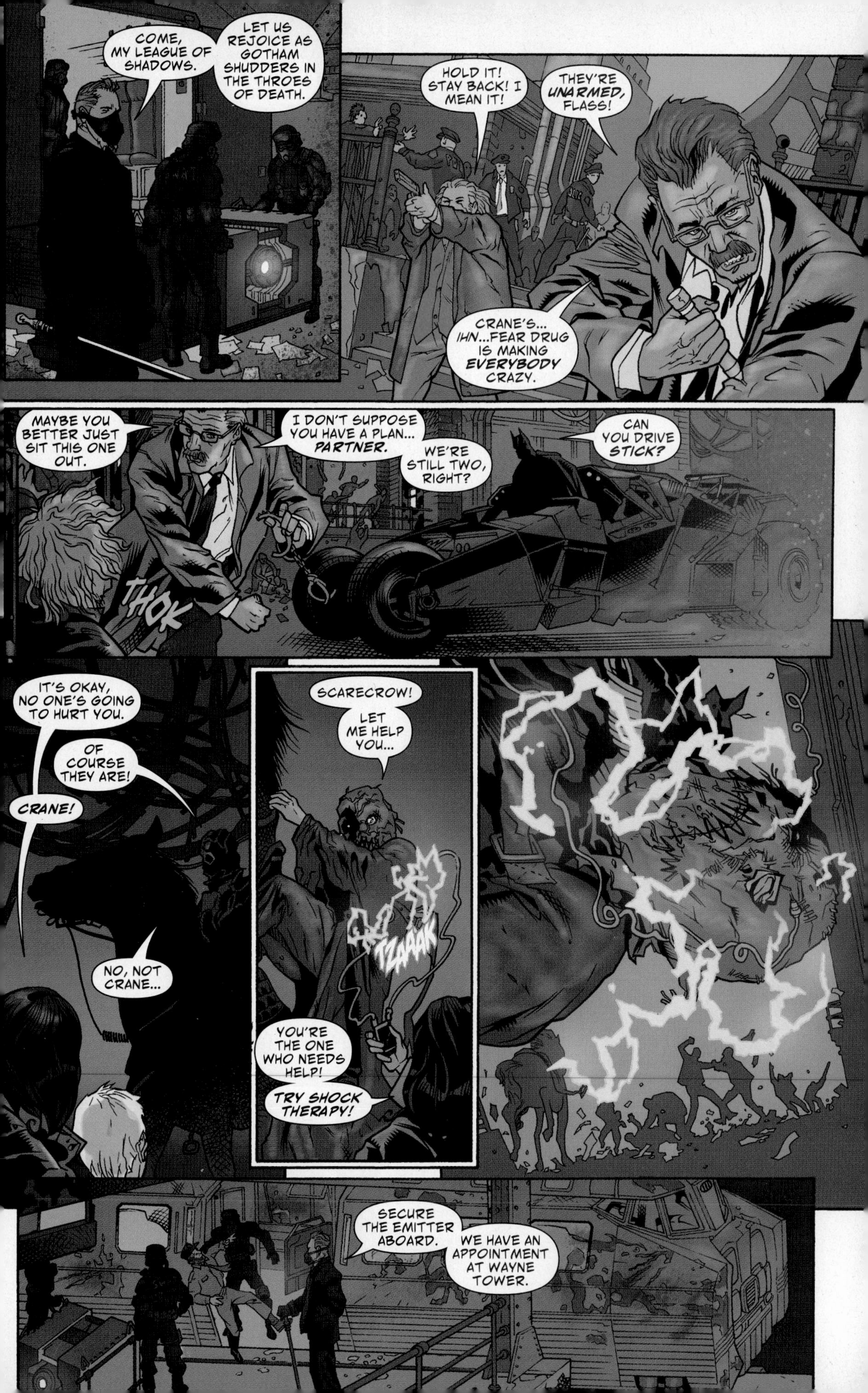
COME, MY LEAGUE OF SHADOWS.
LET US REJOICE AS GOTHAM SHUDDERS IN THE THROES OF DEATH.
HOLD IT! STAY BACK! I MEAN IT!
THEY'RE *UNARMED*, FLASS!
CRANE'S... *IHN*...FEAR DRUG IS MAKING *EVERYBODY* CRAZY.
MAYBE YOU BETTER JUST SIT THIS ONE OUT.
THOK
I DON'T SUPPOSE YOU HAVE A PLAN... *PARTNER*.
WE'RE STILL TWO, RIGHT?
CAN YOU DRIVE *STICK?*
IT'S OKAY, NO ONE'S GOING TO HURT YOU.
OF COURSE THEY ARE!
CRANE!
NO, NOT CRANE...
SCARECROW!
LET ME HELP YOU...
TZAAAK
YOU'RE THE ONE WHO NEEDS HELP!
TRY SHOCK THERAPY!
SECURE THE EMITTER ABOARD.
WE HAVE AN APPOINTMENT AT WAYNE TOWER.

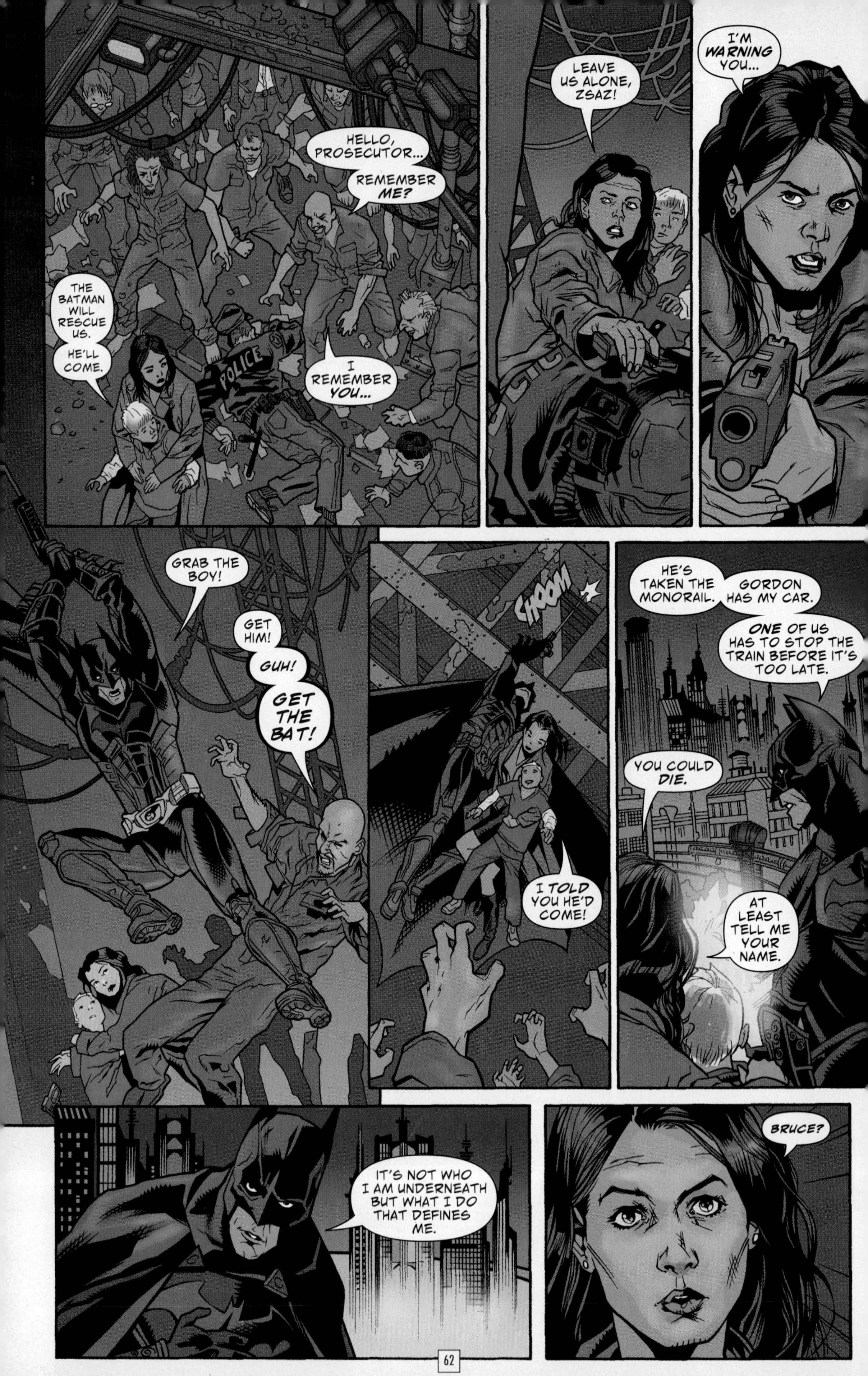
HELLO, PROSECUTOR... REMEMBER ME?
THE BATMAN WILL RESCUE US.
HE'LL COME.
I REMEMBER YOU...
LEAVE US ALONE, ZSAZ!
I'M WARNING YOU...
GRAB THE BOY!
GET HIM!
GUH!
GET THE BAT!
SHOOM
I TOLD YOU HE'D COME!
HE'S TAKEN THE MONORAIL.
GORDON HAS MY CAR.
ONE OF US HAS TO STOP THE TRAIN BEFORE IT'S TOO LATE.
YOU COULD DIE.
AT LEAST TELL ME YOUR NAME.
IT'S NOT WHO I AM UNDERNEATH BUT WHAT I DO THAT DEFINES ME.
BRUCE?

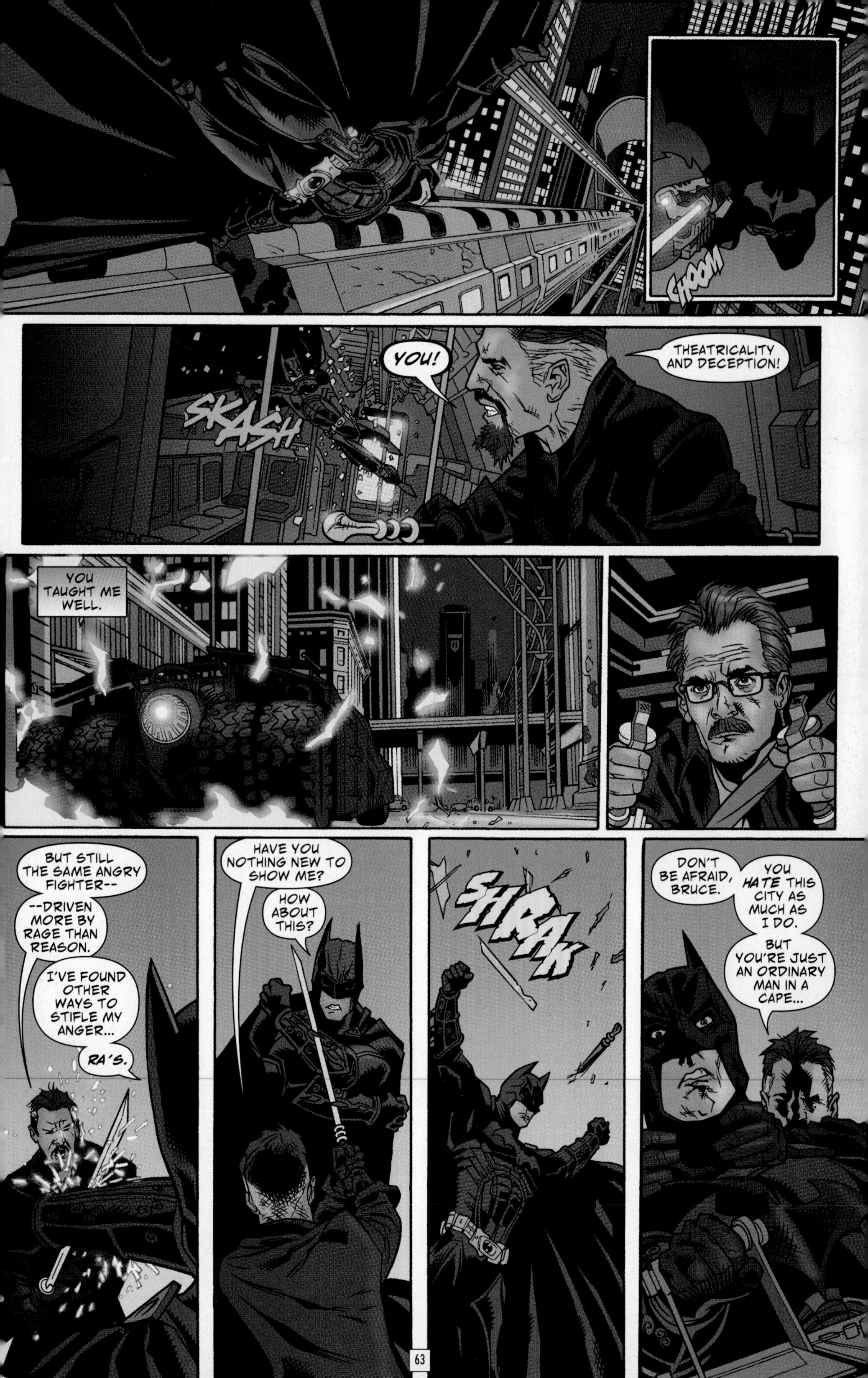

SHOOM
SKASH
YOU!
THEATRICALITY AND DECEPTION!
YOU TAUGHT ME WELL.
BUT STILL THE SAME ANGRY FIGHTER--
--DRIVEN MORE BY RAGE THAN REASON.
I'VE FOUND OTHER WAYS TO STIFLE MY ANGER...
RA'S.
HAVE YOU NOTHING NEW TO SHOW ME?
HOW ABOUT THIS?
SHRAK
DON'T BE AFRAID, BRUCE.
YOU HATE THIS CITY AS MUCH AS I DO.
BUT YOU'RE JUST AN ORDINARY MAN IN A CAPE...

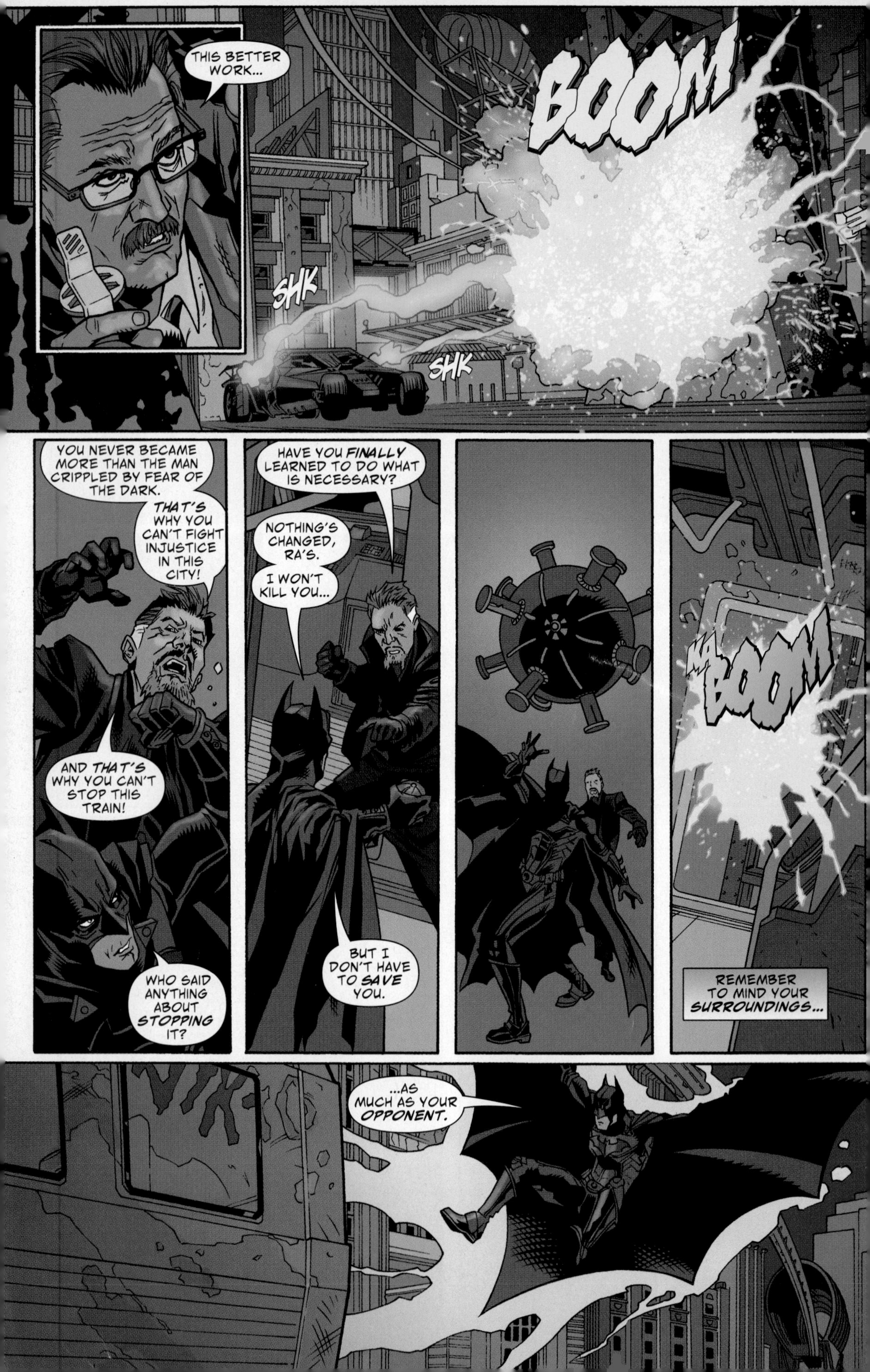

THIS BETTER WORK...
BOOM
SHK
SHK
YOU NEVER BECAME MORE THAN THE MAN CRIPPLED BY FEAR OF THE DARK.
THAT'S WHY YOU CAN'T FIGHT INJUSTICE IN THIS CITY!
AND THAT'S WHY YOU CAN'T STOP THIS TRAIN!
WHO SAID ANYTHING ABOUT STOPPING IT?
HAVE YOU FINALLY LEARNED TO DO WHAT IS NECESSARY?
NOTHING'S CHANGED, RA'S.
I WON'T KILL YOU...
BUT I DON'T HAVE TO SAVE YOU.
KA-BOOM
REMEMBER TO MIND YOUR SURROUNDINGS...
...AS MUCH AS YOUR OPPONENT.

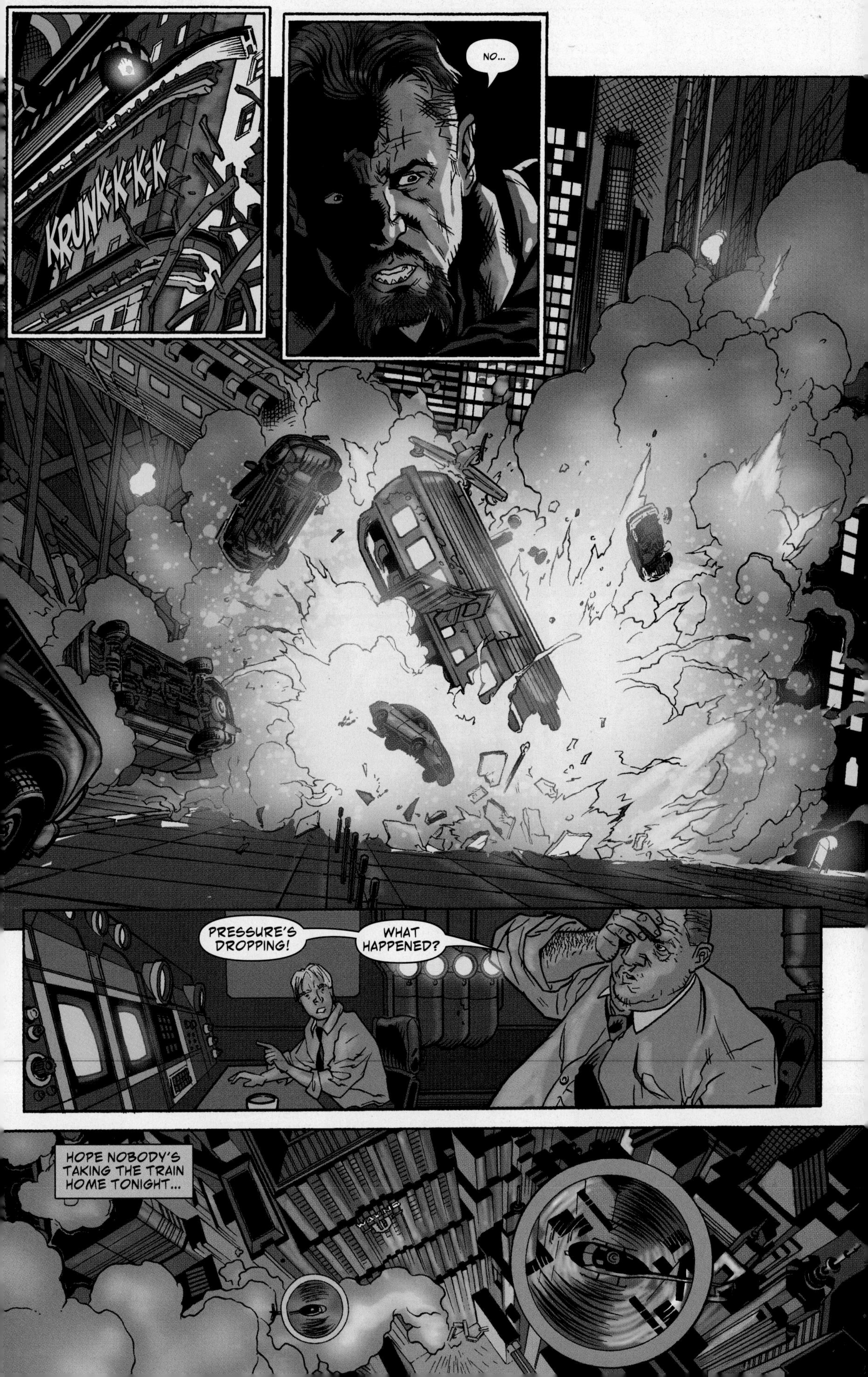
KRUNK-K-K-K
NO...
PRESSURE'S DROPPING!
WHAT HAPPENED?
HOPE NOBODY'S TAKING THE TRAIN HOME TONIGHT...

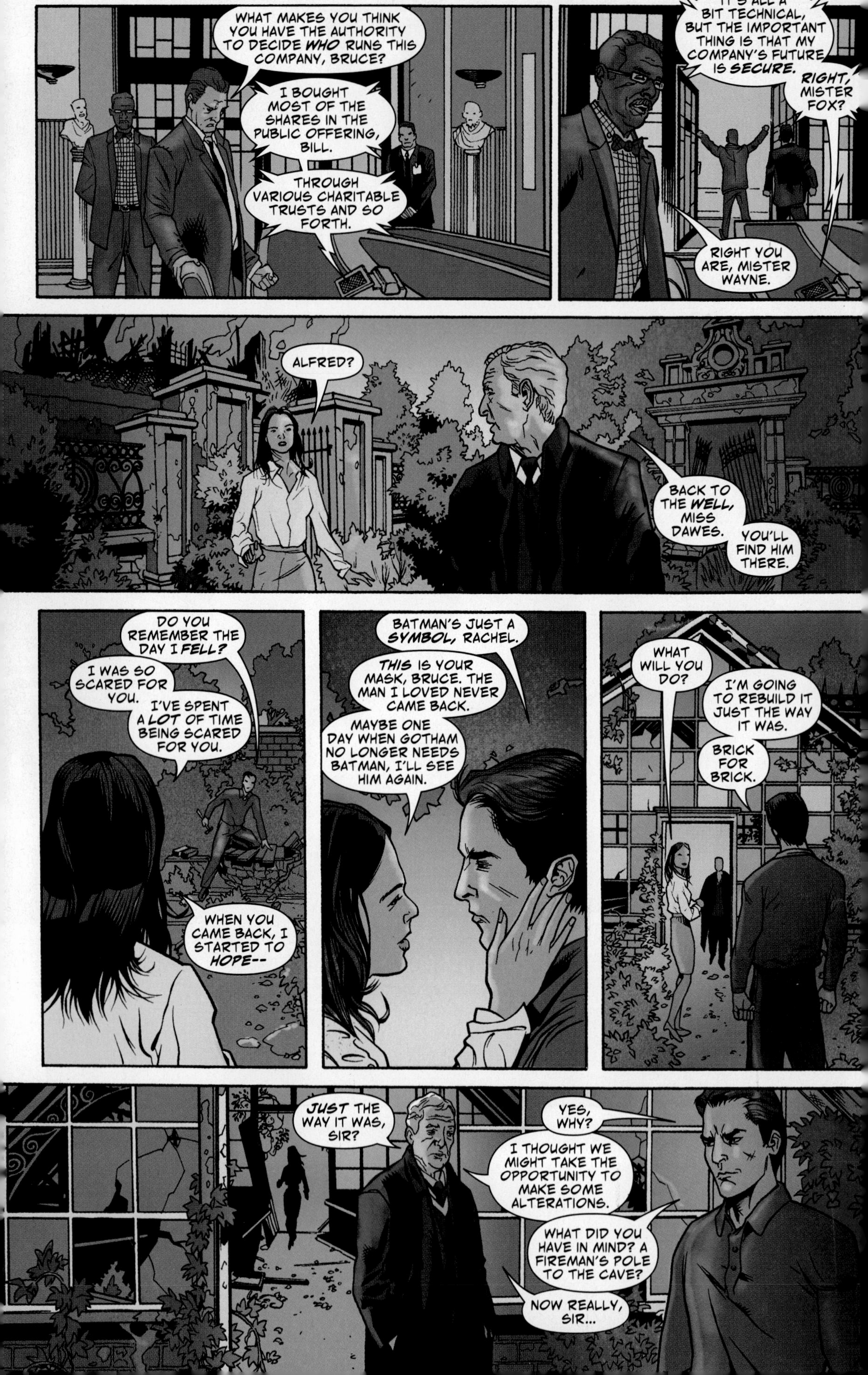
WHAT MAKES YOU THINK YOU HAVE THE AUTHORITY TO DECIDE *WHO* RUNS THIS COMPANY, BRUCE?
I BOUGHT MOST OF THE SHARES IN THE PUBLIC OFFERING, BILL.
THROUGH VARIOUS CHARITABLE TRUSTS AND SO FORTH.
IT'S ALL A BIT TECHNICAL, BUT THE IMPORTANT THING IS THAT MY COMPANY'S FUTURE IS *SECURE.*
RIGHT, MISTER FOX?
RIGHT YOU ARE, MISTER WAYNE.
ALFRED?
BACK TO THE *WELL,* MISS DAWES.
YOU'LL FIND HIM THERE.
DO YOU REMEMBER THE DAY I *FELL?*
I WAS SO SCARED FOR YOU.
I'VE SPENT A *LOT* OF TIME BEING SCARED FOR YOU.
WHEN YOU CAME BACK, I STARTED TO *HOPE--*
BATMAN'S JUST A *SYMBOL,* RACHEL.
THIS IS YOUR MASK, BRUCE. THE MAN I LOVED NEVER CAME BACK.
MAYBE ONE DAY WHEN GOTHAM NO LONGER NEEDS BATMAN, I'LL SEE HIM AGAIN.
WHAT WILL YOU DO?
I'M GOING TO REBUILD IT JUST THE WAY IT WAS.
BRICK FOR BRICK.
JUST THE WAY IT WAS, SIR?
YES, WHY?
I THOUGHT WE MIGHT TAKE THE OPPORTUNITY TO MAKE SOME ALTERATIONS.
WHAT DID YOU HAVE IN MIND? A FIREMAN'S POLE TO THE CAVE?
NOW REALLY, SIR...

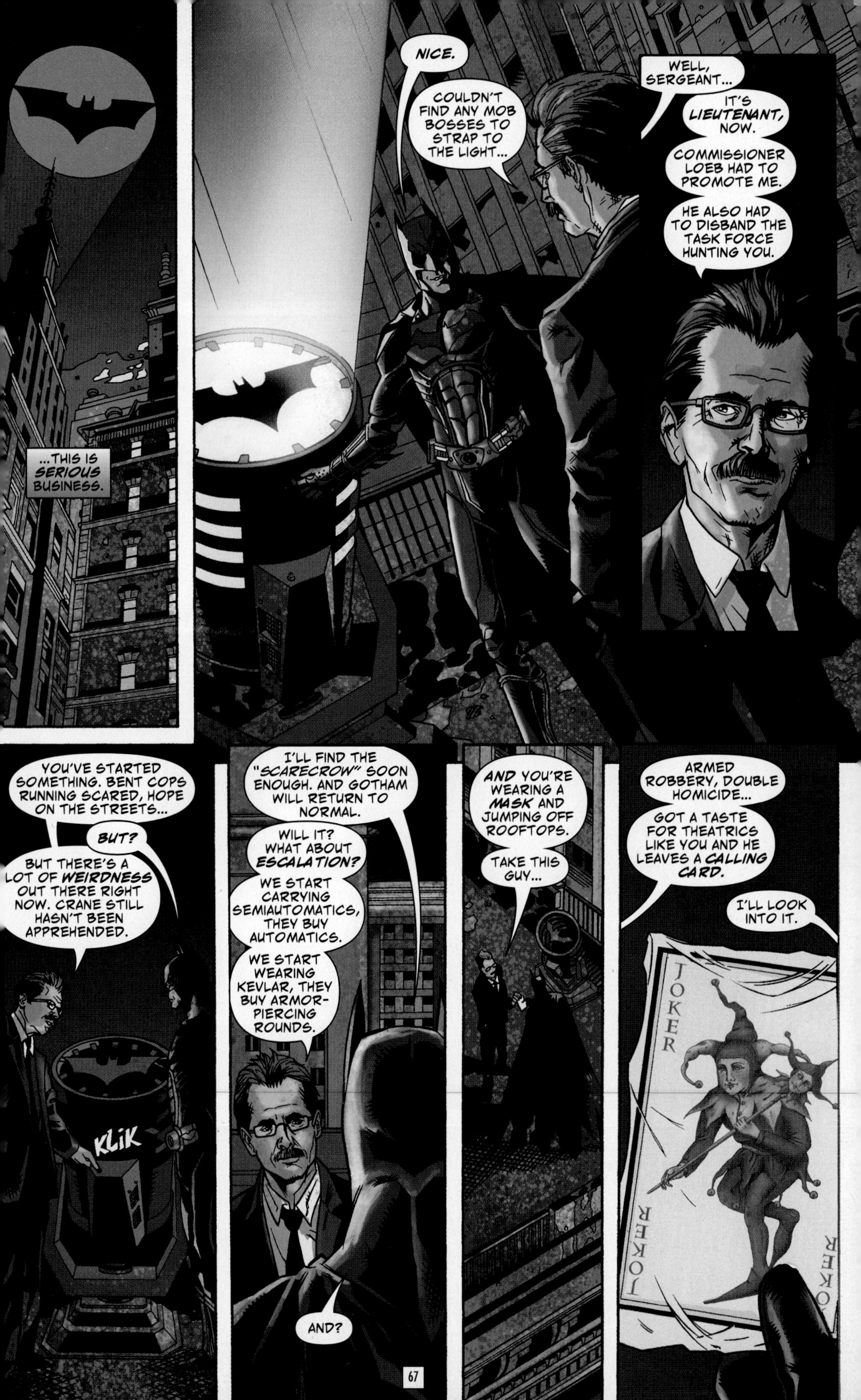
...THIS IS SERIOUS BUSINESS.
NICE.
COULDN'T FIND ANY MOB BOSSES TO STRAP TO THE LIGHT...
WELL, SERGEANT...
IT'S LIEUTENANT, NOW.
COMMISSIONER LOEB HAD TO PROMOTE ME.
HE ALSO HAD TO DISBAND THE TASK FORCE HUNTING YOU.
YOU'VE STARTED SOMETHING. BENT COPS RUNNING SCARED, HOPE ON THE STREETS...
BUT?
BUT THERE'S A LOT OF WEIRDNESS OUT THERE RIGHT NOW. CRANE STILL HASN'T BEEN APPREHENDED.
KLIK
I'LL FIND THE "SCARECROW" SOON ENOUGH. AND GOTHAM WILL RETURN TO NORMAL.
WILL IT? WHAT ABOUT ESCALATION?
WE START CARRYING SEMIAUTOMATICS, THEY BUY AUTOMATICS.
WE START WEARING KEVLAR, THEY BUY ARMOR-PIERCING ROUNDS.
AND?
AND YOU'RE WEARING A MASK AND JUMPING OFF ROOFTOPS.
TAKE THIS GUY...
ARMED ROBBERY, DOUBLE HOMICIDE...
GOT A TASTE FOR THEATRICS LIKE YOU AND HE LEAVES A CALLING CARD.
I'LL LOOK INTO IT.
JOKER
JOKER

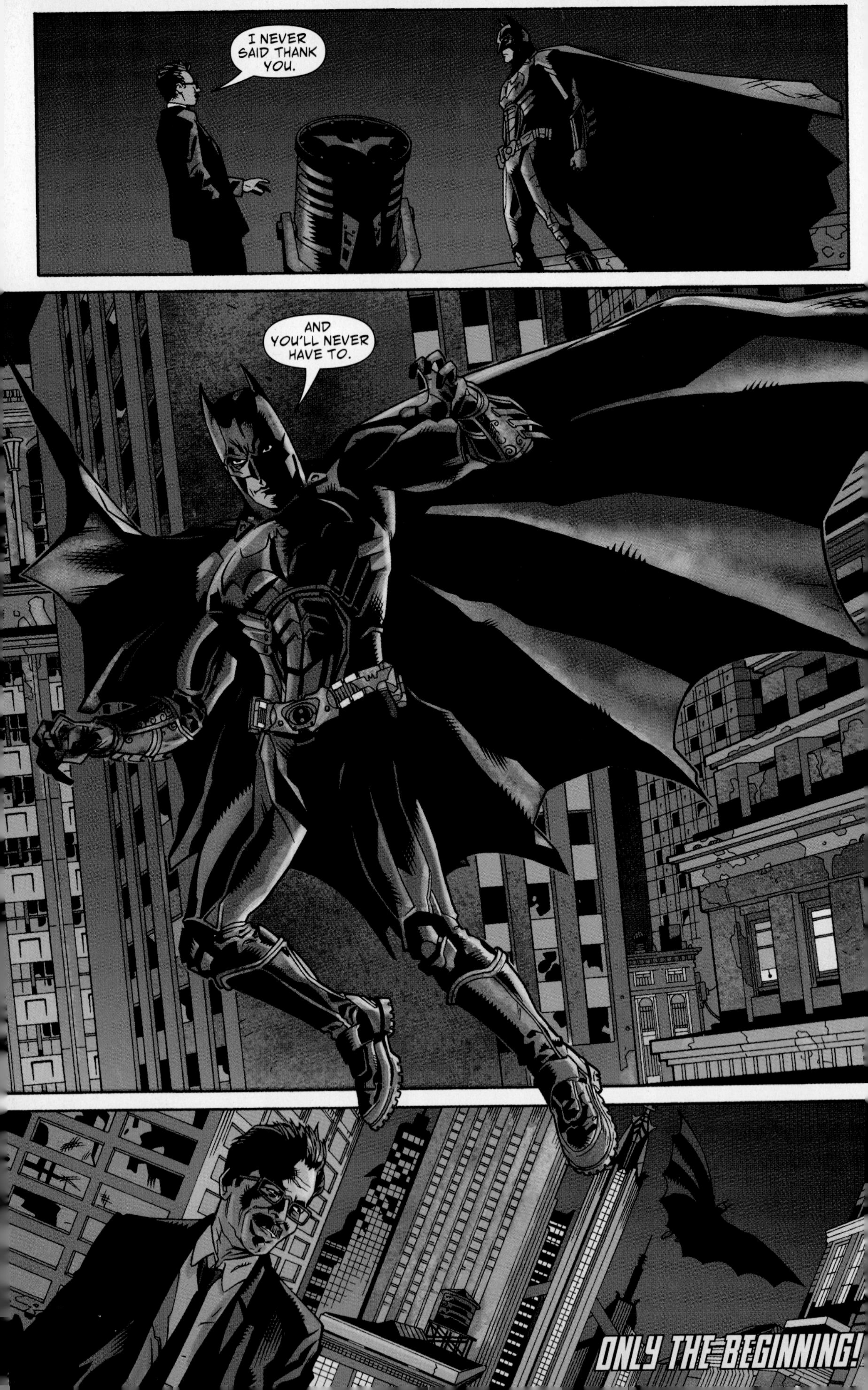
I NEVER SAID THANK YOU.
AND YOU'LL NEVER HAVE TO.
ONLY THE BEGINNING!

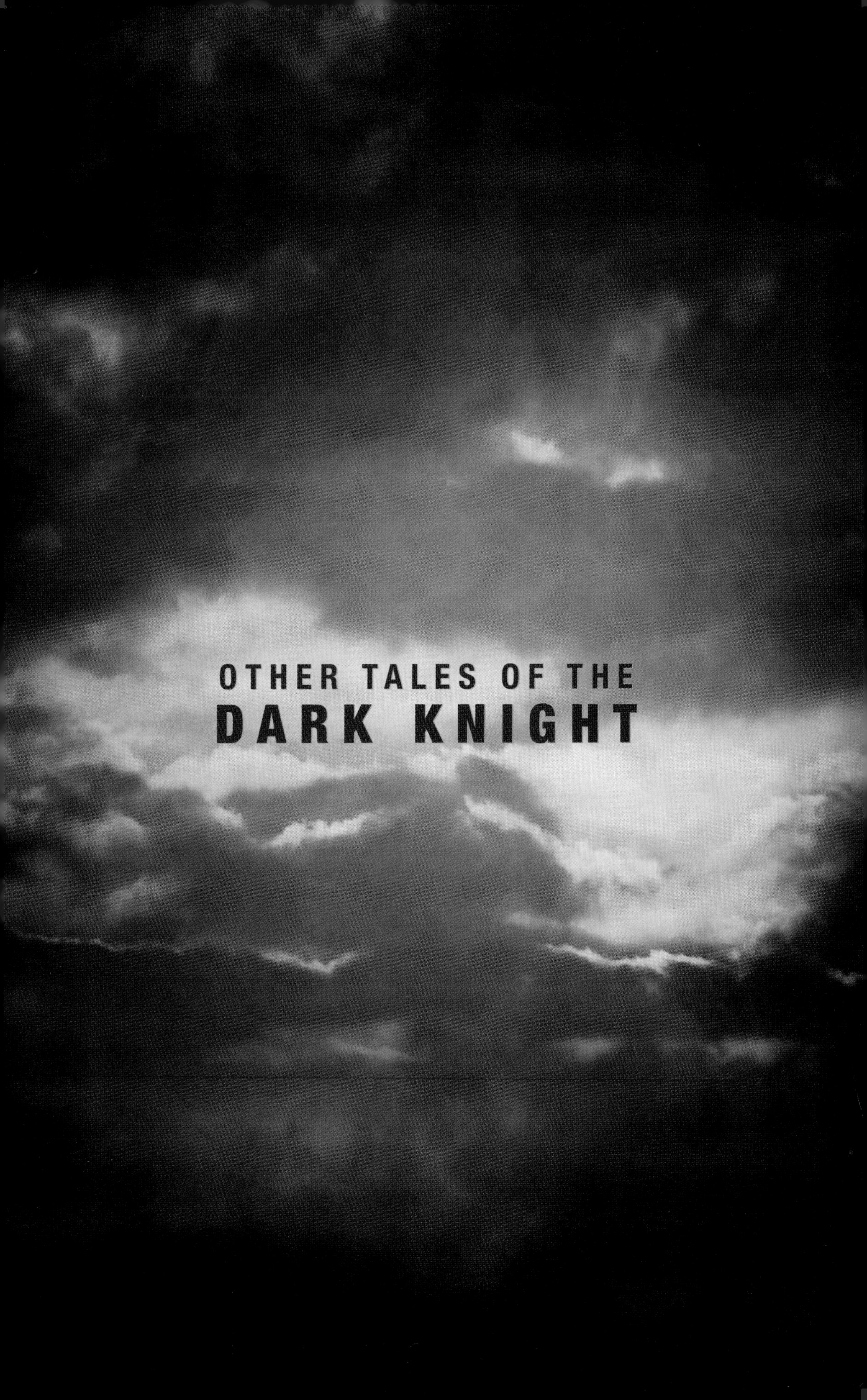
OTHER TALES OF THE
DARK KNIGHT

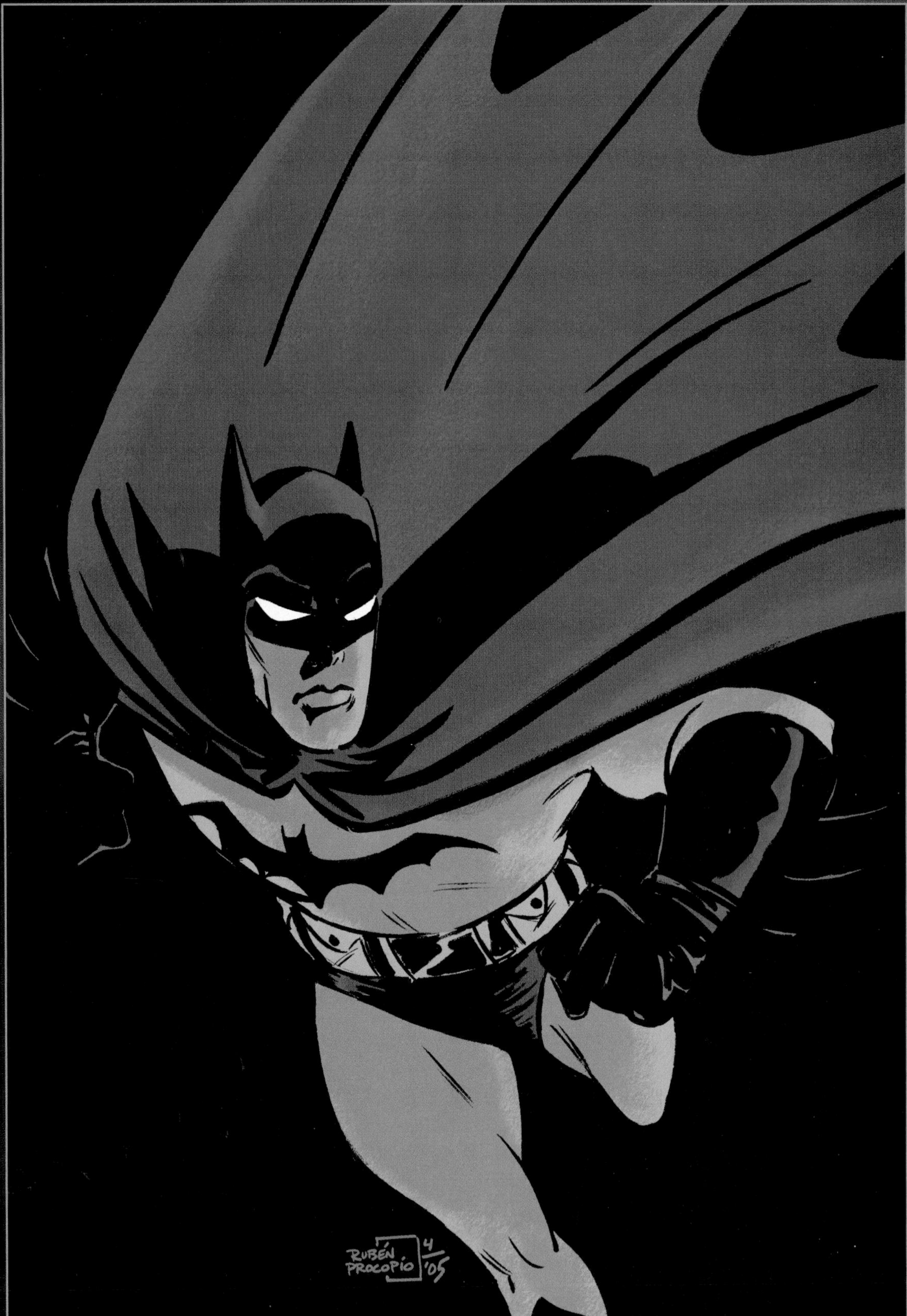
RUBÉN PROCOPIO 4/'05

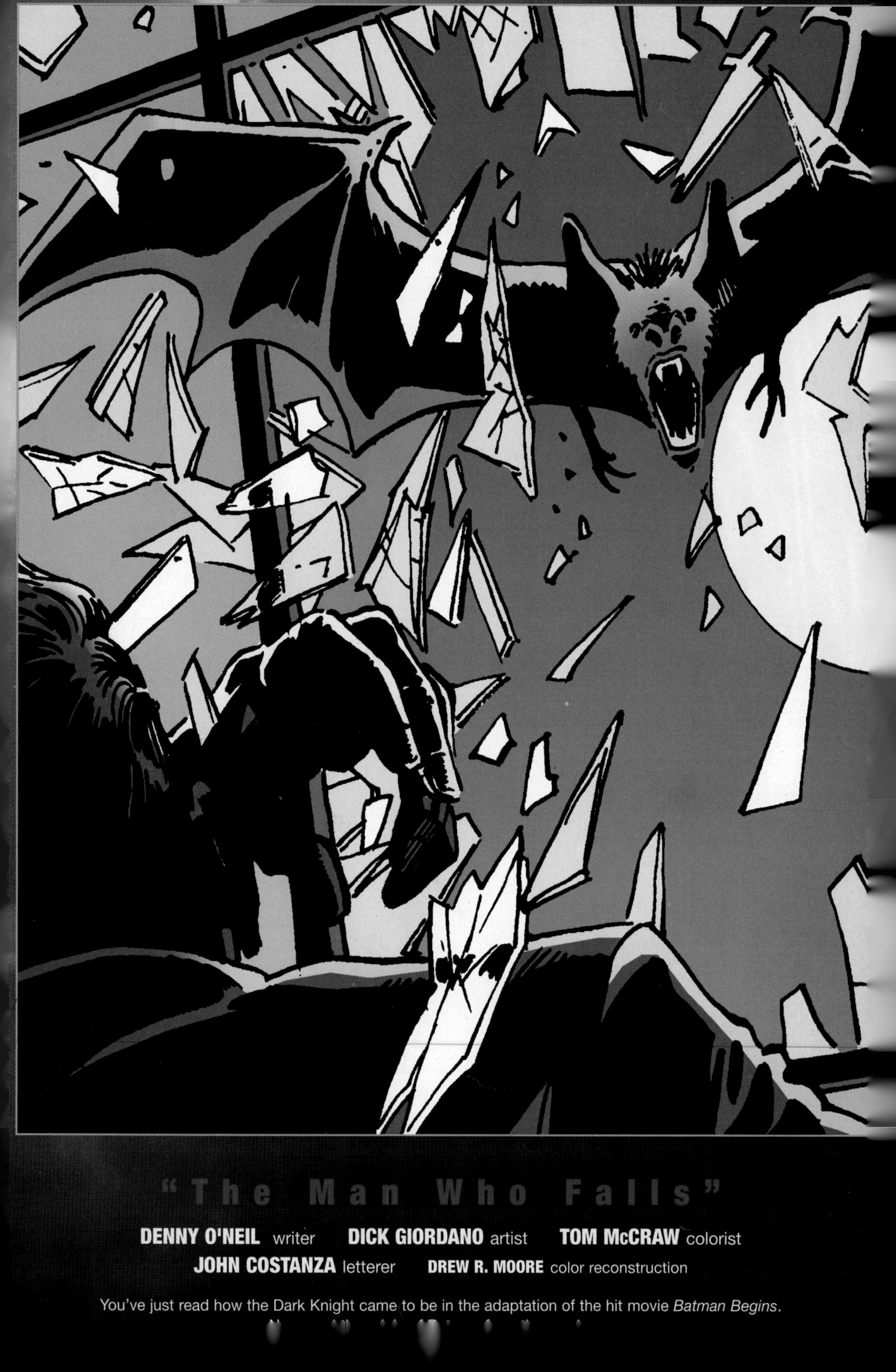

“The Man Who Falls”

DENNY O'NEIL writer **DICK GIORDANO** artist **TOM McCRAW** colorist
JOHN COSTANZA letterer **DREW R. MOORE** color reconstruction

You've just read how the Dark Knight came to be in the adaptation of the hit movie *Batman Begins*.

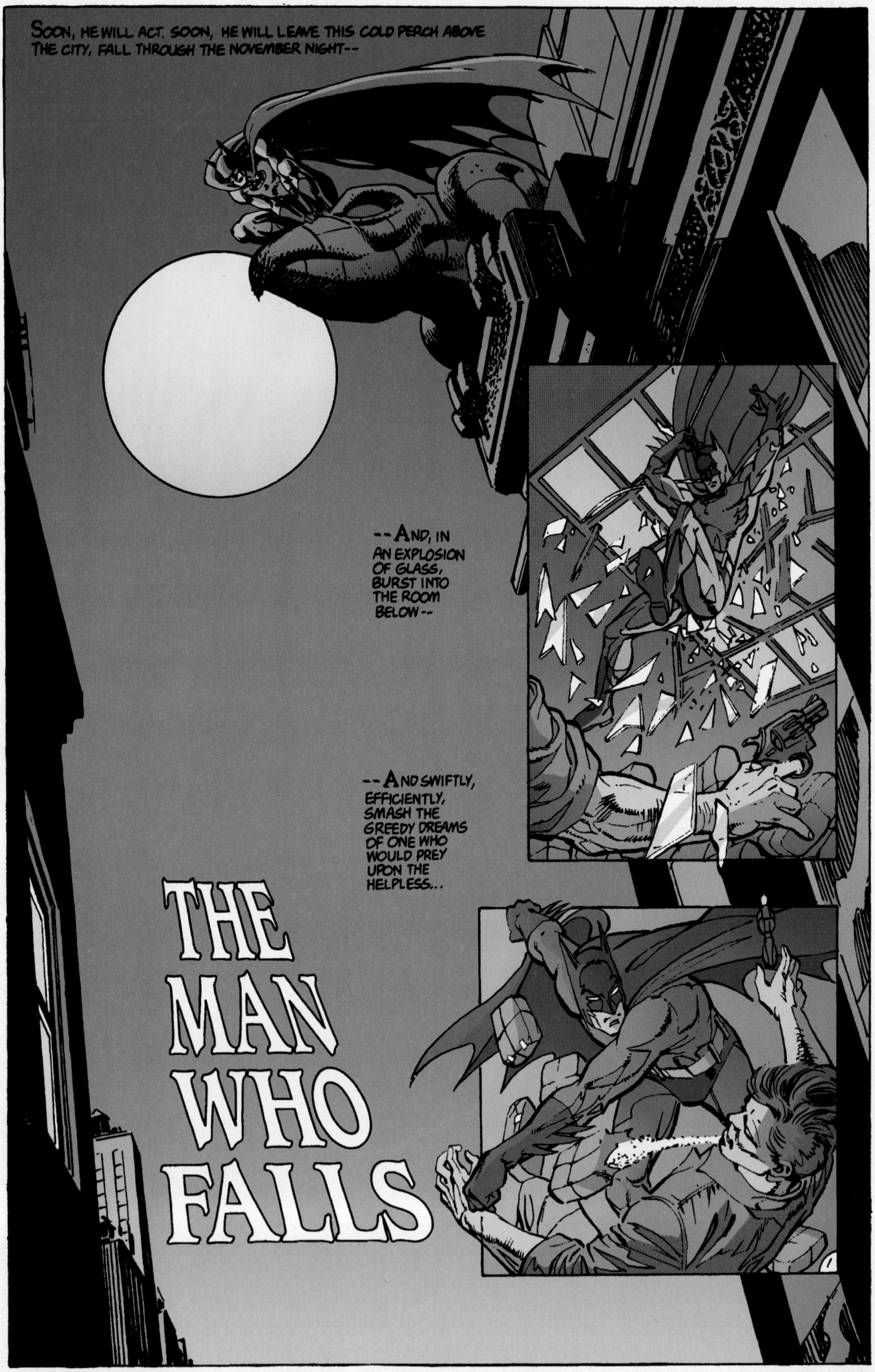
SOON, HE WILL ACT. SOON, HE WILL LEAVE THIS COLD PERCH ABOVE THE CITY, FALL THROUGH THE NOVEMBER NIGHT--
--AND, IN AN EXPLOSION OF GLASS, BURST INTO THE ROOM BELOW--
--AND SWIFTLY, EFFICIENTLY, SMASH THE GREEDY DREAMS OF ONE WHO WOULD PREY UPON THE HELPLESS...
THE MAN WHO FALLS

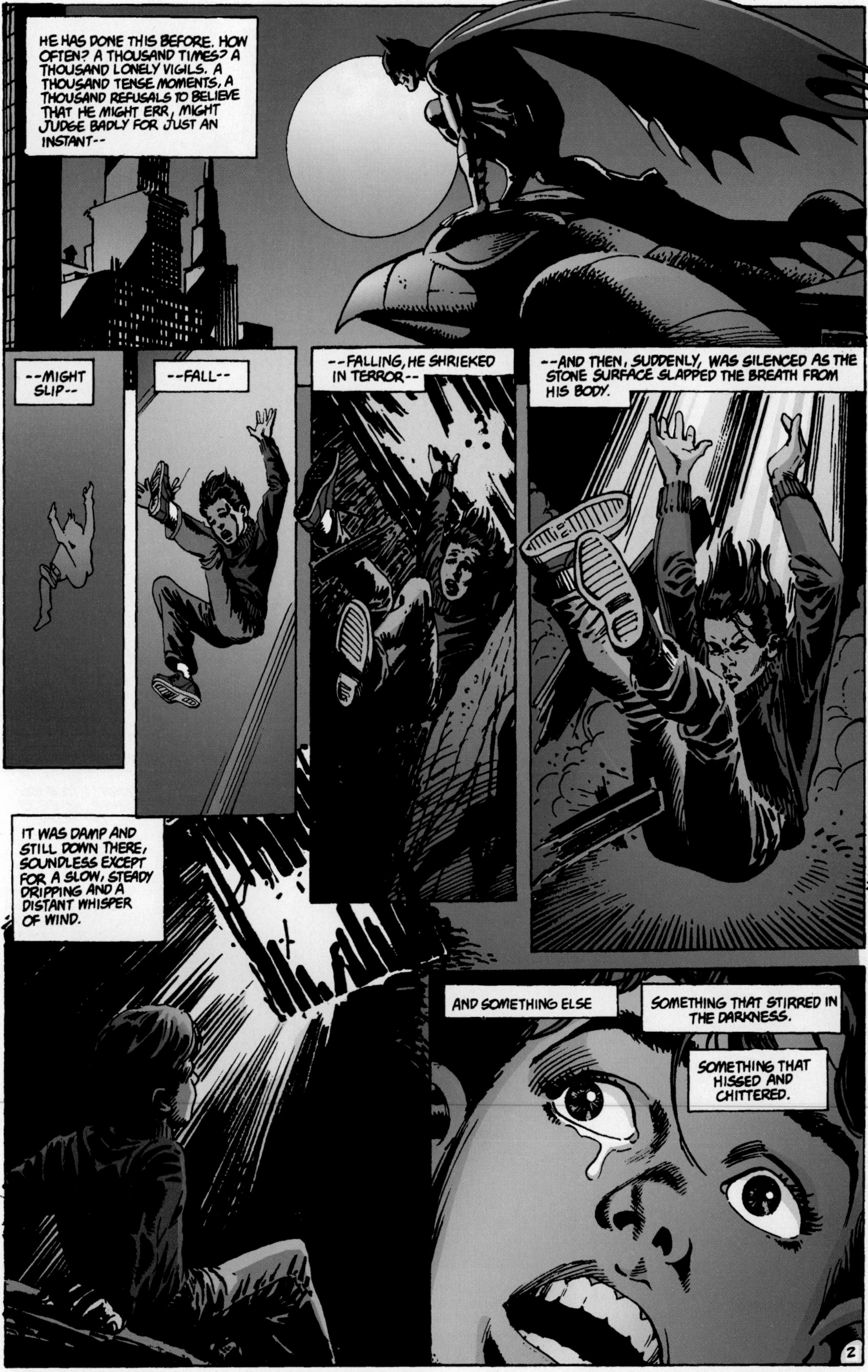
HE HAS DONE THIS BEFORE. HOW OFTEN? A THOUSAND TIMES? A THOUSAND LONELY VIGILS. A THOUSAND TENSE MOMENTS, A THOUSAND REFUSALS TO BELIEVE THAT HE MIGHT ERR, MIGHT JUDGE BADLY FOR JUST AN INSTANT--
--MIGHT SLIP--
--FALL--
--FALLING, HE SHRIEKED IN TERROR--
--AND THEN, SUDDENLY, WAS SILENCED AS THE STONE SURFACE SLAPPED THE BREATH FROM HIS BODY.
IT WAS DAMP AND STILL DOWN THERE, SOUNDLESS EXCEPT FOR A SLOW, STEADY DRIPPING AND A DISTANT WHISPER OF WIND.
AND SOMETHING ELSE
SOMETHING THAT STIRRED IN THE DARKNESS.
SOMETHING THAT HISSED AND CHITTERED.
2

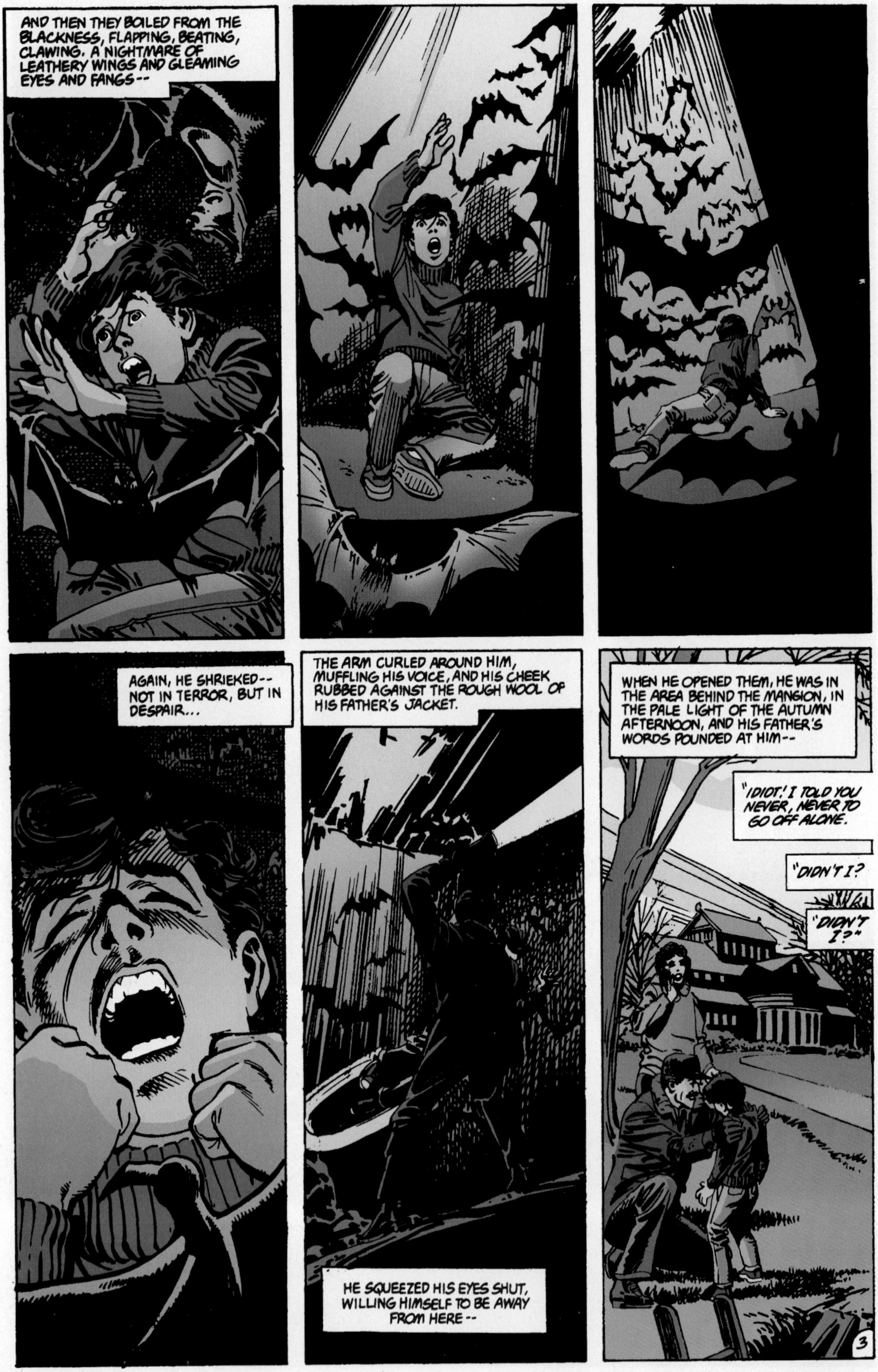
AND THEN THEY BOILED FROM THE BLACKNESS, FLAPPING, BEATING, CLAWING. A NIGHTMARE OF LEATHERY WINGS AND GLEAMING EYES AND FANGS--
AGAIN, HE SHRIEKED-- NOT IN TERROR, BUT IN DESPAIR...
THE ARM CURLED AROUND HIM, MUFFLING HIS VOICE, AND HIS CHEEK RUBBED AGAINST THE ROUGH WOOL OF HIS FATHER'S JACKET.
HE SQUEEZED HIS EYES SHUT, WILLING HIMSELF TO BE AWAY FROM HERE--
WHEN HE OPENED THEM, HE WAS IN THE AREA BEHIND THE MANSION, IN THE PALE LIGHT OF THE AUTUMN AFTERNOON, AND HIS FATHER'S WORDS POUNDED AT HIM--
"IDIOT! I TOLD YOU NEVER, NEVER TO GO OFF ALONE.
"DIDN'T I?
"DIDN'T I?"
3

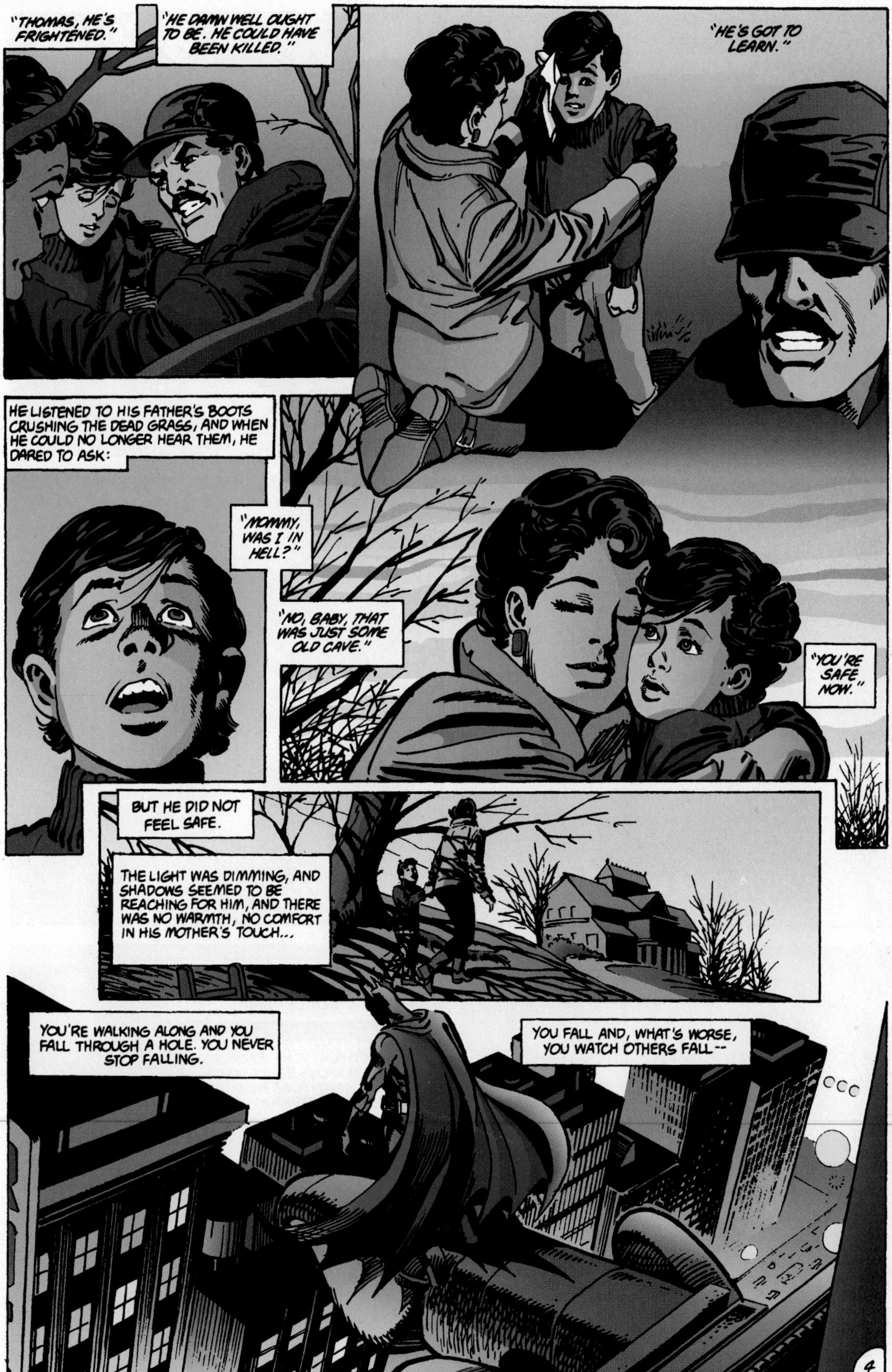
"THOMAS, HE'S FRIGHTENED."
"HE DAMN WELL OUGHT TO BE. HE COULD HAVE BEEN KILLED."
"HE'S GOT TO LEARN."
HE LISTENED TO HIS FATHER'S BOOTS CRUSHING THE DEAD GRASS, AND WHEN HE COULD NO LONGER HEAR THEM, HE DARED TO ASK:
"MOMMY, WAS I IN HELL?"
"NO, BABY, THAT WAS JUST SOME OLD CAVE."
"YOU'RE SAFE NOW."
BUT HE DID NOT FEEL SAFE.
THE LIGHT WAS DIMMING, AND SHADOWS SEEMED TO BE REACHING FOR HIM, AND THERE WAS NO WARMTH, NO COMFORT IN HIS MOTHER'S TOUCH...
YOU'RE WALKING ALONG AND YOU FALL THROUGH A HOLE. YOU NEVER STOP FALLING.
YOU FALL AND, WHAT'S WORSE, YOU WATCH OTHERS FALL--
4

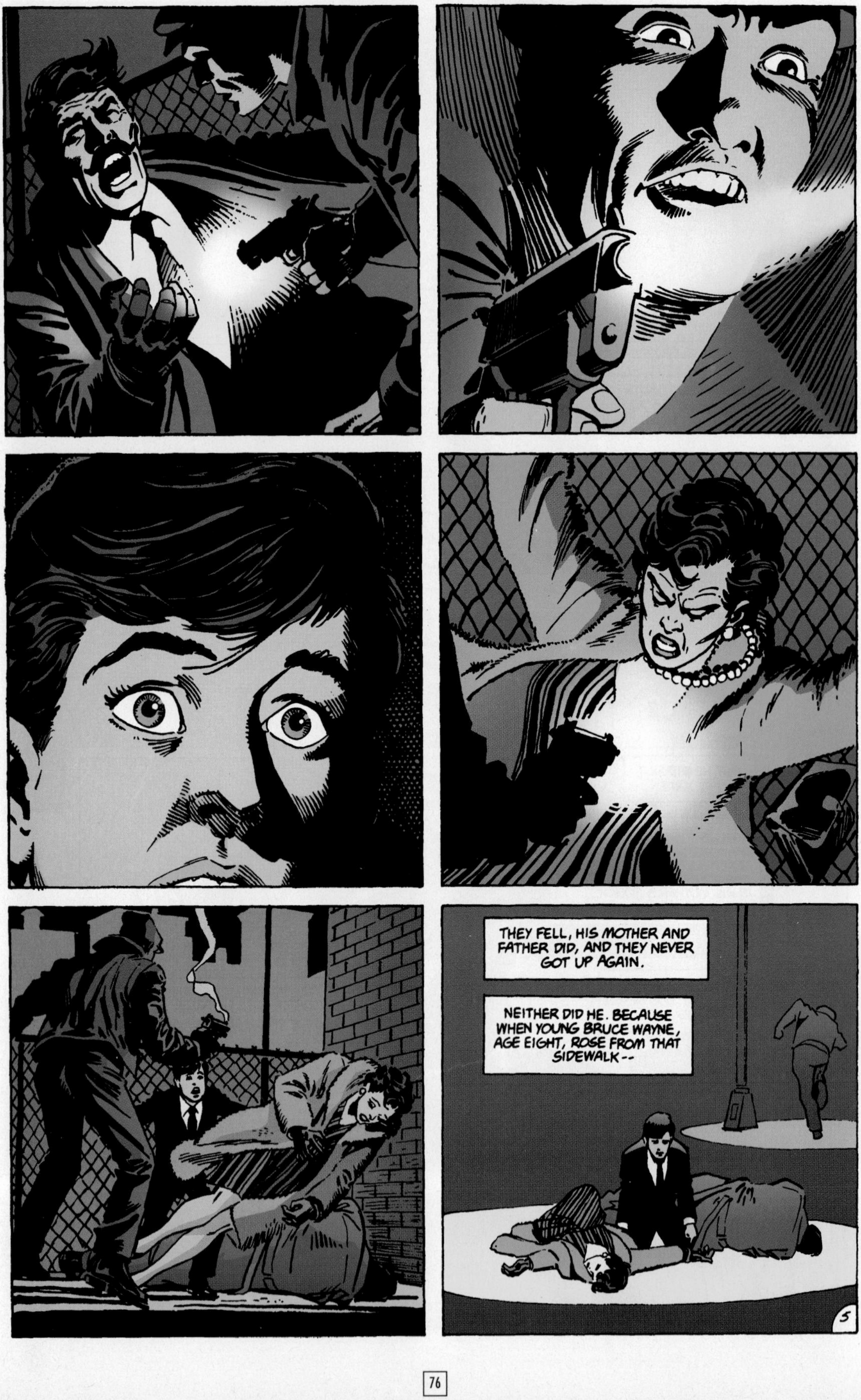
THEY FELL, HIS MOTHER AND FATHER DID, AND THEY NEVER GOT UP AGAIN.
NEITHER DID HE. BECAUSE WHEN YOUNG BRUCE WAYNE, AGE EIGHT, ROSE FROM THAT SIDEWALK--
5

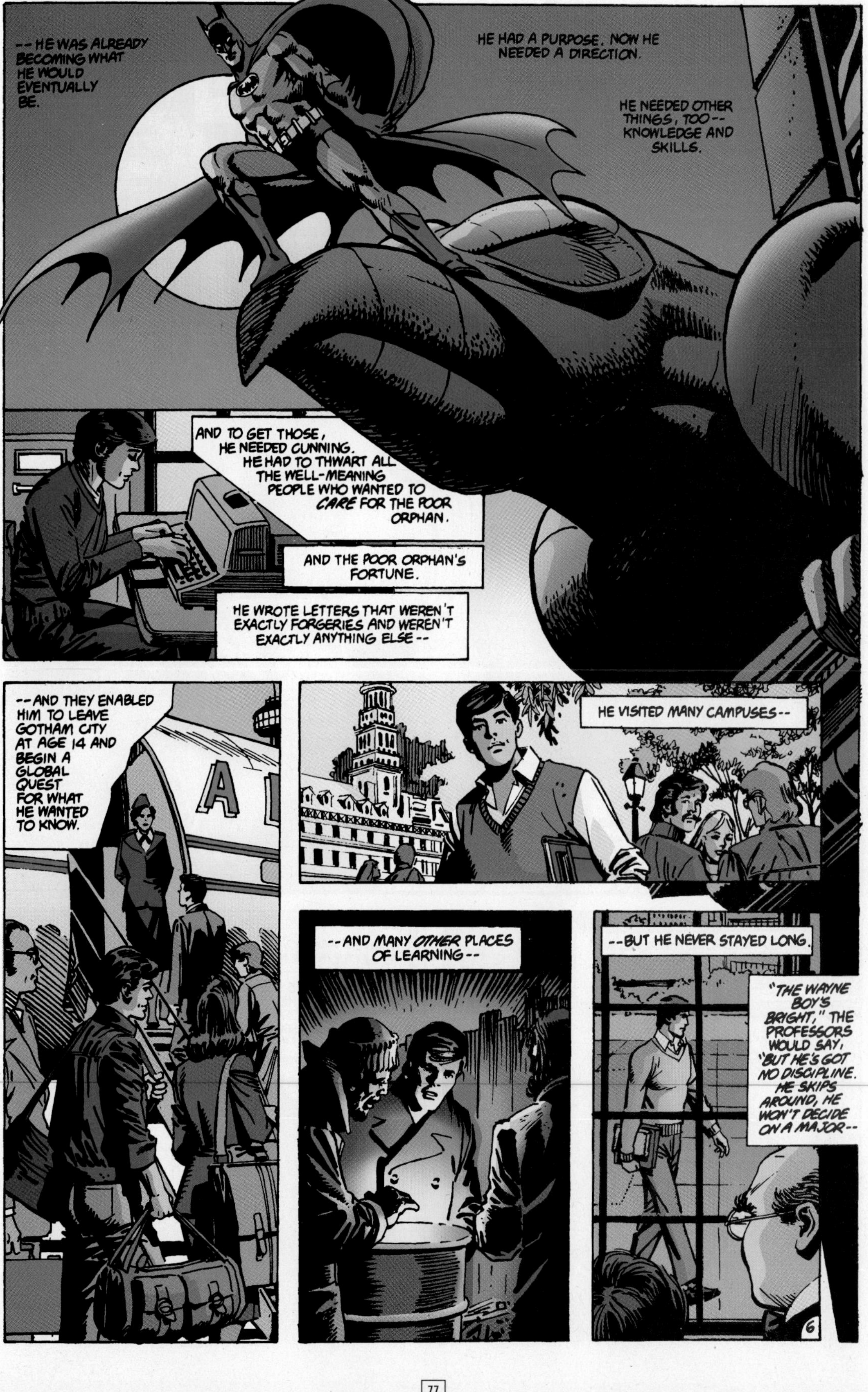
-- HE WAS ALREADY BECOMING WHAT HE WOULD EVENTUALLY BE.
HE HAD A PURPOSE. NOW HE NEEDED A DIRECTION.
HE NEEDED OTHER THINGS, TOO-- KNOWLEDGE AND SKILLS.
AND TO GET THOSE, HE NEEDED CUNNING. HE HAD TO THWART ALL THE WELL-MEANING PEOPLE WHO WANTED TO CARE FOR THE POOR ORPHAN.
AND THE POOR ORPHAN'S FORTUNE.
HE WROTE LETTERS THAT WEREN'T EXACTLY FORGERIES AND WEREN'T EXACTLY ANYTHING ELSE --
-- AND THEY ENABLED HIM TO LEAVE GOTHAM CITY AT AGE 14 AND BEGIN A GLOBAL QUEST FOR WHAT HE WANTED TO KNOW.
A
HE VISITED MANY CAMPUSES --
-- AND MANY OTHER PLACES OF LEARNING --
-- BUT HE NEVER STAYED LONG.
"THE WAYNE BOY'S BRIGHT," THE PROFESSORS WOULD SAY, "BUT HE'S GOT NO DISCIPLINE. HE SKIPS AROUND, HE WON'T DECIDE ON A MAJOR --
6

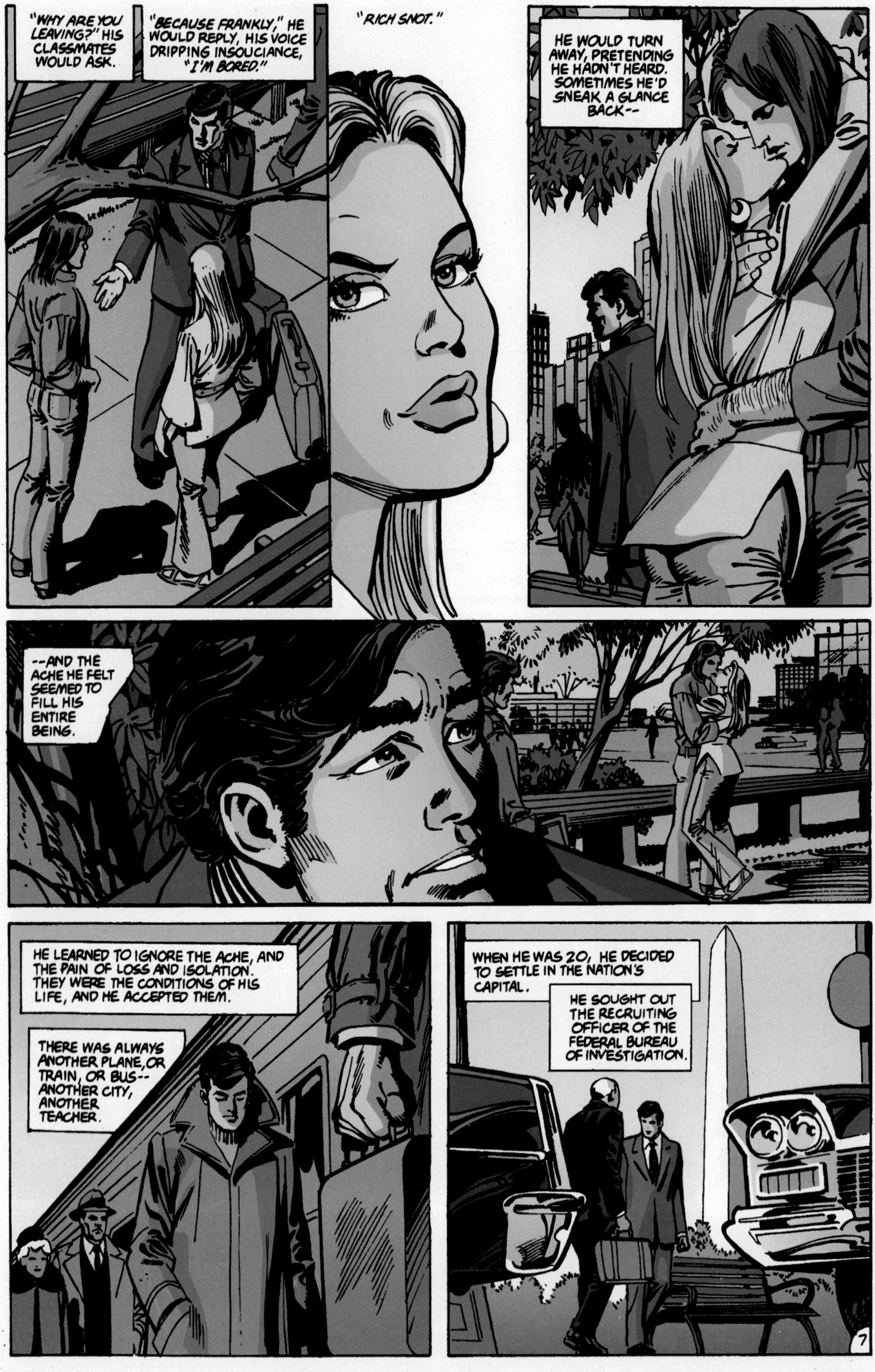
"WHY ARE YOU LEAVING?" HIS CLASSMATES WOULD ASK.
"BECAUSE FRANKLY," HE WOULD REPLY, HIS VOICE DRIPPING INSOUCIANCE, "I'M BORED."
"RICH SNOT."
HE WOULD TURN AWAY, PRETENDING HE HADN'T HEARD. SOMETIMES HE'D SNEAK A GLANCE BACK--
--AND THE ACHE HE FELT SEEMED TO FILL HIS ENTIRE BEING.
HE LEARNED TO IGNORE THE ACHE, AND THE PAIN OF LOSS AND ISOLATION. THEY WERE THE CONDITIONS OF HIS LIFE, AND HE ACCEPTED THEM.
THERE WAS ALWAYS ANOTHER PLANE, OR TRAIN, OR BUS-- ANOTHER CITY, ANOTHER TEACHER.
WHEN HE WAS 20, HE DECIDED TO SETTLE IN THE NATION'S CAPITAL.
HE SOUGHT OUT THE RECRUITING OFFICER OF THE FEDERAL BUREAU OF INVESTIGATION.
7

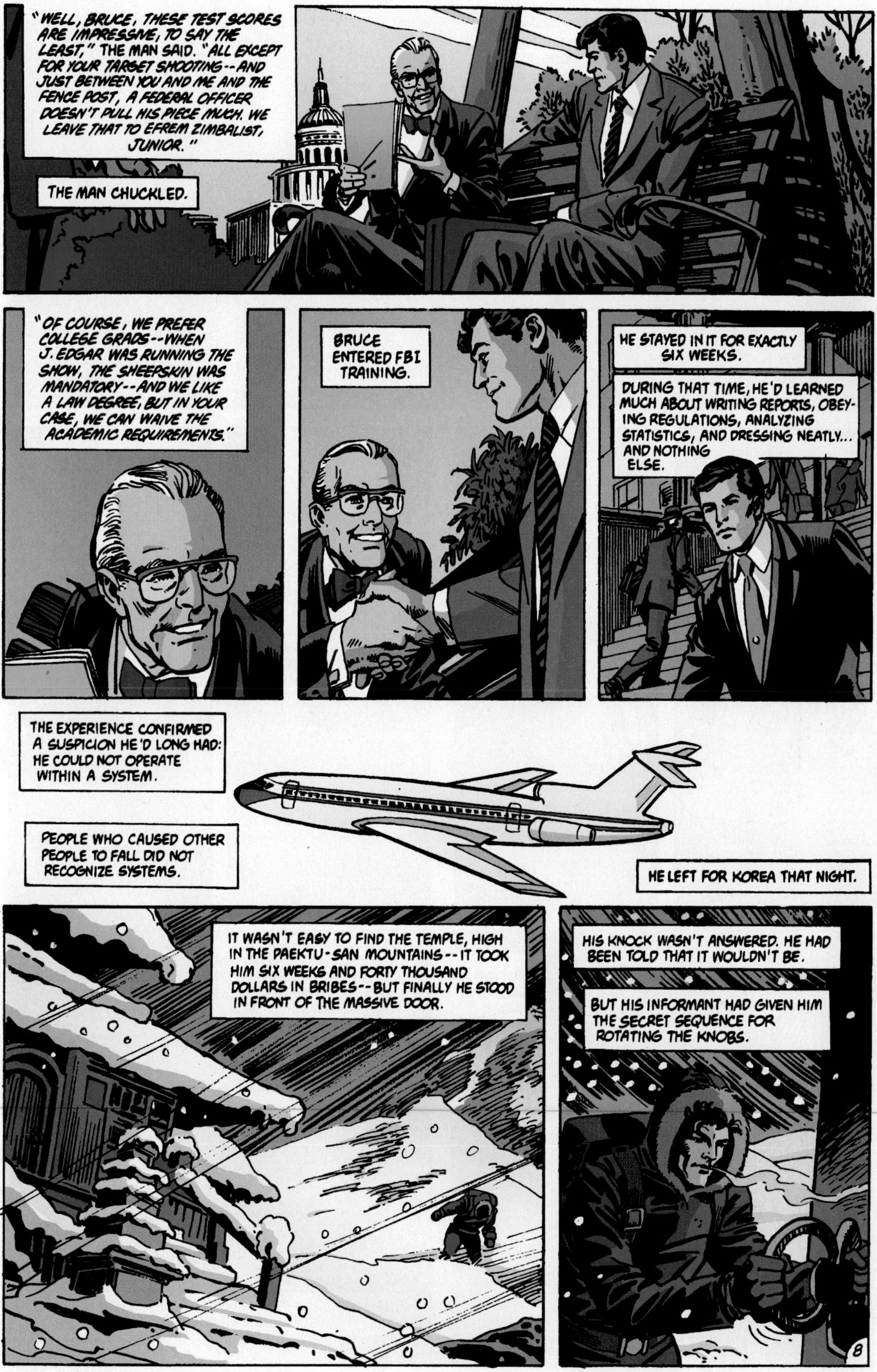
"WELL, BRUCE, THESE TEST SCORES ARE IMPRESSIVE, TO SAY THE LEAST," THE MAN SAID. "ALL EXCEPT FOR YOUR TARGET SHOOTING--AND JUST BETWEEN YOU AND ME AND THE FENCE POST, A FEDERAL OFFICER DOESN'T PULL HIS PIECE MUCH. WE LEAVE THAT TO EFREM ZIMBALIST, JUNIOR."
THE MAN CHUCKLED.
"OF COURSE, WE PREFER COLLEGE GRADS--WHEN J. EDGAR WAS RUNNING THE SHOW, THE SHEEPSKIN WAS MANDATORY--AND WE LIKE A LAW DEGREE, BUT IN YOUR CASE, WE CAN WAIVE THE ACADEMIC REQUIREMENTS."
BRUCE ENTERED FBI TRAINING.
HE STAYED IN IT FOR EXACTLY SIX WEEKS.
DURING THAT TIME, HE'D LEARNED MUCH ABOUT WRITING REPORTS, OBEYING REGULATIONS, ANALYZING STATISTICS, AND DRESSING NEATLY... AND NOTHING ELSE.
THE EXPERIENCE CONFIRMED A SUSPICION HE'D LONG HAD: HE COULD NOT OPERATE WITHIN A SYSTEM.
PEOPLE WHO CAUSED OTHER PEOPLE TO FALL DID NOT RECOGNIZE SYSTEMS.
HE LEFT FOR KOREA THAT NIGHT.
IT WASN'T EASY TO FIND THE TEMPLE, HIGH IN THE PAEKTU-SAN MOUNTAINS--IT TOOK HIM SIX WEEKS AND FORTY THOUSAND DOLLARS IN BRIBES--BUT FINALLY HE STOOD IN FRONT OF THE MASSIVE DOOR.
HIS KNOCK WASN'T ANSWERED. HE HAD BEEN TOLD THAT IT WOULDN'T BE.
BUT HIS INFORMANT HAD GIVEN HIM THE SECRET SEQUENCE FOR ROTATING THE KNOBS.
8

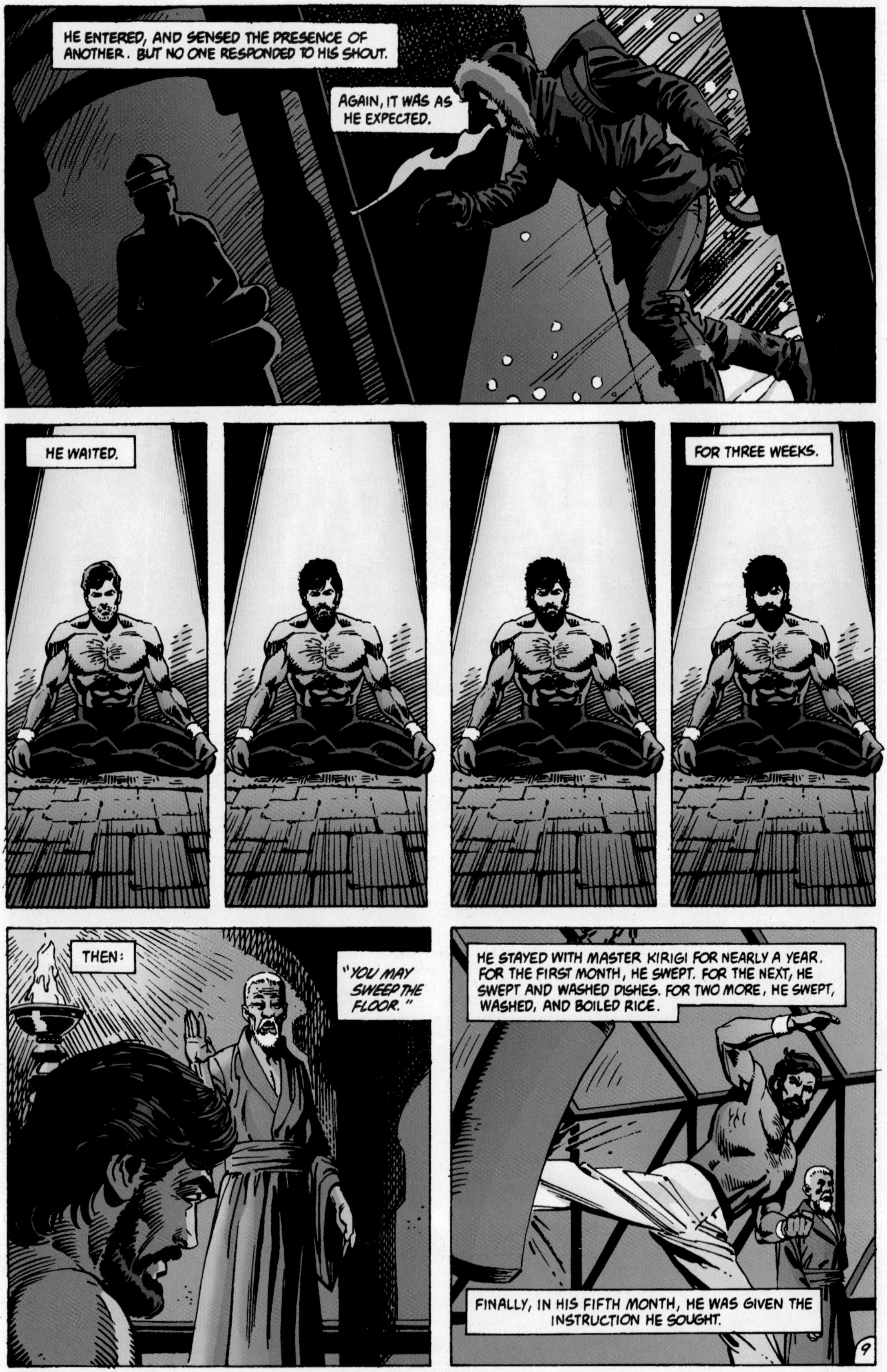

HE ENTERED, AND SENSED THE PRESENCE OF ANOTHER. BUT NO ONE RESPONDED TO HIS SHOUT.
AGAIN, IT WAS AS HE EXPECTED.
HE WAITED.
FOR THREE WEEKS.
THEN:
"YOU MAY SWEEP THE FLOOR."
HE STAYED WITH MASTER KIRIGI FOR NEARLY A YEAR. FOR THE FIRST MONTH, HE SWEPT. FOR THE NEXT, HE SWEPT AND WASHED DISHES. FOR TWO MORE, HE SWEPT, WASHED, AND BOILED RICE.
FINALLY, IN HIS FIFTH MONTH, HE WAS GIVEN THE INSTRUCTION HE SOUGHT.
9

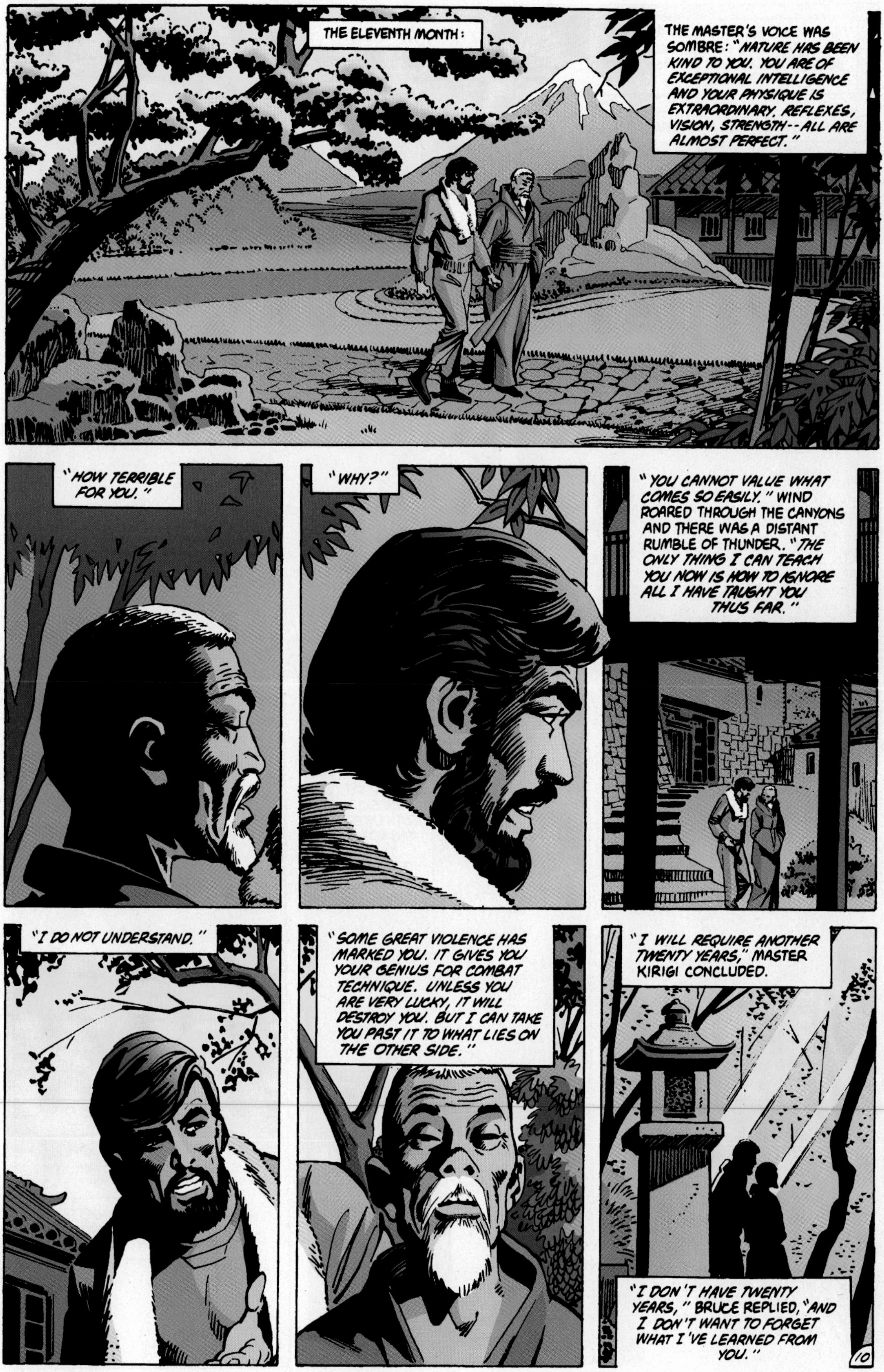
THE ELEVENTH MONTH:
THE MASTER'S VOICE WAS SOMBRE: "NATURE HAS BEEN KIND TO YOU. YOU ARE OF EXCEPTIONAL INTELLIGENCE AND YOUR PHYSIQUE IS EXTRAORDINARY. REFLEXES, VISION, STRENGTH--ALL ARE ALMOST PERFECT."
"HOW TERRIBLE FOR YOU."
"WHY?"
"YOU CANNOT VALUE WHAT COMES SO EASILY." WIND ROARED THROUGH THE CANYONS AND THERE WAS A DISTANT RUMBLE OF THUNDER. "THE ONLY THING I CAN TEACH YOU NOW IS HOW TO IGNORE ALL I HAVE TAUGHT YOU THUS FAR."
"I DO NOT UNDERSTAND."
"SOME GREAT VIOLENCE HAS MARKED YOU. IT GIVES YOU YOUR GENIUS FOR COMBAT TECHNIQUE. UNLESS YOU ARE VERY LUCKY, IT WILL DESTROY YOU. BUT I CAN TAKE YOU PAST IT TO WHAT LIES ON THE OTHER SIDE."
"I WILL REQUIRE ANOTHER TWENTY YEARS," MASTER KIRIGI CONCLUDED.
"I DON'T HAVE TWENTY YEARS," BRUCE REPLIED, "AND I DON'T WANT TO FORGET WHAT I'VE LEARNED FROM YOU."
10

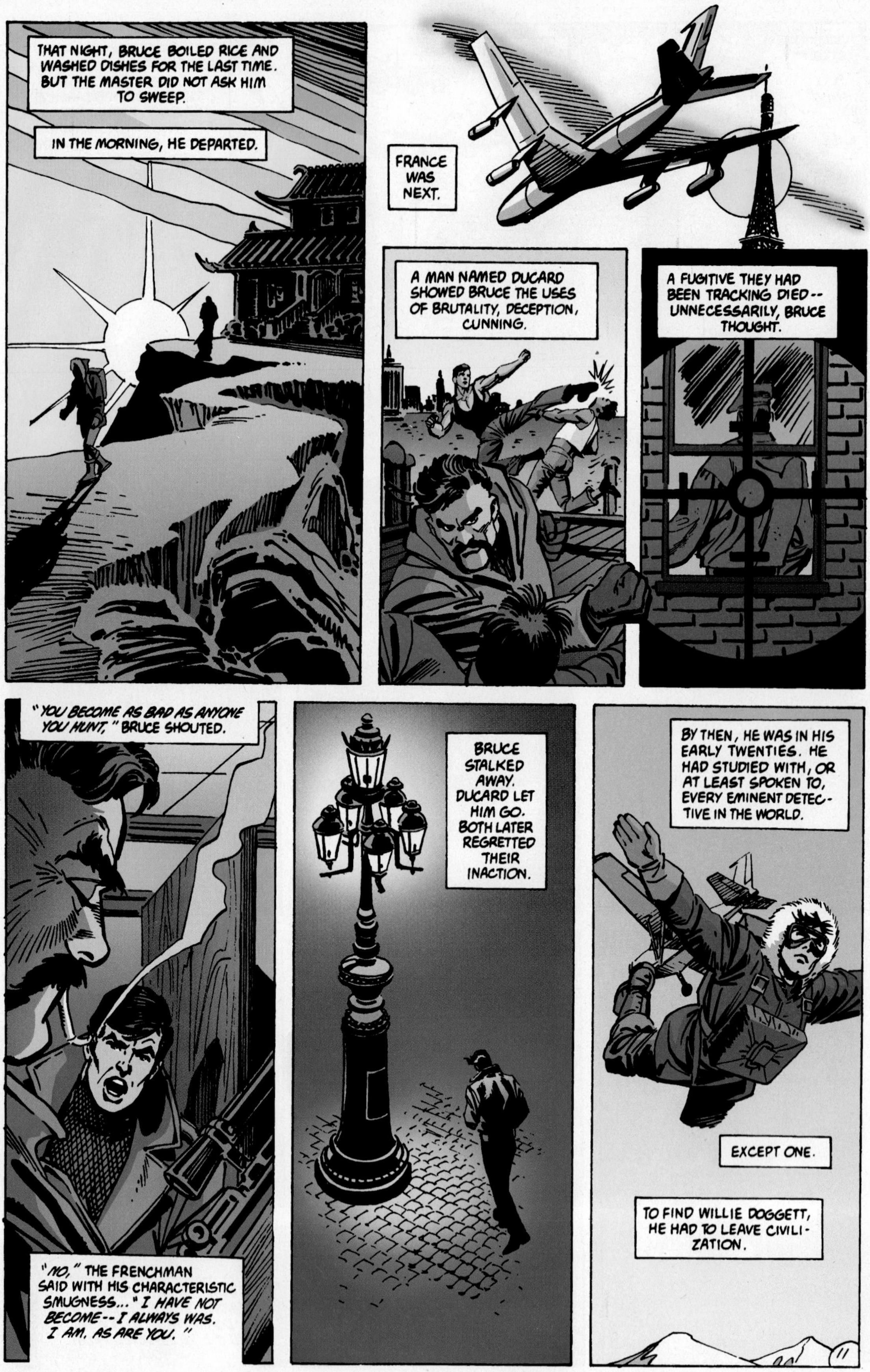
THAT NIGHT, BRUCE BOILED RICE AND WASHED DISHES FOR THE LAST TIME. BUT THE MASTER DID NOT ASK HIM TO SWEEP.
IN THE MORNING, HE DEPARTED.
FRANCE WAS NEXT.
A MAN NAMED DUCARD SHOWED BRUCE THE USES OF BRUTALITY, DECEPTION, CUNNING.
A FUGITIVE THEY HAD BEEN TRACKING DIED-- UNNECESSARILY, BRUCE THOUGHT.
"YOU BECOME AS BAD AS ANYONE YOU HUNT," BRUCE SHOUTED.
"NO," THE FRENCHMAN SAID WITH HIS CHARACTERISTIC SMUGNESS... "I HAVE NOT BECOME--I ALWAYS WAS. I AM. AS ARE YOU."
BRUCE STALKED AWAY. DUCARD LET HIM GO. BOTH LATER REGRETTED THEIR INACTION.
BY THEN, HE WAS IN HIS EARLY TWENTIES. HE HAD STUDIED WITH, OR AT LEAST SPOKEN TO, EVERY EMINENT DETECTIVE IN THE WORLD.
EXCEPT ONE.
TO FIND WILLIE DOGGETT, HE HAD TO LEAVE CIVILIZATION.

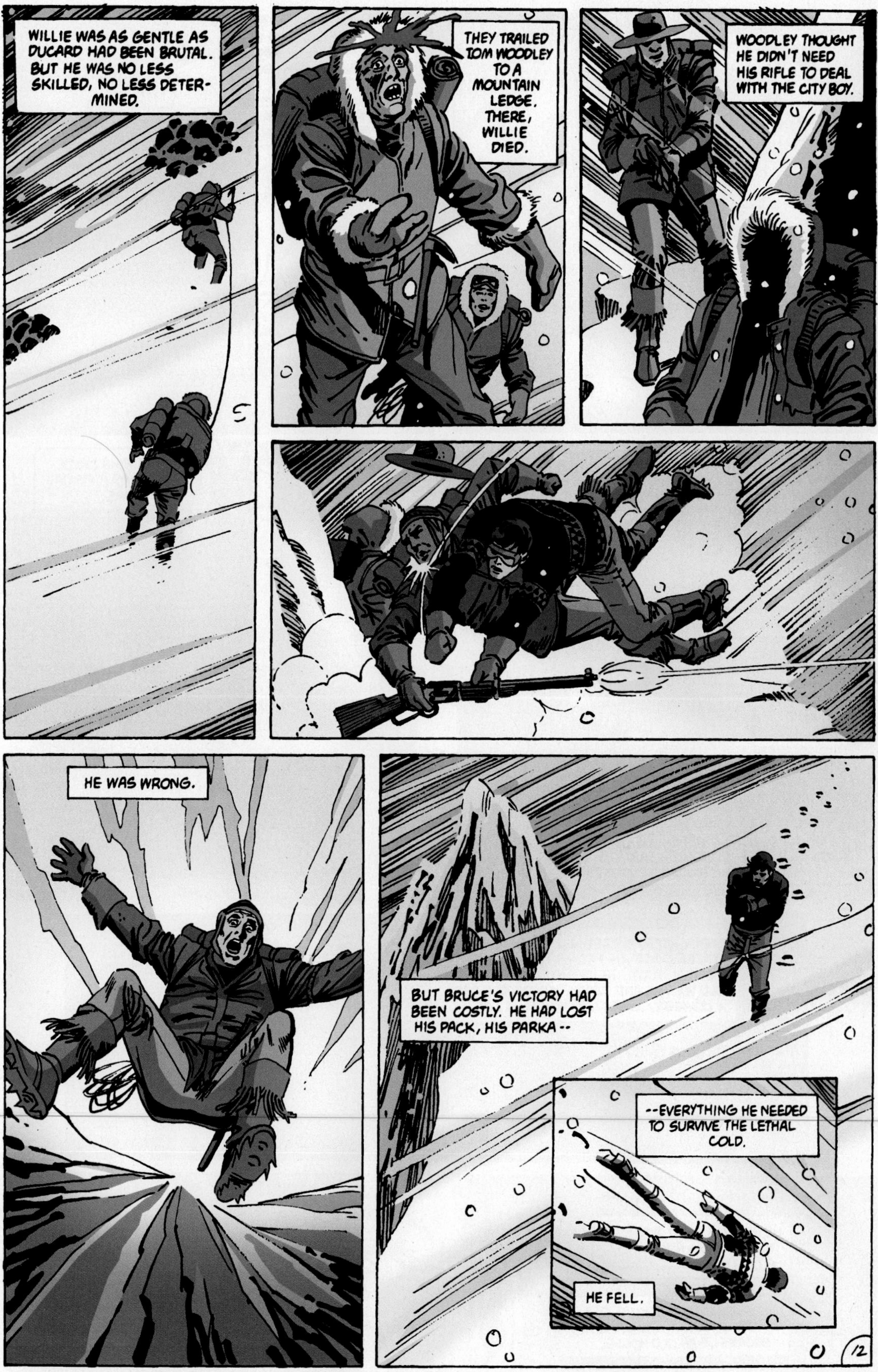
WILLIE WAS AS GENTLE AS DUCARD HAD BEEN BRUTAL. BUT HE WAS NO LESS SKILLED, NO LESS DETERMINED.
THEY TRAILED TOM WOODLEY TO A MOUNTAIN LEDGE. THERE, WILLIE DIED.
WOODLEY THOUGHT HE DIDN'T NEED HIS RIFLE TO DEAL WITH THE CITY BOY.
HE WAS WRONG.
BUT BRUCE'S VICTORY HAD BEEN COSTLY. HE HAD LOST HIS PACK, HIS PARKA --
--EVERYTHING HE NEEDED TO SURVIVE THE LETHAL COLD.
HE FELL.
12

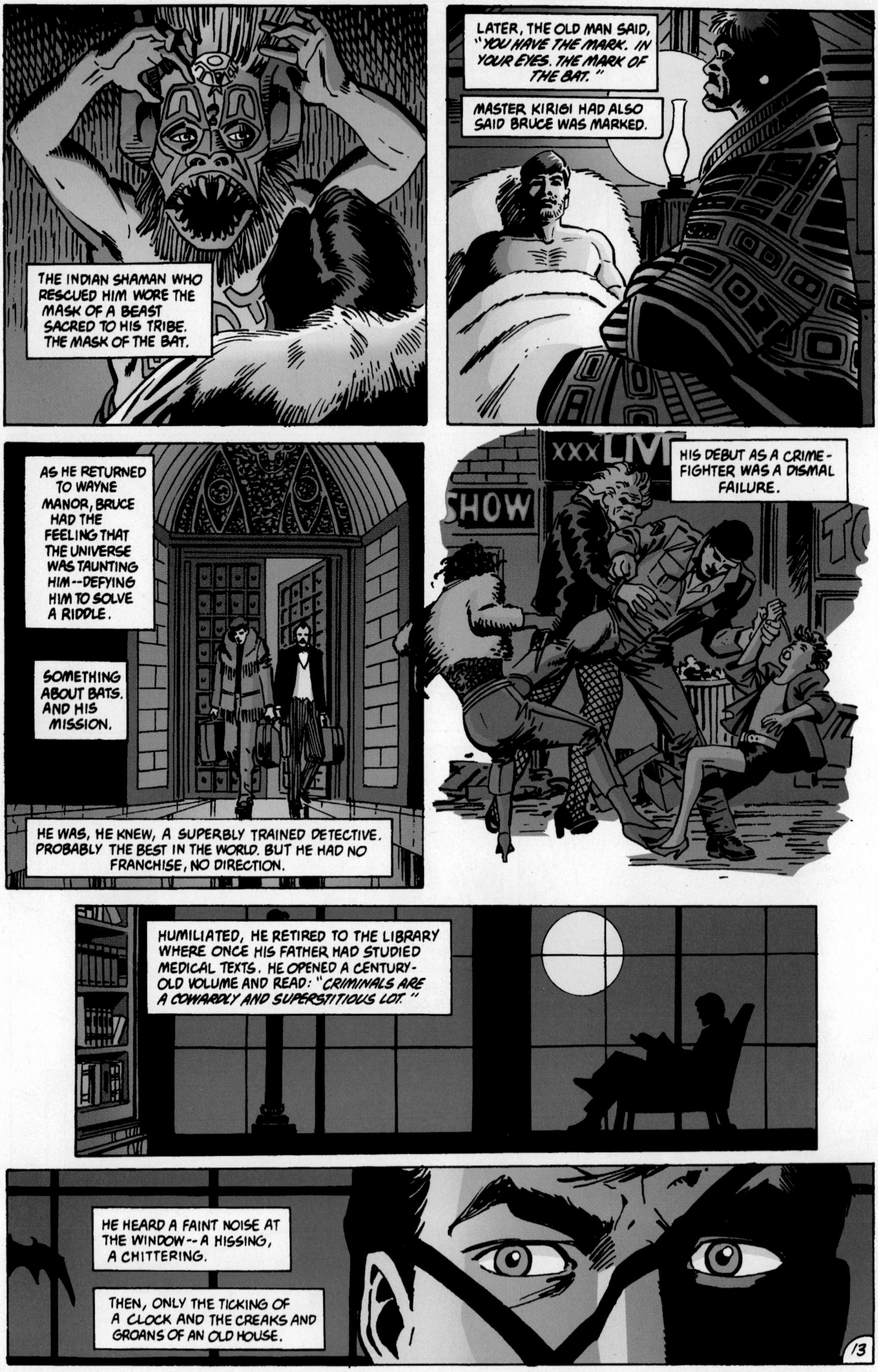
THE INDIAN SHAMAN WHO RESCUED HIM WORE THE MASK OF A BEAST SACRED TO HIS TRIBE. THE MASK OF THE BAT.
LATER, THE OLD MAN SAID, "YOU HAVE THE MARK. IN YOUR EYES. THE MARK OF THE BAT."
MASTER KIRIGI HAD ALSO SAID BRUCE WAS MARKED.
AS HE RETURNED TO WAYNE MANOR, BRUCE HAD THE FEELING THAT THE UNIVERSE WAS TAUNTING HIM--DEFYING HIM TO SOLVE A RIDDLE.
SOMETHING ABOUT BATS. AND HIS MISSION.
HE WAS, HE KNEW, A SUPERBLY TRAINED DETECTIVE. PROBABLY THE BEST IN THE WORLD. BUT HE HAD NO FRANCHISE, NO DIRECTION.
XXX LIVE
SHOW
HIS DEBUT AS A CRIME-FIGHTER WAS A DISMAL FAILURE.
HUMILIATED, HE RETIRED TO THE LIBRARY WHERE ONCE HIS FATHER HAD STUDIED MEDICAL TEXTS. HE OPENED A CENTURY-OLD VOLUME AND READ: "CRIMINALS ARE A COWARDLY AND SUPERSTITIOUS LOT."
HE HEARD A FAINT NOISE AT THE WINDOW--A HISSING, A CHITTERING.
THEN, ONLY THE TICKING OF A CLOCK AND THE CREAKS AND GROANS OF AN OLD HOUSE.
13

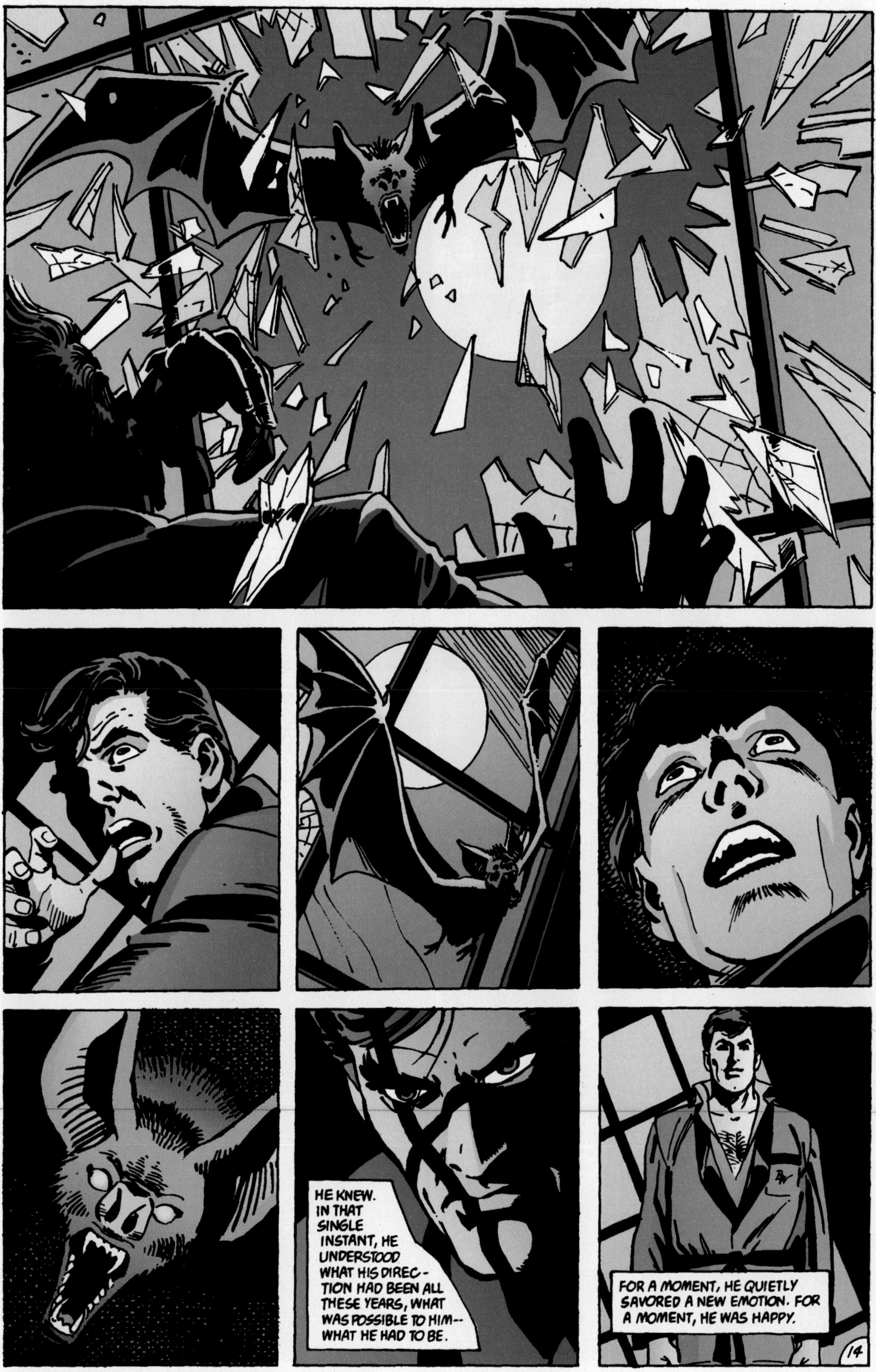
HE KNEW. IN THAT SINGLE INSTANT, HE UNDERSTOOD WHAT HIS DIREC-TION HAD BEEN ALL THESE YEARS, WHAT WAS POSSIBLE TO HIM-- WHAT HE HAD TO BE.
FOR A MOMENT, HE QUIETLY SAVORED A NEW EMOTION. FOR A MOMENT, HE WAS HAPPY.
14

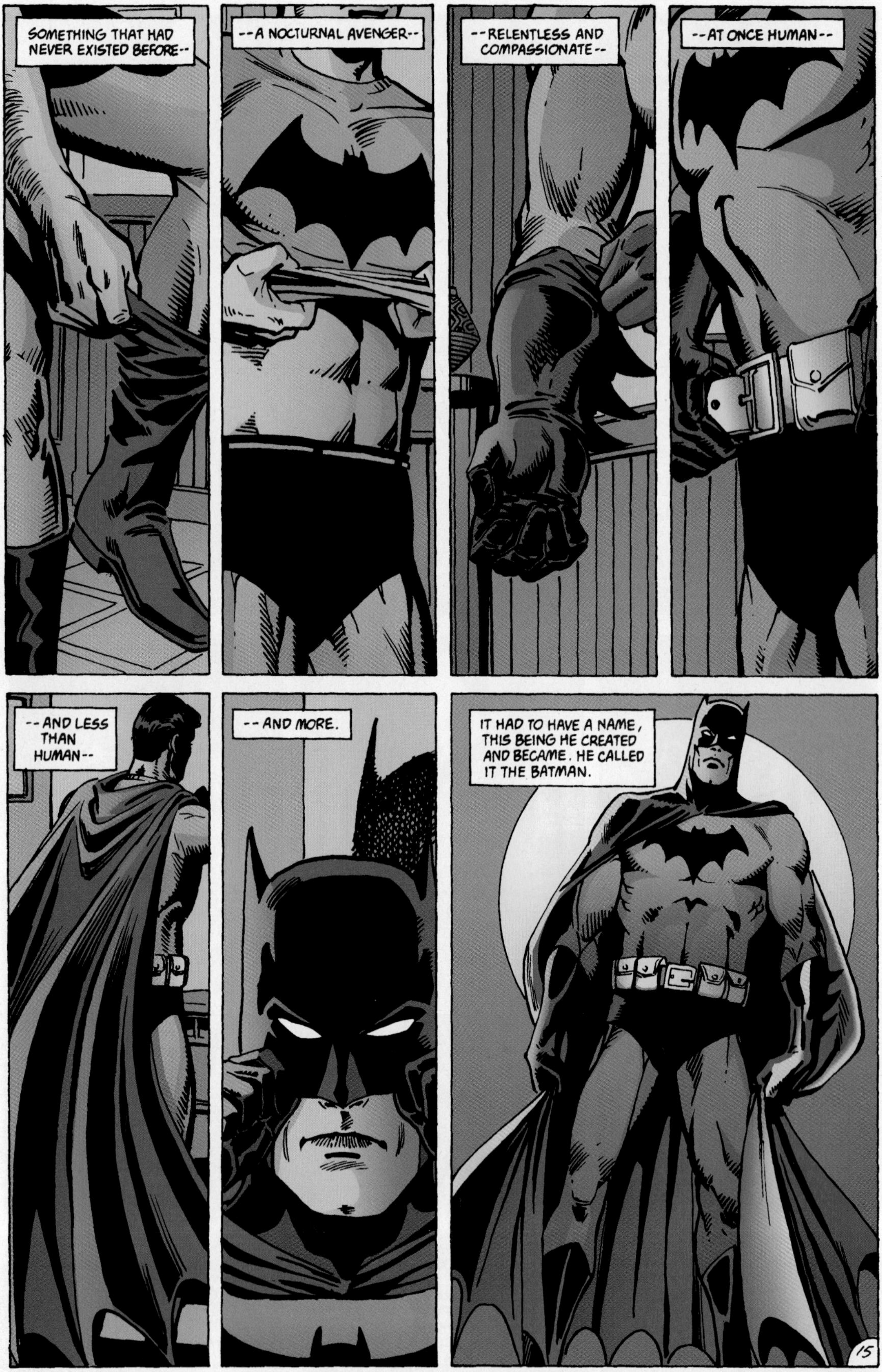
SOMETHING THAT HAD NEVER EXISTED BEFORE--
--A NOCTURNAL AVENGER--
--RELENTLESS AND COMPASSIONATE--
--AT ONCE HUMAN--
--AND LESS THAN HUMAN--
--AND MORE.
IT HAD TO HAVE A NAME, THIS BEING HE CREATED AND BECAME. HE CALLED IT THE BATMAN.
15

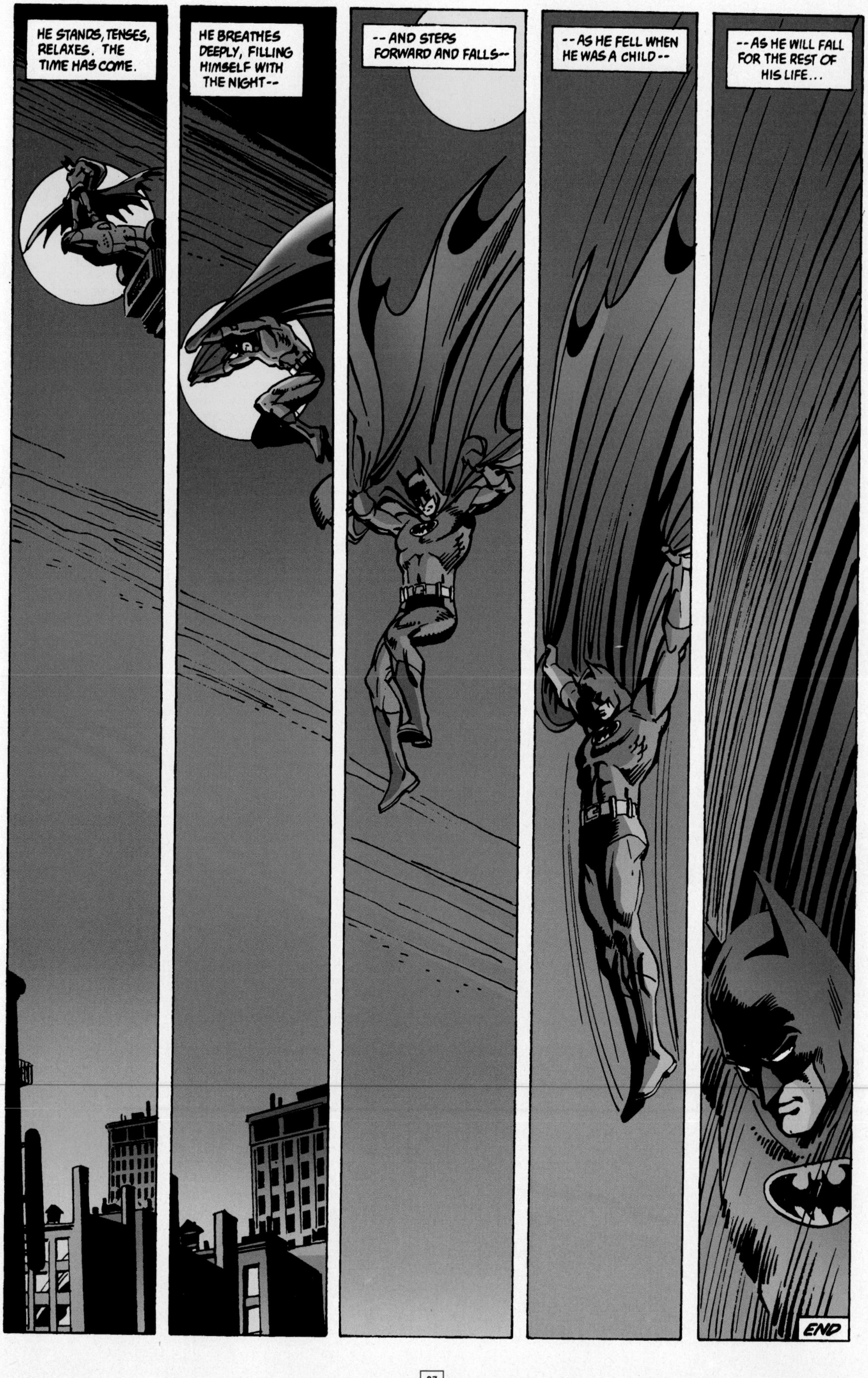
HE STANDS, TENSES, RELAXES. THE TIME HAS COME.
HE BREATHES DEEPLY, FILLING HIMSELF WITH THE NIGHT--
--AND STEPS FORWARD AND FALLS--
--AS HE FELL WHEN HE WAS A CHILD--
--AS HE WILL FALL FOR THE REST OF HIS LIFE...
END

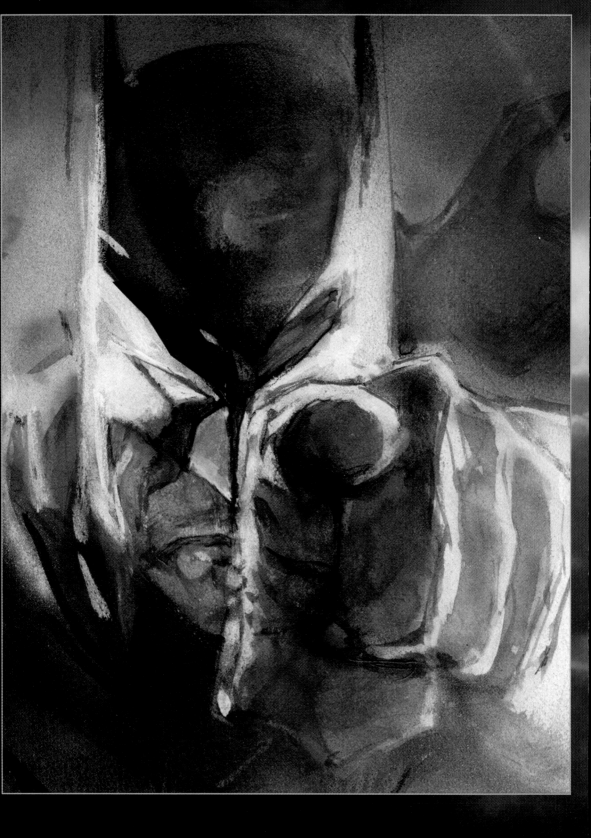

pinup by **BILL SIENKIEWICZ**

Originally seen in the *VS. System* trading card game from Upper Deck Entertainment.

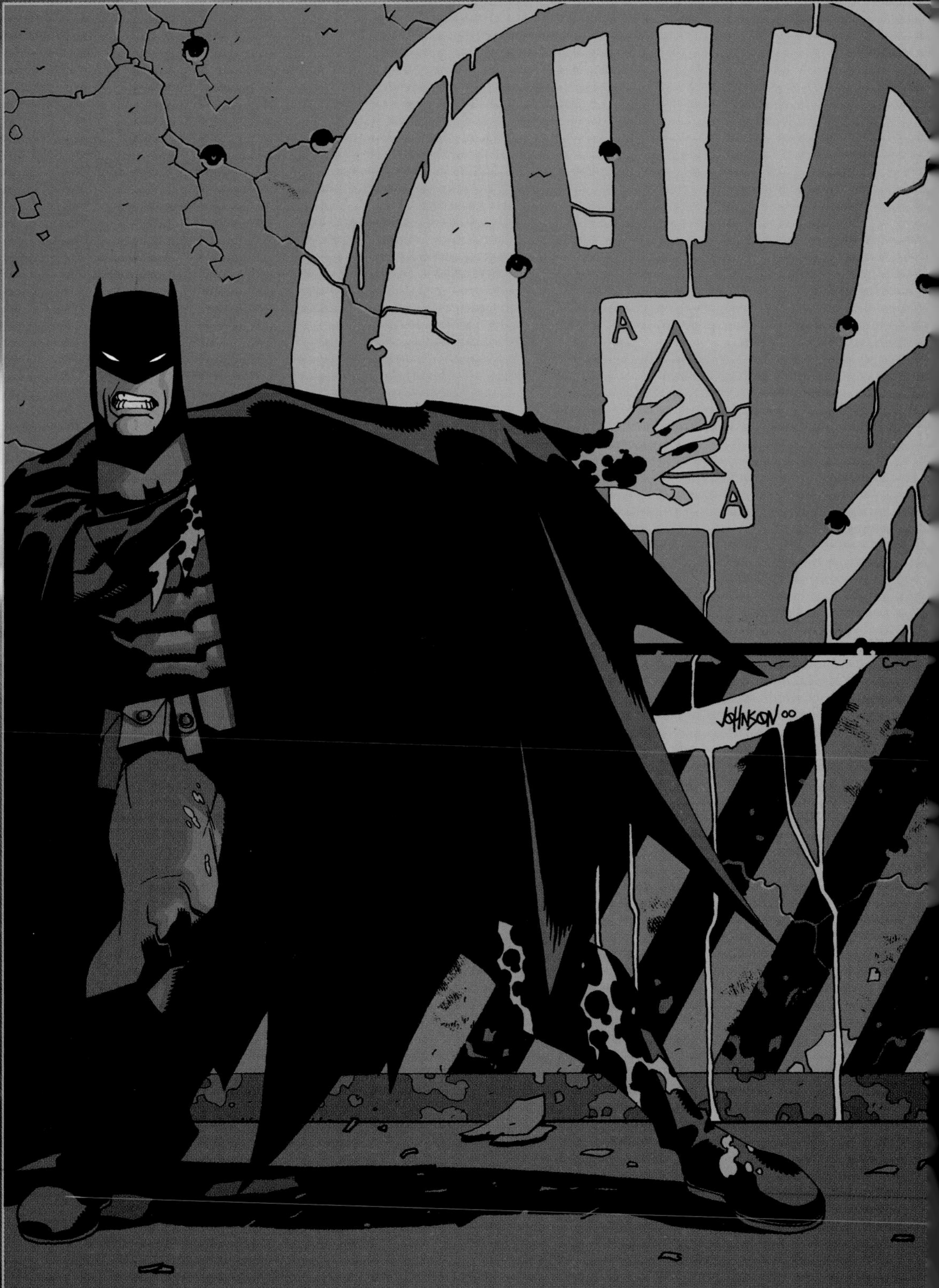
JOHNSON 00

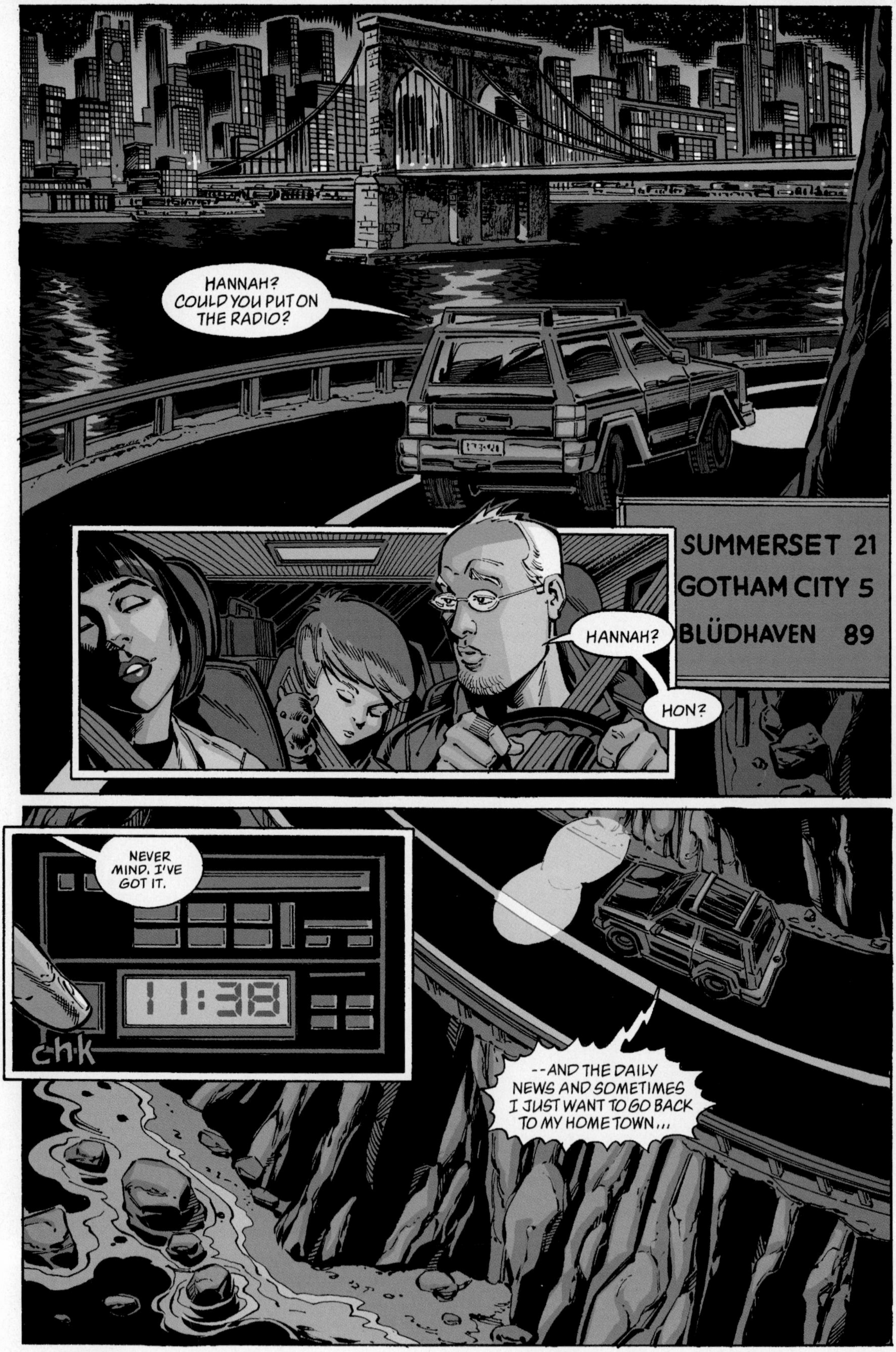
HANNAH? COULD YOU PUT ON THE RADIO?
SUMMERSET 21
GOTHAM CITY 5
BLÜDHAVEN 89
HANNAH?
HON?
NEVER MIND. I'VE GOT IT.
11:38
chk
--AND THE DAILY NEWS AND SOMETIMES I JUST WANT TO GO BACK TO MY HOME TOWN...

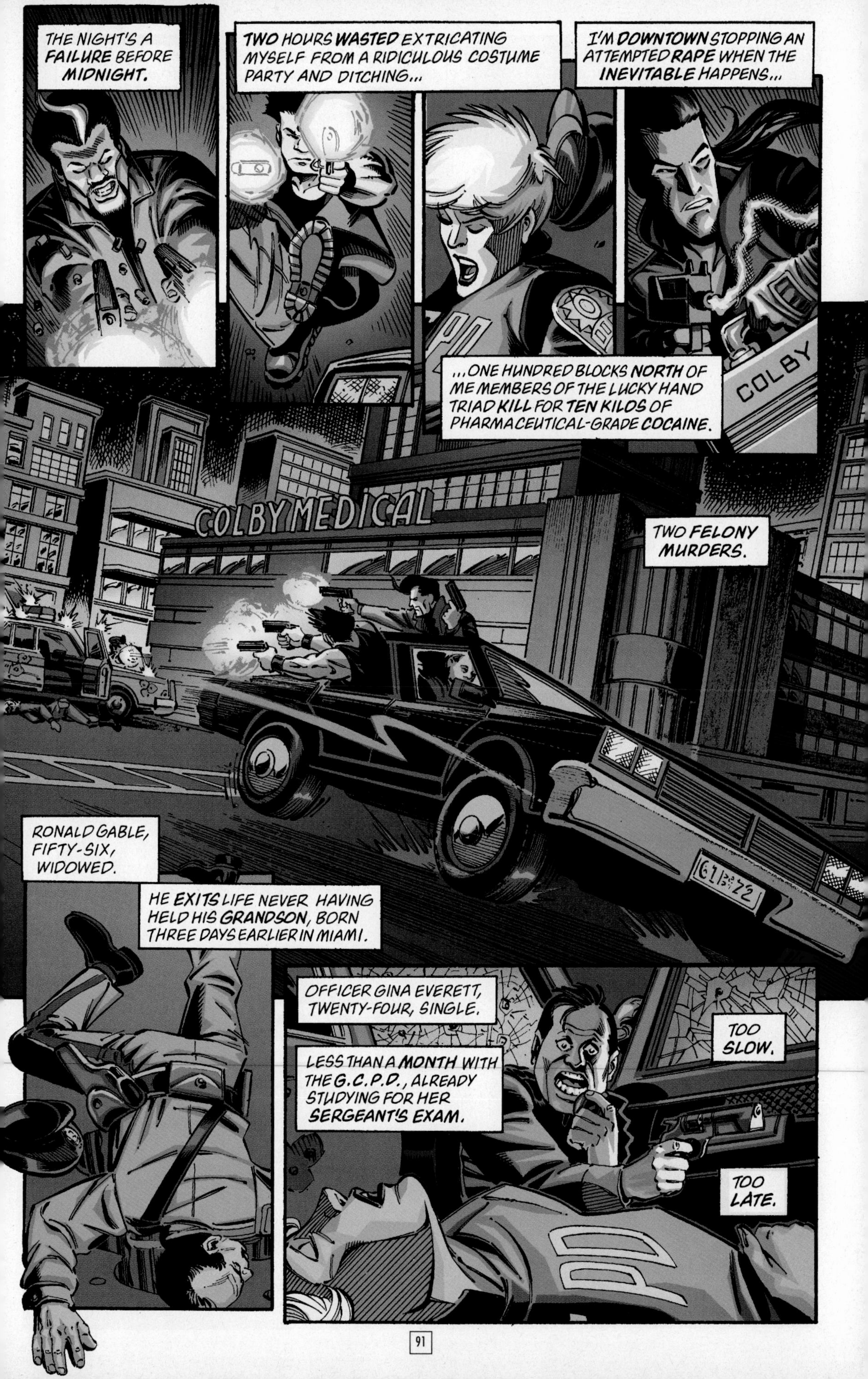
THE NIGHT'S A FAILURE BEFORE MIDNIGHT.
TWO HOURS WASTED EXTRICATING MYSELF FROM A RIDICULOUS COSTUME PARTY AND DITCHING...
I'M DOWNTOWN STOPPING AN ATTEMPTED RAPE WHEN THE INEVITABLE HAPPENS...
COLBY
...ONE HUNDRED BLOCKS NORTH OF ME MEMBERS OF THE LUCKY HAND TRIAD KILL FOR TEN KILOS OF PHARMACEUTICAL-GRADE COCAINE.
COLBY MEDICAL
TWO FELONY MURDERS.
RONALD GABLE, FIFTY-SIX, WIDOWED.
HE EXITS LIFE NEVER HAVING HELD HIS GRANDSON, BORN THREE DAYS EARLIER IN MIAMI.
OFFICER GINA EVERETT, TWENTY-FOUR, SINGLE.
LESS THAN A MONTH WITH THE G.C.P.D., ALREADY STUDYING FOR HER SERGEANT'S EXAM.
TOO SLOW.
TOO LATE.

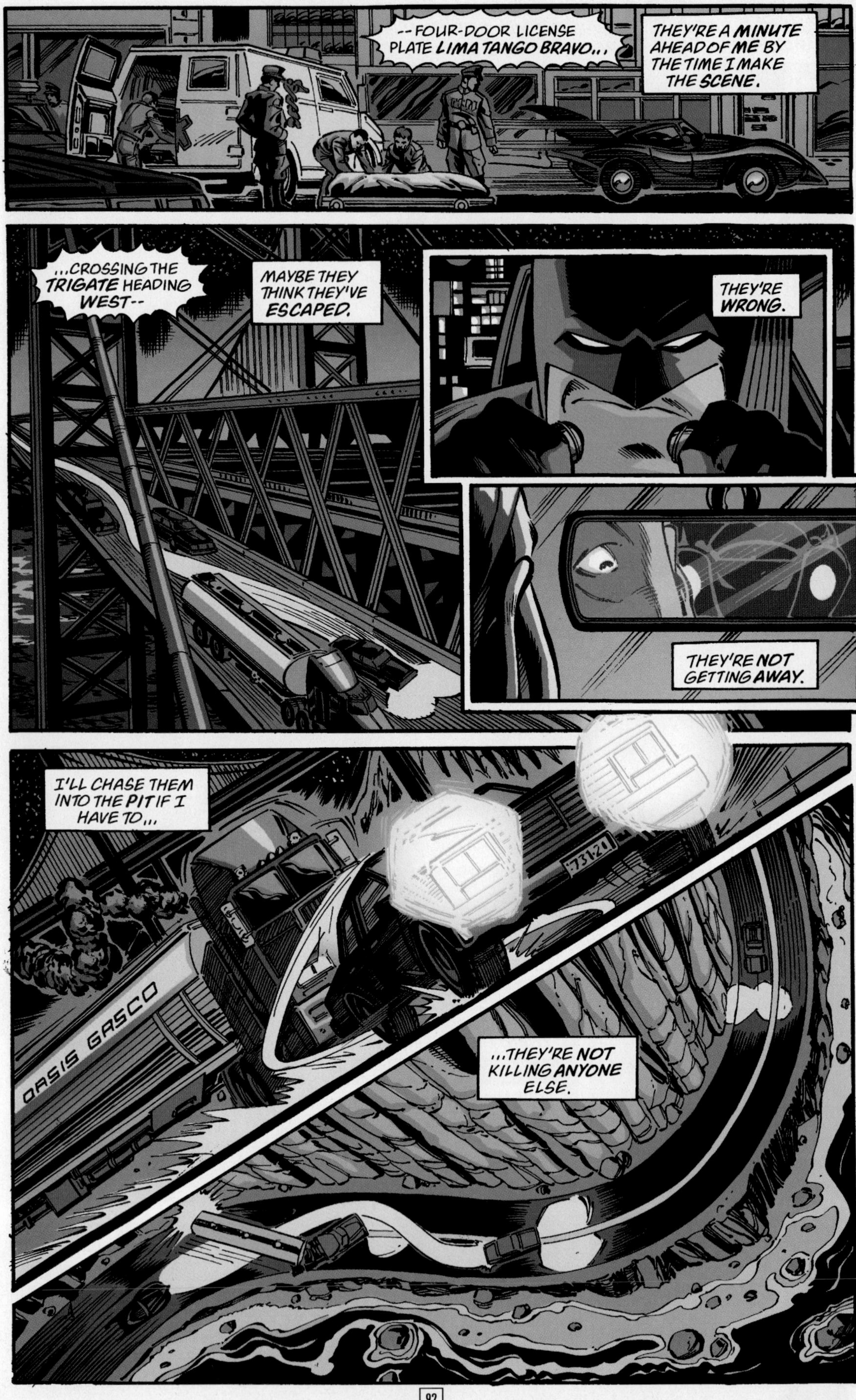
--FOUR-DOOR LICENSE PLATE LIMA TANGO BRAVO...
THEY'RE A MINUTE AHEAD OF ME BY THE TIME I MAKE THE SCENE.
...CROSSING THE TRIGATE HEADING WEST--
MAYBE THEY THINK THEY'VE ESCAPED.
THEY'RE WRONG.
THEY'RE NOT GETTING AWAY.
I'LL CHASE THEM INTO THE PIT IF I HAVE TO...
...THEY'RE NOT KILLING ANYONE ELSE.
OASIS GASCO
731-21

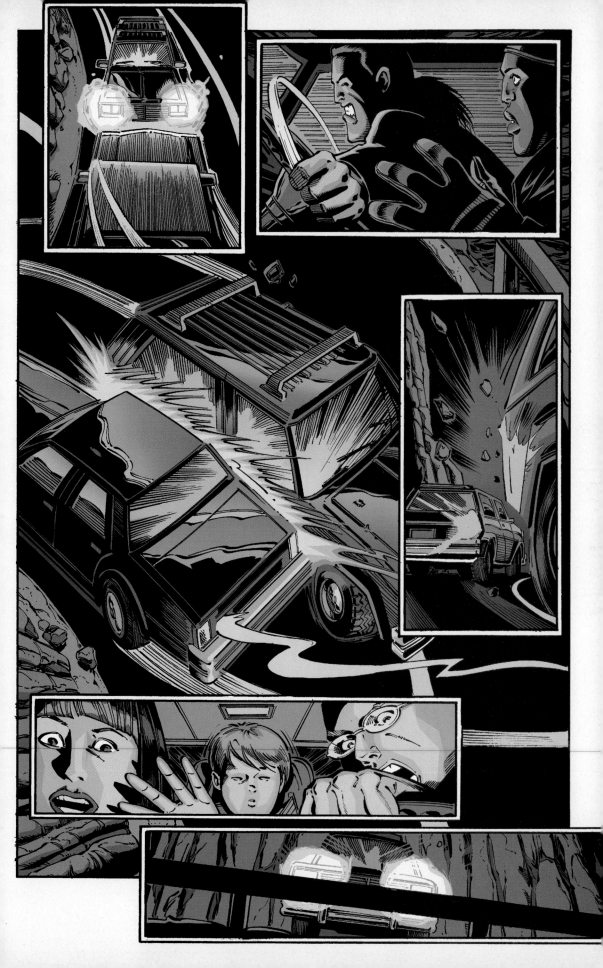

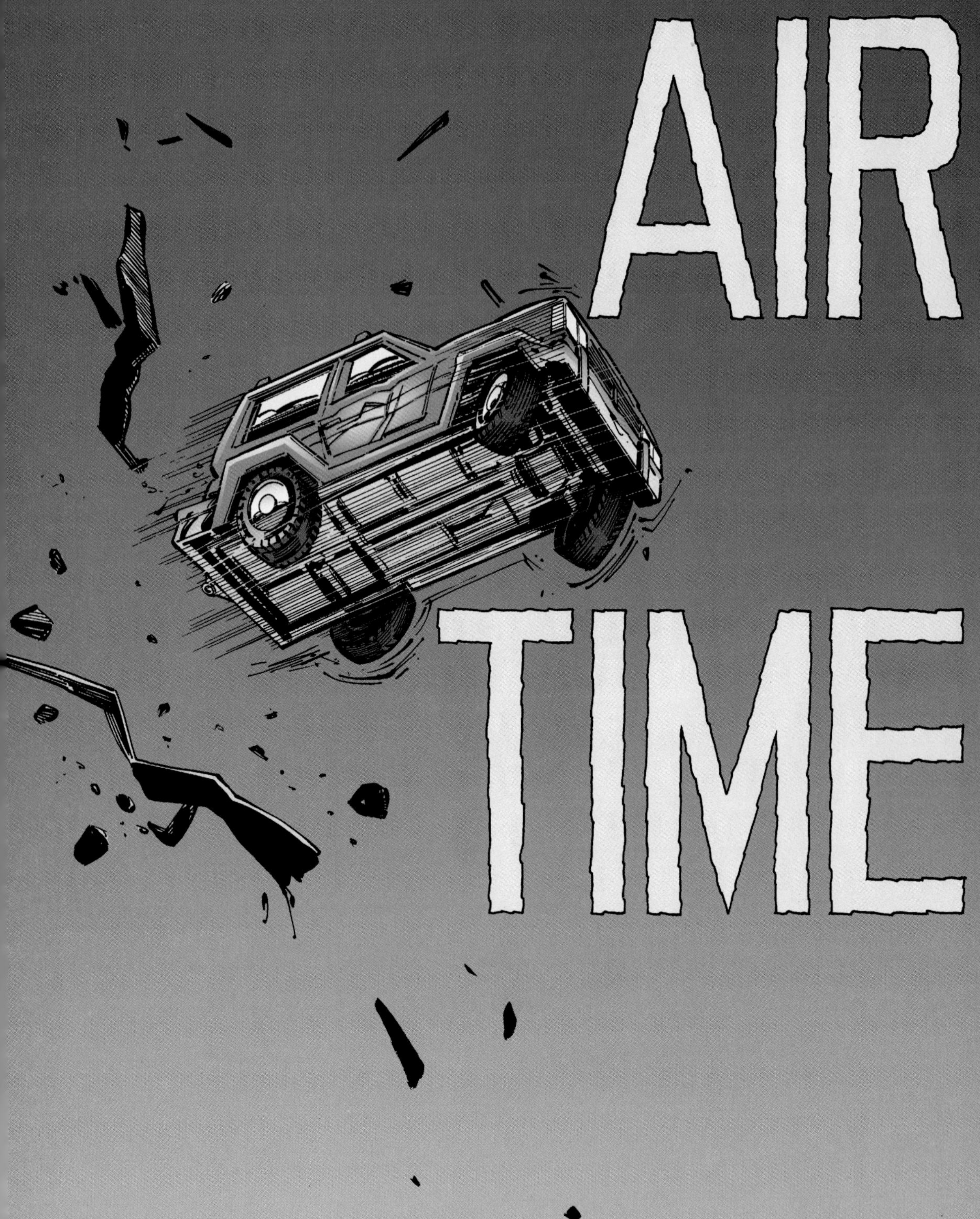
AIR
TIME

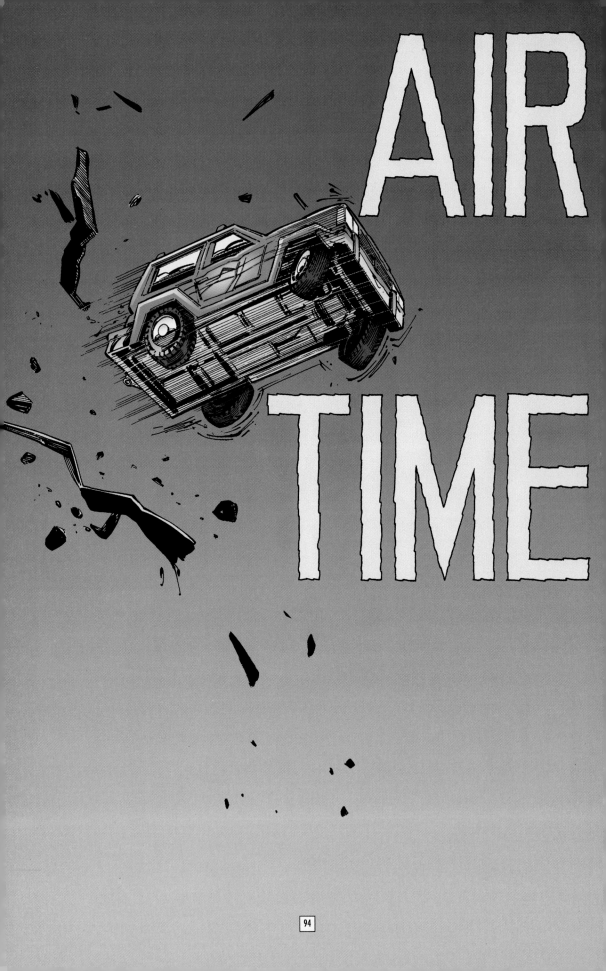

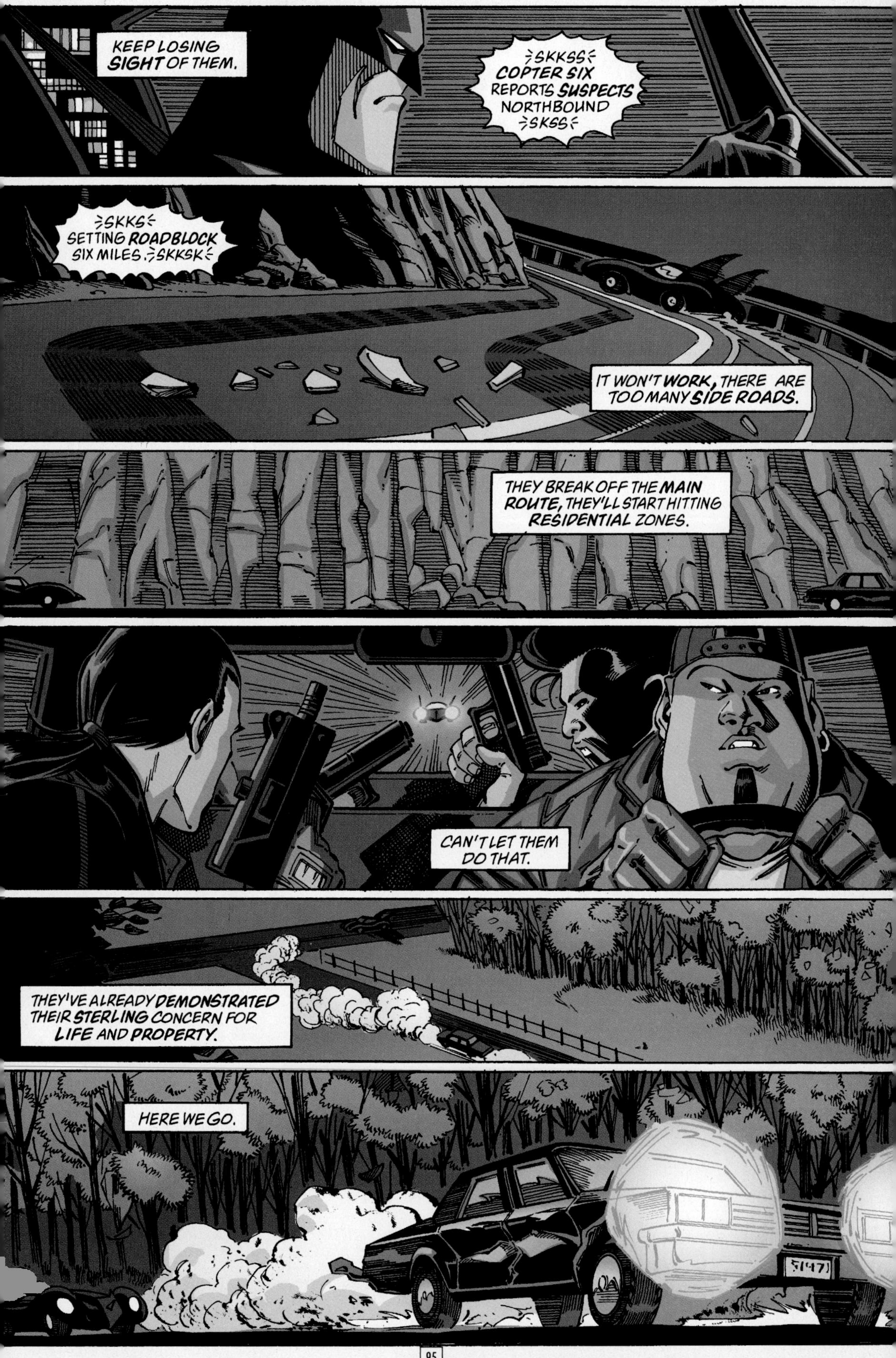
KEEP LOSING SIGHT OF THEM.
⚡SKKSS⚡ COPTER SIX REPORTS SUSPECTS NORTHBOUND ⚡SKSS⚡
⚡SKKS⚡ SETTING ROADBLOCK SIX MILES. ⚡SKKSK⚡
IT WON'T WORK, THERE ARE TOO MANY SIDE ROADS.
THEY BREAK OFF THE MAIN ROUTE, THEY'LL START HITTING RESIDENTIAL ZONES.
CAN'T LET THEM DO THAT.
THEY'VE ALREADY DEMONSTRATED THEIR STERLING CONCERN FOR LIFE AND PROPERTY.
HERE WE GO.

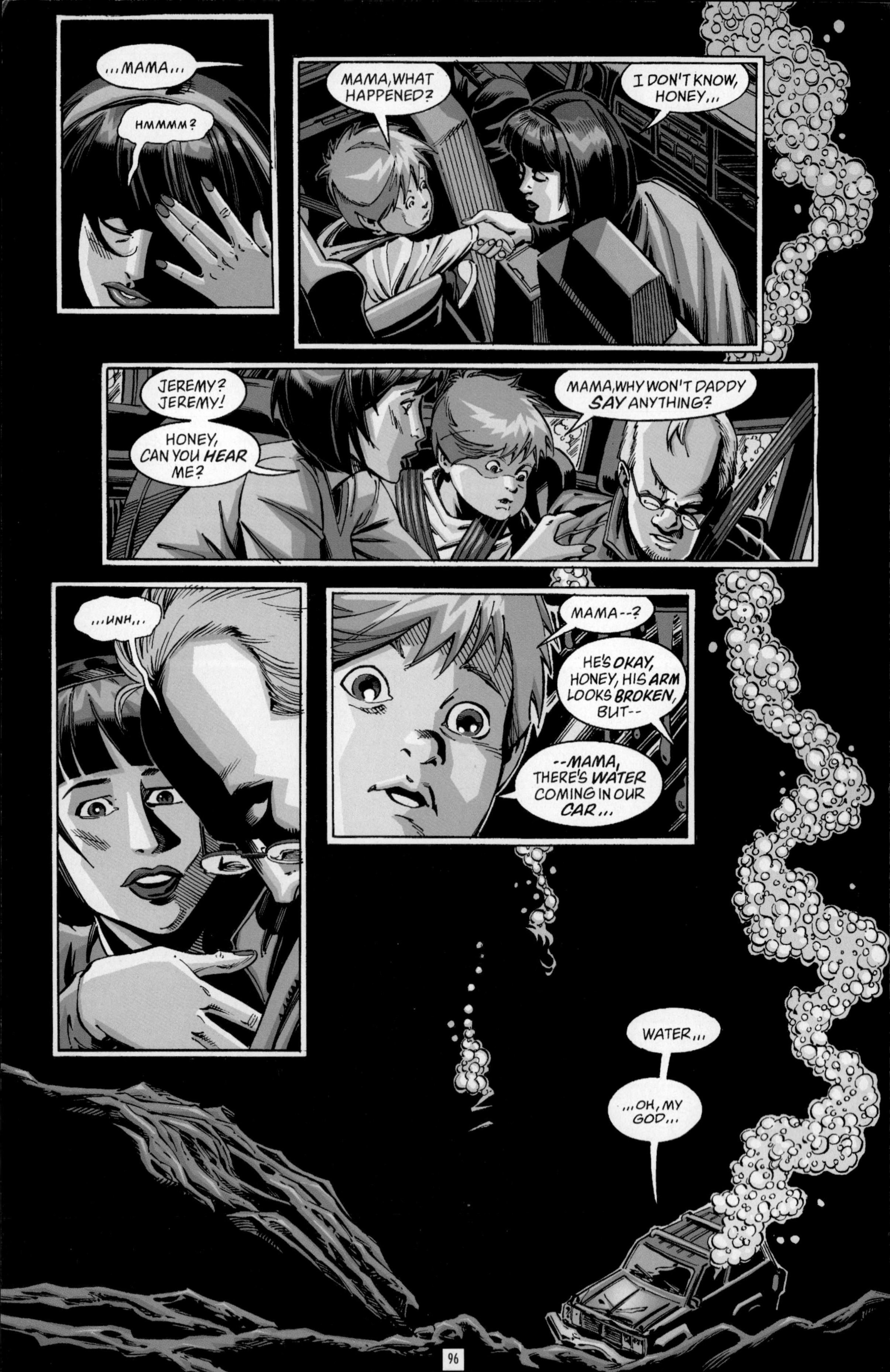
...MAMA...
HMMMM?
MAMA, WHAT HAPPENED?
I DON'T KNOW, HONEY...
JEREMY? JEREMY!
HONEY, CAN YOU HEAR ME?
MAMA, WHY WON'T DADDY SAY ANYTHING?
...UNH...
MAMA--?
HE'S OKAY, HONEY, HIS ARM LOOKS BROKEN, BUT--
--MAMA, THERE'S WATER COMING IN OUR CAR...
WATER...
...OH, MY GOD...

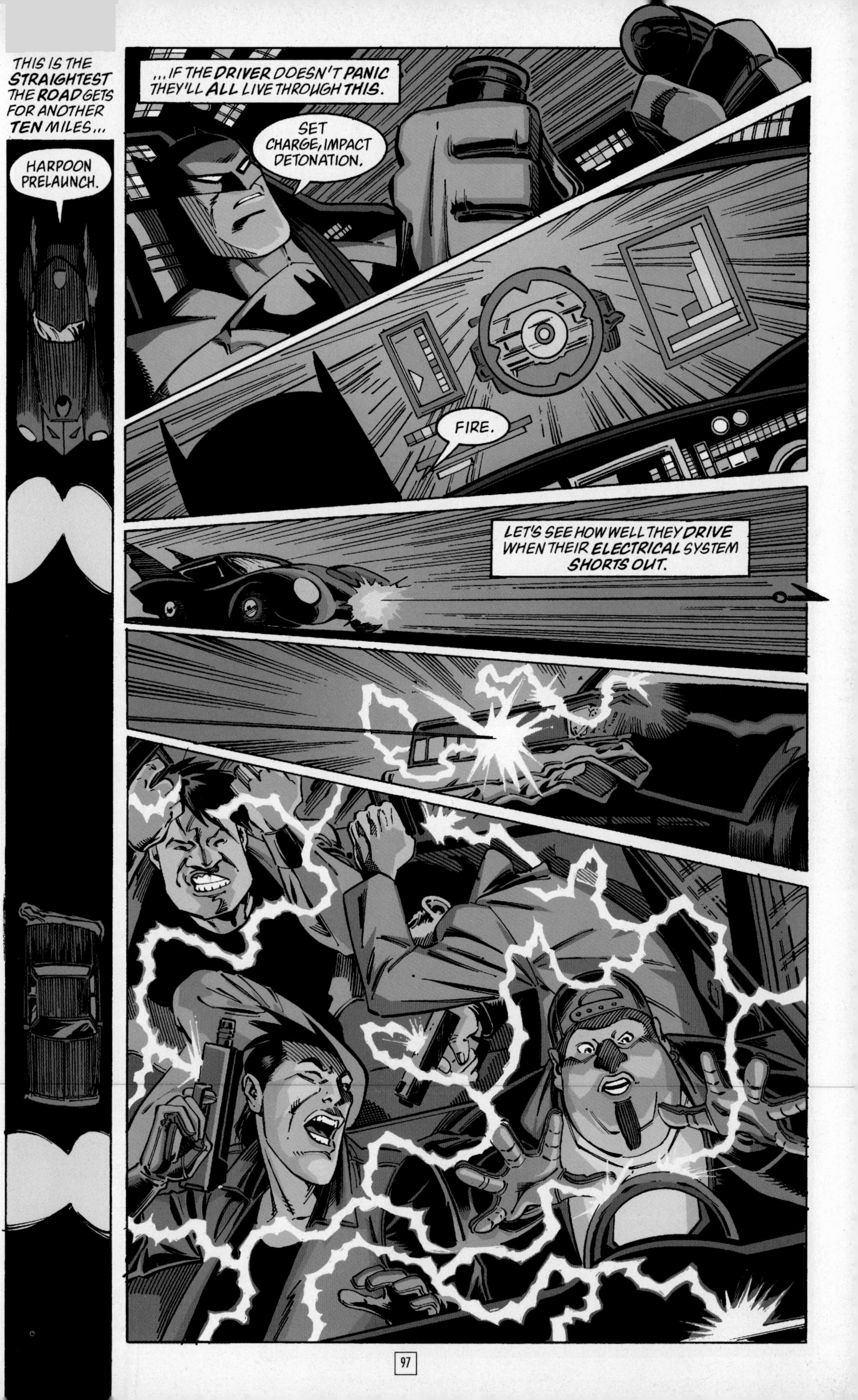
THIS IS THE STRAIGHTEST THE ROAD GETS FOR ANOTHER TEN MILES...
...IF THE DRIVER DOESN'T PANIC THEY'LL ALL LIVE THROUGH THIS.
HARPOON PRELAUNCH.
SET CHARGE, IMPACT DETONATION.
FIRE.
LET'S SEE HOW WELL THEY DRIVE WHEN THEIR ELECTRICAL SYSTEM SHORTS OUT.

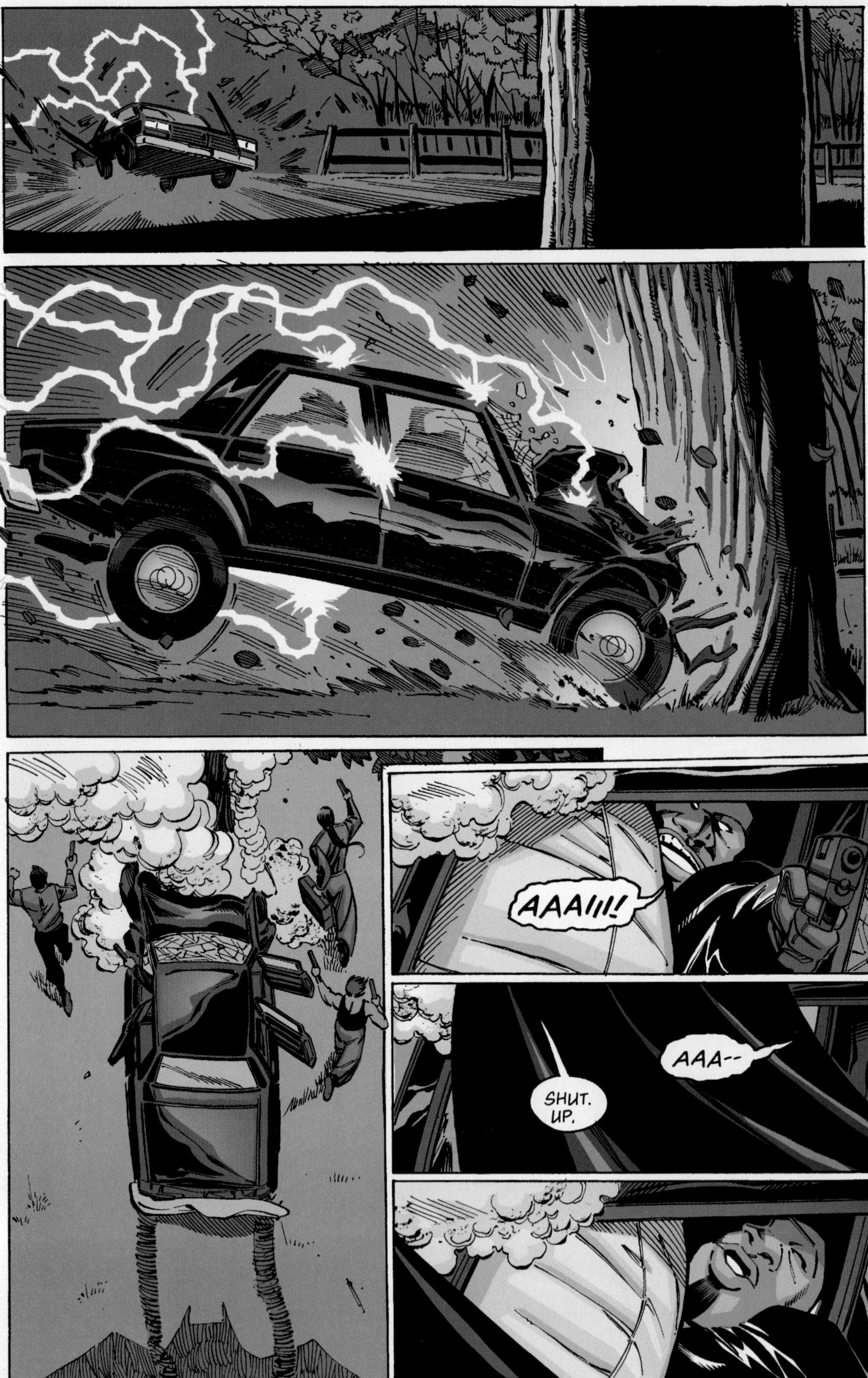
AAAIII!
AAA--
SHUT. UP.

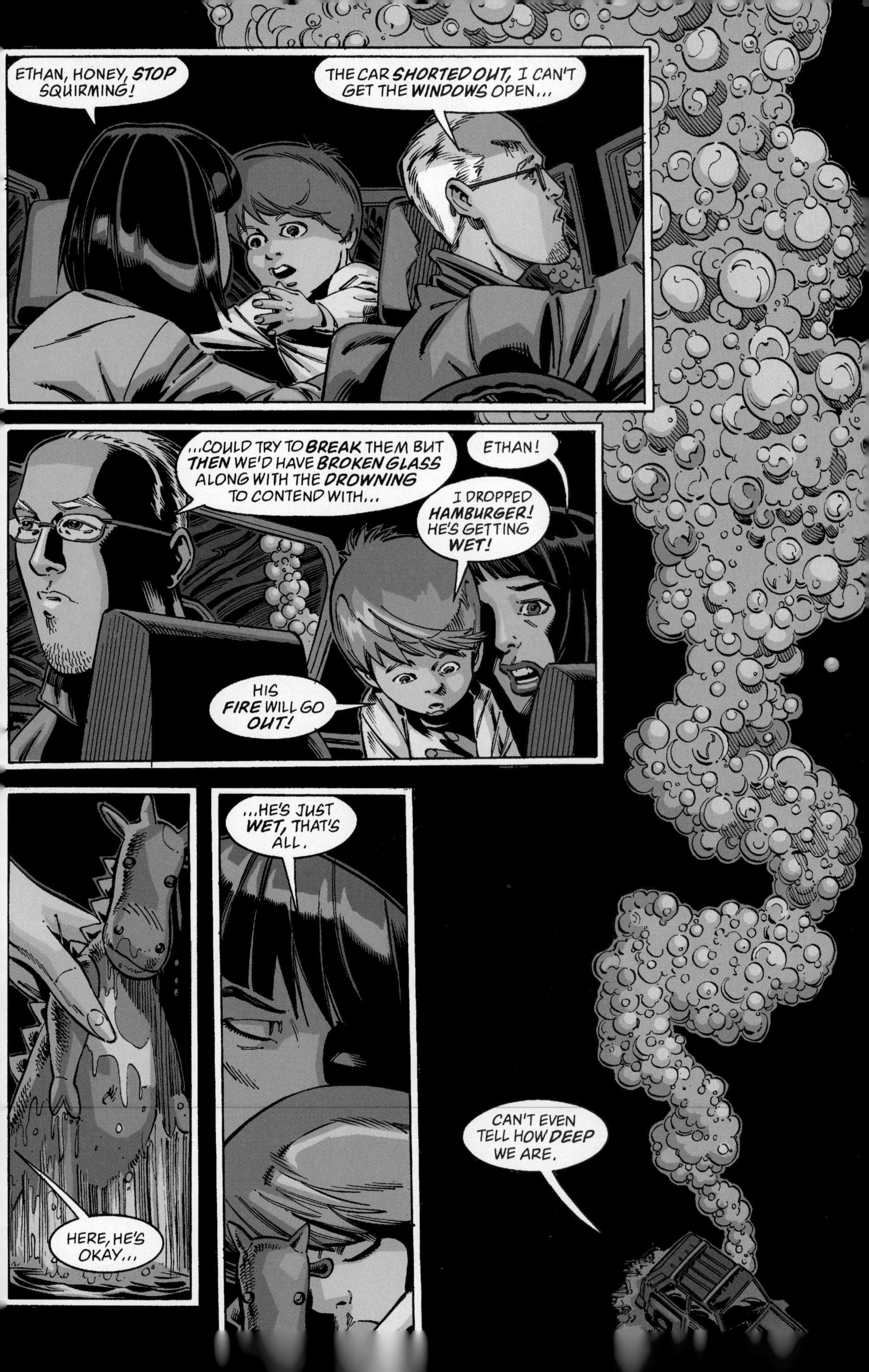
ETHAN, HONEY, STOP SQUIRMING!
THE CAR SHORTED OUT, I CAN'T GET THE WINDOWS OPEN...
...COULD TRY TO BREAK THEM BUT THEN WE'D HAVE BROKEN GLASS ALONG WITH THE DROWNING TO CONTEND WITH...
ETHAN!
I DROPPED HAMBURGER! HE'S GETTING WET!
HIS FIRE WILL GO OUT!
HERE, HE'S OKAY...
...HE'S JUST WET, THAT'S ALL.
CAN'T EVEN TELL HOW DEEP WE ARE.

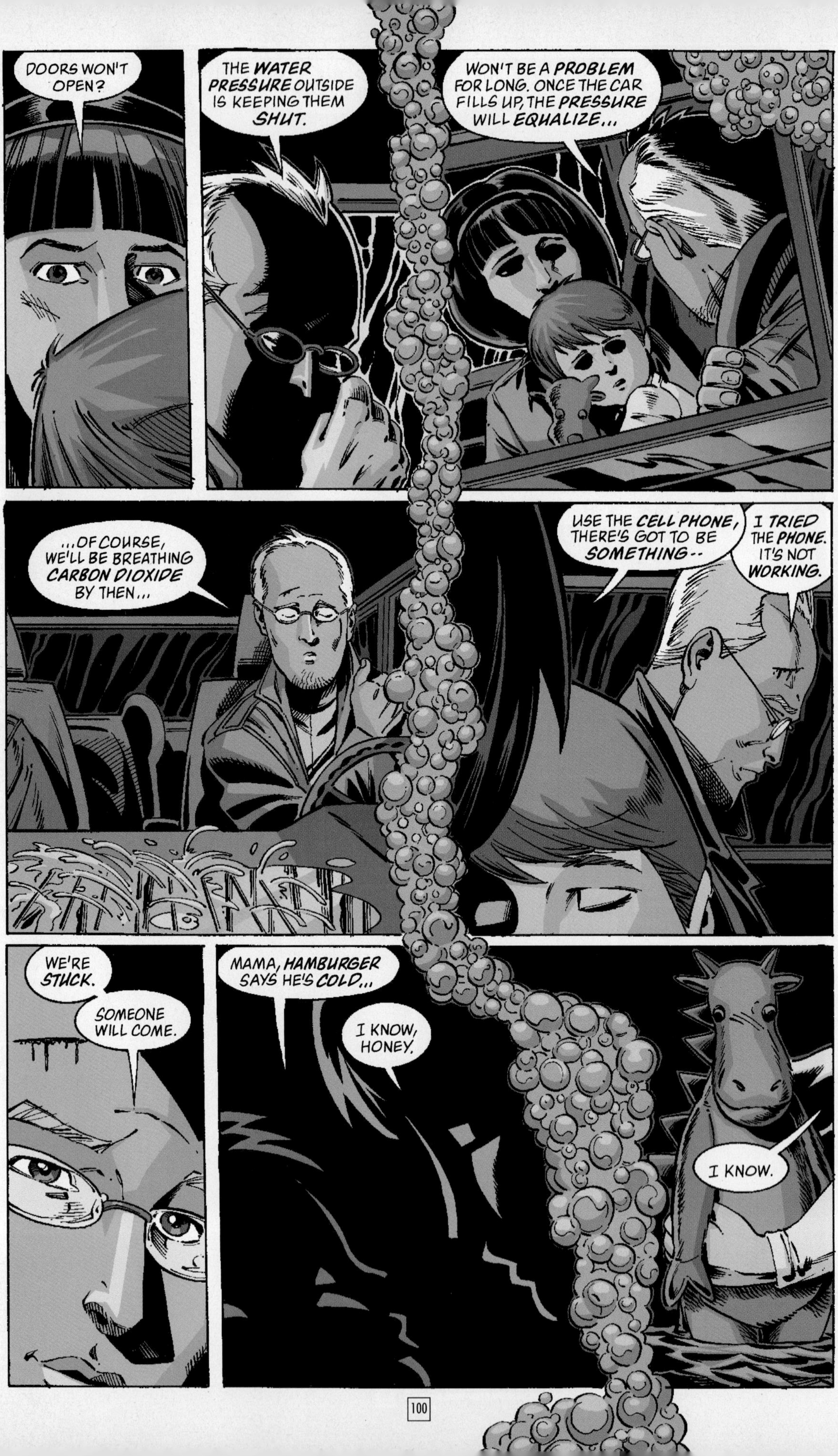
DOORS WON'T OPEN?
THE WATER PRESSURE OUTSIDE IS KEEPING THEM SHUT.
WON'T BE A PROBLEM FOR LONG. ONCE THE CAR FILLS UP, THE PRESSURE WILL EQUALIZE...
...OF COURSE, WE'LL BE BREATHING CARBON DIOXIDE BY THEN...
USE THE CELL PHONE, THERE'S GOT TO BE SOMETHING--
I TRIED THE PHONE. IT'S NOT WORKING.
WE'RE STUCK.
SOMEONE WILL COME.
MAMA, HAMBURGER SAYS HE'S COLD...
I KNOW, HONEY.
I KNOW.

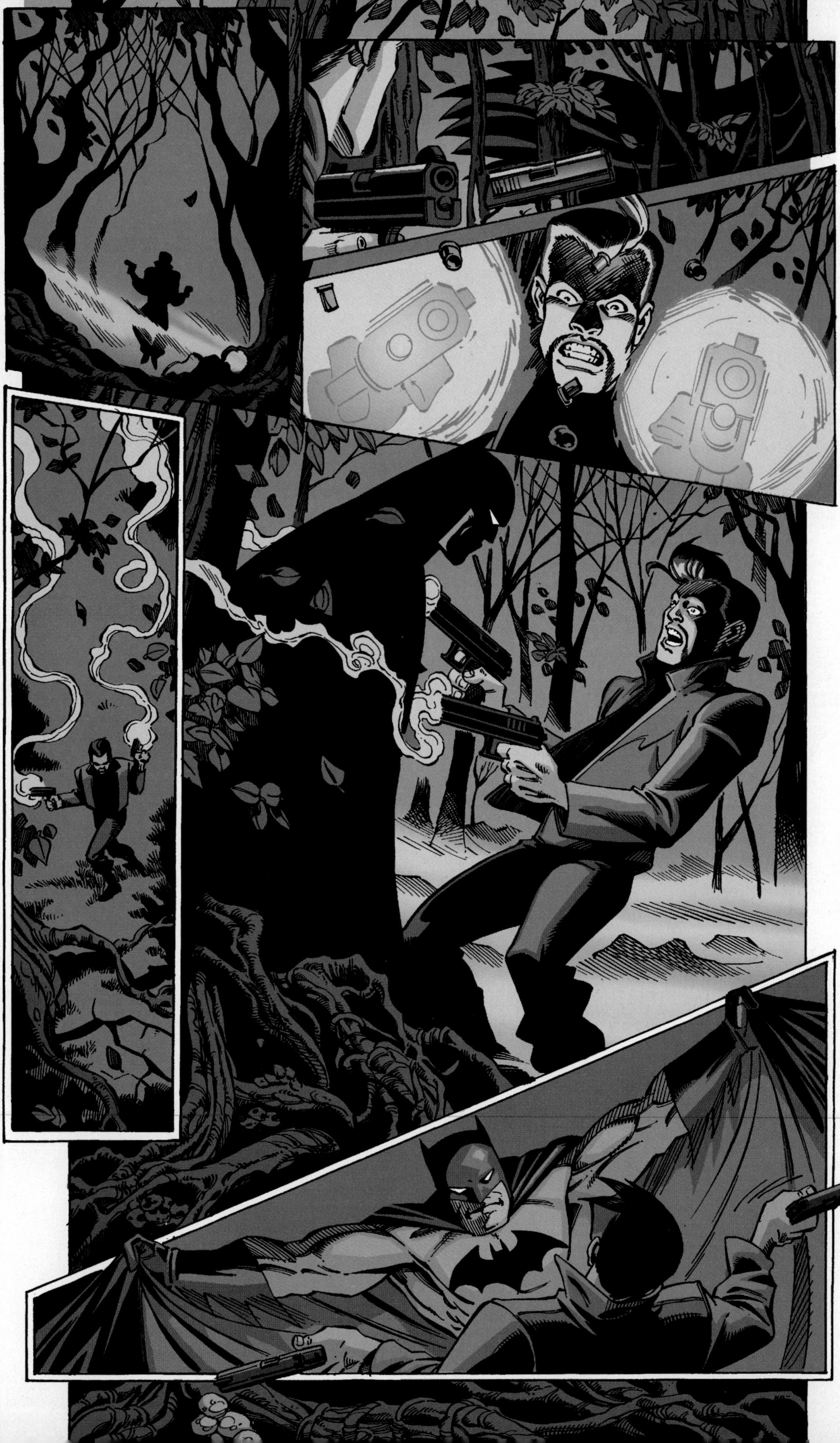

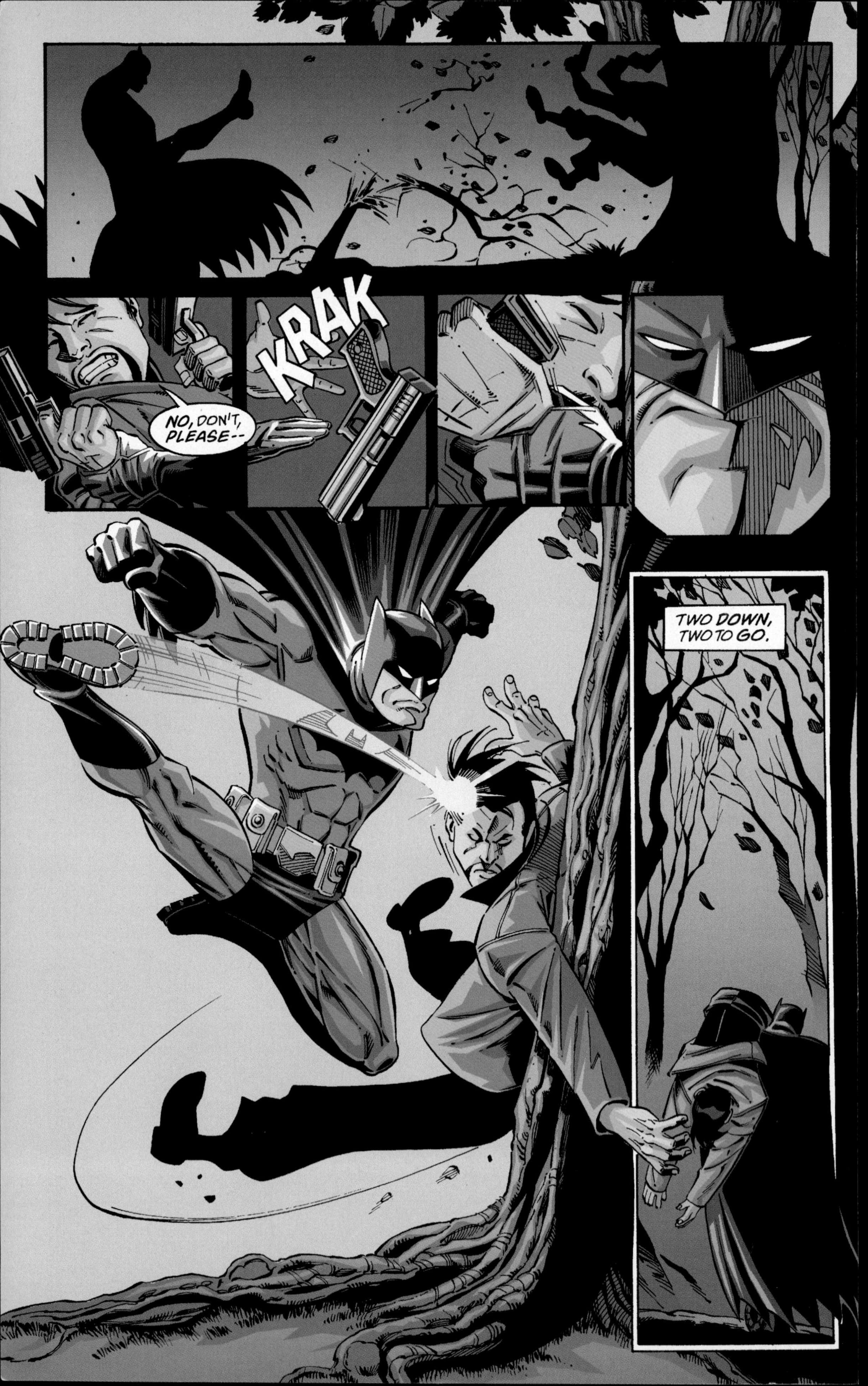
NO, DON'T, PLEASE--
KRAK
TWO DOWN, TWO TO GO.

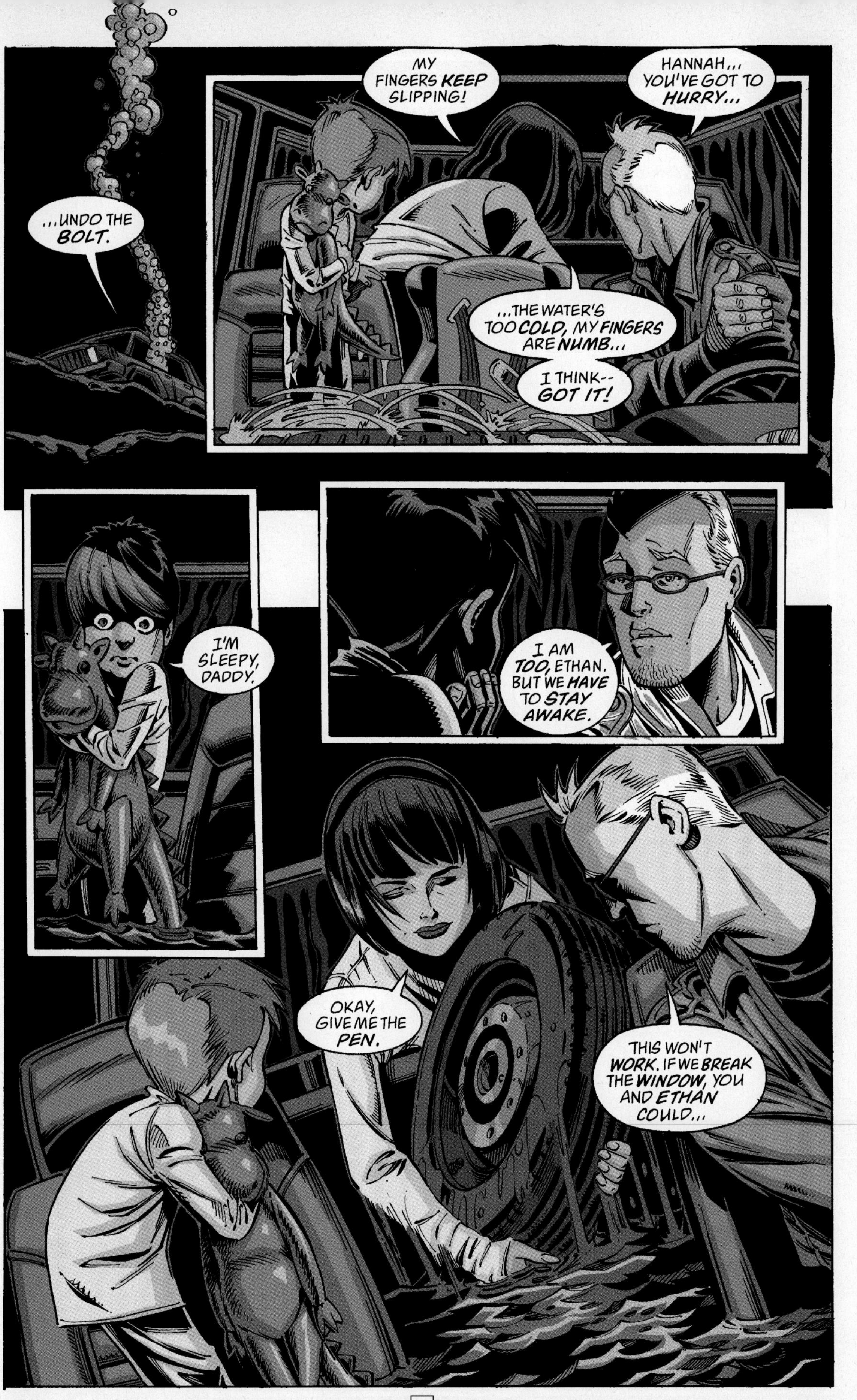
MY FINGERS KEEP SLIPPING!
HANNAH... YOU'VE GOT TO HURRY...
...UNDO THE BOLT.
...THE WATER'S TOO COLD, MY FINGERS ARE NUMB...
I THINK-- GOT IT!
I'M SLEEPY, DADDY.
I AM TOO, ETHAN. BUT WE HAVE TO STAY AWAKE.
OKAY, GIVE ME THE PEN.
THIS WON'T WORK. IF WE BREAK THE WINDOW, YOU AND ETHAN COULD...

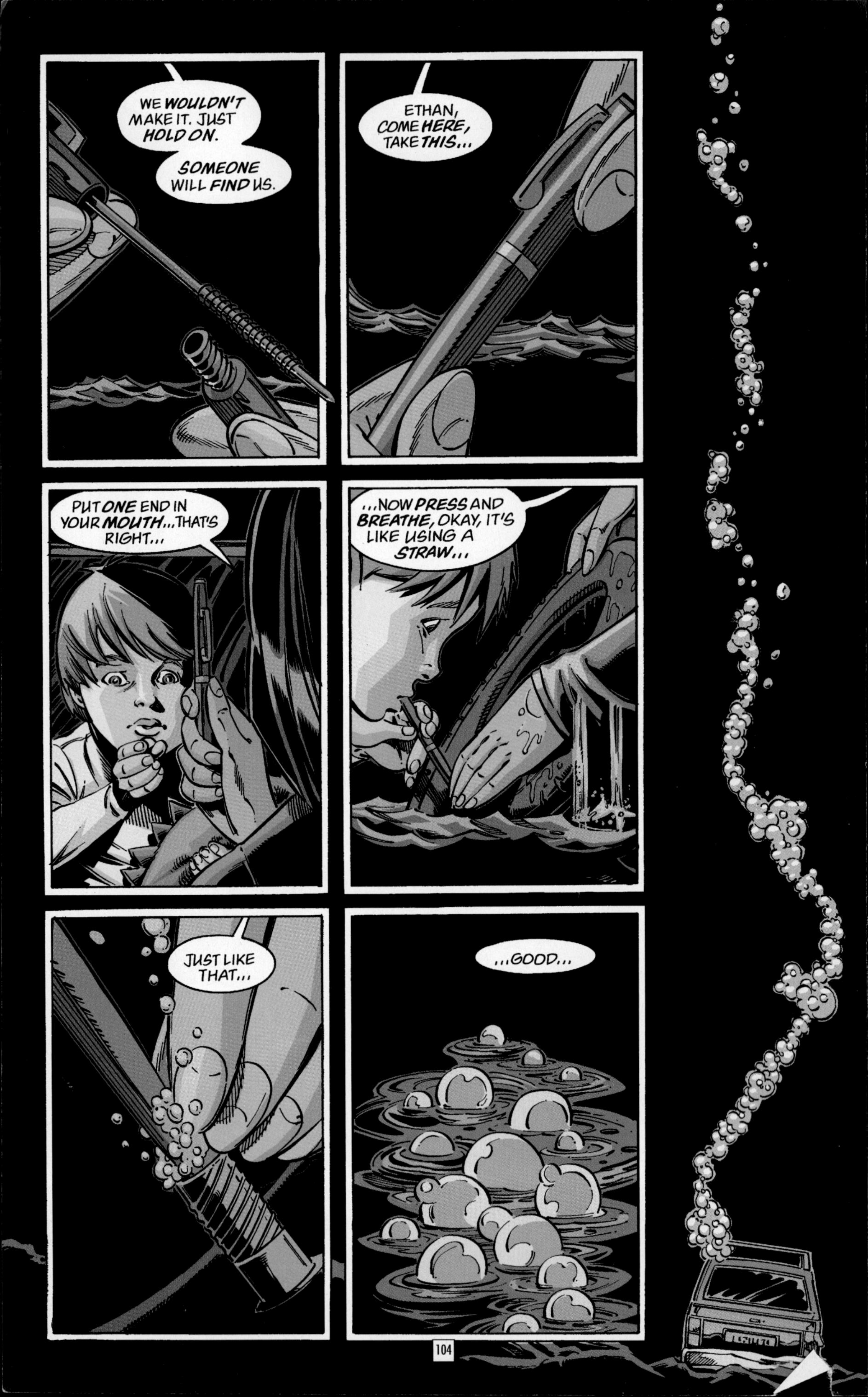
WE WOULDN'T MAKE IT. JUST HOLD ON.
SOMEONE WILL FIND US.
ETHAN, COME HERE, TAKE THIS...
PUT ONE END IN YOUR MOUTH...THAT'S RIGHT...
...NOW PRESS AND BREATHE, OKAY, IT'S LIKE USING A STRAW...
JUST LIKE THAT...
...GOOD...

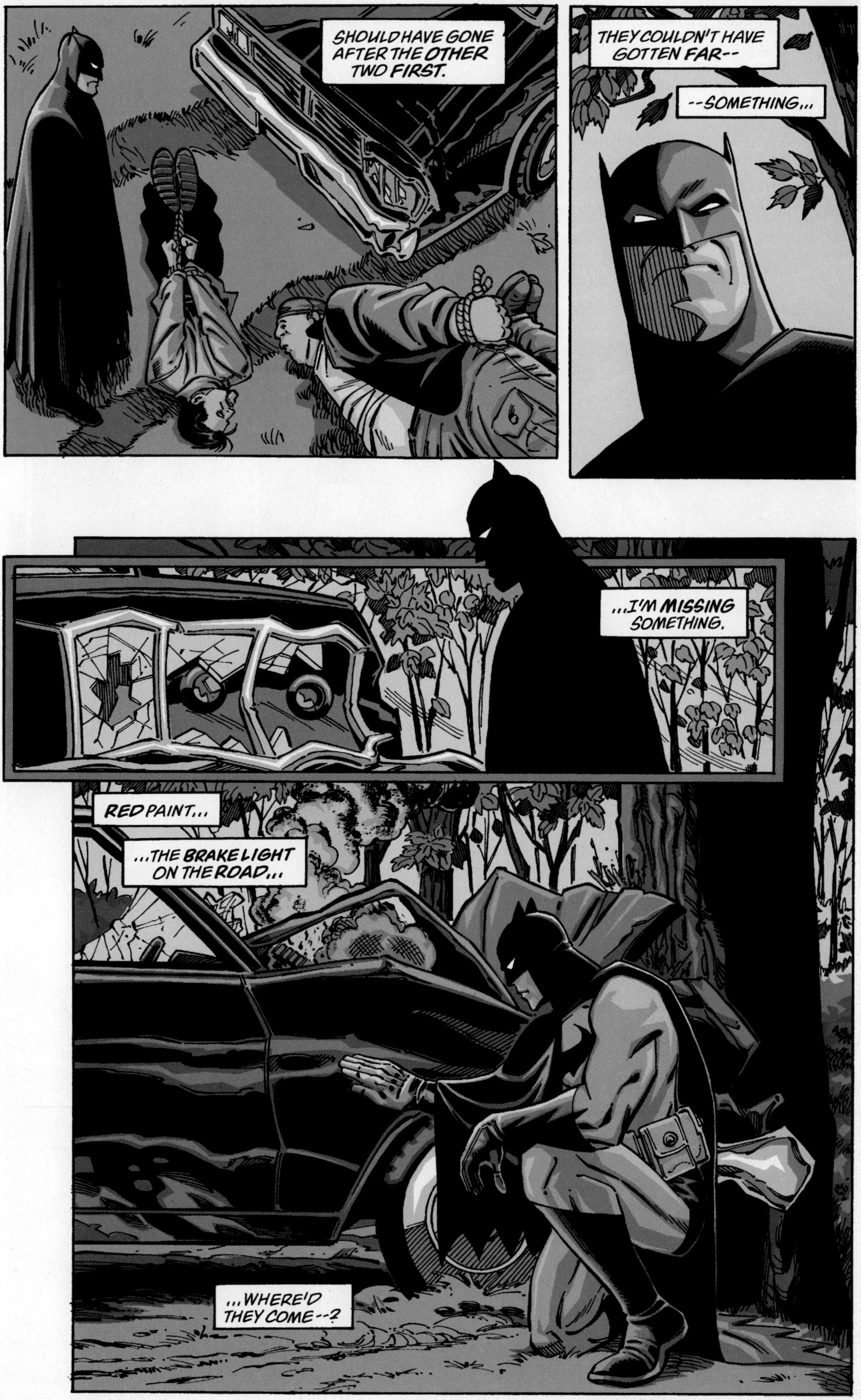
SHOULD HAVE GONE AFTER THE OTHER TWO FIRST.
THEY COULDN'T HAVE GOTTEN FAR--
--SOMETHING...
...I'M MISSING SOMETHING.
RED PAINT...
...THE BRAKE LIGHT ON THE ROAD...
...WHERE'D THEY COME--?

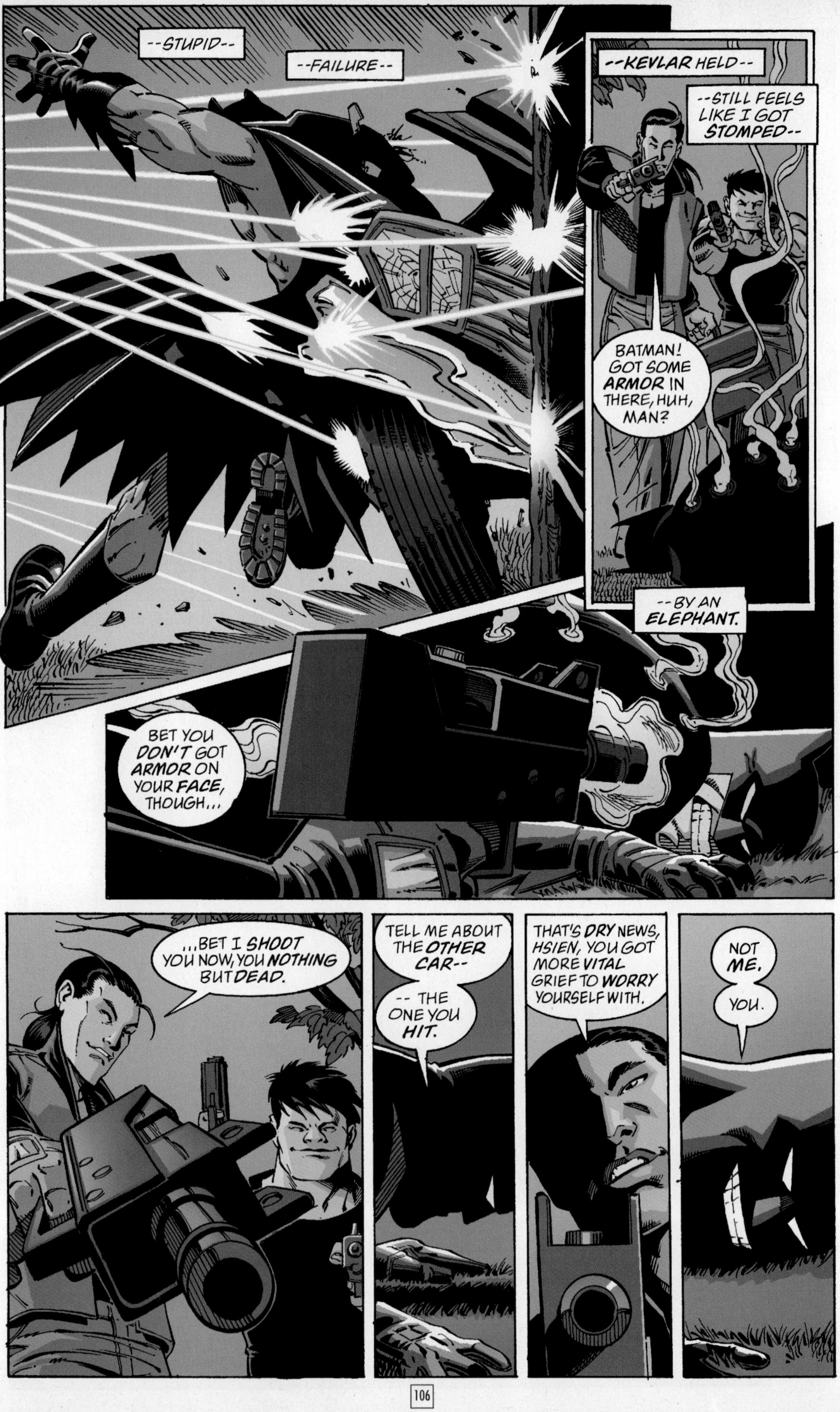
--STUPID--
--FAILURE--
--KEVLAR HELD--
--STILL FEELS LIKE I GOT STOMPED--
BATMAN! GOT SOME ARMOR IN THERE, HUH, MAN?
--BY AN ELEPHANT.
BET YOU DON'T GOT ARMOR ON YOUR FACE, THOUGH...
...BET I SHOOT YOU NOW, YOU NOTHING BUT DEAD.
TELL ME ABOUT THE OTHER CAR--
-- THE ONE YOU HIT.
THAT'S DRY NEWS, HSIEN, YOU GOT MORE VITAL GRIEF TO WORRY YOURSELF WITH.
NOT ME.
YOU.

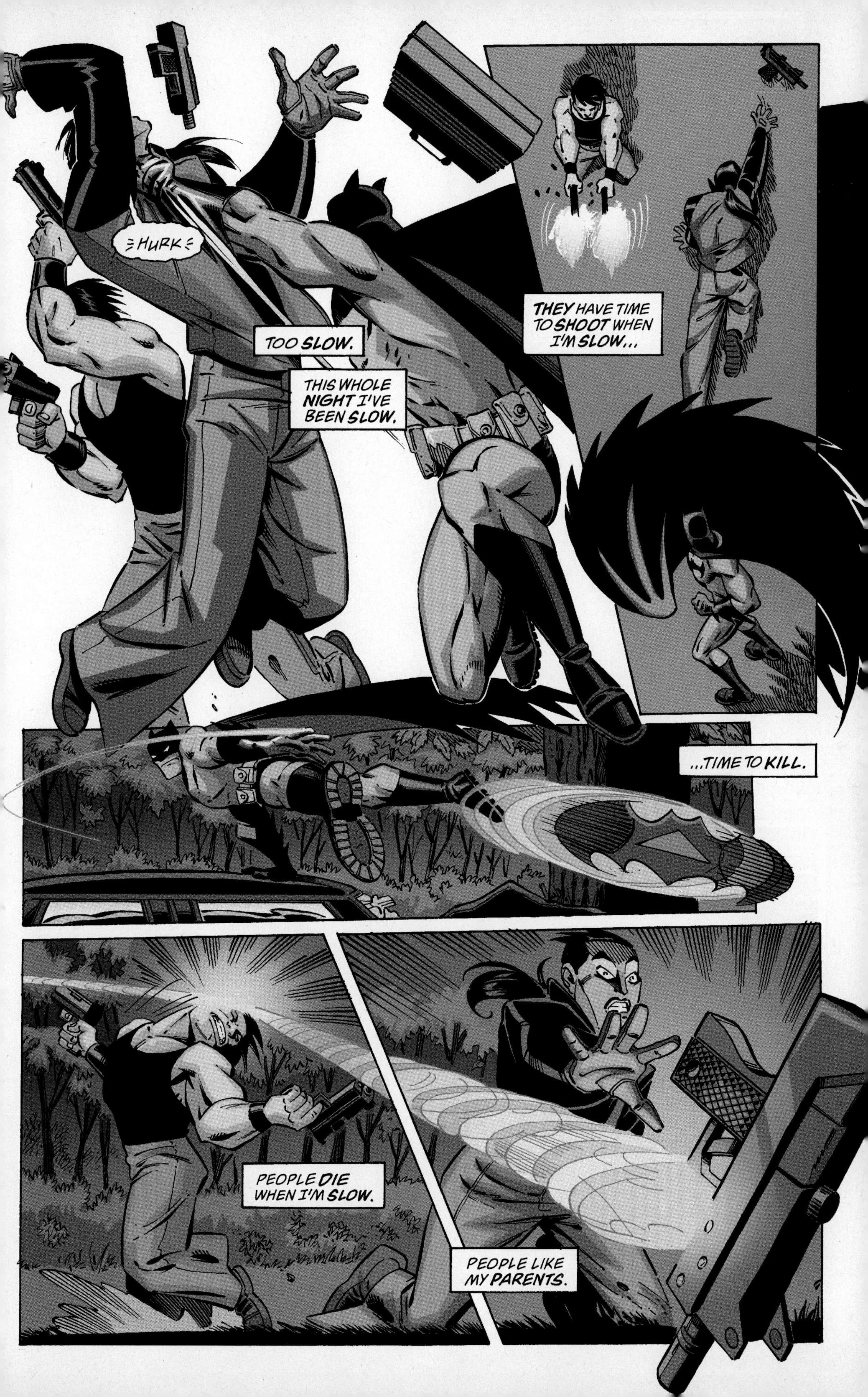
HURK
TOO SLOW.
THIS WHOLE NIGHT I'VE BEEN SLOW.
THEY HAVE TIME TO SHOOT WHEN I'M SLOW...
...TIME TO KILL.
PEOPLE DIE WHEN I'M SLOW.
PEOPLE LIKE MY PARENTS.

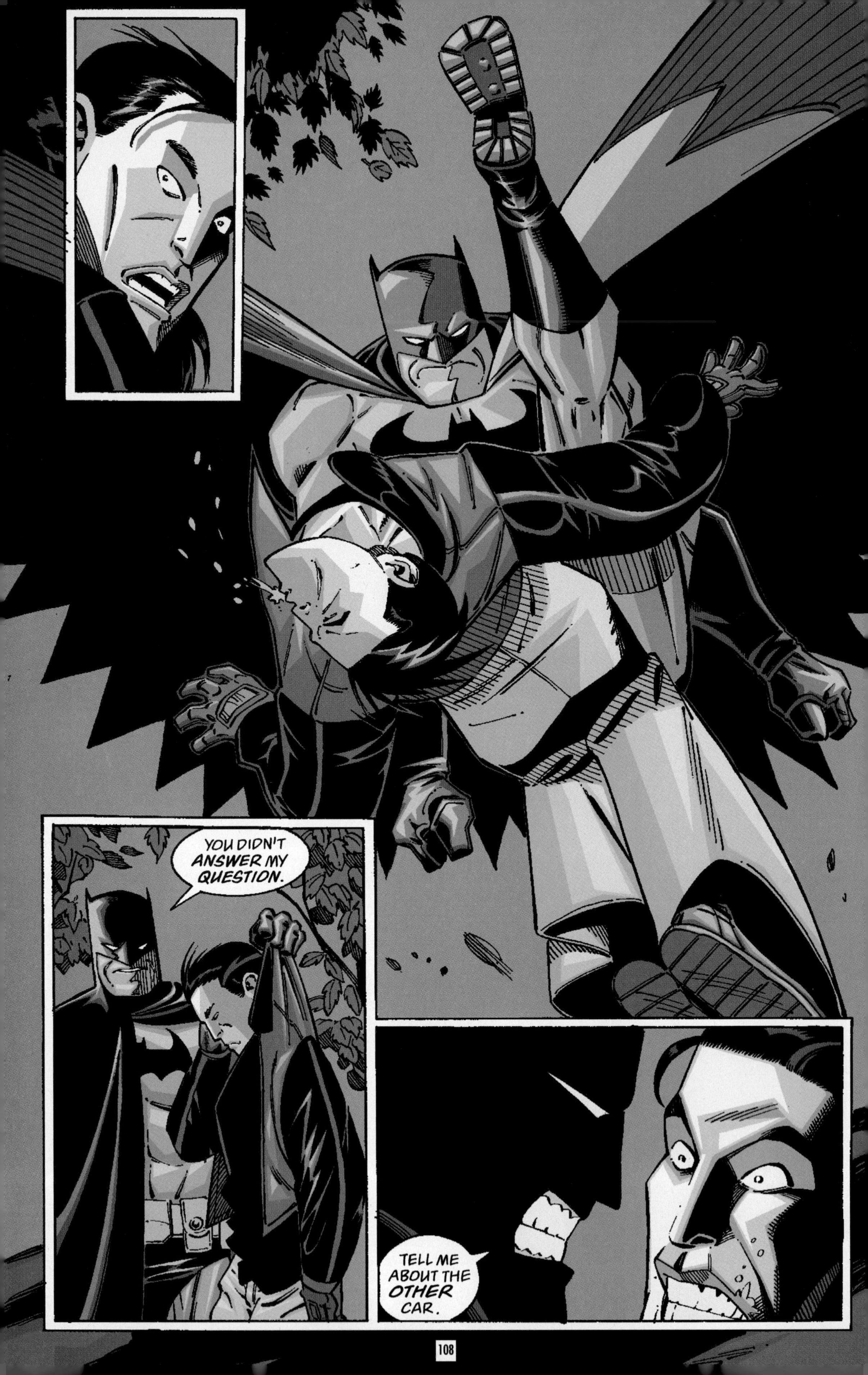
YOU DIDN'T ANSWER MY QUESTION.
TELL ME ABOUT THE OTHER CAR.

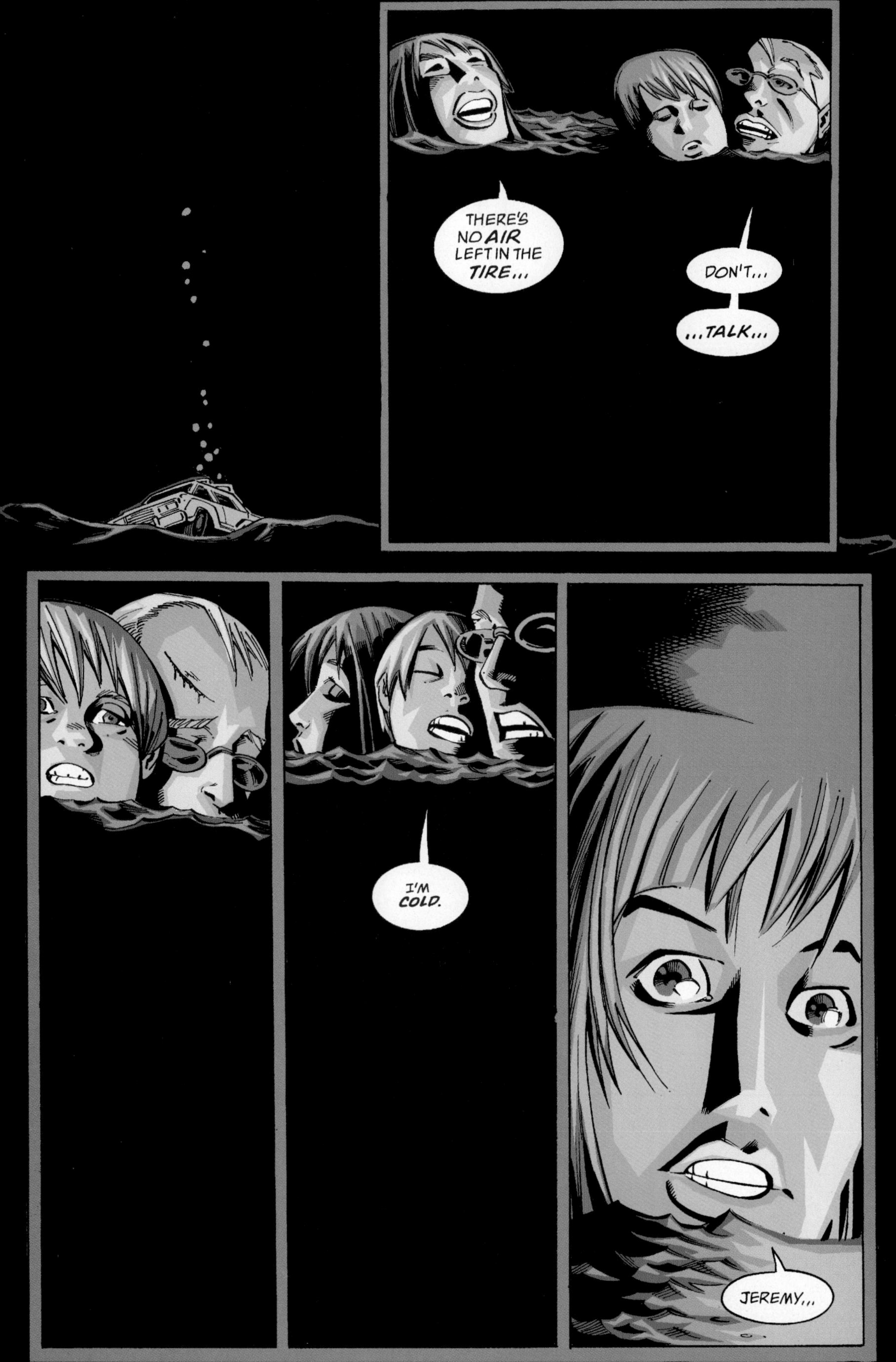
THERE'S NO AIR LEFT IN THE TIRE...
DON'T...
...TALK...
I'M COLD.
JEREMY...

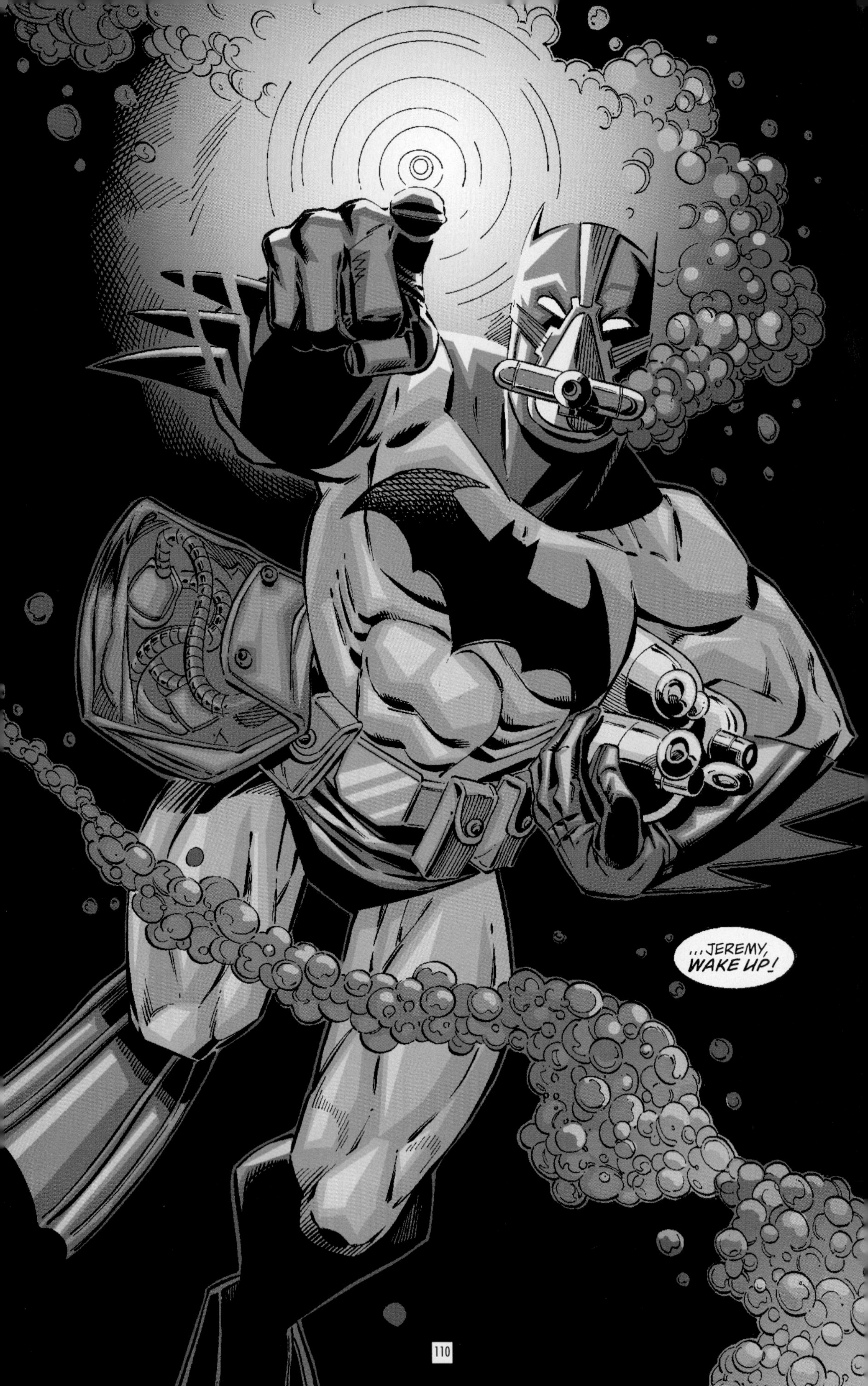
...JEREMY, WAKE UP!

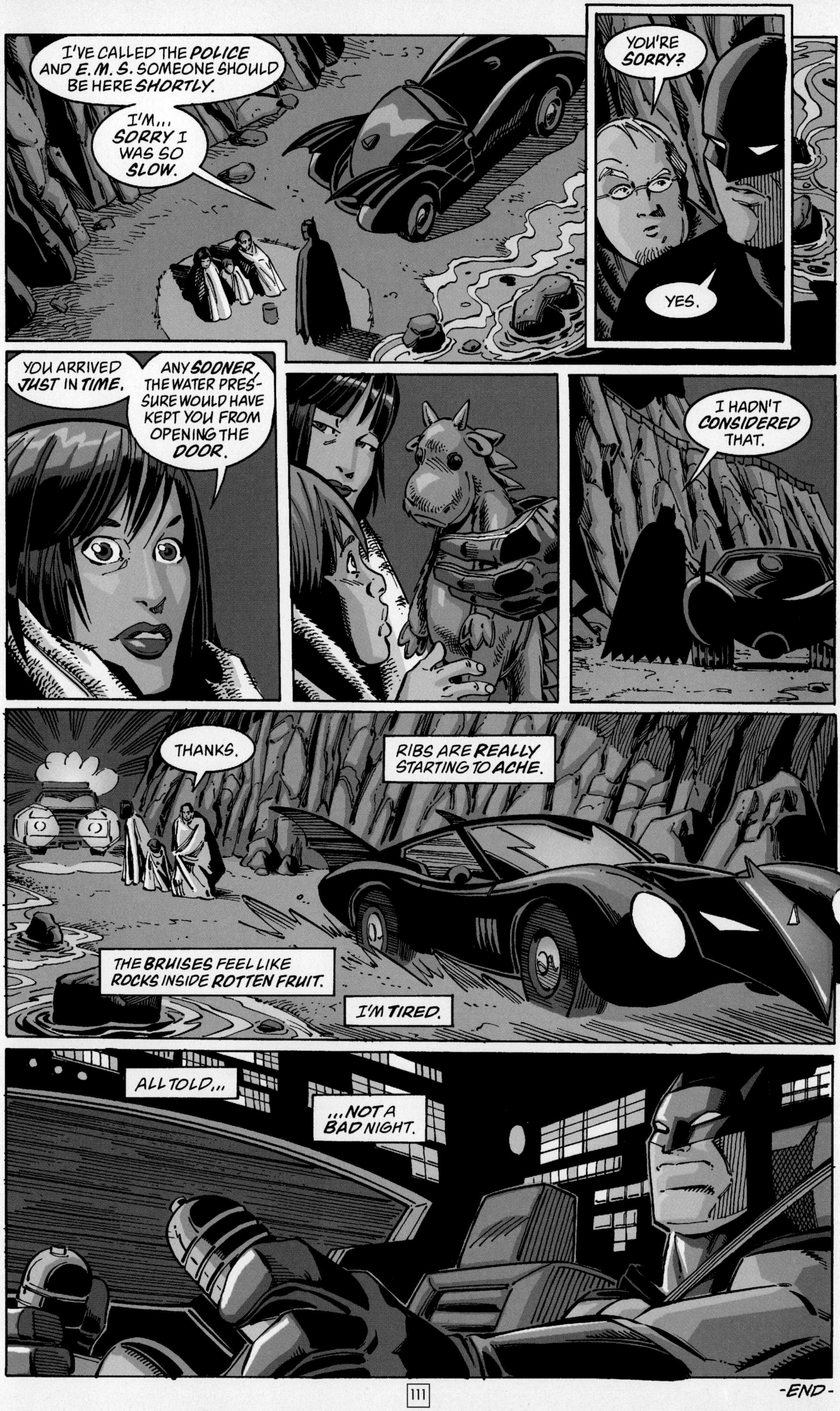
I'VE CALLED THE POLICE AND E.M.S. SOMEONE SHOULD BE HERE SHORTLY.
I'M... SORRY I WAS SO SLOW.
YOU'RE SORRY?
YES.
YOU ARRIVED JUST IN TIME.
ANY SOONER, THE WATER PRES-SURE WOULD HAVE KEPT YOU FROM OPENING THE DOOR.
I HADN'T CONSIDERED THAT.
THANKS.
RIBS ARE REALLY STARTING TO ACHE.
THE BRUISES FEEL LIKE ROCKS INSIDE ROTTEN FRUIT.
I'M TIRED.
ALL TOLD...
...NOT A BAD NIGHT.
-END-

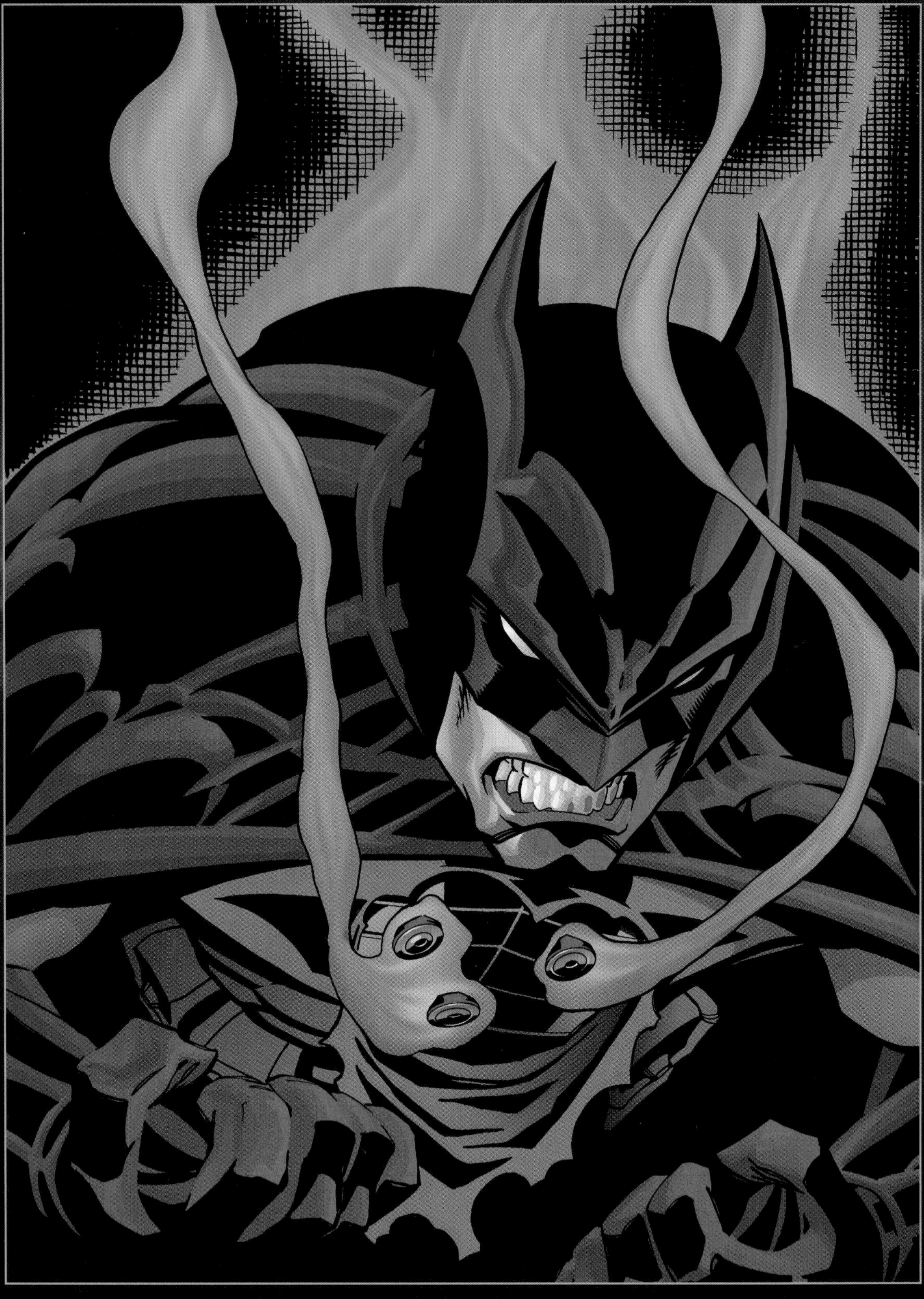

"Reasons"

ED BRUBAKER writer **SCOTT MCDANIEL** penciller & cover artist
ANDY OWENS inker **GREGORY WRIGHT** colorist **JOHN COSTANZA** letterer

In this story, taken from the pages of the monthly BATMAN title, our hero encounters the feline fatale Catwoman, and discovers a new aspect about himself.

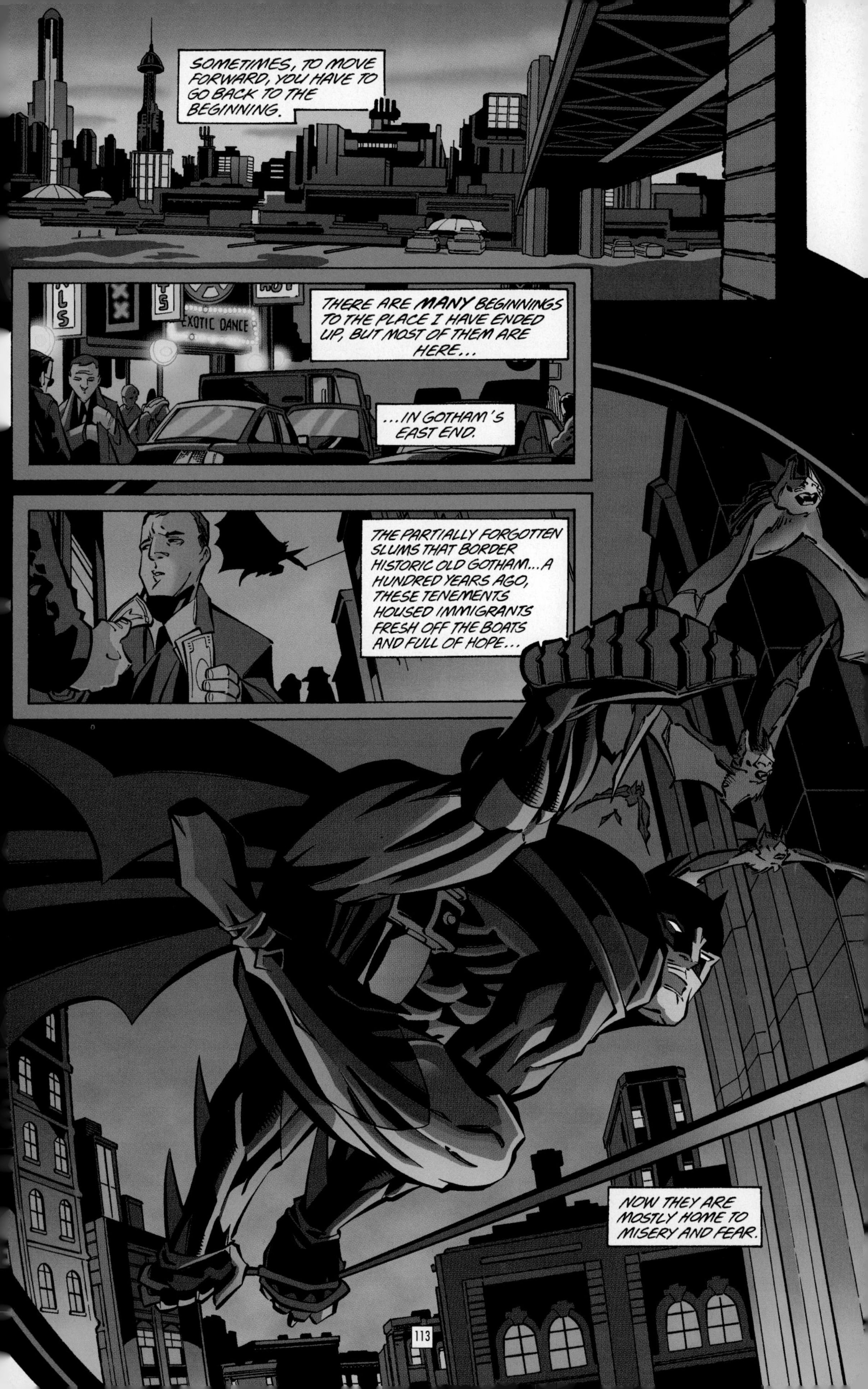
SOMETIMES, TO MOVE FORWARD, YOU HAVE TO GO BACK TO THE BEGINNING.
EXOTIC DANCE
THERE ARE MANY BEGINNINGS TO THE PLACE I HAVE ENDED UP, BUT MOST OF THEM ARE HERE...
...IN GOTHAM'S EAST END.
THE PARTIALLY FORGOTTEN SLUMS THAT BORDER HISTORIC OLD GOTHAM... A HUNDRED YEARS AGO, THESE TENEMENTS HOUSED IMMIGRANTS FRESH OFF THE BOATS AND FULL OF HOPE...
NOW THEY ARE MOSTLY HOME TO MISERY AND FEAR.

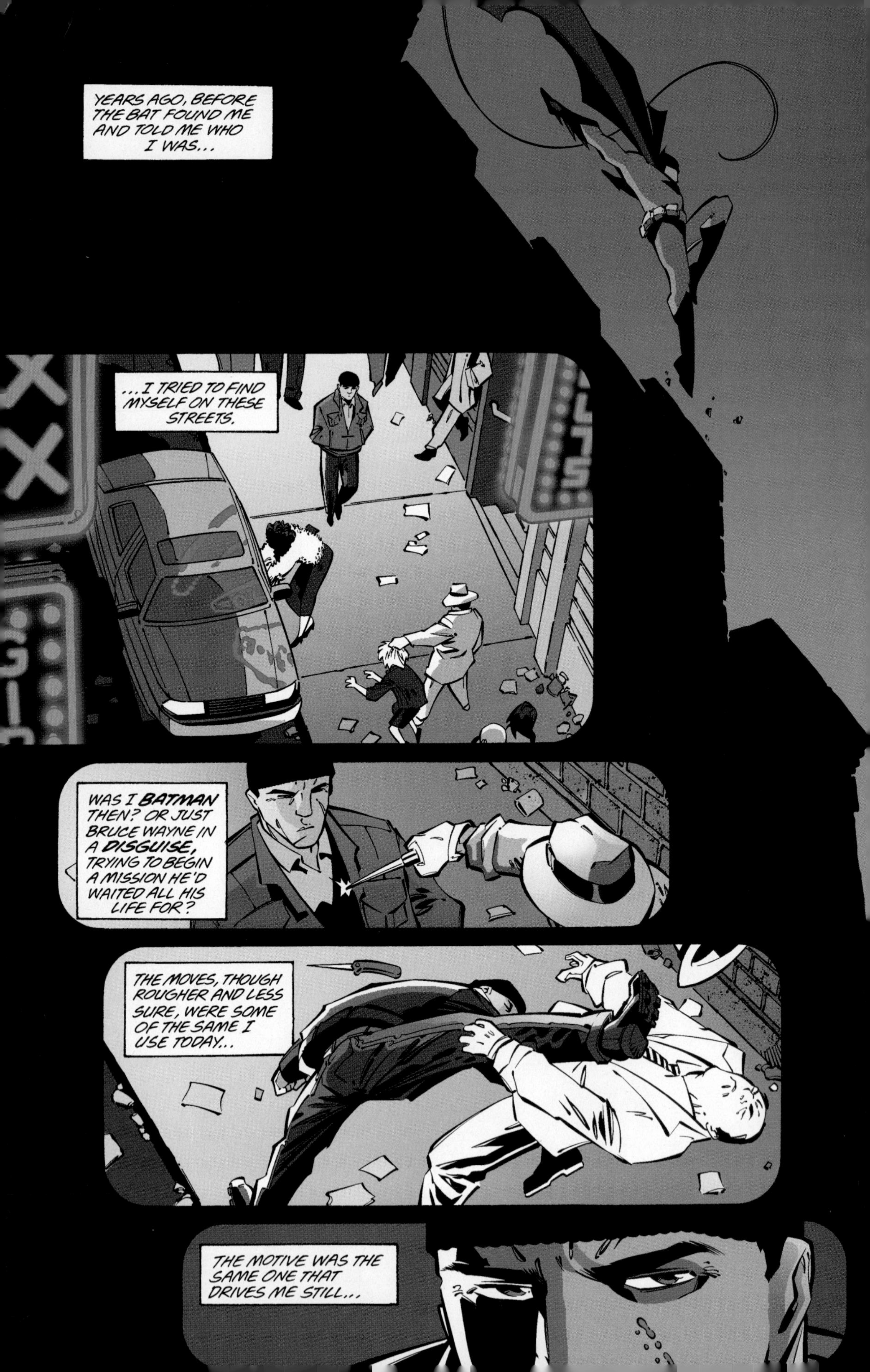
YEARS AGO, BEFORE THE BAT FOUND ME AND TOLD ME WHO I WAS...
...I TRIED TO FIND MYSELF ON THESE STREETS.
WAS I BATMAN THEN? OR JUST BRUCE WAYNE IN A DISGUISE, TRYING TO BEGIN A MISSION HE'D WAITED ALL HIS LIFE FOR?
THE MOVES, THOUGH ROUGHER AND LESS SURE, WERE SOME OF THE SAME I USE TODAY...
THE MOTIVE WAS THE SAME ONE THAT DRIVES ME STILL...

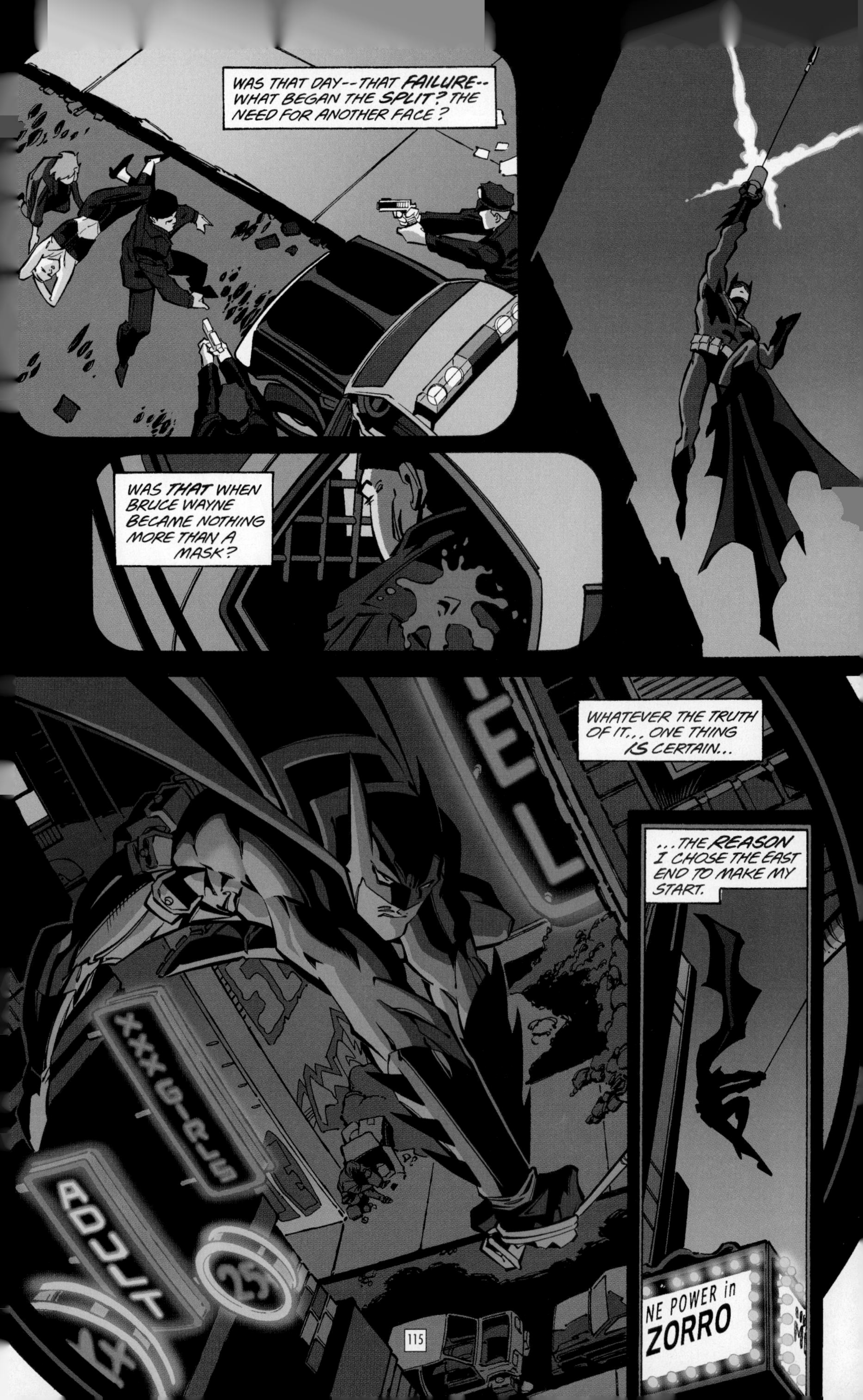
WAS THAT DAY--THAT FAILURE--WHAT BEGAN THE SPLIT? THE NEED FOR ANOTHER FACE?
WAS THAT WHEN BRUCE WAYNE BECAME NOTHING MORE THAN A MASK?
WHATEVER THE TRUTH OF IT... ONE THING IS CERTAIN...
...THE REASON I CHOSE THE EAST END TO MAKE MY START.
XXX GIRLS
ADULT
25¢
NE POWER in
ZORRO

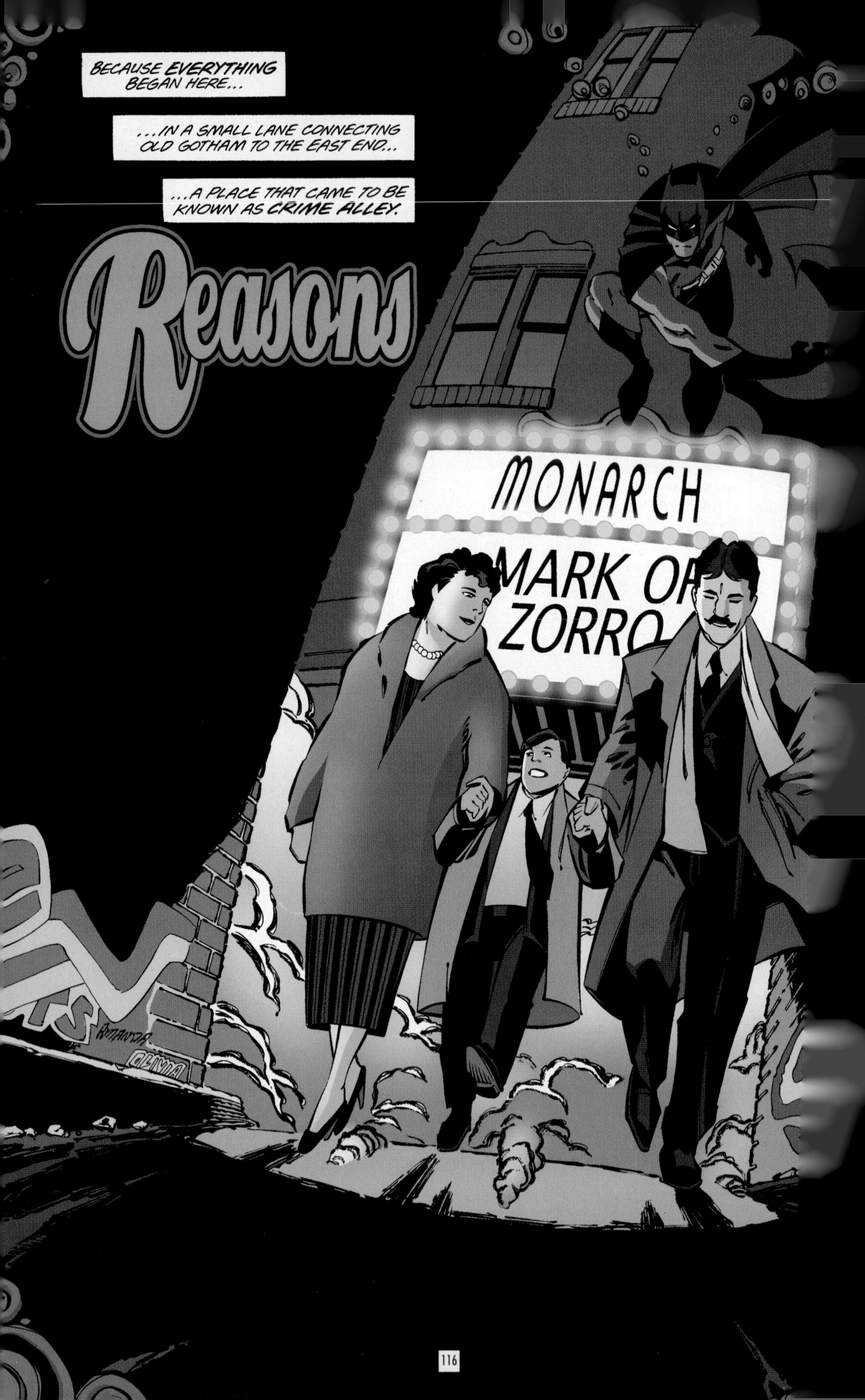
BECAUSE EVERYTHING BEGAN HERE...
...IN A SMALL LANE CONNECTING OLD GOTHAM TO THE EAST END...
...A PLACE THAT CAME TO BE KNOWN AS CRIME ALLEY.
Reasons
MONARCH
MARK OF ZORRO

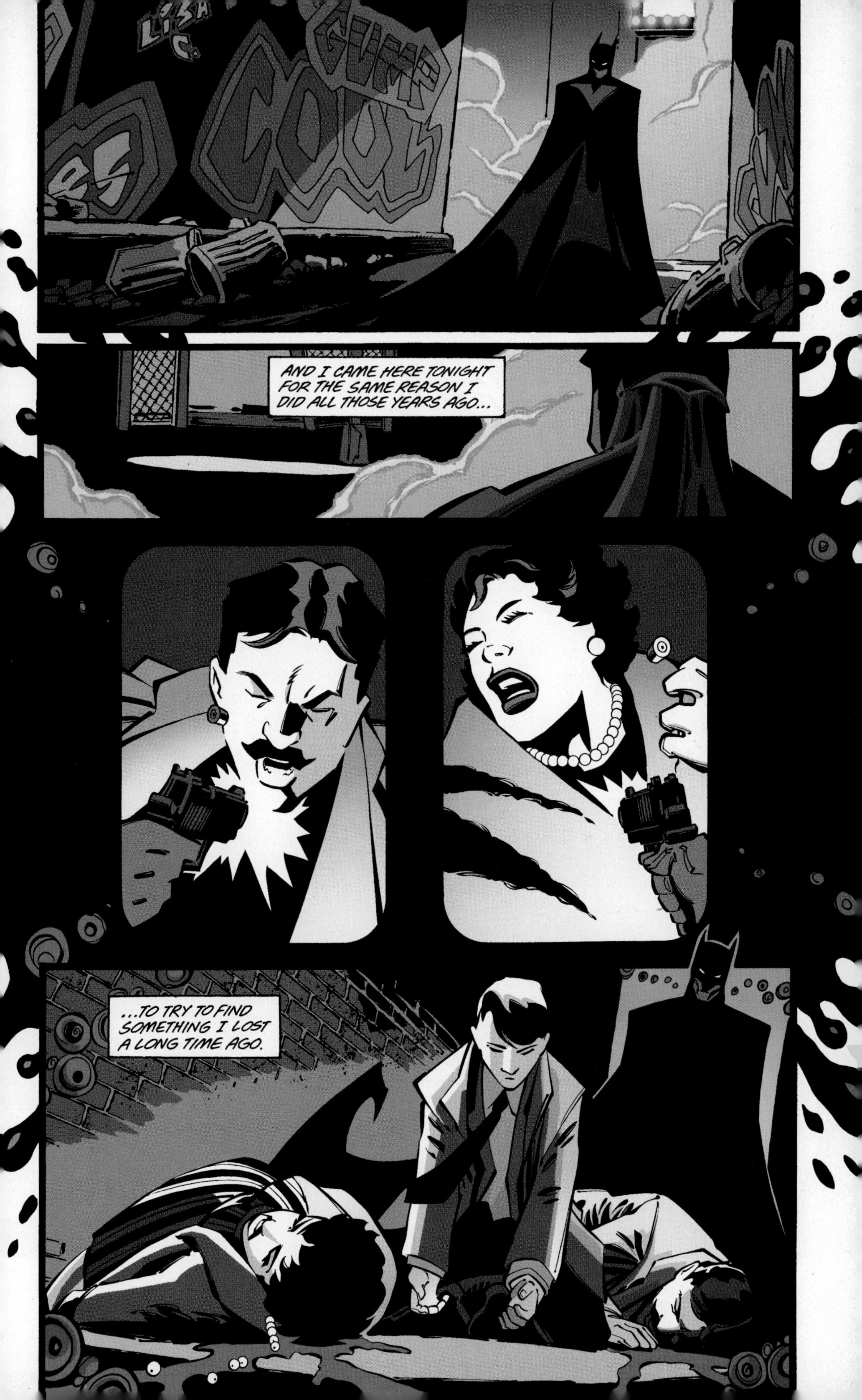
AND I CAME HERE TONIGHT FOR THE SAME REASON I DID ALL THOSE YEARS AGO...
...TO TRY TO FIND SOMETHING I LOST A LONG TIME AGO.

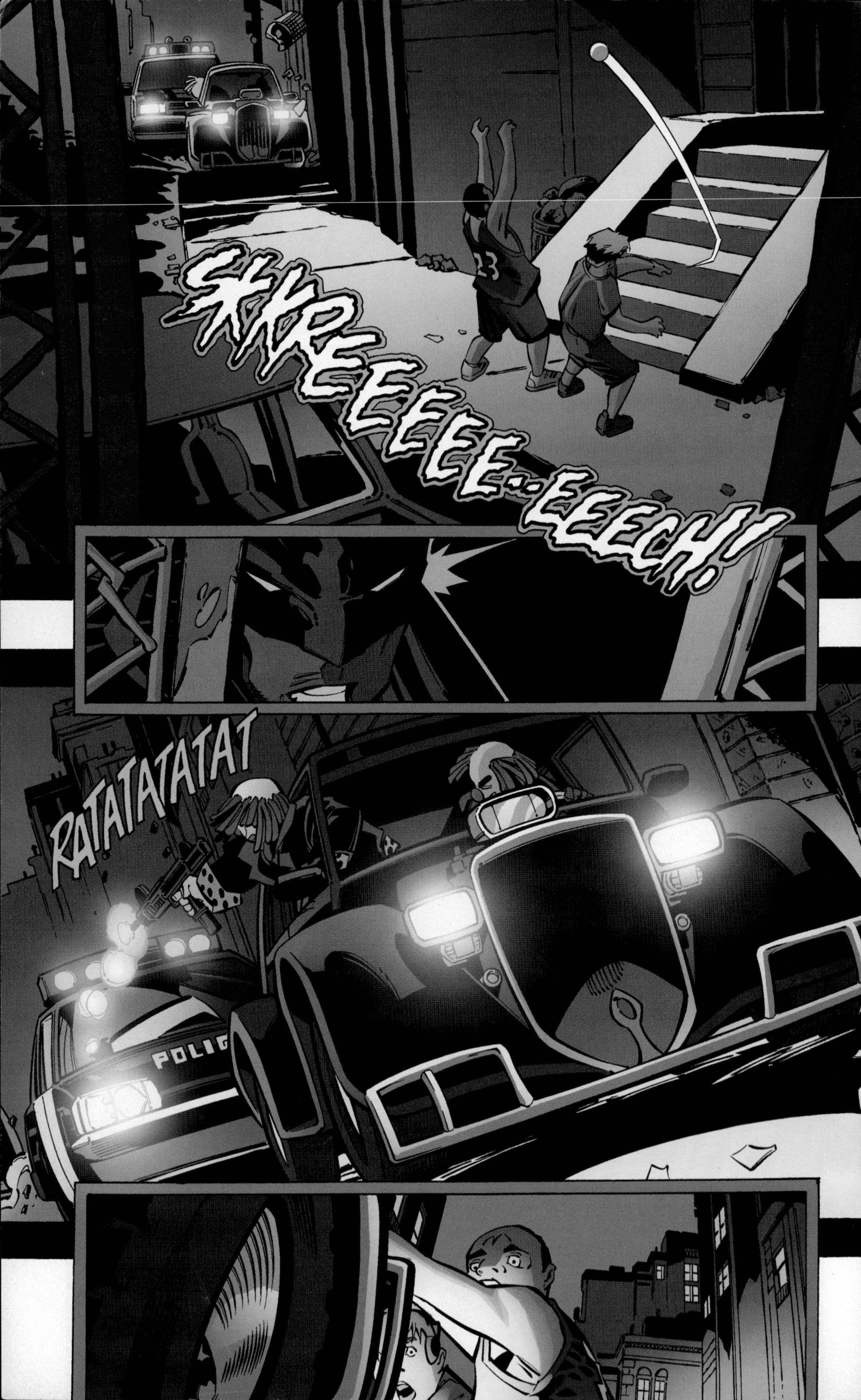
SKREEEEEE--EEECH!
RATATATATAT
POLIC

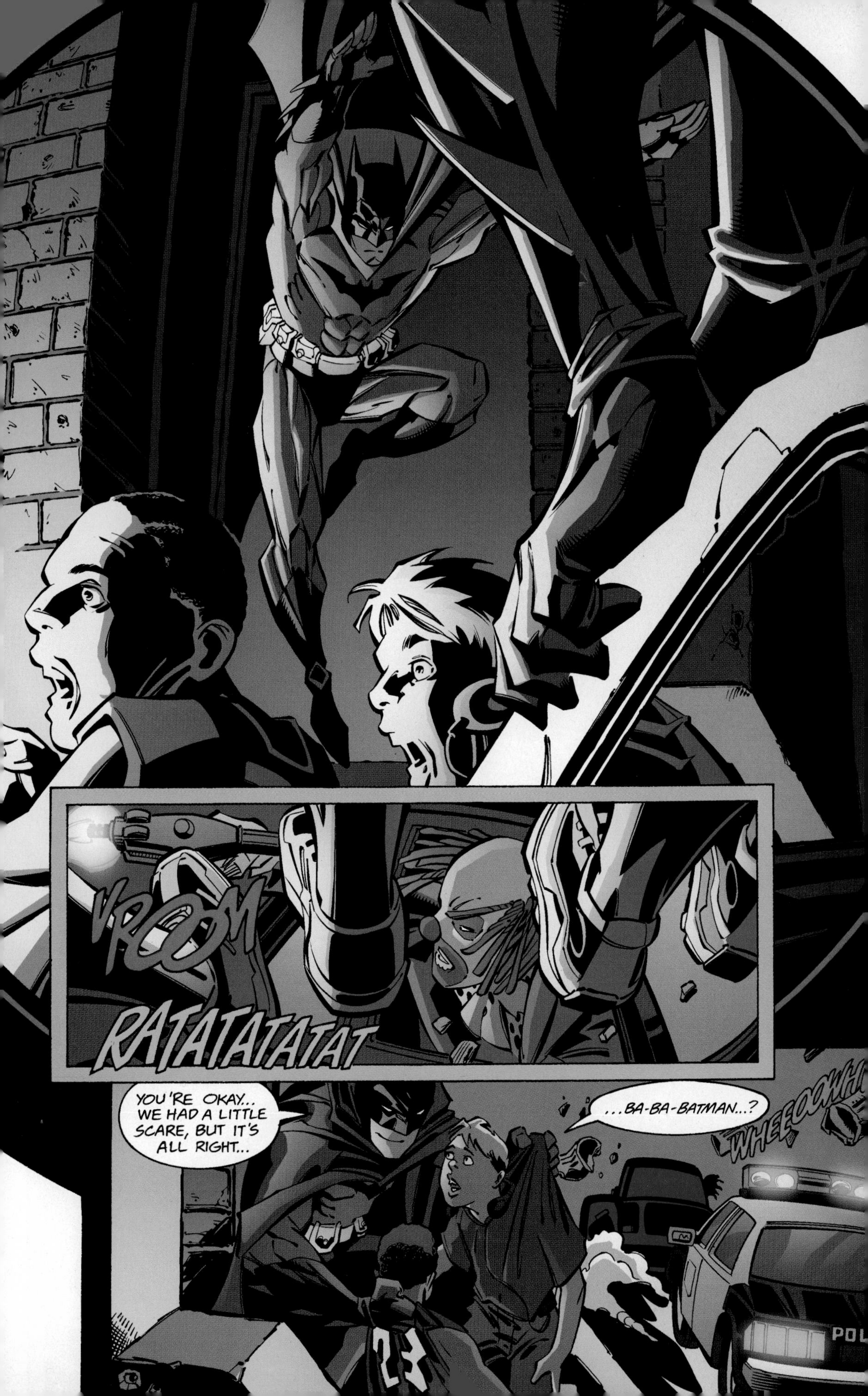
VROOM
RATATATATATAT
YOU'RE OKAY... WE HAD A LITTLE SCARE, BUT IT'S ALL RIGHT...
...BA-BA-BATMAN...?
WHEEOOWH
POL

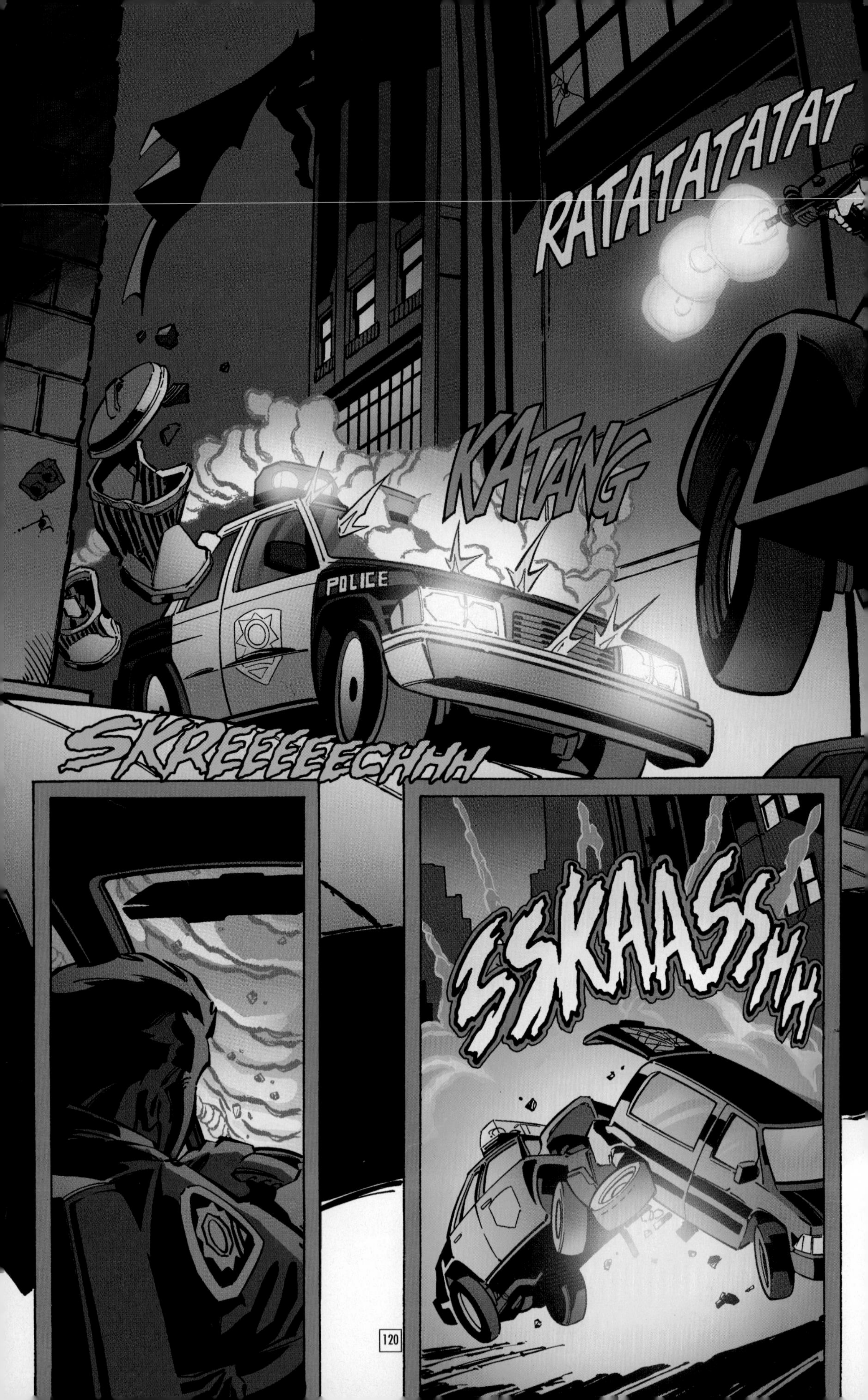
RATATATATAT
KATANG
POLICE
SKREEEEEECHHH
SSKAASSHH

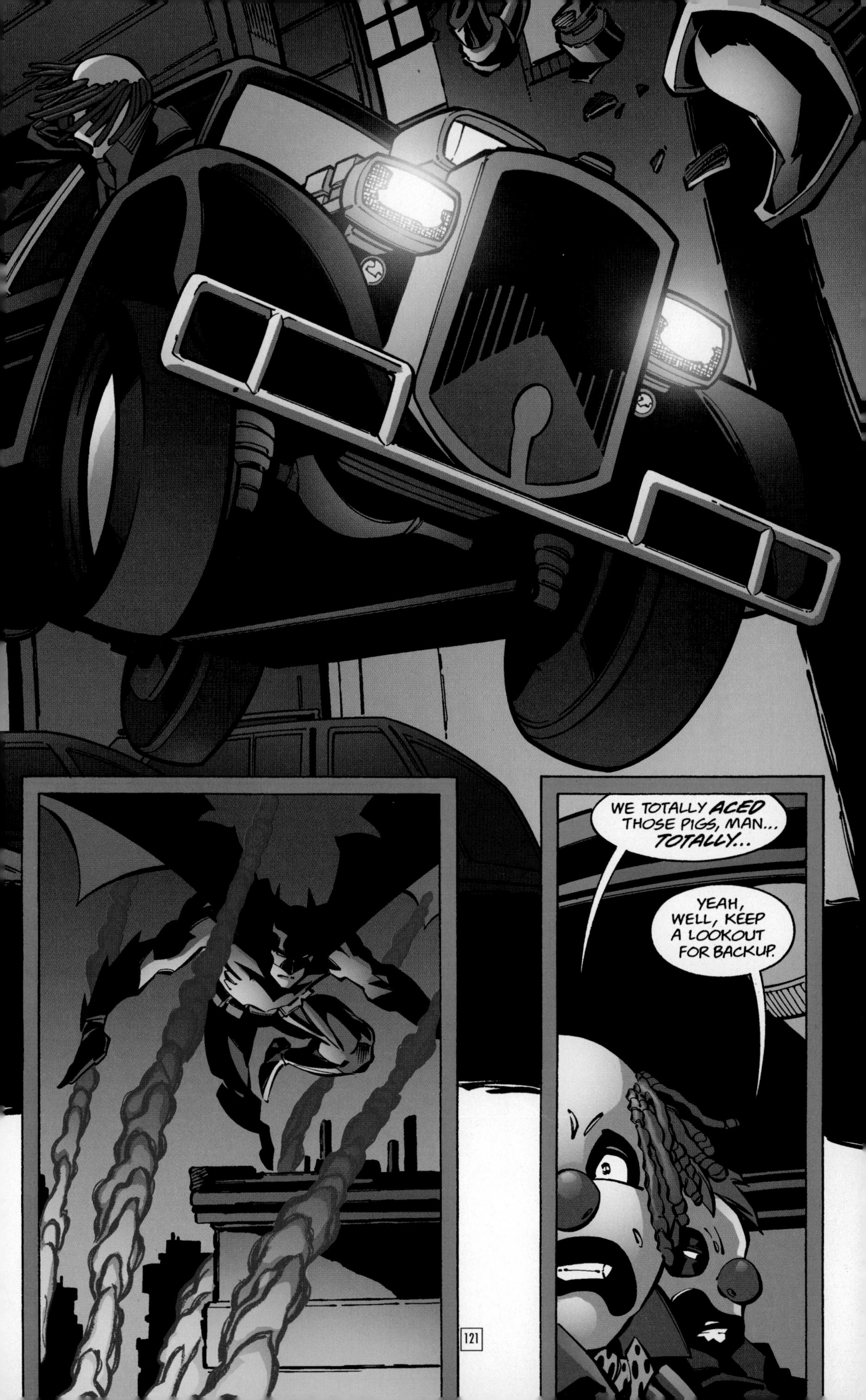
WE TOTALLY ACED THOSE PIGS, MAN... TOTALLY...
YEAH, WELL, KEEP A LOOKOUT FOR BACKUP.

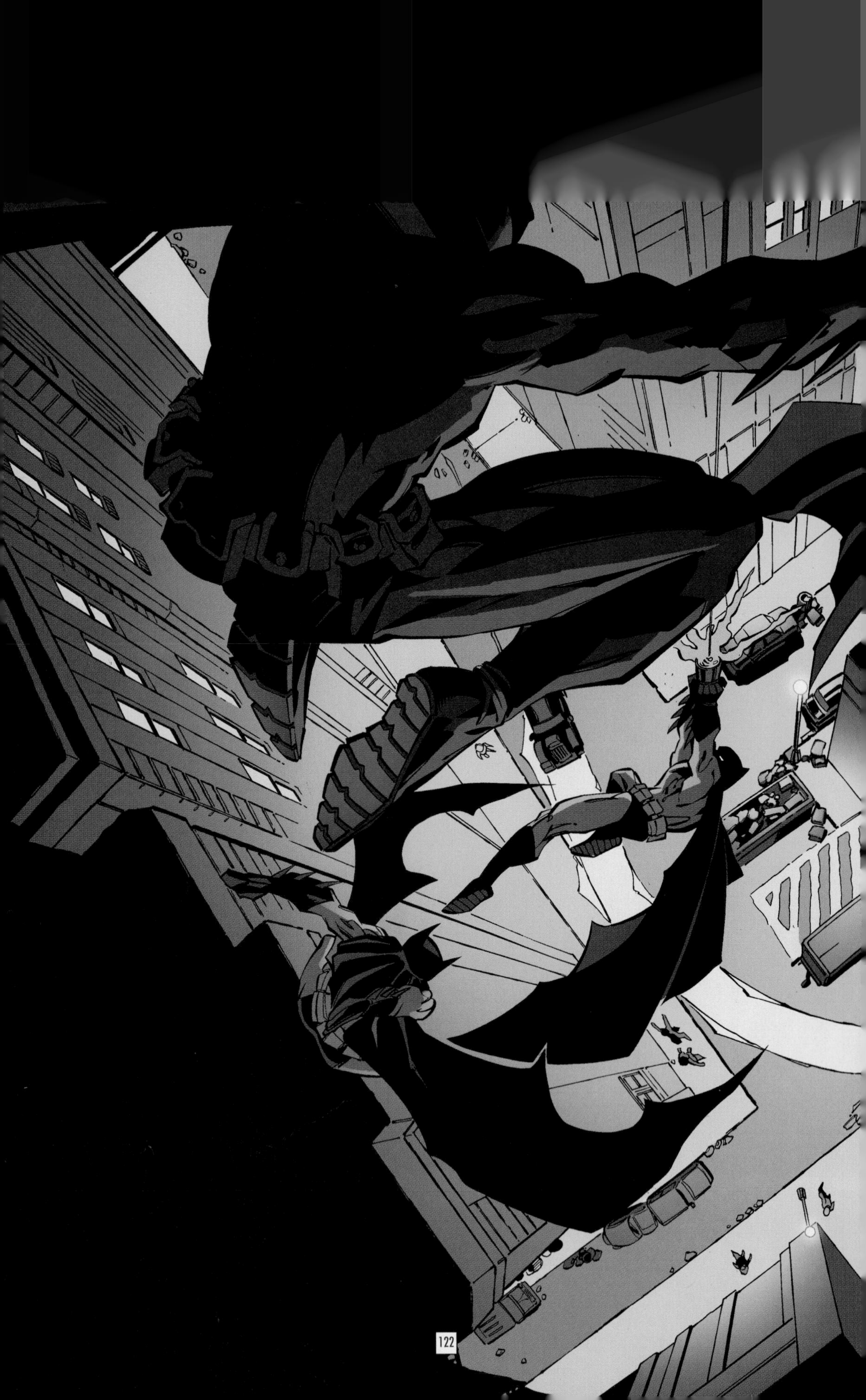

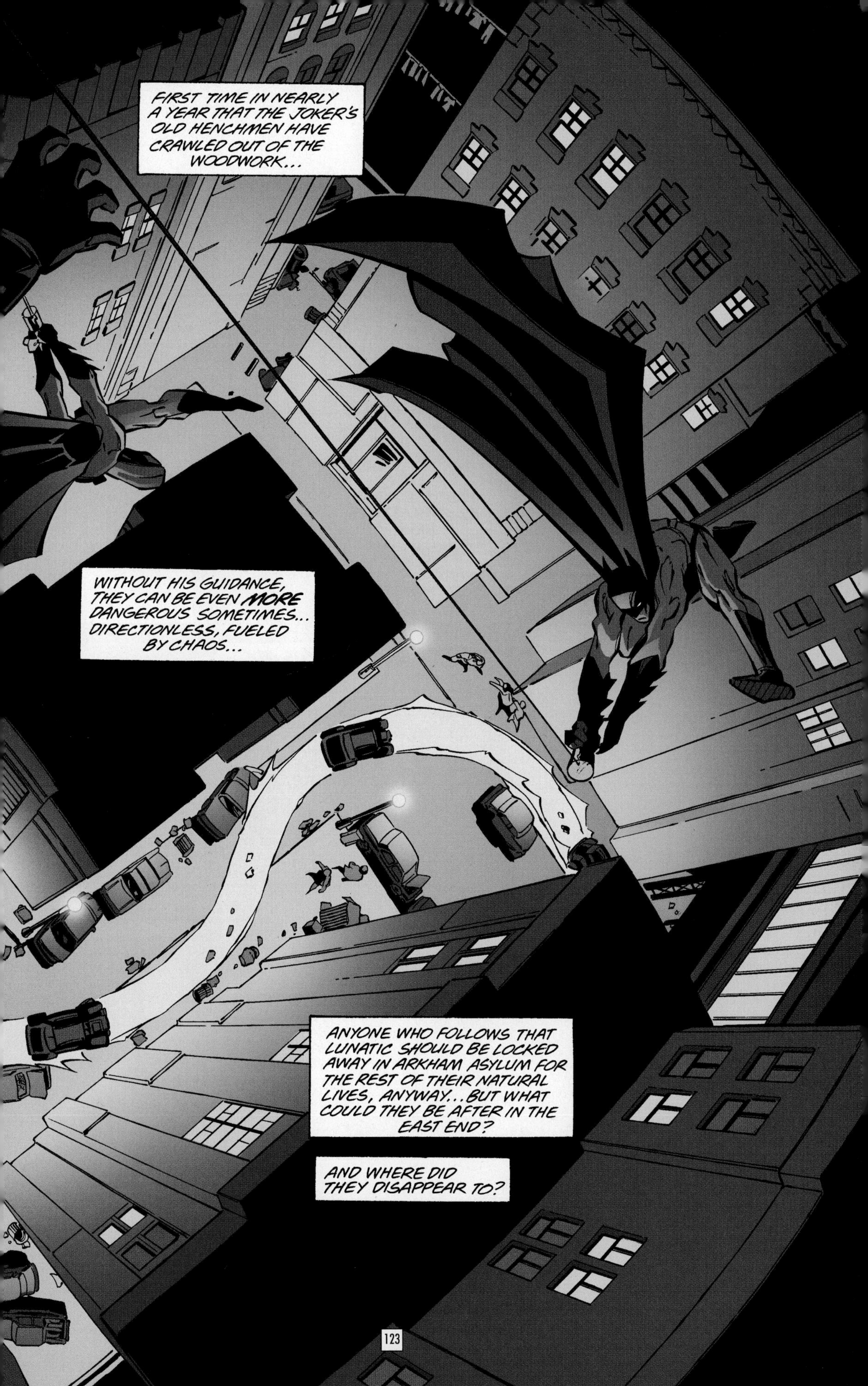
FIRST TIME IN NEARLY A YEAR THAT THE JOKER'S OLD HENCHMEN HAVE CRAWLED OUT OF THE WOODWORK...
WITHOUT HIS GUIDANCE, THEY CAN BE EVEN MORE DANGEROUS SOMETIMES... DIRECTIONLESS, FUELED BY CHAOS...
ANYONE WHO FOLLOWS THAT LUNATIC SHOULD BE LOCKED AWAY IN ARKHAM ASYLUM FOR THE REST OF THEIR NATURAL LIVES, ANYWAY... BUT WHAT COULD THEY BE AFTER IN THE EAST END?
AND WHERE DID THEY DISAPPEAR TO?

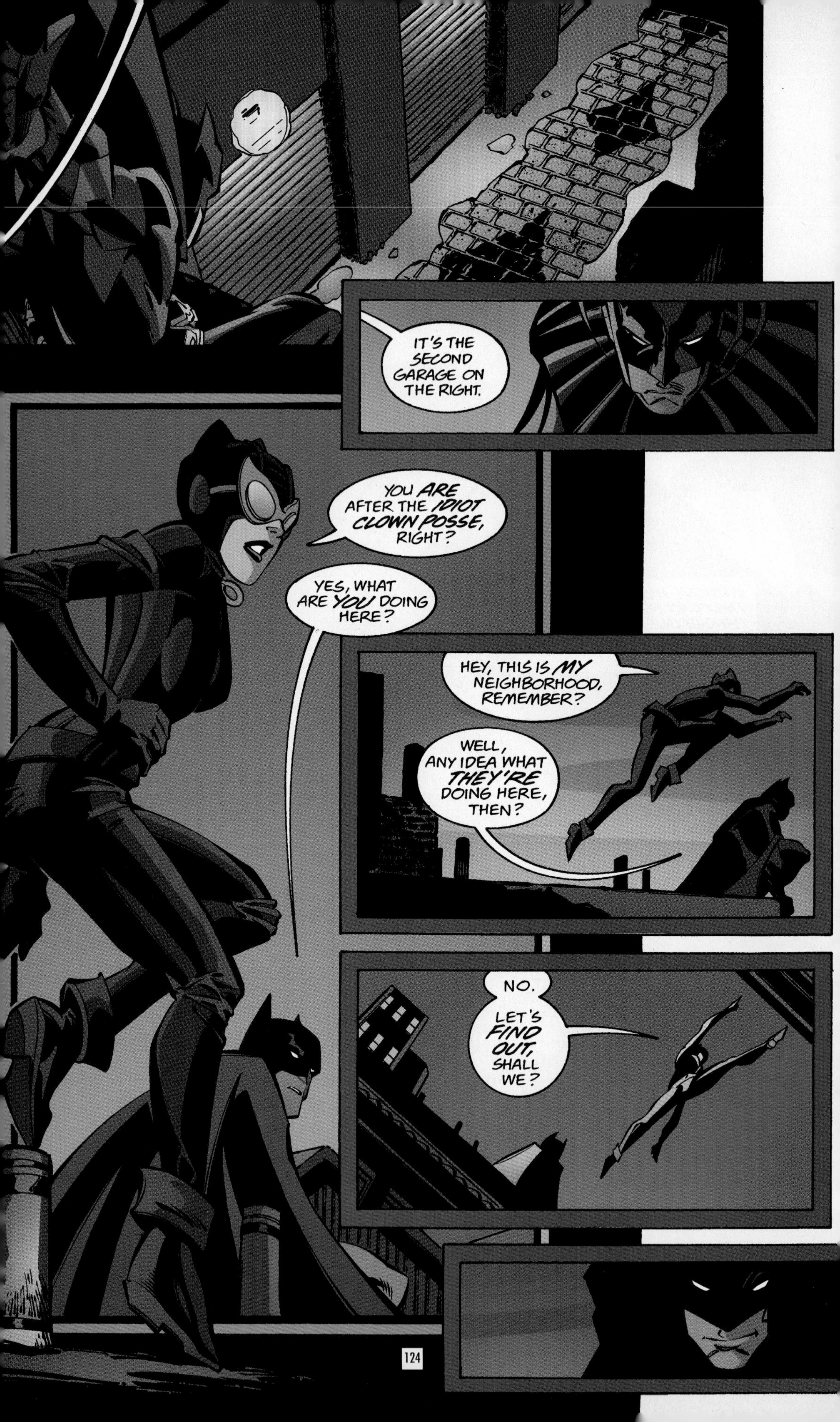

IT'S THE SECOND GARAGE ON THE RIGHT.
YOU ARE AFTER THE IDIOT CLOWN POSSE, RIGHT?
YES, WHAT ARE YOU DOING HERE?
HEY, THIS IS MY NEIGHBORHOOD, REMEMBER?
WELL, ANY IDEA WHAT THEY'RE DOING HERE, THEN?
NO.
LET'S FIND OUT, SHALL WE?

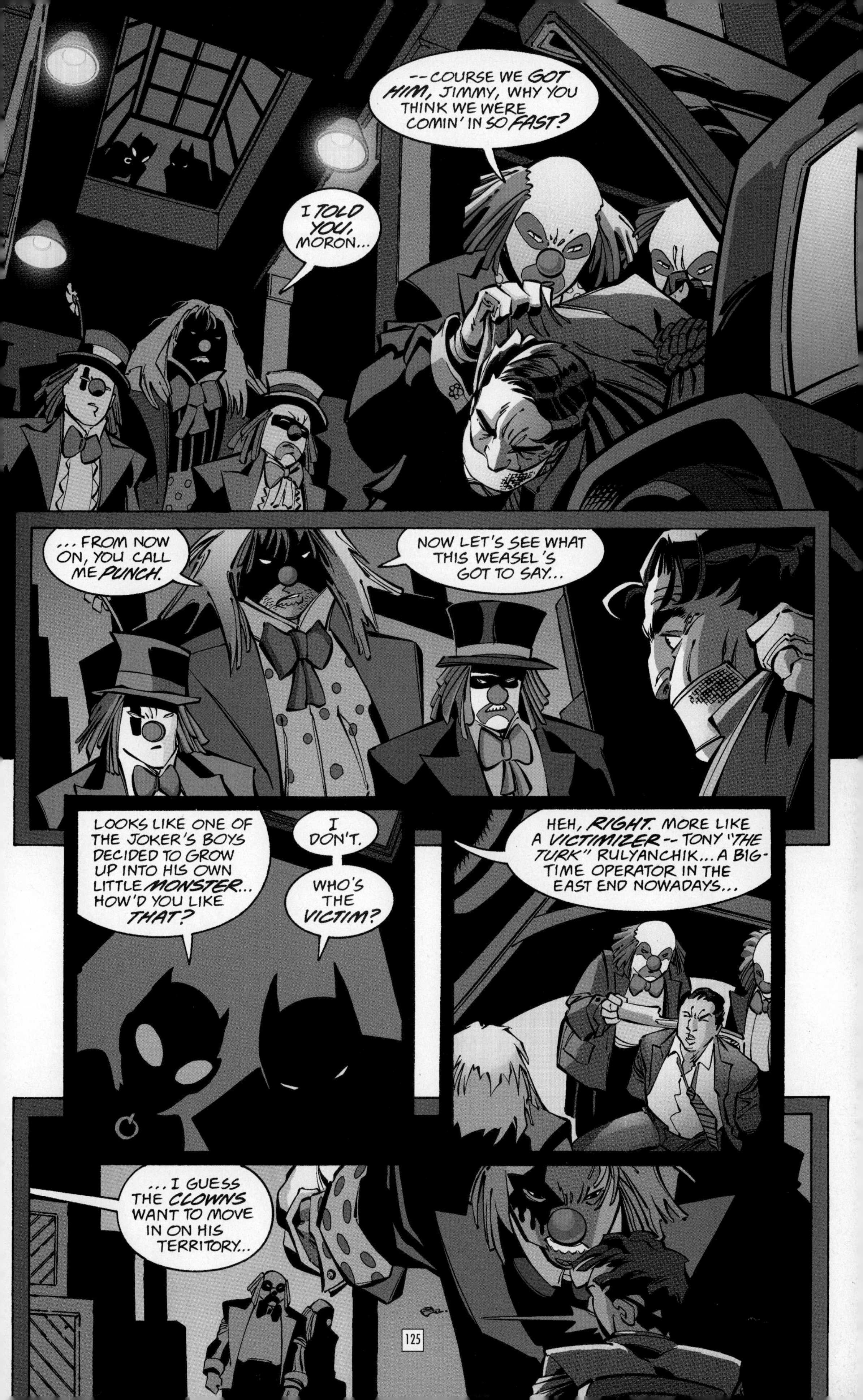

I TOLD YOU, MORON...
--COURSE WE GOT HIM, JIMMY, WHY YOU THINK WE WERE COMIN' IN SO FAST?
...FROM NOW ON, YOU CALL ME PUNCH.
NOW LET'S SEE WHAT THIS WEASEL'S GOT TO SAY...
LOOKS LIKE ONE OF THE JOKER'S BOYS DECIDED TO GROW UP INTO HIS OWN LITTLE MONSTER... HOW'D YOU LIKE THAT?
I DON'T.
WHO'S THE VICTIM?
HEH, RIGHT. MORE LIKE A VICTIMIZER -- TONY "THE TURK" RULYANCHIK... A BIG-TIME OPERATOR IN THE EAST END NOWADAYS...
...I GUESS THE CLOWNS WANT TO MOVE IN ON HIS TERRITORY...

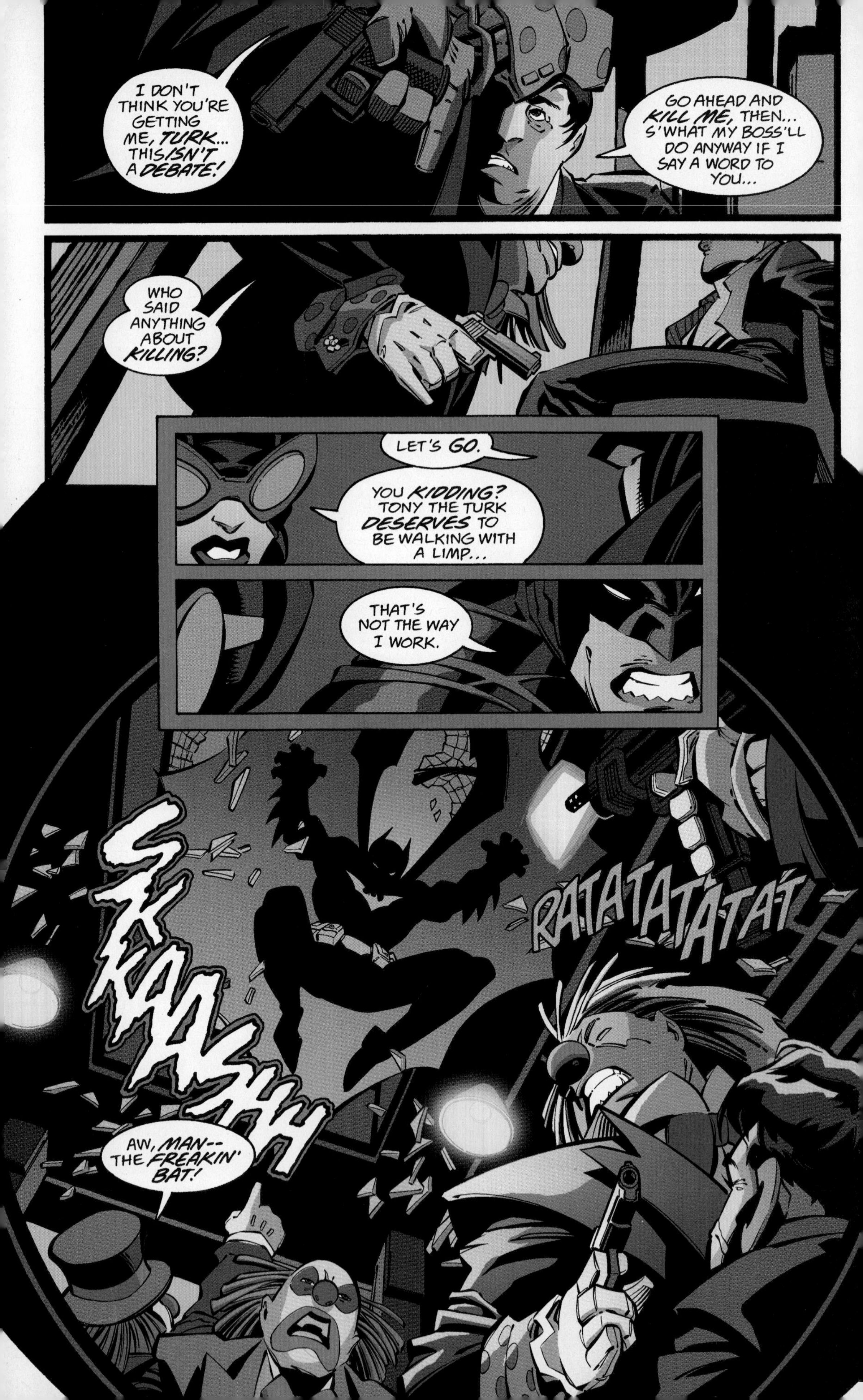
I DON'T THINK YOU'RE GETTING ME, TURK... THIS ISN'T A DEBATE!
GO AHEAD AND KILL ME, THEN... S'WHAT MY BOSS'LL DO ANYWAY IF I SAY A WORD TO YOU...
WHO SAID ANYTHING ABOUT KILLING?
LET'S GO.
YOU KIDDING? TONY THE TURK DESERVES TO BE WALKING WITH A LIMP...
THAT'S NOT THE WAY I WORK.
SKRASHH
RATATATATATAT
AW, MAN-- THE FREAKIN' BAT!

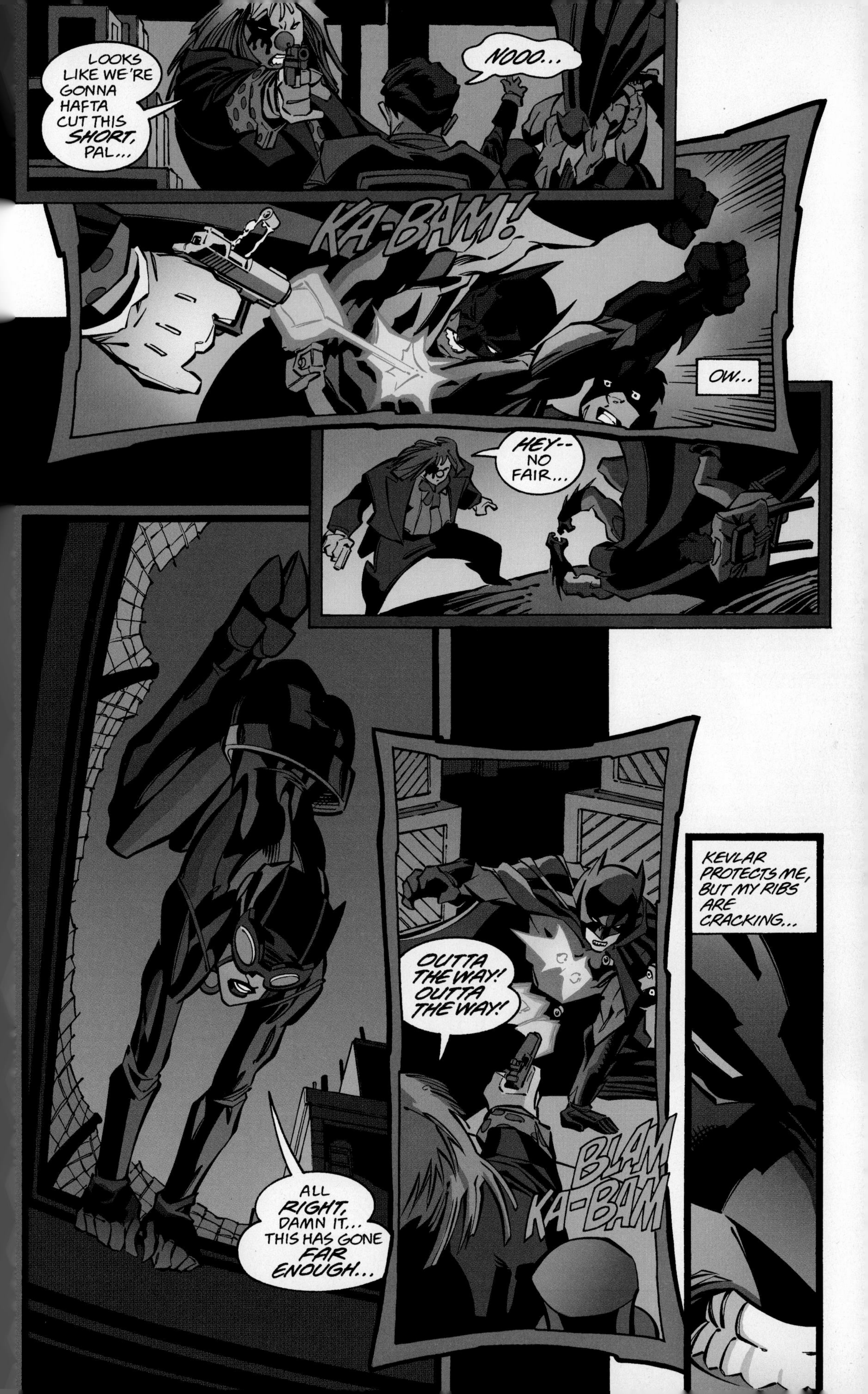

LOOKS LIKE WE'RE GONNA HAFTA CUT THIS SHORT, PAL...
NOOO...
KA-BAM!
OW...
HEY-- NO FAIR...
KEVLAR PROTECTS ME, BUT MY RIBS ARE CRACKING...
OUTTA THE WAY! OUTTA THE WAY!
BLAM KA-BAM
ALL RIGHT, DAMN IT... THIS HAS GONE FAR ENOUGH...

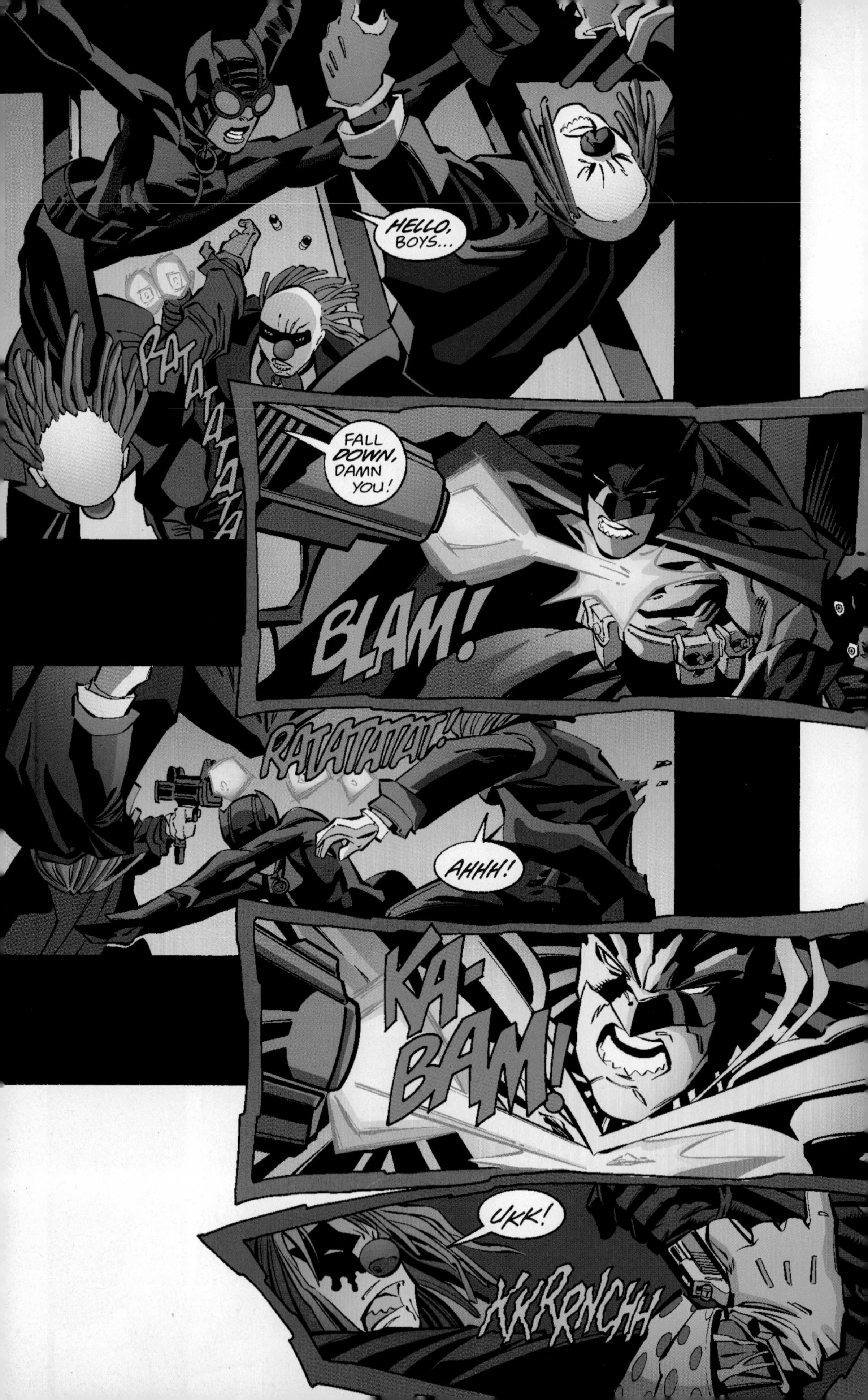

HELLO, BOYS...
RATATATATATA
FALL DOWN, DAMN YOU!
BLAM!
RATATATAT!
AHHH!
KA-BAM!
UKK!
KKRNCHH

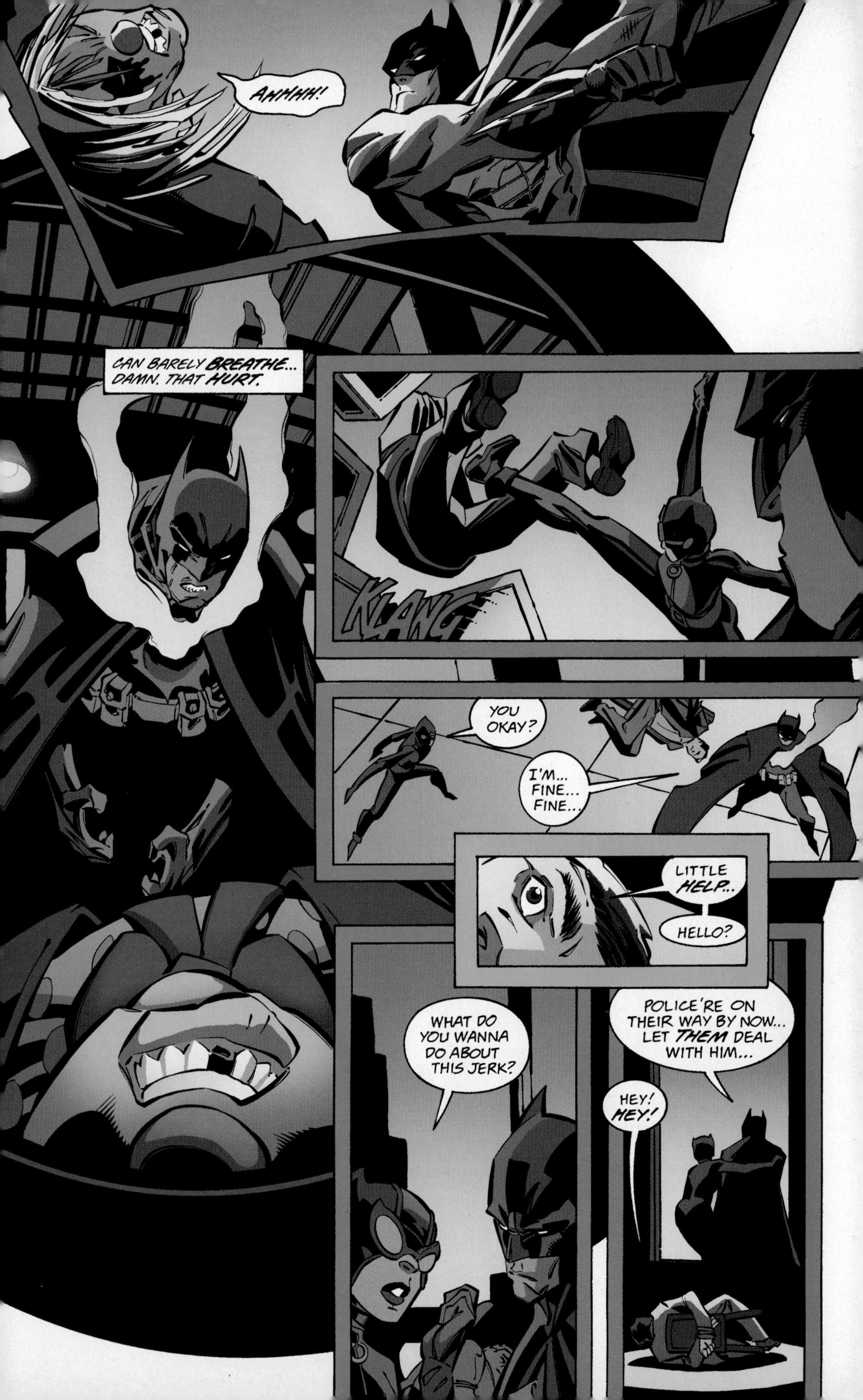

AHHHH!
CAN BARELY BREATHE... DAMN. THAT HURT.
KLANG
YOU OKAY?
I'M... FINE... FINE...
LITTLE HELP...
HELLO?
WHAT DO YOU WANNA DO ABOUT THIS JERK?
POLICE'RE ON THEIR WAY BY NOW... LET THEM DEAL WITH HIM...
HEY! HEY!

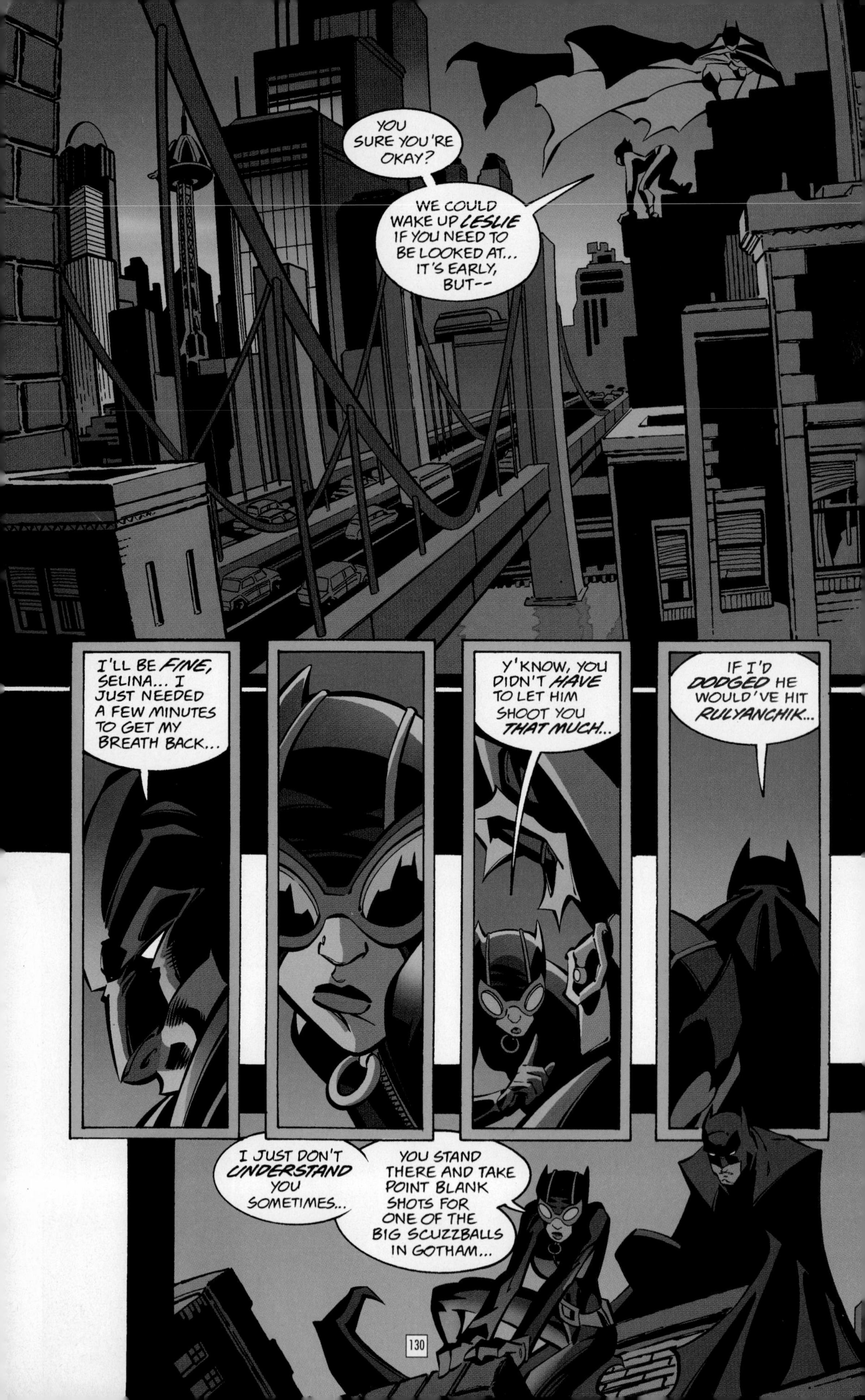
YOU SURE YOU'RE OKAY?
WE COULD WAKE UP LESLIE IF YOU NEED TO BE LOOKED AT... IT'S EARLY, BUT--
I'LL BE FINE, SELINA... I JUST NEEDED A FEW MINUTES TO GET MY BREATH BACK...
Y'KNOW, YOU DIDN'T HAVE TO LET HIM SHOOT YOU THAT MUCH...
IF I'D DODGED HE WOULD'VE HIT RULYANCHIK...
I JUST DON'T UNDERSTAND YOU SOMETIMES...
YOU STAND THERE AND TAKE POINT BLANK SHOTS FOR ONE OF THE BIG SCUZZBALLS IN GOTHAM...

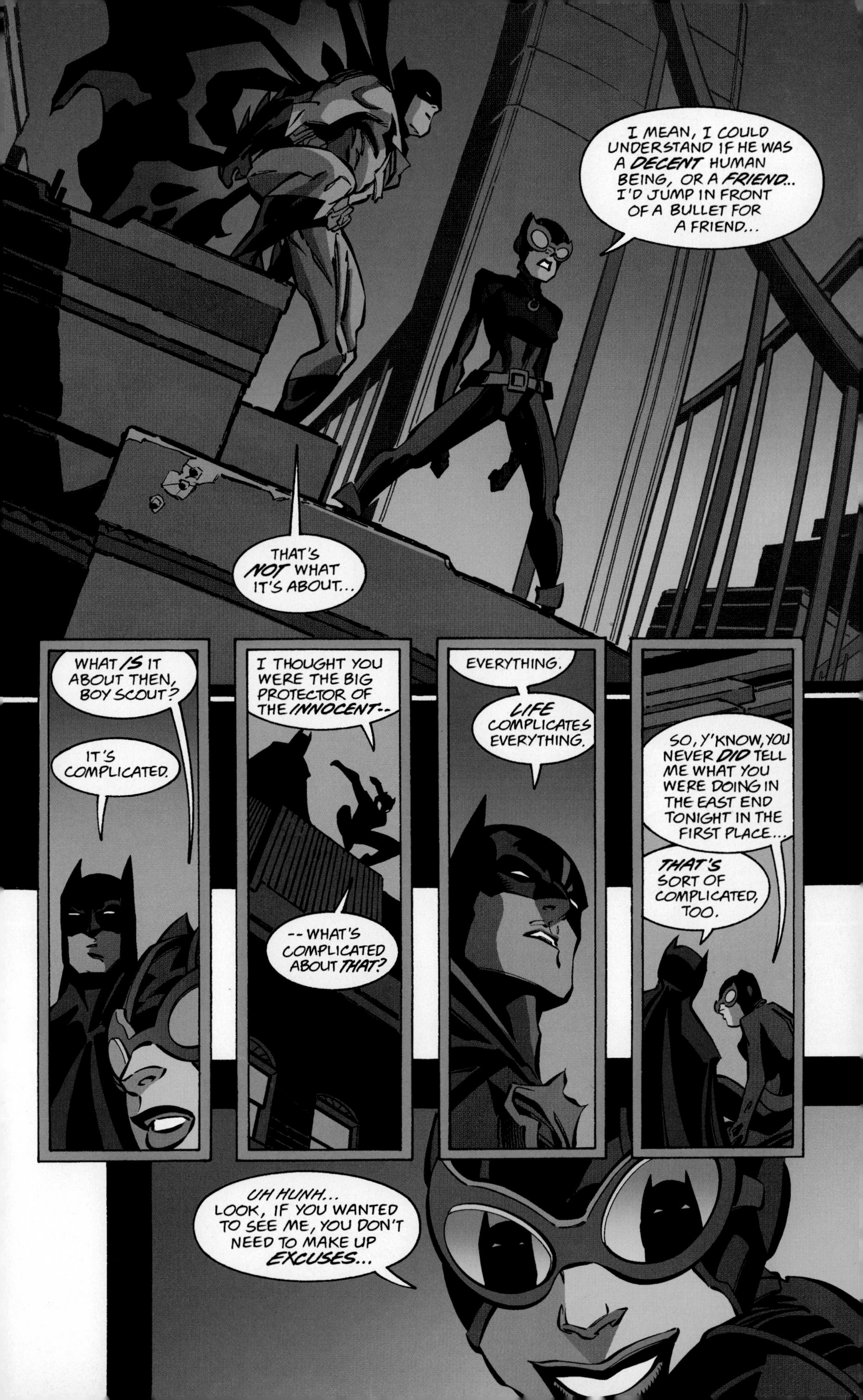
I MEAN, I COULD UNDERSTAND IF HE WAS A DECENT HUMAN BEING, OR A FRIEND... I'D JUMP IN FRONT OF A BULLET FOR A FRIEND...
THAT'S NOT WHAT IT'S ABOUT...
WHAT IS IT ABOUT THEN, BOY SCOUT?
IT'S COMPLICATED.
I THOUGHT YOU WERE THE BIG PROTECTOR OF THE INNOCENT--
--WHAT'S COMPLICATED ABOUT THAT?
EVERYTHING.
LIFE COMPLICATES EVERYTHING.
SO, Y'KNOW, YOU NEVER DID TELL ME WHAT YOU WERE DOING IN THE EAST END TONIGHT IN THE FIRST PLACE...
THAT'S SORT OF COMPLICATED, TOO.
UH HUNH... LOOK, IF YOU WANTED TO SEE ME, YOU DON'T NEED TO MAKE UP EXCUSES...

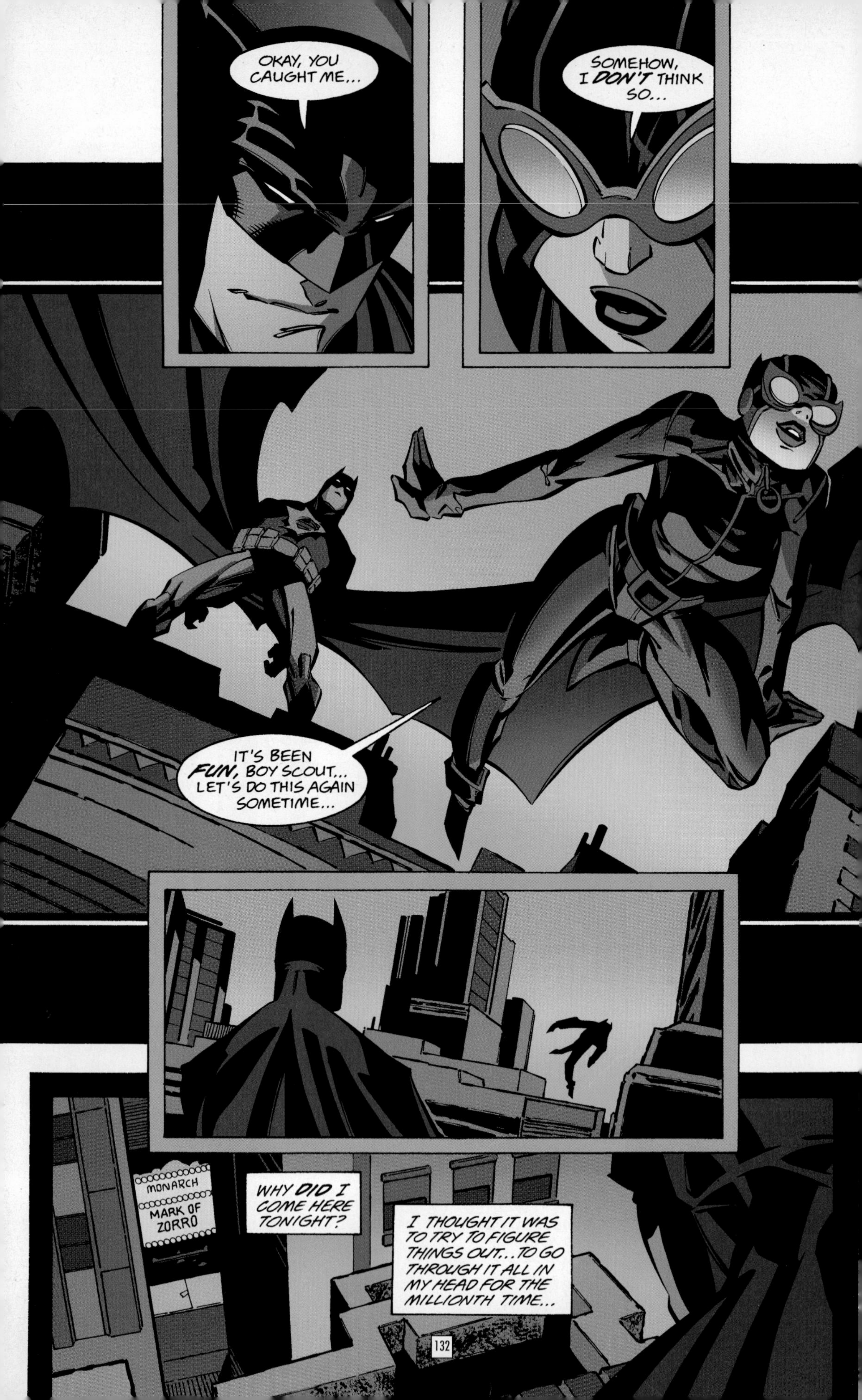
OKAY, YOU CAUGHT ME...
SOMEHOW, I DON'T THINK SO...
IT'S BEEN FUN, BOY SCOUT... LET'S DO THIS AGAIN SOMETIME...
MONARCH
MARK OF ZORRO
WHY DID I COME HERE TONIGHT?
I THOUGHT IT WAS TO TRY TO FIGURE THINGS OUT...TO GO THROUGH IT ALL IN MY HEAD FOR THE MILLIONTH TIME...

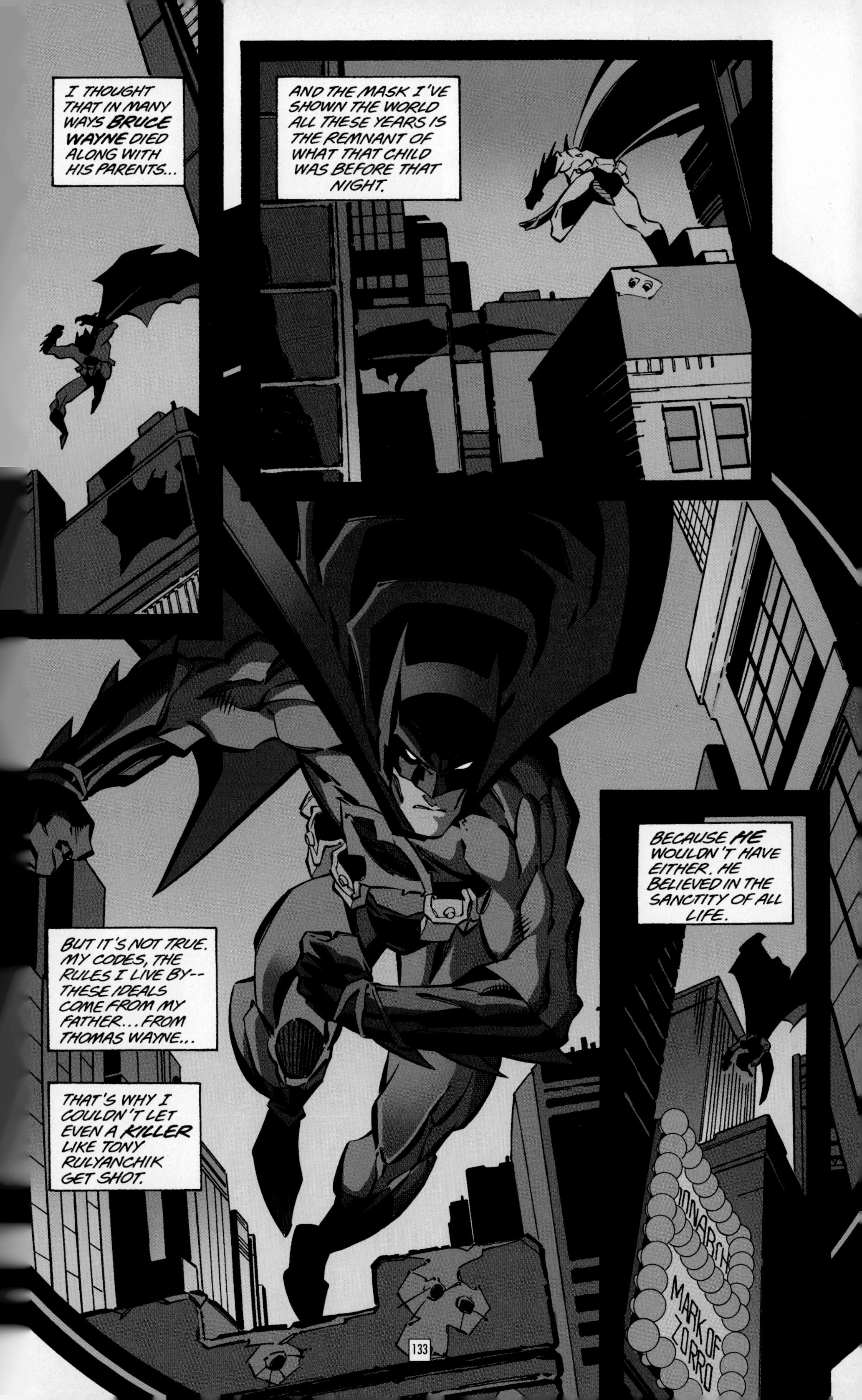
I THOUGHT THAT IN MANY WAYS BRUCE WAYNE DIED ALONG WITH HIS PARENTS...
AND THE MASK I'VE SHOWN THE WORLD ALL THESE YEARS IS THE REMNANT OF WHAT THAT CHILD WAS BEFORE THAT NIGHT.
BUT IT'S NOT TRUE. MY CODES, THE RULES I LIVE BY-- THESE IDEALS COME FROM MY FATHER...FROM THOMAS WAYNE...
THAT'S WHY I COULDN'T LET EVEN A KILLER LIKE TONY RULYANCHIK GET SHOT.
BECAUSE HE WOULDN'T HAVE EITHER. HE BELIEVED IN THE SANCTITY OF ALL LIFE.
MARK OF ZORRO

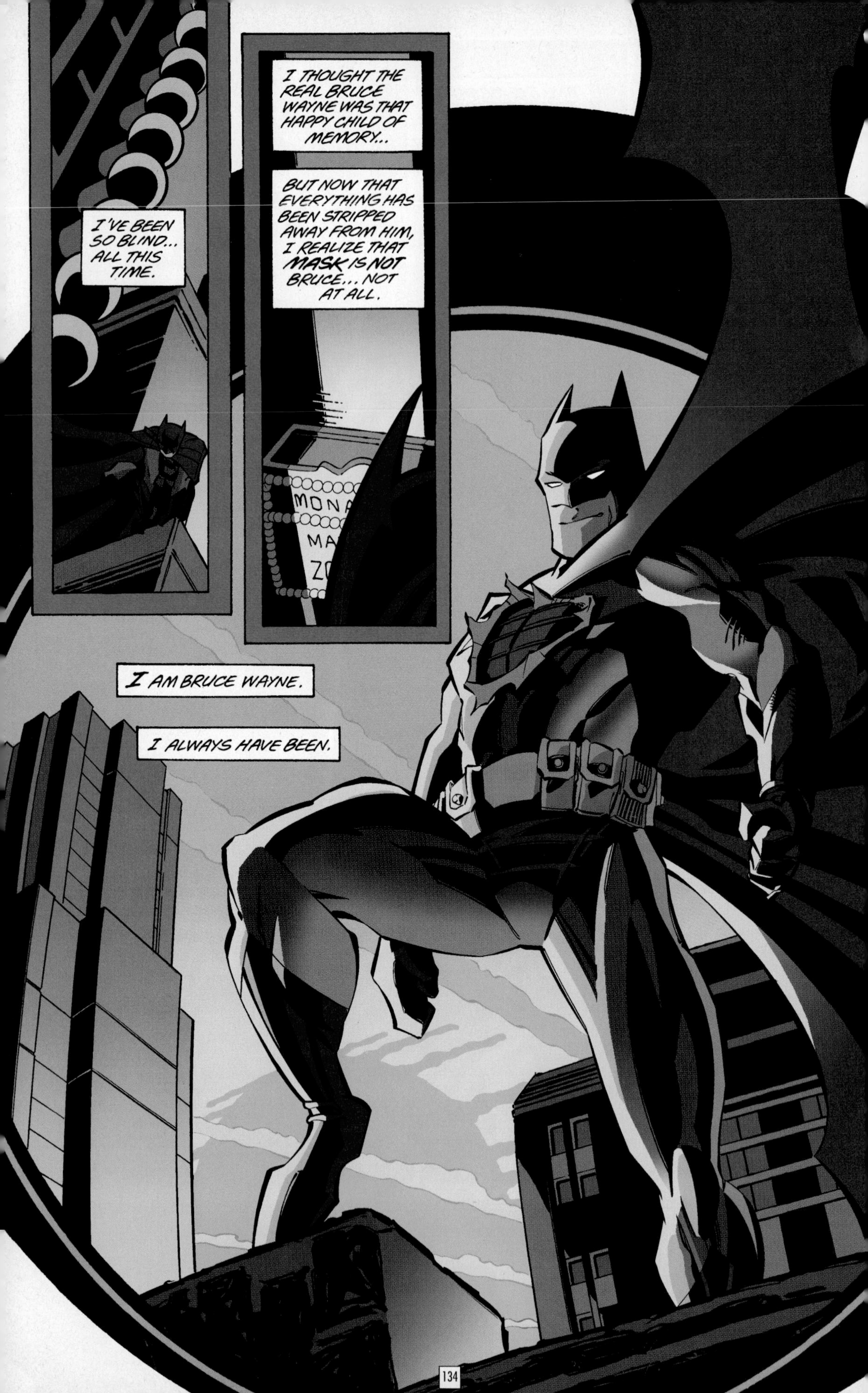
I'VE BEEN SO BLIND... ALL THIS TIME.
I THOUGHT THE REAL BRUCE WAYNE WAS THAT HAPPY CHILD OF MEMORY...
BUT NOW THAT EVERYTHING HAS BEEN STRIPPED AWAY FROM HIM, I REALIZE THAT MASK IS NOT BRUCE... NOT AT ALL.
I AM BRUCE WAYNE.
I ALWAYS HAVE BEEN.

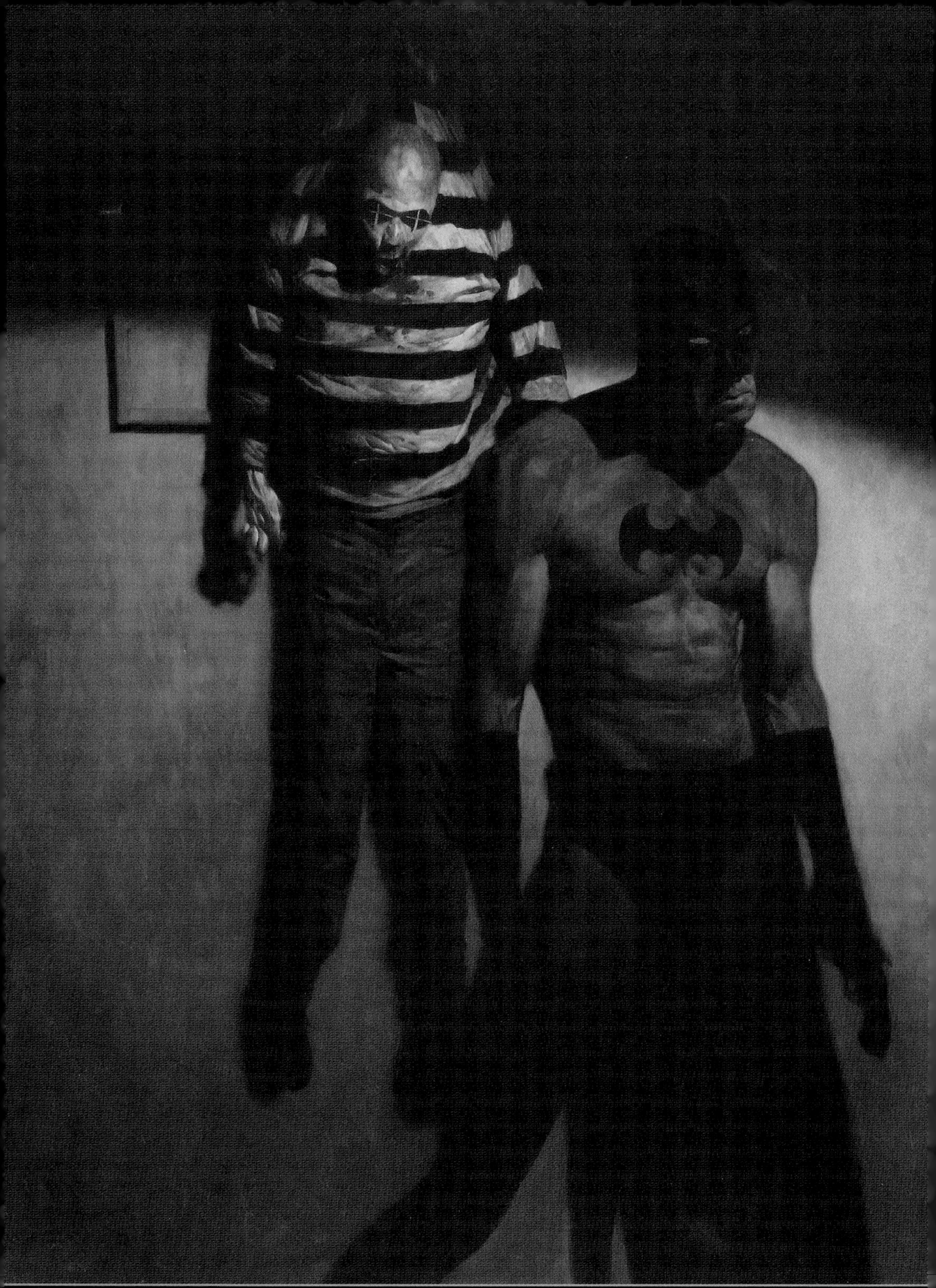

"Urban Legend"

BILL WILLINGHAM writer **TOM FOWLER** artist
JAMES SINCLAIR inker **KURT HATHAWAY** colorist **PHIL HALE** cover artist

From the pages of the showcase title, BATMAN: LEGENDS OF THE DARK KNIGHT, comes this harrowing tale of a badly beaten-up Batman who has no memory of how he came to be this way.

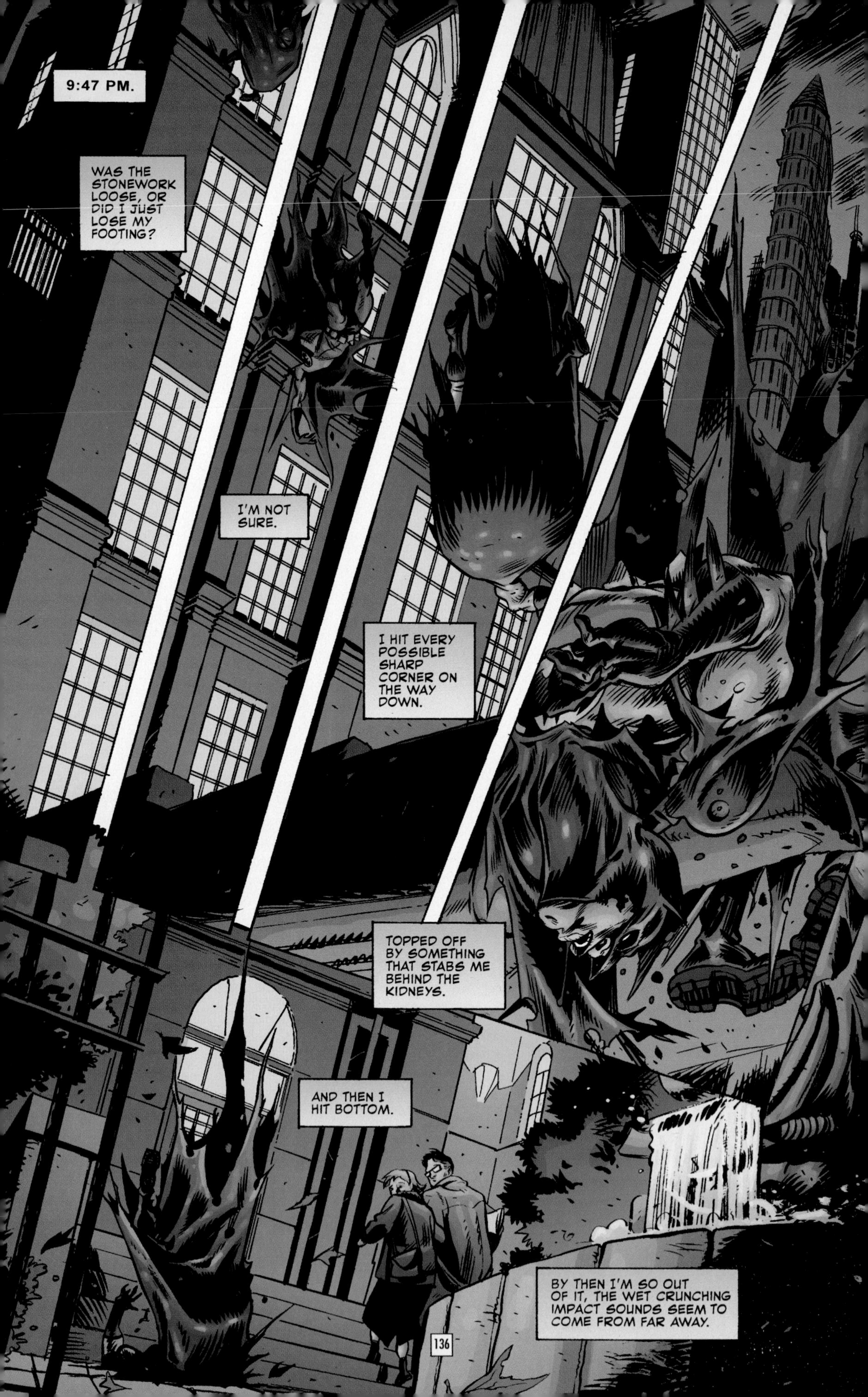
9:47 PM.
WAS THE STONEWORK LOOSE, OR DID I JUST LOSE MY FOOTING?
I'M NOT SURE.
I HIT EVERY POSSIBLE SHARP CORNER ON THE WAY DOWN.
TOPPED OFF BY SOMETHING THAT STABS ME BEHIND THE KIDNEYS.
AND THEN I HIT BOTTOM.
BY THEN I'M SO OUT OF IT, THE WET CRUNCHING IMPACT SOUNDS SEEM TO COME FROM FAR AWAY.

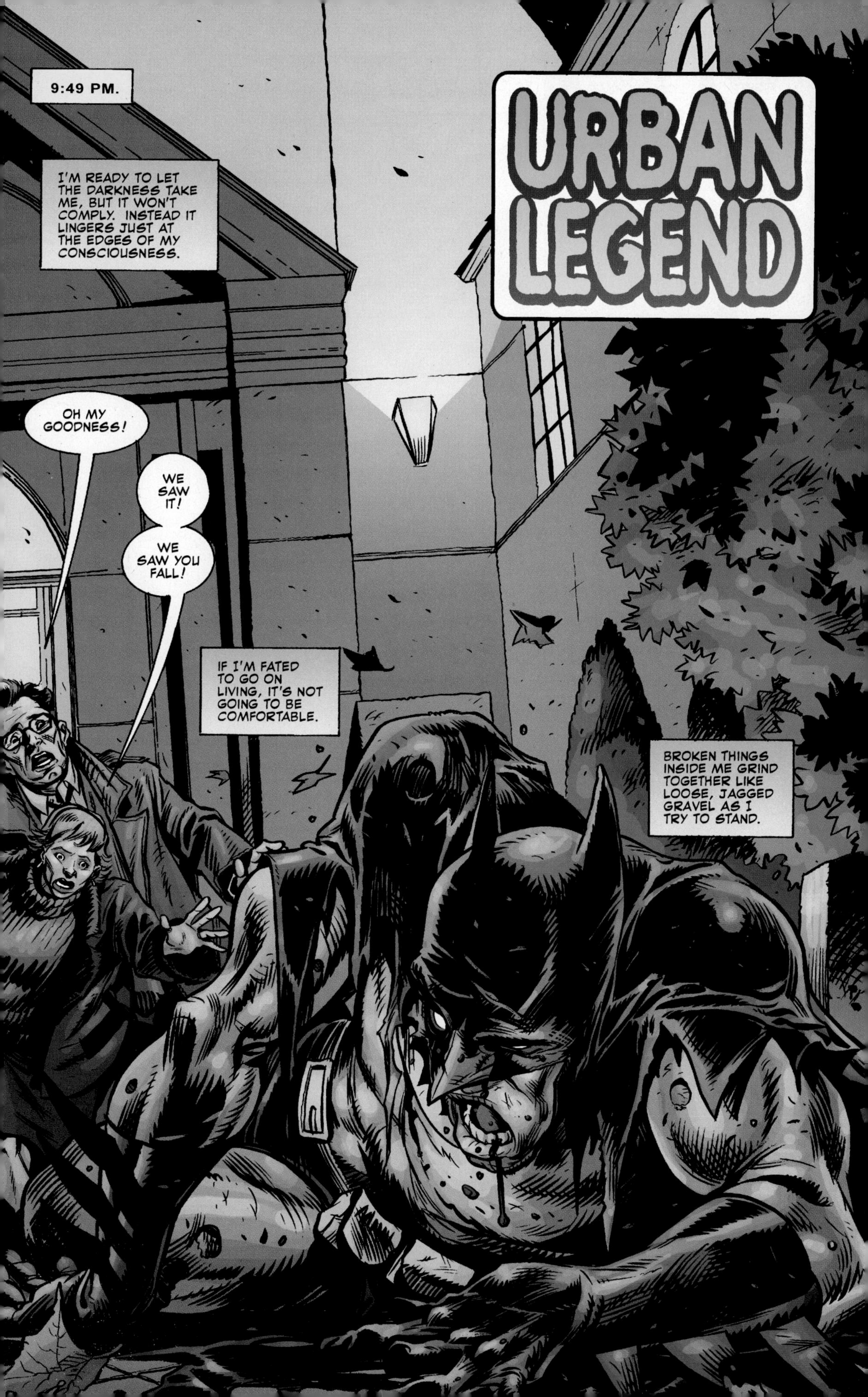
9:49 PM.
URBAN LEGEND
I'M READY TO LET THE DARKNESS TAKE ME, BUT IT WON'T COMPLY. INSTEAD IT LINGERS JUST AT THE EDGES OF MY CONSCIOUSNESS.
OH MY GOODNESS!
WE SAW IT!
WE SAW YOU FALL!
IF I'M FATED TO GO ON LIVING, IT'S NOT GOING TO BE COMFORTABLE.
BROKEN THINGS INSIDE ME GRIND TOGETHER LIKE LOOSE, JAGGED GRAVEL AS I TRY TO STAND.

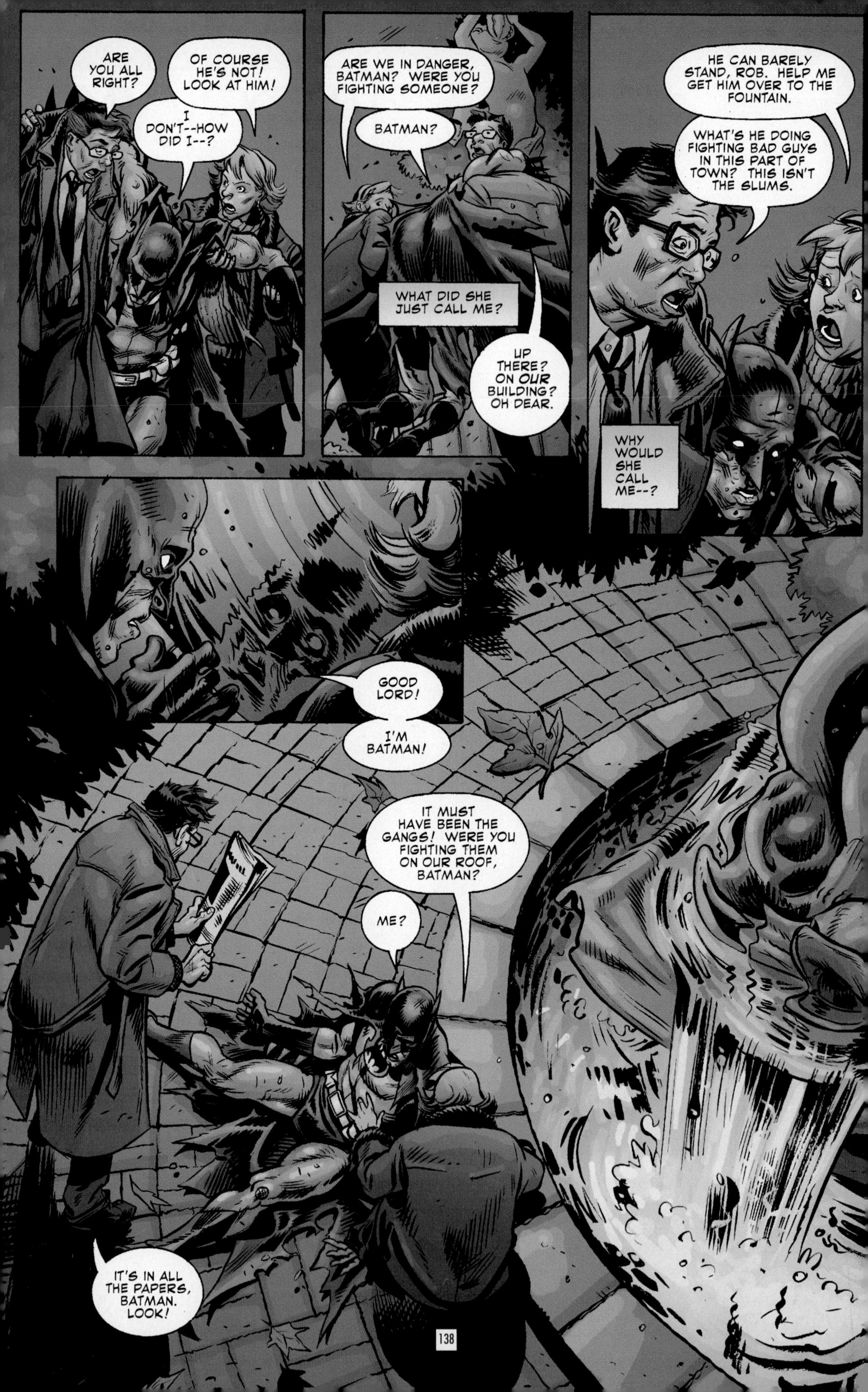
ARE YOU ALL RIGHT?
OF COURSE HE'S NOT! LOOK AT HIM!
I DON'T--HOW DID I--?
ARE WE IN DANGER, BATMAN? WERE YOU FIGHTING SOMEONE?
BATMAN?
WHAT DID SHE JUST CALL ME?
UP THERE? ON OUR BUILDING? OH DEAR.
HE CAN BARELY STAND, ROB. HELP ME GET HIM OVER TO THE FOUNTAIN.
WHAT'S HE DOING FIGHTING BAD GUYS IN THIS PART OF TOWN? THIS ISN'T THE SLUMS.
WHY WOULD SHE CALL ME--?
GOOD LORD!
I'M BATMAN!
IT MUST HAVE BEEN THE GANGS! WERE YOU FIGHTING THEM ON OUR ROOF, BATMAN?
ME?
IT'S IN ALL THE PAPERS, BATMAN. LOOK!

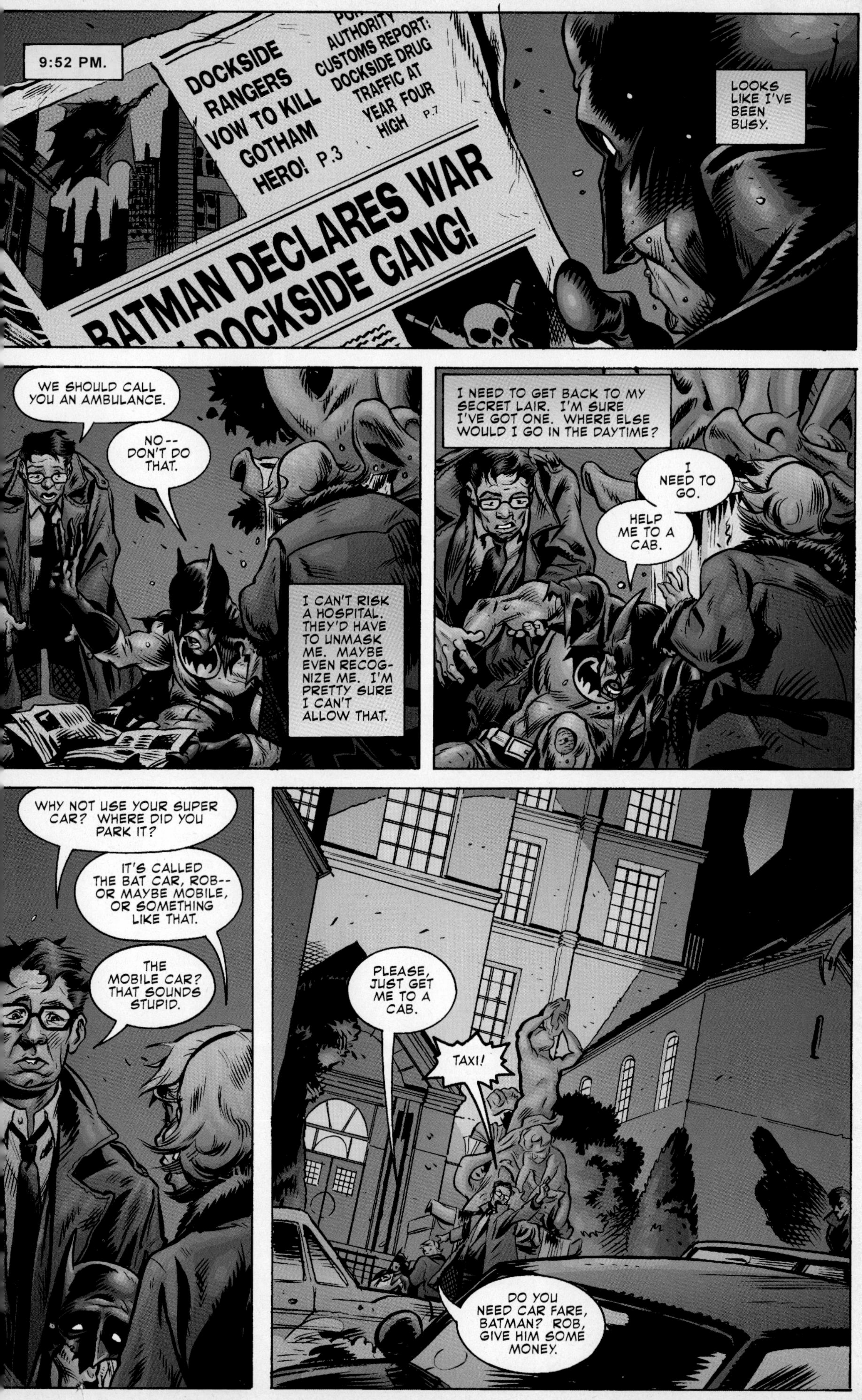
9:52 PM.
DOCKSIDE RANGERS VOW TO KILL GOTHAM HERO! P.3
PORT AUTHORITY CUSTOMS REPORT: DOCKSIDE DRUG TRAFFIC AT YEAR FOUR HIGH P.7
BATMAN DECLARES WAR ON DOCKSIDE GANG!
LOOKS LIKE I'VE BEEN BUSY.
WE SHOULD CALL YOU AN AMBULANCE.
NO-- DON'T DO THAT.
I CAN'T RISK A HOSPITAL. THEY'D HAVE TO UNMASK ME. MAYBE EVEN RECOGNIZE ME. I'M PRETTY SURE I CAN'T ALLOW THAT.
I NEED TO GET BACK TO MY SECRET LAIR. I'M SURE I'VE GOT ONE. WHERE ELSE WOULD I GO IN THE DAYTIME?
I NEED TO GO.
HELP ME TO A CAB.
WHY NOT USE YOUR SUPER CAR? WHERE DID YOU PARK IT?
IT'S CALLED THE BAT CAR, ROB-- OR MAYBE MOBILE, OR SOMETHING LIKE THAT.
THE MOBILE CAR? THAT SOUNDS STUPID.
PLEASE, JUST GET ME TO A CAB.
TAXI!
DO YOU NEED CAR FARE, BATMAN? ROB, GIVE HIM SOME MONEY.

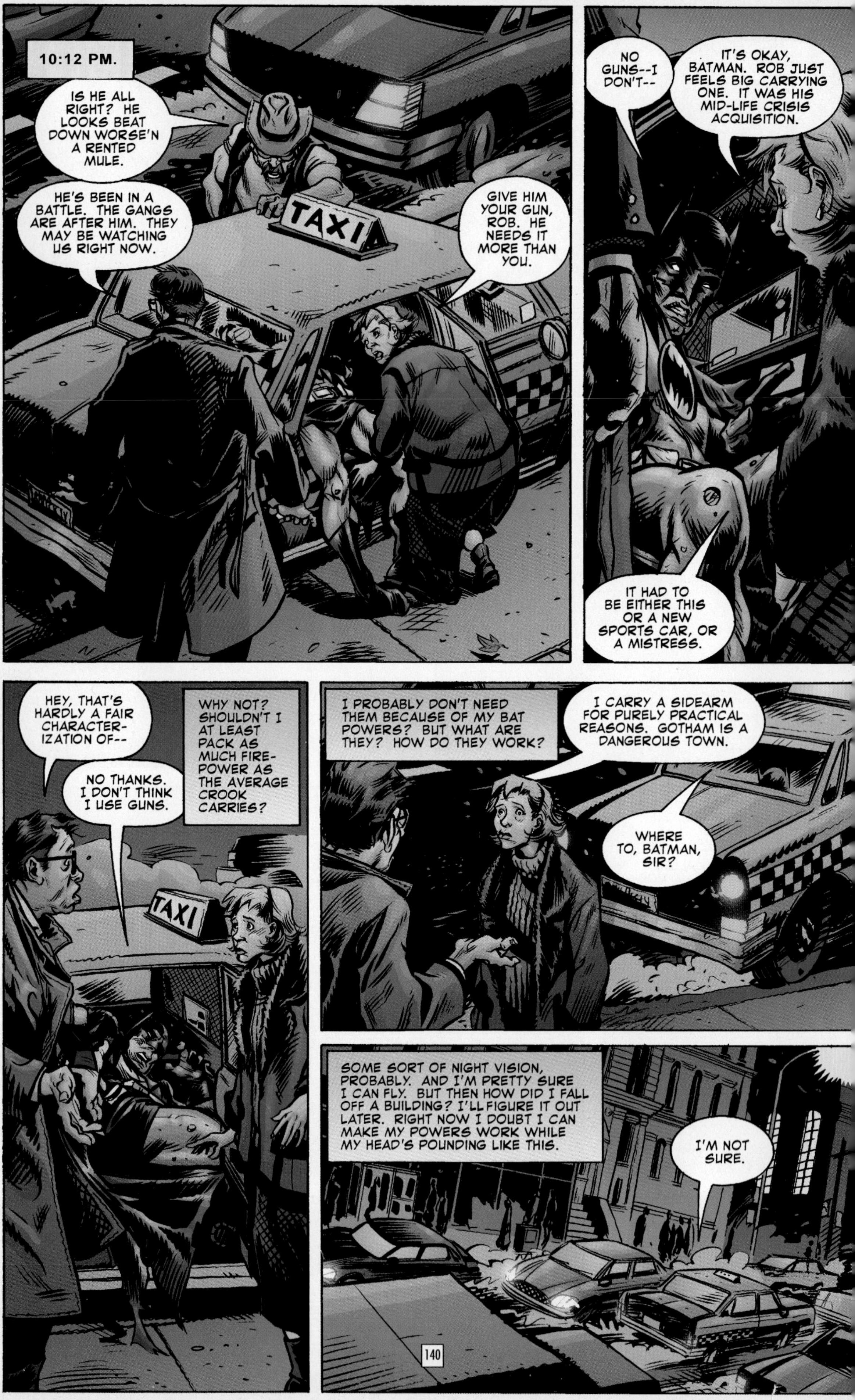
10:12 PM.
IS HE ALL RIGHT? HE LOOKS BEAT DOWN WORSE'N A RENTED MULE.
HE'S BEEN IN A BATTLE. THE GANGS ARE AFTER HIM. THEY MAY BE WATCHING US RIGHT NOW.
TAXI
GIVE HIM YOUR GUN, ROB. HE NEEDS IT MORE THAN YOU.
NO GUNS--I DON'T--
IT'S OKAY, BATMAN. ROB JUST FEELS BIG CARRYING ONE. IT WAS HIS MID-LIFE CRISIS ACQUISITION.
IT HAD TO BE EITHER THIS OR A NEW SPORTS CAR, OR A MISTRESS.
HEY, THAT'S HARDLY A FAIR CHARACTER-IZATION OF--
NO THANKS. I DON'T THINK I USE GUNS.
WHY NOT? SHOULDN'T I AT LEAST PACK AS MUCH FIRE-POWER AS THE AVERAGE CROOK CARRIES?
TAXI
I PROBABLY DON'T NEED THEM BECAUSE OF MY BAT POWERS? BUT WHAT ARE THEY? HOW DO THEY WORK?
I CARRY A SIDEARM FOR PURELY PRACTICAL REASONS. GOTHAM IS A DANGEROUS TOWN.
WHERE TO, BATMAN, SIR?
SOME SORT OF NIGHT VISION, PROBABLY. AND I'M PRETTY SURE I CAN FLY. BUT THEN HOW DID I FALL OFF A BUILDING? I'LL FIGURE IT OUT LATER. RIGHT NOW I DOUBT I CAN MAKE MY POWERS WORK WHILE MY HEAD'S POUNDING LIKE THIS.
I'M NOT SURE.

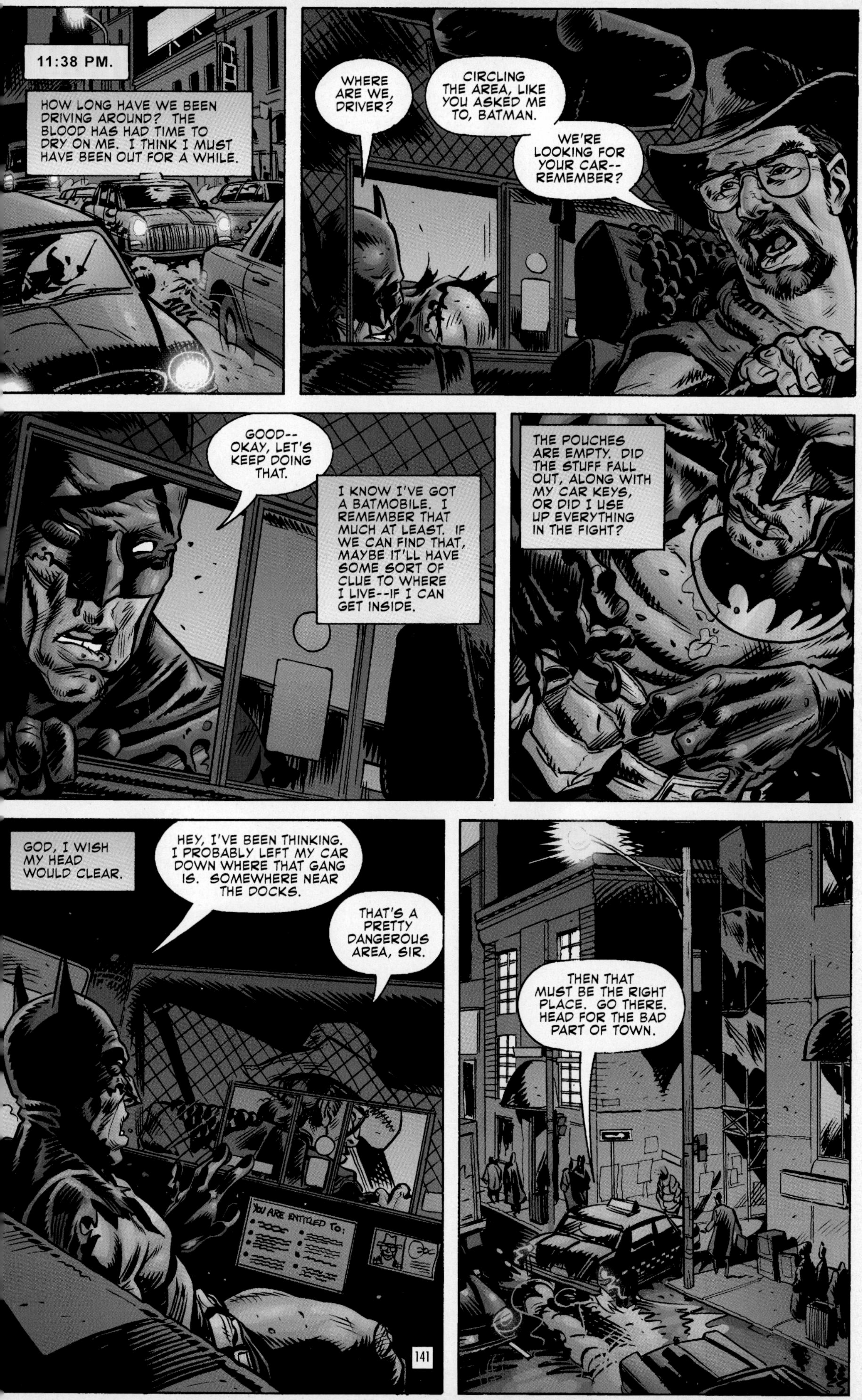

11:38 PM.
HOW LONG HAVE WE BEEN DRIVING AROUND? THE BLOOD HAS HAD TIME TO DRY ON ME. I THINK I MUST HAVE BEEN OUT FOR A WHILE.
WHERE ARE WE, DRIVER?
CIRCLING THE AREA, LIKE YOU ASKED ME TO, BATMAN.
WE'RE LOOKING FOR YOUR CAR-- REMEMBER?
GOOD-- OKAY, LET'S KEEP DOING THAT.
I KNOW I'VE GOT A BATMOBILE. I REMEMBER THAT MUCH AT LEAST. IF WE CAN FIND THAT, MAYBE IT'LL HAVE SOME SORT OF CLUE TO WHERE I LIVE--IF I CAN GET INSIDE.
THE POUCHES ARE EMPTY. DID THE STUFF FALL OUT, ALONG WITH MY CAR KEYS, OR DID I USE UP EVERYTHING IN THE FIGHT?
GOD, I WISH MY HEAD WOULD CLEAR.
HEY, I'VE BEEN THINKING. I PROBABLY LEFT MY CAR DOWN WHERE THAT GANG IS. SOMEWHERE NEAR THE DOCKS.
THAT'S A PRETTY DANGEROUS AREA, SIR.
YOU ARE ENTITLED TO:
THEN THAT MUST BE THE RIGHT PLACE. GO THERE. HEAD FOR THE BAD PART OF TOWN.

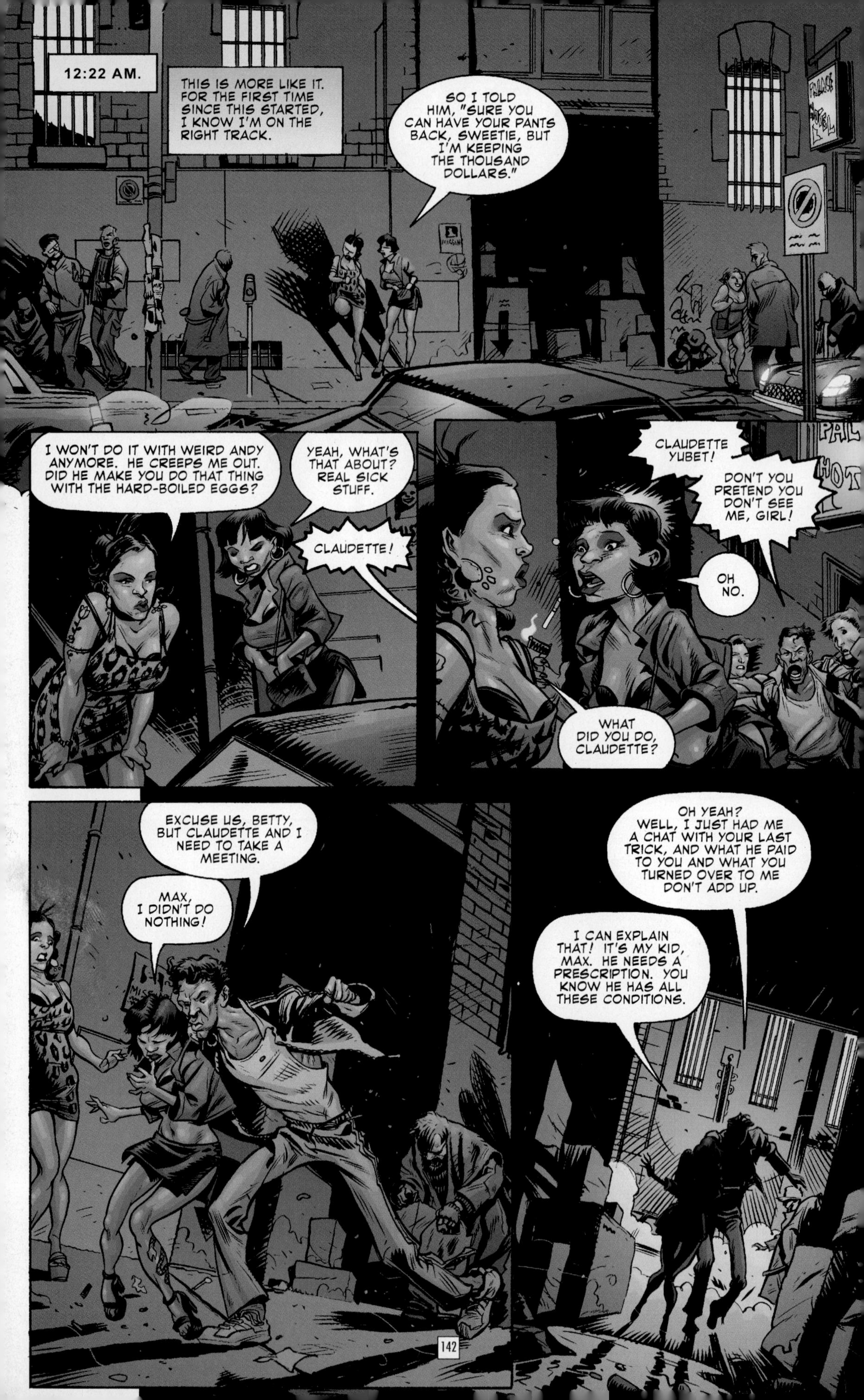
12:22 AM.
THIS IS MORE LIKE IT. FOR THE FIRST TIME SINCE THIS STARTED, I KNOW I'M ON THE RIGHT TRACK.
SO I TOLD HIM, "SURE YOU CAN HAVE YOUR PANTS BACK, SWEETIE, BUT I'M KEEPING THE THOUSAND DOLLARS."
I WON'T DO IT WITH WEIRD ANDY ANYMORE. HE CREEPS ME OUT. DID HE MAKE YOU DO THAT THING WITH THE HARD-BOILED EGGS?
YEAH, WHAT'S THAT ABOUT? REAL SICK STUFF.
CLAUDETTE!
CLAUDETTE YUBET!
DON'T YOU PRETEND YOU DON'T SEE ME, GIRL!
OH NO.
WHAT DID YOU DO, CLAUDETTE?
EXCUSE US, BETTY, BUT CLAUDETTE AND I NEED TO TAKE A MEETING.
MAX, I DIDN'T DO NOTHING!
OH YEAH? WELL, I JUST HAD ME A CHAT WITH YOUR LAST TRICK, AND WHAT HE PAID TO YOU AND WHAT YOU TURNED OVER TO ME DON'T ADD UP.
I CAN EXPLAIN THAT! IT'S MY KID, MAX. HE NEEDS A PRESCRIPTION. YOU KNOW HE HAS ALL THESE CONDITIONS.

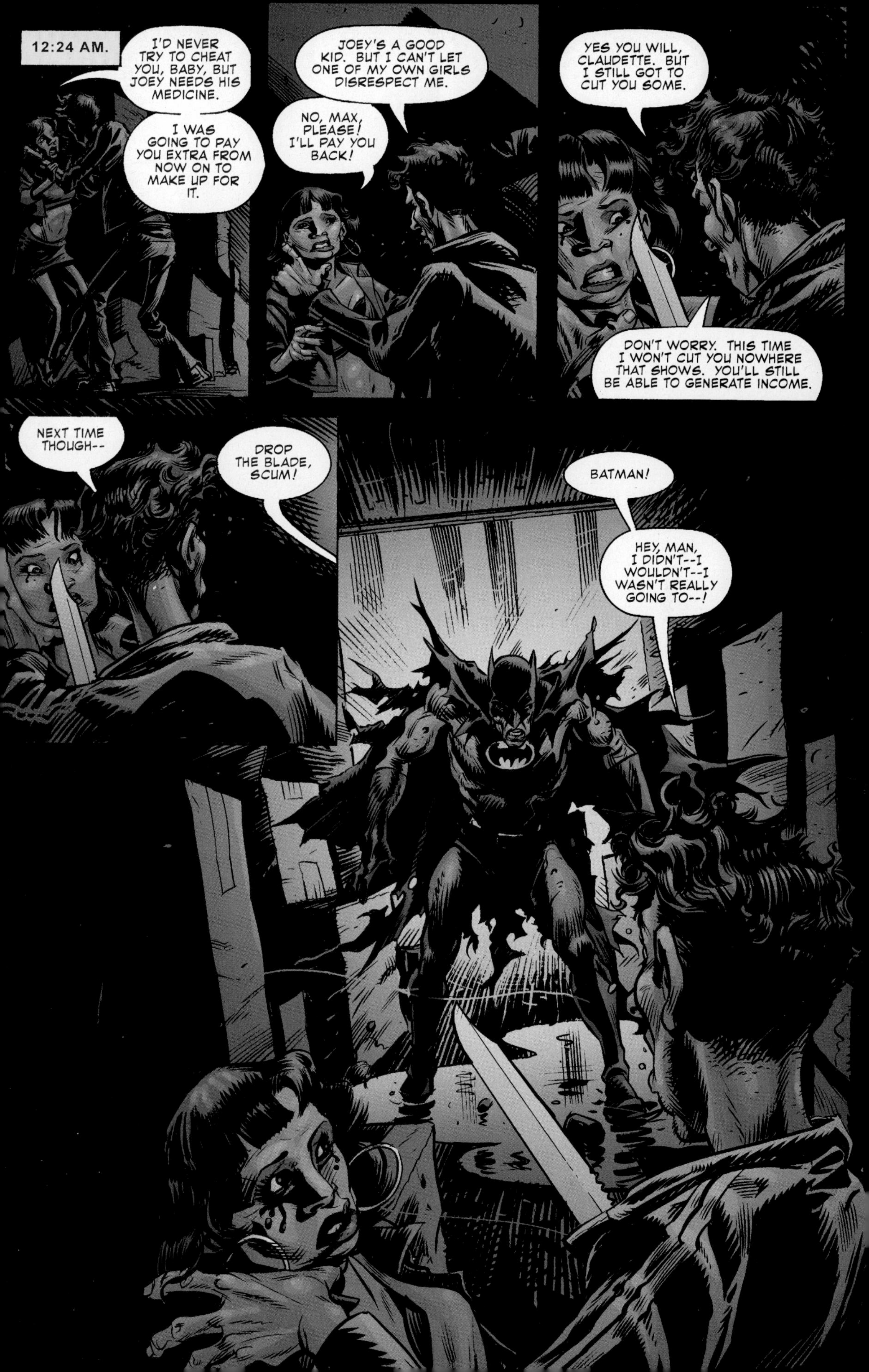
12:24 AM.
I'D NEVER TRY TO CHEAT YOU, BABY, BUT JOEY NEEDS HIS MEDICINE.
I WAS GOING TO PAY YOU EXTRA FROM NOW ON TO MAKE UP FOR IT.
JOEY'S A GOOD KID. BUT I CAN'T LET ONE OF MY OWN GIRLS DISRESPECT ME.
NO, MAX, PLEASE! I'LL PAY YOU BACK!
YES YOU WILL, CLAUDETTE. BUT I STILL GOT TO CUT YOU SOME.
DON'T WORRY. THIS TIME I WON'T CUT YOU NOWHERE THAT SHOWS. YOU'LL STILL BE ABLE TO GENERATE INCOME.
NEXT TIME THOUGH--
DROP THE BLADE, SCUM!
BATMAN!
HEY, MAN, I DIDN'T--I WOULDN'T--I WASN'T REALLY GOING TO--!

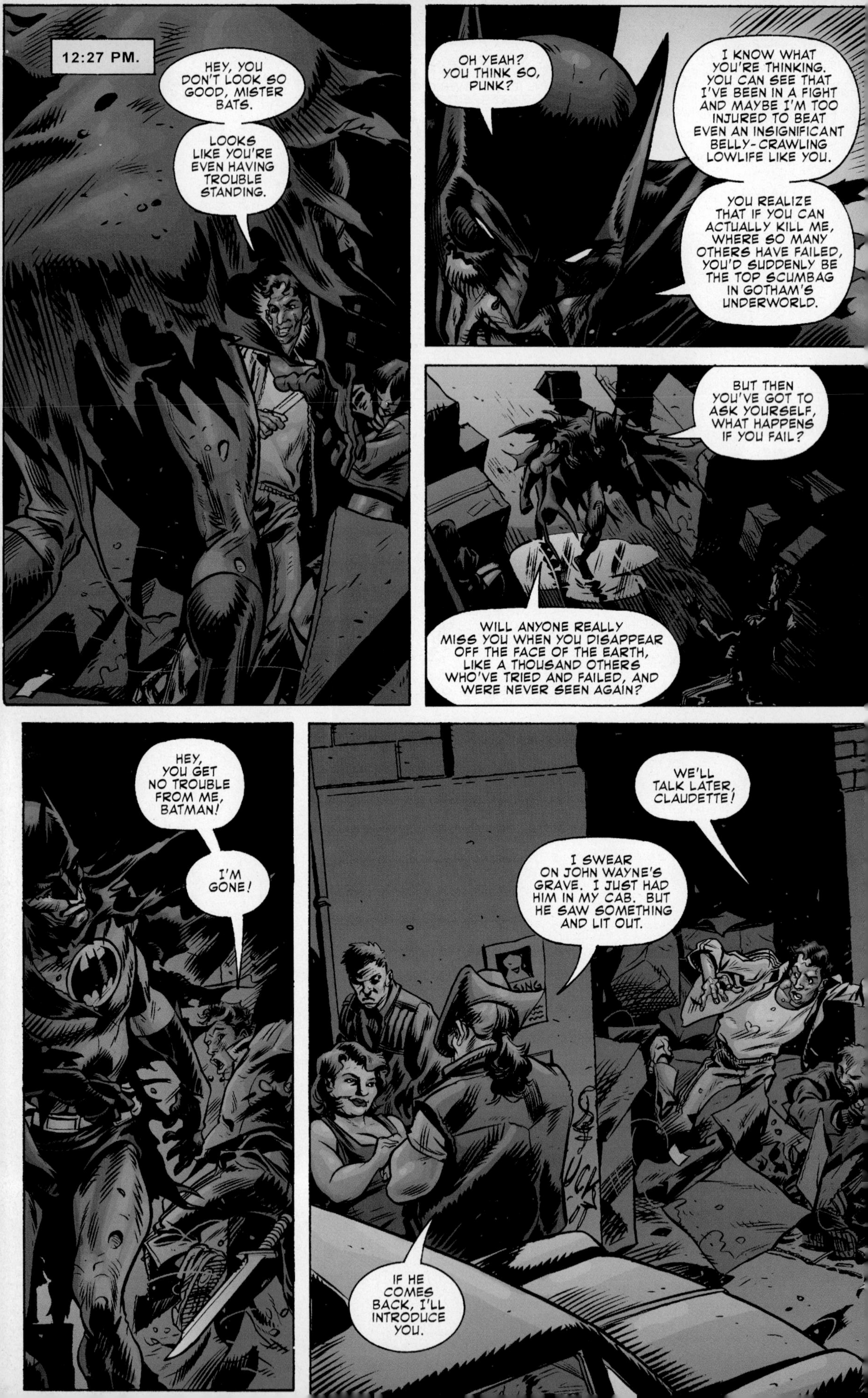
12:27 PM.
HEY, YOU DON'T LOOK SO GOOD, MISTER BATS.
LOOKS LIKE YOU'RE EVEN HAVING TROUBLE STANDING.
OH YEAH? YOU THINK SO, PUNK?
I KNOW WHAT YOU'RE THINKING. YOU CAN SEE THAT I'VE BEEN IN A FIGHT AND MAYBE I'M TOO INJURED TO BEAT EVEN AN INSIGNIFICANT BELLY-CRAWLING LOWLIFE LIKE YOU.
YOU REALIZE THAT IF YOU CAN ACTUALLY KILL ME, WHERE SO MANY OTHERS HAVE FAILED, YOU'D SUDDENLY BE THE TOP SCUMBAG IN GOTHAM'S UNDERWORLD.
BUT THEN YOU'VE GOT TO ASK YOURSELF, WHAT HAPPENS IF YOU FAIL?
WILL ANYONE REALLY MISS YOU WHEN YOU DISAPPEAR OFF THE FACE OF THE EARTH, LIKE A THOUSAND OTHERS WHO'VE TRIED AND FAILED, AND WERE NEVER SEEN AGAIN?
HEY, YOU GET NO TROUBLE FROM ME, BATMAN!
I'M GONE!
WE'LL TALK LATER, CLAUDETTE!
I SWEAR ON JOHN WAYNE'S GRAVE. I JUST HAD HIM IN MY CAB. BUT HE SAW SOMETHING AND LIT OUT.
IF HE COMES BACK, I'LL INTRODUCE YOU.

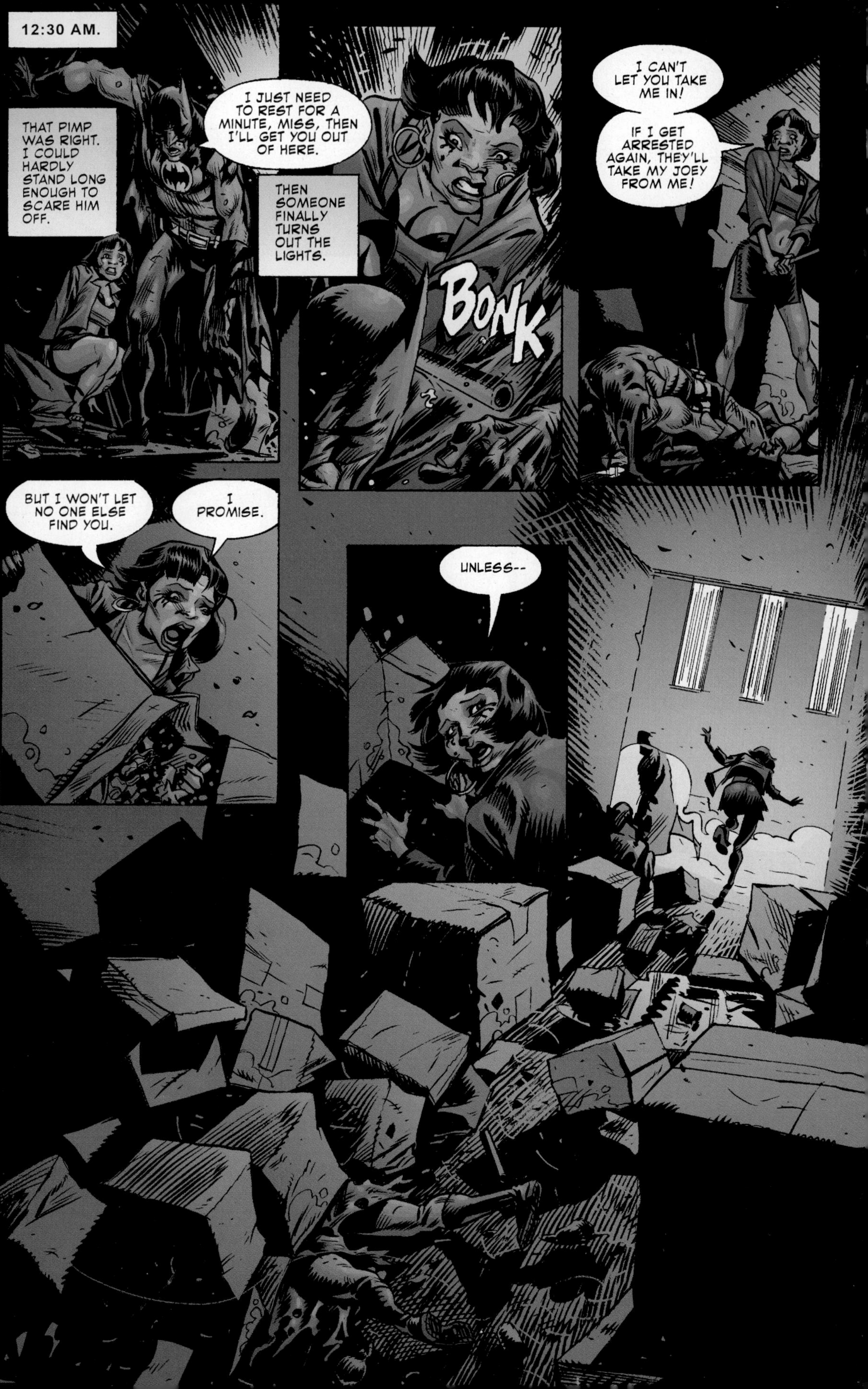
12:30 AM.
THAT PIMP WAS RIGHT. I COULD HARDLY STAND LONG ENOUGH TO SCARE HIM OFF.
I JUST NEED TO REST FOR A MINUTE, MISS, THEN I'LL GET YOU OUT OF HERE.
THEN SOMEONE FINALLY TURNS OUT THE LIGHTS.
BONK
I CAN'T LET YOU TAKE ME IN!
IF I GET ARRESTED AGAIN, THEY'LL TAKE MY JOEY FROM ME!
BUT I WON'T LET NO ONE ELSE FIND YOU.
I PROMISE.
UNLESS--

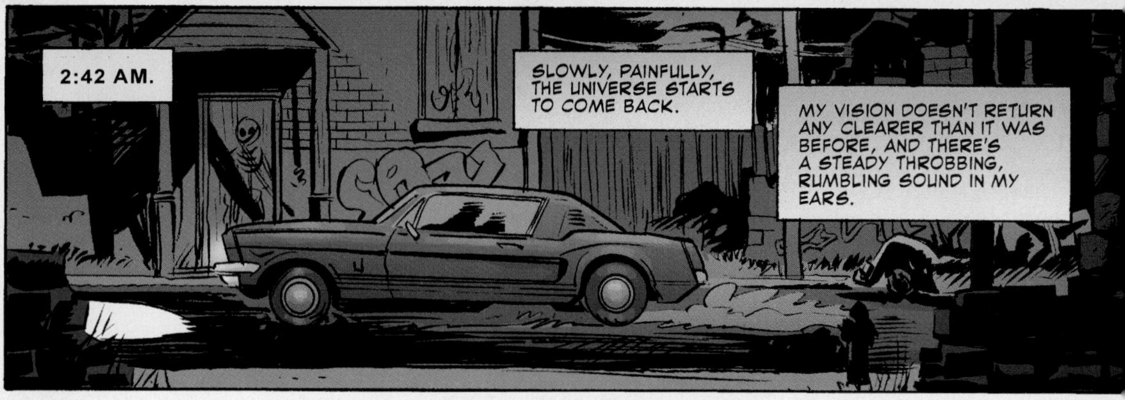
2:42 AM.
SLOWLY, PAINFULLY, THE UNIVERSE STARTS TO COME BACK.
MY VISION DOESN'T RETURN ANY CLEARER THAN IT WAS BEFORE, AND THERE'S A STEADY THROBBING, RUMBLING SOUND IN MY EARS.

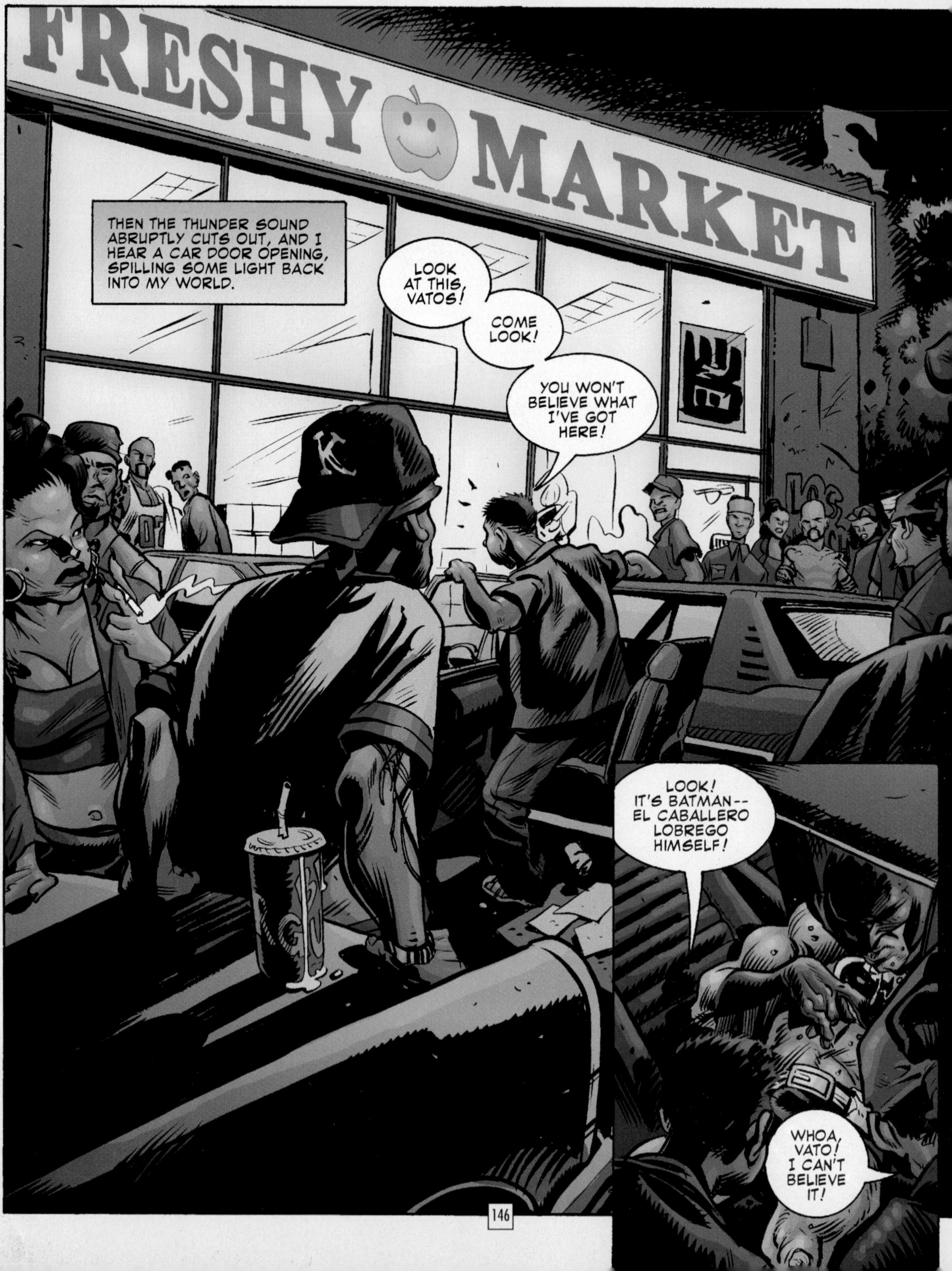
FRESHY MARKET
THEN THE THUNDER SOUND ABRUPTLY CUTS OUT, AND I HEAR A CAR DOOR OPENING, SPILLING SOME LIGHT BACK INTO MY WORLD.
LOOK AT THIS, VATOS!
COME LOOK!
YOU WON'T BELIEVE WHAT I'VE GOT HERE!
LOOK! IT'S BATMAN-- EL CABALLERO LOBREGO HIMSELF!
WHOA, VATO! I CAN'T BELIEVE IT!

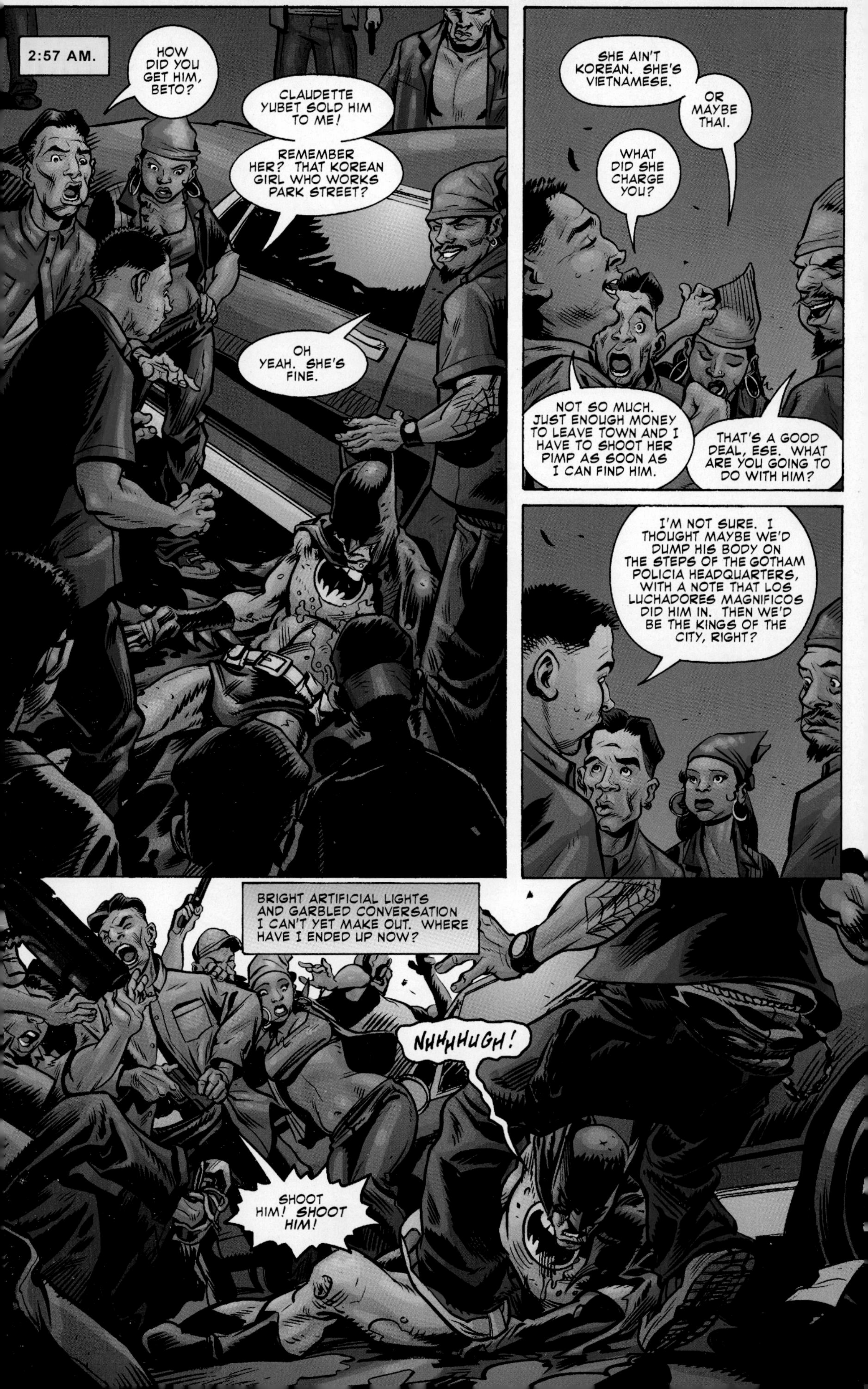
2:57 AM.
HOW DID YOU GET HIM, BETO?
CLAUDETTE YUBET SOLD HIM TO ME!
REMEMBER HER? THAT KOREAN GIRL WHO WORKS PARK STREET?
OH YEAH. SHE'S FINE.
SHE AIN'T KOREAN. SHE'S VIETNAMESE.
OR MAYBE THAI.
WHAT DID SHE CHARGE YOU?
NOT SO MUCH. JUST ENOUGH MONEY TO LEAVE TOWN AND I HAVE TO SHOOT HER PIMP AS SOON AS I CAN FIND HIM.
THAT'S A GOOD DEAL, ESE. WHAT ARE YOU GOING TO DO WITH HIM?
I'M NOT SURE. I THOUGHT MAYBE WE'D DUMP HIS BODY ON THE STEPS OF THE GOTHAM POLICIA HEADQUARTERS, WITH A NOTE THAT LOS LUCHADORES MAGNIFICOS DID HIM IN. THEN WE'D BE THE KINGS OF THE CITY, RIGHT?
BRIGHT ARTIFICIAL LIGHTS AND GARBLED CONVERSATION I CAN'T YET MAKE OUT. WHERE HAVE I ENDED UP NOW?
NHHHHUGH!
SHOOT HIM! SHOOT HIM!

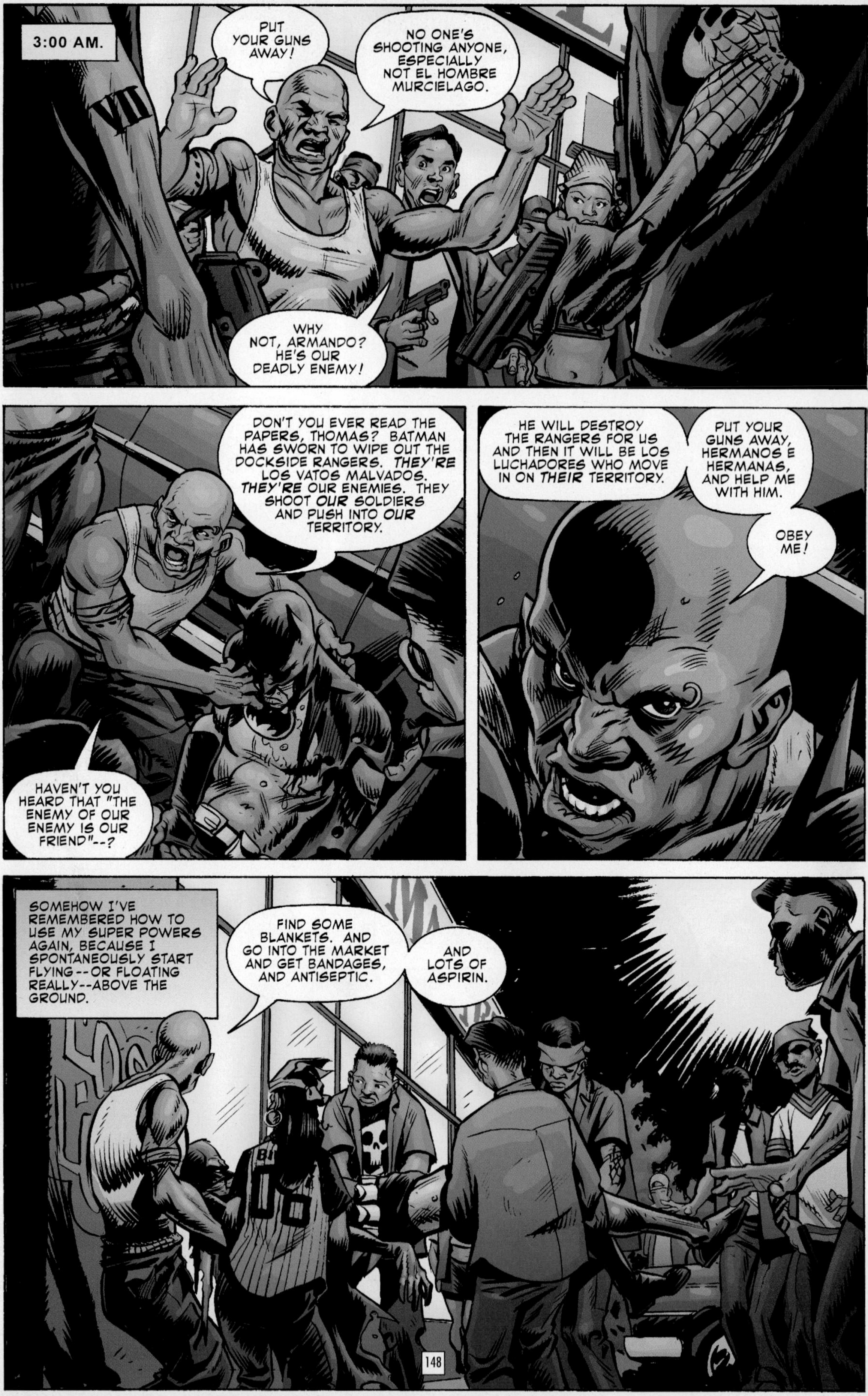
3:00 AM.
PUT YOUR GUNS AWAY!
NO ONE'S SHOOTING ANYONE, ESPECIALLY NOT EL HOMBRE MURCIELAGO.
WHY NOT, ARMANDO? HE'S OUR DEADLY ENEMY!
DON'T YOU EVER READ THE PAPERS, THOMAS? BATMAN HAS SWORN TO WIPE OUT THE DOCKSIDE RANGERS. THEY'RE LOS VATOS MALVADOS. THEY'RE OUR ENEMIES. THEY SHOOT OUR SOLDIERS AND PUSH INTO OUR TERRITORY.
HAVEN'T YOU HEARD THAT "THE ENEMY OF OUR ENEMY IS OUR FRIEND"--?
HE WILL DESTROY THE RANGERS FOR US AND THEN IT WILL BE LOS LUCHADORES WHO MOVE IN ON THEIR TERRITORY.
PUT YOUR GUNS AWAY, HERMANOS E HERMANAS, AND HELP ME WITH HIM.
OBEY ME!
SOMEHOW I'VE REMEMBERED HOW TO USE MY SUPER POWERS AGAIN, BECAUSE I SPONTANEOUSLY START FLYING--OR FLOATING REALLY--ABOVE THE GROUND.
FIND SOME BLANKETS. AND GO INTO THE MARKET AND GET BANDAGES, AND ANTISEPTIC.
AND LOTS OF ASPIRIN.

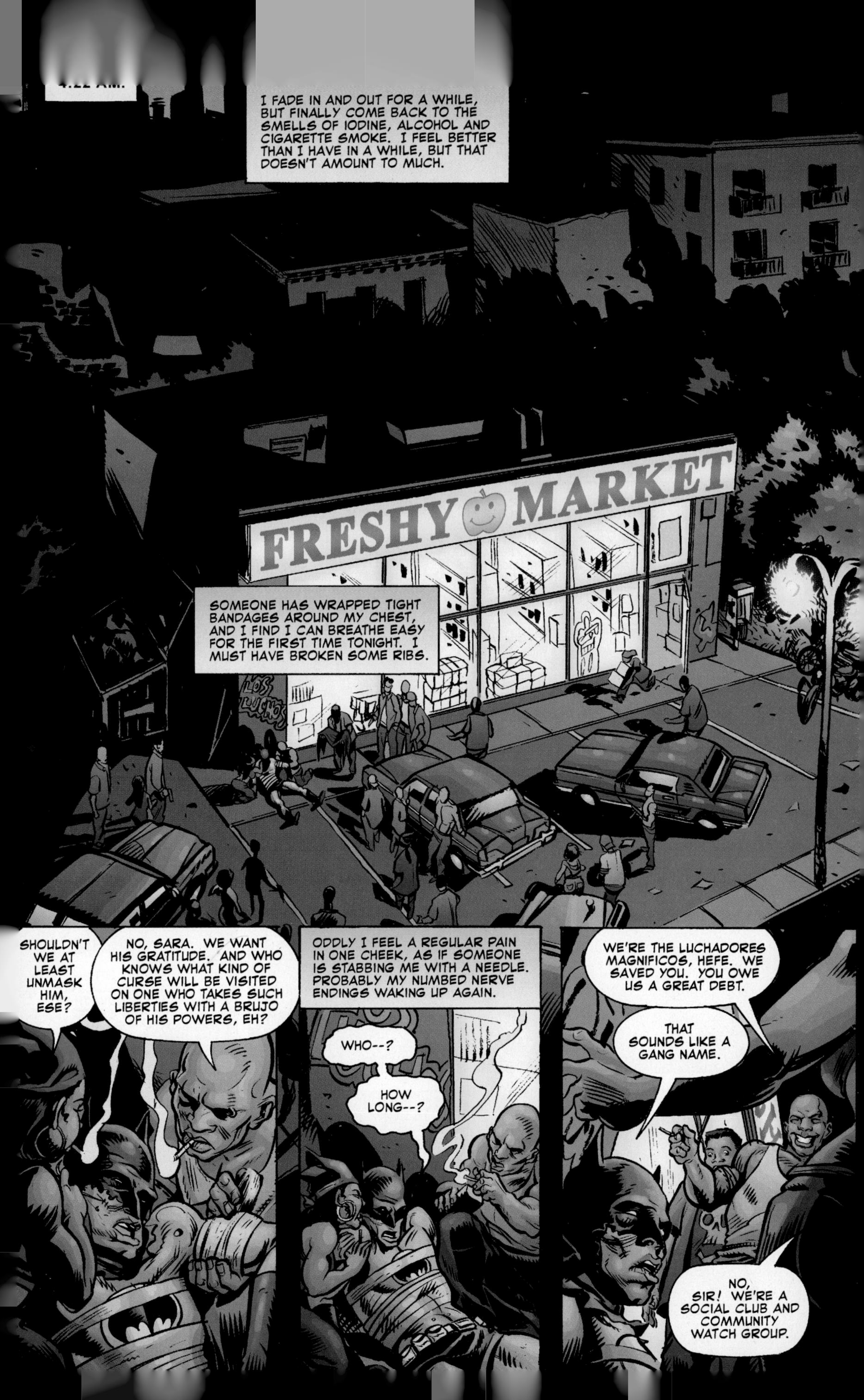

I FADE IN AND OUT FOR A WHILE, BUT FINALLY COME BACK TO THE SMELLS OF IODINE, ALCOHOL AND CIGARETTE SMOKE. I FEEL BETTER THAN I HAVE IN A WHILE, BUT THAT DOESN'T AMOUNT TO MUCH.
FRESHY MARKET
SOMEONE HAS WRAPPED TIGHT BANDAGES AROUND MY CHEST, AND I FIND I CAN BREATHE EASY FOR THE FIRST TIME TONIGHT. I MUST HAVE BROKEN SOME RIBS.
SHOULDN'T WE AT LEAST UNMASK HIM, ESE?
NO, SARA. WE WANT HIS GRATITUDE. AND WHO KNOWS WHAT KIND OF CURSE WILL BE VISITED ON ONE WHO TAKES SUCH LIBERTIES WITH A BRUJO OF HIS POWERS, EH?
ODDLY I FEEL A REGULAR PAIN IN ONE CHEEK, AS IF SOMEONE IS STABBING ME WITH A NEEDLE. PROBABLY MY NUMBED NERVE ENDINGS WAKING UP AGAIN.
WHO--?
HOW LONG--?
WE'RE THE LUCHADORES MAGNIFICOS, HEFE. WE SAVED YOU. YOU OWE US A GREAT DEBT.
THAT SOUNDS LIKE A GANG NAME.
NO, SIR! WE'RE A SOCIAL CLUB AND COMMUNITY WATCH GROUP.

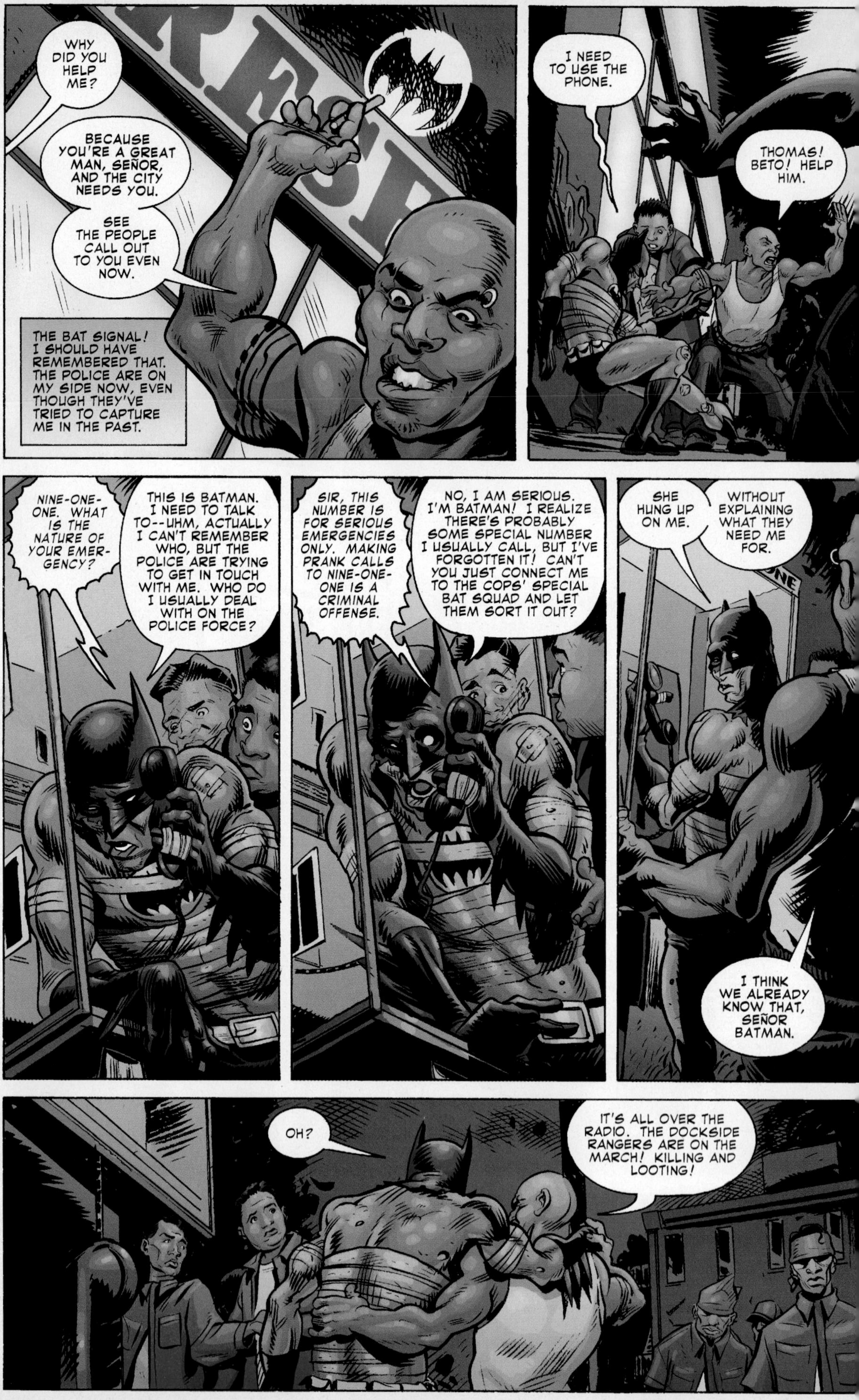
WHY DID YOU HELP ME?
BECAUSE YOU'RE A GREAT MAN, SEÑOR, AND THE CITY NEEDS YOU.
SEE THE PEOPLE CALL OUT TO YOU EVEN NOW.
THE BAT SIGNAL! I SHOULD HAVE REMEMBERED THAT. THE POLICE ARE ON MY SIDE NOW, EVEN THOUGH THEY'VE TRIED TO CAPTURE ME IN THE PAST.
I NEED TO USE THE PHONE.
THOMAS! BETO! HELP HIM.
NINE-ONE-ONE. WHAT IS THE NATURE OF YOUR EMERGENCY?
THIS IS BATMAN. I NEED TO TALK TO--UHM, ACTUALLY I CAN'T REMEMBER WHO, BUT THE POLICE ARE TRYING TO GET IN TOUCH WITH ME. WHO DO I USUALLY DEAL WITH ON THE POLICE FORCE?
SIR, THIS NUMBER IS FOR SERIOUS EMERGENCIES ONLY. MAKING PRANK CALLS TO NINE-ONE-ONE IS A CRIMINAL OFFENSE.
NO, I AM SERIOUS. I'M BATMAN! I REALIZE THERE'S PROBABLY SOME SPECIAL NUMBER I USUALLY CALL, BUT I'VE FORGOTTEN IT! CAN'T YOU JUST CONNECT ME TO THE COPS' SPECIAL BAT SQUAD AND LET THEM SORT IT OUT?
SHE HUNG UP ON ME.
WITHOUT EXPLAINING WHAT THEY NEED ME FOR.
I THINK WE ALREADY KNOW THAT, SEÑOR BATMAN.
OH?
IT'S ALL OVER THE RADIO. THE DOCKSIDE RANGERS ARE ON THE MARCH! KILLING AND LOOTING!

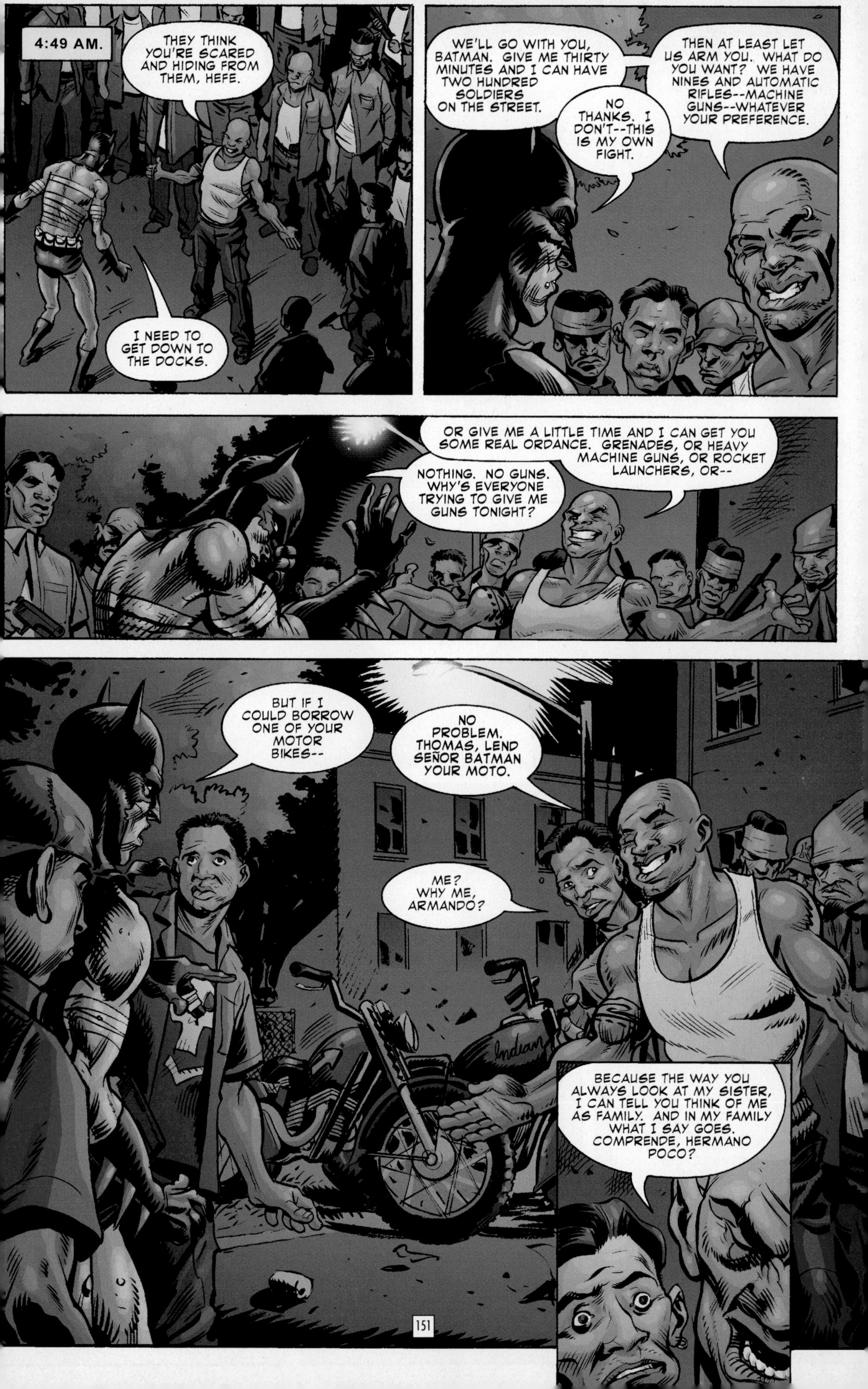
4:49 AM.
THEY THINK YOU'RE SCARED AND HIDING FROM THEM, HEFE.
I NEED TO GET DOWN TO THE DOCKS.
WE'LL GO WITH YOU, BATMAN. GIVE ME THIRTY MINUTES AND I CAN HAVE TWO HUNDRED SOLDIERS ON THE STREET.
NO THANKS. I DON'T--THIS IS MY OWN FIGHT.
THEN AT LEAST LET US ARM YOU. WHAT DO YOU WANT? WE HAVE NINES AND AUTOMATIC RIFLES--MACHINE GUNS--WHATEVER YOUR PREFERENCE.
OR GIVE ME A LITTLE TIME AND I CAN GET YOU SOME REAL ORDANCE. GRENADES, OR HEAVY MACHINE GUNS, OR ROCKET LAUNCHERS, OR--
NOTHING. NO GUNS. WHY'S EVERYONE TRYING TO GIVE ME GUNS TONIGHT?
BUT IF I COULD BORROW ONE OF YOUR MOTOR BIKES--
NO PROBLEM. THOMAS, LEND SEÑOR BATMAN YOUR MOTO.
ME? WHY ME, ARMANDO?
BECAUSE THE WAY YOU ALWAYS LOOK AT MY SISTER, I CAN TELL YOU THINK OF ME AS FAMILY. AND IN MY FAMILY WHAT I SAY GOES. COMPRENDE, HERMANO POCO?

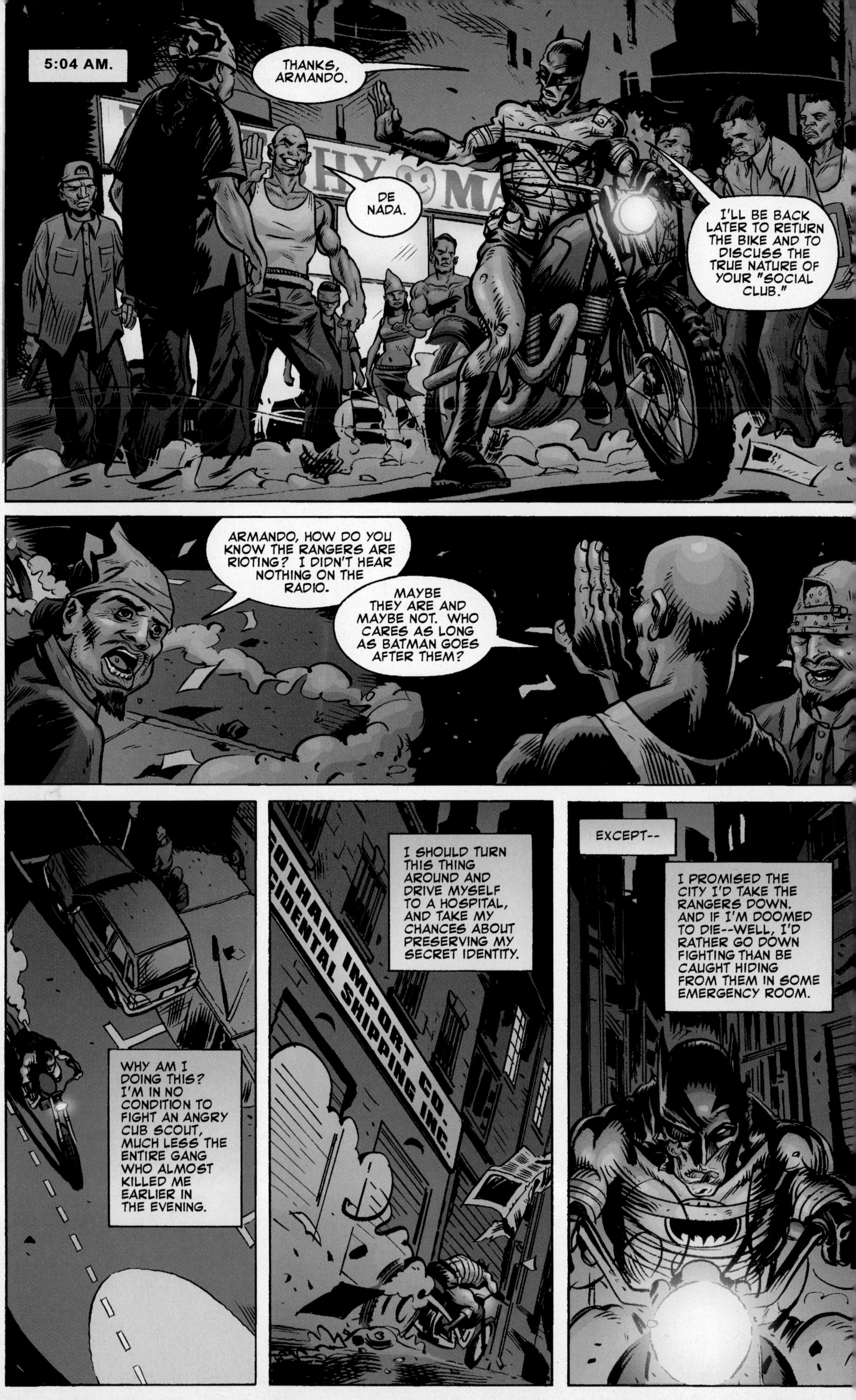

5:04 AM.
THANKS, ARMANDO.
DE NADA.
I'LL BE BACK LATER TO RETURN THE BIKE AND TO DISCUSS THE TRUE NATURE OF YOUR "SOCIAL CLUB."
ARMANDO, HOW DO YOU KNOW THE RANGERS ARE RIOTING? I DIDN'T HEAR NOTHING ON THE RADIO.
MAYBE THEY ARE AND MAYBE NOT. WHO CARES AS LONG AS BATMAN GOES AFTER THEM?
WHY AM I DOING THIS? I'M IN NO CONDITION TO FIGHT AN ANGRY CUB SCOUT, MUCH LESS THE ENTIRE GANG WHO ALMOST KILLED ME EARLIER IN THE EVENING.
I SHOULD TURN THIS THING AROUND AND DRIVE MYSELF TO A HOSPITAL, AND TAKE MY CHANCES ABOUT PRESERVING MY SECRET IDENTITY.
GOTHAM IMPORT CO.
CIDENTAL SHIPPING INC.
EXCEPT--
I PROMISED THE CITY I'D TAKE THE RANGERS DOWN. AND IF I'M DOOMED TO DIE--WELL, I'D RATHER GO DOWN FIGHTING THAN BE CAUGHT HIDING FROM THEM IN SOME EMERGENCY ROOM.

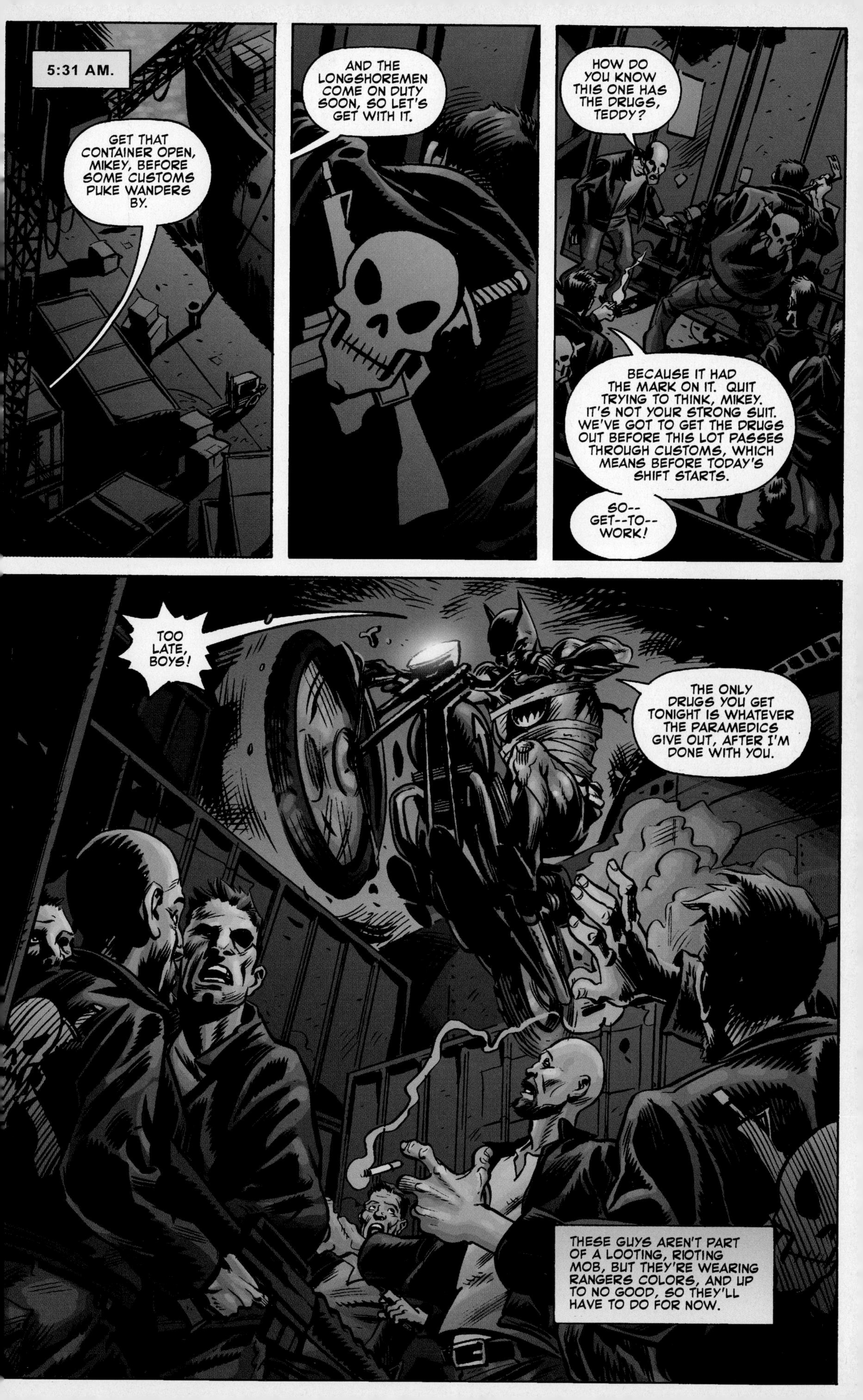

5:31 AM.
GET THAT CONTAINER OPEN, MIKEY, BEFORE SOME CUSTOMS PUKE WANDERS BY.
AND THE LONGSHOREMEN COME ON DUTY SOON, SO LET'S GET WITH IT.
HOW DO YOU KNOW THIS ONE HAS THE DRUGS, TEDDY?
BECAUSE IT HAD THE MARK ON IT. QUIT TRYING TO THINK, MIKEY. IT'S NOT YOUR STRONG SUIT. WE'VE GOT TO GET THE DRUGS OUT BEFORE THIS LOT PASSES THROUGH CUSTOMS, WHICH MEANS BEFORE TODAY'S SHIFT STARTS.
SO--GET--TO--WORK!
TOO LATE, BOYS!
THE ONLY DRUGS YOU GET TONIGHT IS WHATEVER THE PARAMEDICS GIVE OUT, AFTER I'M DONE WITH YOU.
THESE GUYS AREN'T PART OF A LOOTING, RIOTING MOB, BUT THEY'RE WEARING RANGERS COLORS, AND UP TO NO GOOD, SO THEY'LL HAVE TO DO FOR NOW.

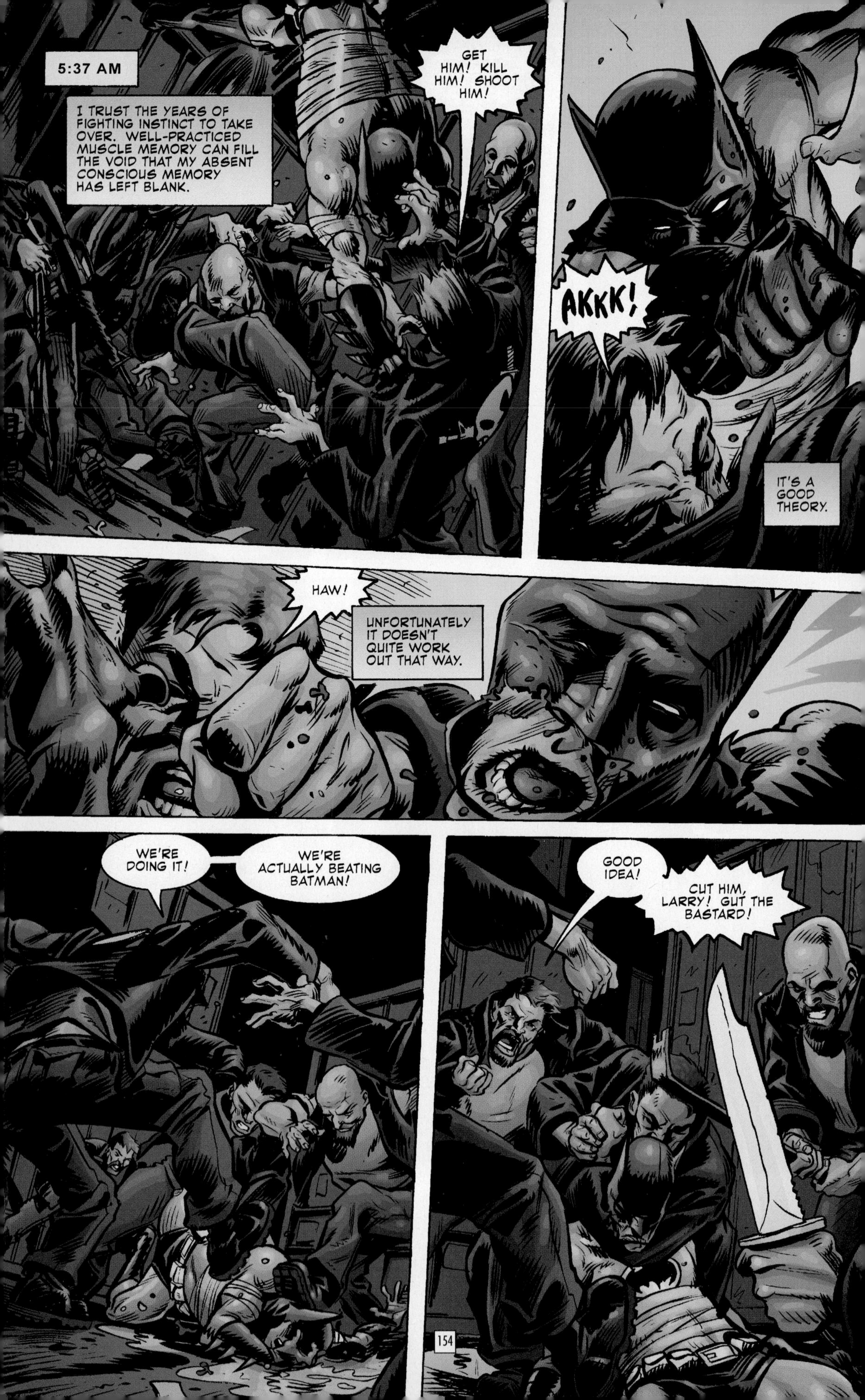

5:37 AM
I TRUST THE YEARS OF FIGHTING INSTINCT TO TAKE OVER. WELL-PRACTICED MUSCLE MEMORY CAN FILL THE VOID THAT MY ABSENT CONSCIOUS MEMORY HAS LEFT BLANK.
GET HIM! KILL HIM! SHOOT HIM!
AKKK!
IT'S A GOOD THEORY.
HAW!
UNFORTUNATELY IT DOESN'T QUITE WORK OUT THAT WAY.
WE'RE DOING IT!
WE'RE ACTUALLY BEATING BATMAN!
GOOD IDEA!
CUT HIM, LARRY! GUT THE BASTARD!

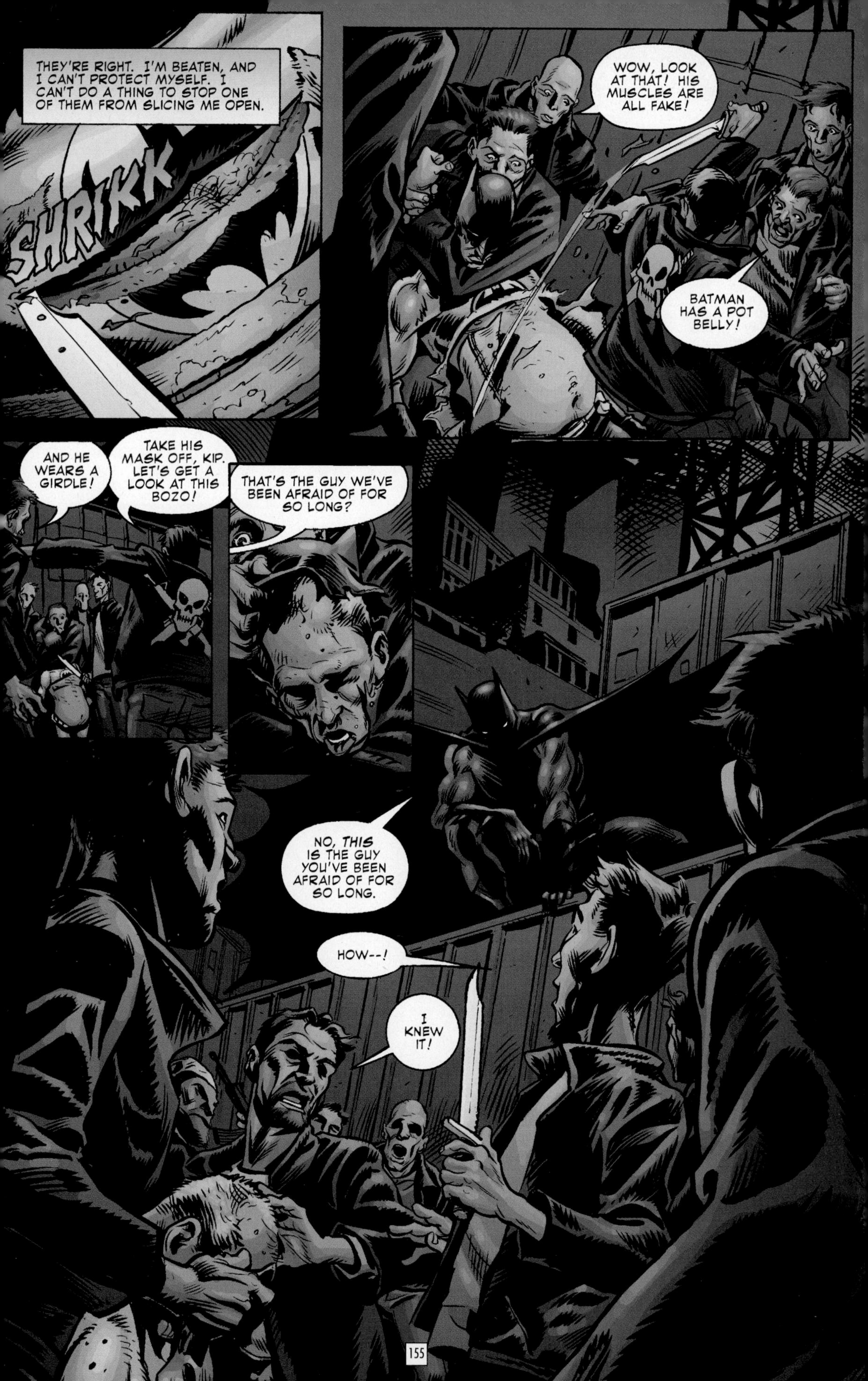
THEY'RE RIGHT. I'M BEATEN, AND I CAN'T PROTECT MYSELF. I CAN'T DO A THING TO STOP ONE OF THEM FROM SLICING ME OPEN.
SHRIKK
WOW, LOOK AT THAT! HIS MUSCLES ARE ALL FAKE!
BATMAN HAS A POT BELLY!
AND HE WEARS A GIRDLE!
TAKE HIS MASK OFF, KIP. LET'S GET A LOOK AT THIS BOZO!
THAT'S THE GUY WE'VE BEEN AFRAID OF FOR SO LONG?
NO, *THIS* IS THE GUY YOU'VE BEEN AFRAID OF FOR SO LONG.
HOW--!
I KNEW IT!

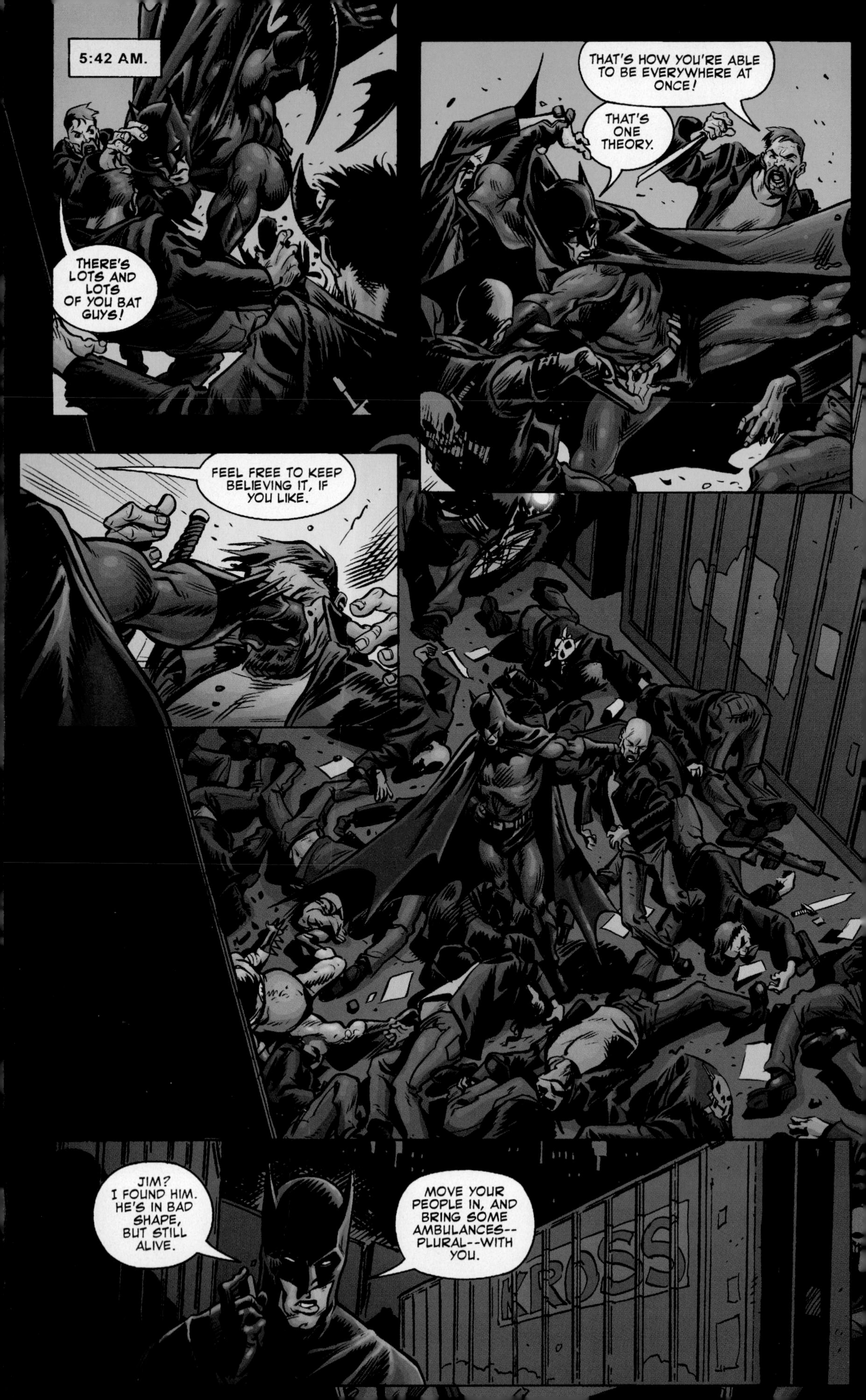
5:42 AM.
THERE'S LOTS AND LOTS OF YOU BAT GUYS!
THAT'S HOW YOU'RE ABLE TO BE EVERYWHERE AT ONCE!
THAT'S ONE THEORY.
FEEL FREE TO KEEP BELIEVING IT, IF YOU LIKE.
JIM? I FOUND HIM. HE'S IN BAD SHAPE, BUT STILL ALIVE.
MOVE YOUR PEOPLE IN, AND BRING SOME AMBULANCES--PLURAL--WITH YOU.
KROSS

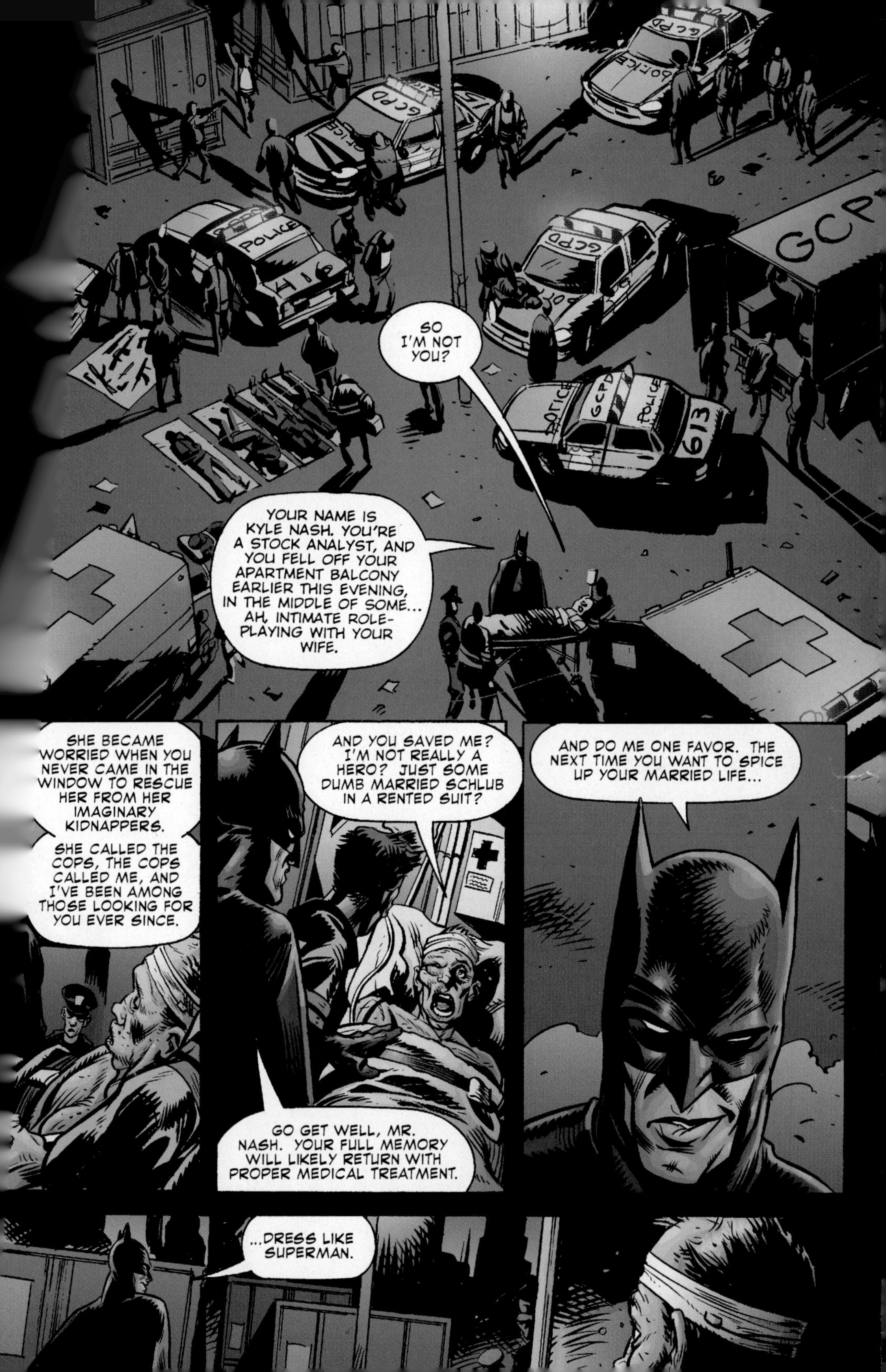
GCPD
POLICE
SO I'M NOT YOU?
YOUR NAME IS KYLE NASH. YOU'RE A STOCK ANALYST, AND YOU FELL OFF YOUR APARTMENT BALCONY EARLIER THIS EVENING, IN THE MIDDLE OF SOME... AH, INTIMATE ROLE-PLAYING WITH YOUR WIFE.
SHE BECAME WORRIED WHEN YOU NEVER CAME IN THE WINDOW TO RESCUE HER FROM HER IMAGINARY KIDNAPPERS.
SHE CALLED THE COPS, THE COPS CALLED ME, AND I'VE BEEN AMONG THOSE LOOKING FOR YOU EVER SINCE.
AND YOU SAVED ME? I'M NOT REALLY A HERO? JUST SOME DUMB MARRIED SCHLUB IN A RENTED SUIT?
GO GET WELL, MR. NASH. YOUR FULL MEMORY WILL LIKELY RETURN WITH PROPER MEDICAL TREATMENT.
AND DO ME ONE FAVOR. THE NEXT TIME YOU WANT TO SPICE UP YOUR MARRIED LIFE...
...DRESS LIKE SUPERMAN.

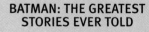

BATMAN:
THE LONG HALLOWEEN

JEPH LOEB TIM SALE
BATMAN
THE LONG HALLOWEEN

JEPH LOEB/TIM SALE

BATMAN:
DARK VICTORY

JEPH LOEB TIM SALE
BATMAN Dark Victory

JEPH LOEB/TIM SALE

BATMAN:
HAUNTED KNIGHT

From the Eisner Award-winning creators
JEPH LOEB TIM SALE
BATMAN
HAUNTED KNIGHT

JEPH LOEB/TIM SALE

BATMAN:
SCARECROW TALES

BATMAN
SCARECROW TALES

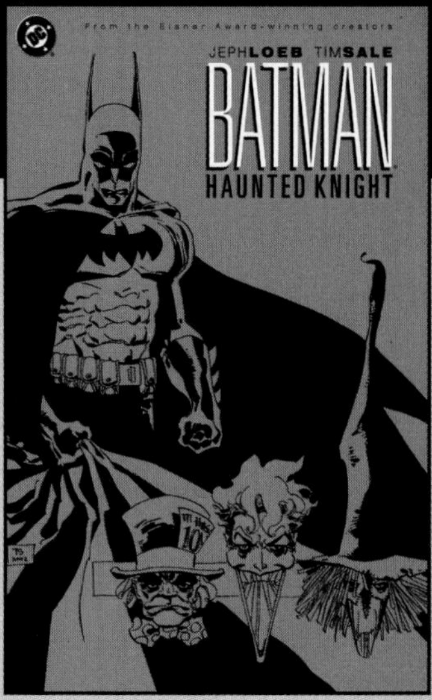

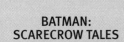

VARIOUS

8 CHILLING TALES
FEATURING
THE MASTER OF FEAR!

BATMAN:
BLIND JUSTICE

BATMAN
BLIND JUSTICE
SAM HAMM
DENYS COWAN
DICK GIORDANO

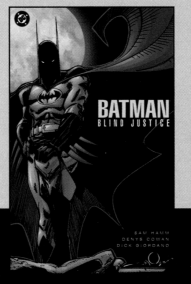

**SAM HAMM/DENYS COWAN/
DICK GIORDANO**

INTRODUCING
HENRI DUCARD
THE MAN WHO TRAINED
BRUCE WAYNE!

BATMAN:
TALES OF THE DEMON

BATMAN
TALES OF THE
DEMON

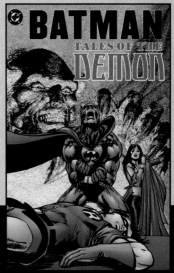

**DENNIS O'NEIL/
NEAL ADAMS/VARIOUS**

FEATURING BATMAN'S
DEADLIEST OPPONENT
RA'S AL GHUL!

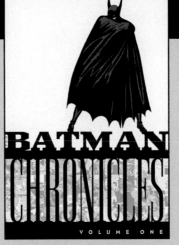

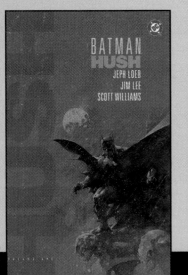